C-6

U. S. History   1st 12 -

6

The American Planner
Biographies and Recollections

The American Planner

Biographies and Recollections

Edited by
Donald A. Krueckeberg

Methuen
New York and London

First published in 1983 by
Methuen, Inc.
733 Third Avenue, New York, NY 10017

Published in Great Britain by
Methuen & Co. Ltd
11 New Fetter Lane, London EC4P 4EE

This collection © 1983 Methuen, Inc.

Typeset in Great Britain by
Scarborough Typesetting Services
and printed in the United States of America

*Library of Congress Cataloging in Publication
Data*

Main entry under title:
The American planner.
    Includes index.
    1. City planners – United States –
Addresses, essays, lectures.   2. City
planners – United States – Biography –
Addresses, essays, lectures.   3. Regional
planning – United States – Addresses,
essays, lectures.
I. Krueckeberg, Donald A.
HT167.A5767   307'.12'0922 [B]   82–6461
ISBN 0–416–33360–5   AACR2

*British Library Cataloguing in Publication
Data*

The American planner.
1. Regional planning – United States –
History   I. Krueckeberg, Donald A.
307'.12'0973   HT392 (expanded)
ISBN 0–416–33360–5

Contents

List of plates

List of figures

Notes on the contributors

Eugenie Ladner Birch is assistant professor of Urban Planning at Hunter College, New York.

Henry Churchill (deceased) is the author of *The City is the People* (Harcourt, Brace & World, 1945) and practiced architecture and planning in New York City and Philadelphia.

Laurence C. Gerckens is professor of City and Regional Planning at the Ohio State University, Columbus, Ohio.

Park Dixon Goist is associate professor of American Studies at Case Western Reserve University, Cleveland, Ohio.

John Hancock is professor of Urban Planning at the University of Washington, Seattle, Washington.

Norman J. Johnston is professor of Urban Planning at the University of Washington, Seattle, Washington.

Harvey Kantor (deceased) was assistant professor of American Urban History at the University of Rhode Island, Kingston, Rhode Island.

Donald A. Krueckeberg is professor of urban planning and policy development at Rutgers University, New Brunswick, New Jersey.

David Myhra is a consultant to industry and government and assistant professional lecturer in Urban Planning at George Washington University, Washington, D.C.

John R. Ross, former assistant professor of History at Virginia Polytechnic Institute and State University, resides in Portland, Oregon.

Thomas J. Schlereth is associate professor of American Studies at the University of Notre Dame, Notre Dame, Indiana.

Bernard Taper is professor of Journalism at the University of California, Berkeley, California.

Sydney H. Williams is a Partner in Williams & Mocine/City and Regional Planning, San Rafael, California.

Acknowledgments

The editor and publisher would like to thank the following for permission to reproduce copyright material:

Ch. 2. John Hancock (1960) "John Nolen: the background of a pioneer planner," *Journal of the American Institute of Planners*, 26 (4), 302–12; Ch. 3. Harvey A. Kantor (1974) "Benjamin C. Marsh and the fight over population congestion," *Journal of the American Institute of Planners*, 40 (6), 422–9; Ch. 4. Thomas J. Schlereth (1981) "Burnham's *Plan* and Moody's *Manual*: city planning as progressive reform," *Journal of the American Planning Association*, 47 (1); Ch. 5. Edward M. Bassett (1939) *The Autobiography of Edward M. Bassett*, New York, The Harbor Press, pp. 105–34; Ch. 7. Eugenie Ladner Birch (1978) "Woman-made America: the case of early public housing policy," *Journal of the American Institute of Planners*, 44 (2), 130–44; Ch. 8. Harvey A. Kantor (1973) "Charles Dyer Norton and the origins of the Regional Plan of New York," *Journal of the American Institute of Planners*, 39 (1), 35–44; Ch. 9. John R. Ross (1975) "Benton MacKaye: the Appalachian Trail," *Journal of the American Institute of Planners*, 41 (2), 110–14; Ch. 10. Henry Churchill (1960) "Henry Wright: 1878–1936," *Journal of the American Institute of Planners*, 26 (4), 293–301; Ch. 11. David Myhra (1973) "Rexford Guy Tugwell: initiator of America's Greenbelt New Towns, 1935 to 1936," *Journal of the American Institute of Planners*, 40 (3), 176–88; Ch. 12. Park Dixon Goist (1972) "Seeing things whole: a consideration of Lewis Mumford," *Journal of the American Institute of Planners*, 38 (6), 379–91; Ch. 13. Norman J. Johnston (1973) "Harland Bartholomew: precedent for the profession," *Journal of the American Institute of Planners*, 39 (2), 115–24; Ch. 14. Sydney H. Williams (1980) *The Ladislas Segoe Tapes*, Washington, D.C. and Chicago, The American Planning Association, v. p.; Ch. 16. Donald A. Krueckeberg (1980) "From the backyard garden to the whole USA: a conversation with Charles W. Eliot, 2nd," *Journal of the American Planning Association*, 46 (4), 440–8; Ch. 17. Bernard Taper (1967) "Charles Abrams: a lover of cities," *The New Yorker*, February 11.

My deepest gratitude is owed to Lee Krueckeberg. Her enthusiasm, encouragement, and good ideas have been a steady source of support from the beginning. To my son, John, I am also very thankful for his genuine interest and many good suggestions. From our trip to the First International Conference of the Planning History Group, in London, down to the very end, the book has been something of a family project.

Great thanks also go to each of the authors of the works included. I consider each of their efforts excellent and I am grateful for their generous permission to include them in this collection. Special appreciation is offered to Eugenie Ladner Birch and Laurence C. Gerckens for their original contributions and many helpful suggestions.

Other helpful reviews and suggestions came from many colleagues and friends, especially Bob Beauregard, Richard Brail, Mike Greenberg, Jim Hughes, and John Pucher of Rutgers University. Thanks also to Jerry Kaufman of the University of Wisconsin, John Mullin of the University of Massachusetts, Milt Patton of Lexington, Kentucky, Laird Klingler of the Rutgers University Library, Nancy Dean of the Olin Library, Cornell University, and to an anonymous British reviewer.

Ken Pearlman, editor of the *Journal of the American Planning Association* got me started when he encouraged me to write a history of the *Journal* that led to the interviews and then to the concept of the present book. My thanks to him and to Pat Stack, managing editor of the *Journal*, for their assistance and genuine interest in the project. Thanks similarly to Frank So, Deputy Executive Director of the American Planning Association, who shares our interest in the history of planning.

Many of the chapters included here first appeared in the AIP/APA *Journal* and I wish to recognize the contribution of the editors who preceded Ken Pearlman and myself for their part in generating many of these papers, particularly that special impetus given to historical biography by John Hancock in association with Dave Godschalk and Dick Bolan.

Everyone I ever sought assistance from has been most gracious: Frederick J. Adams, his wife Keith and his son Thomas Frederick; Charles W. Eliot, 2nd; Ladislas Segoe; Coleman Woodbury; each hold intimate shares in the final product for which I am very grateful. Thanks similarly to John Howard, Ruth Abrams, and Rose Churchill for their assistance.

I also wish to thank Janice Price and Paul Lee of Methuen for their warm support of the idea and their patient encouragement.

That the book is finished at last is in large measure due to the skill and devotion of Vera Lee who once again, with the commitment of a co-author, typed and retyped and contributed numerous good ideas of her own. Thanks also go to Marilyn Watterson who very skillfully and cheerfully transcribed most of the original tapes of interviews and recollections. Special thanks also to Barbara Swan, Kathy Bignell, and Nancy Swan for friendly and faithful assistance.

I wish also to thank the Rutgers University Research Council for a small grant to assist in the final preparations and to acknowledge the Faculty Academic Study Program of Rutgers for time to devote to finishing the work.

Finally, I wish to express my deep appreciation to Warren Susman, professor of American History at Rutgers University, whose lectures have been for me a stimulating source of ideas and insight into American thought.

My measure of debts is very great, but final responsibility for the remaining shortcomings is, of course, mine alone.

Donald A. Krueckeberg
New Brunswick, New Jersey
December 1981

1 Introduction to the American planner

Donald A. Krueckeberg

Yet there are men, a diminishing few, who will not be molded and
who will not follow blindly. They go their lonely and uncomfortable
ways in mental nakedness, unprotected and unhampered by the
conformity with which their years should have clothed them,
poking and prying and shaking the established order into new
forms. They practice thinking rather than acceptance. They arm
themselves with keen and penetrating queries, and when they
attack the carnage is fearful. . . .
   There was a time when most planners were among the naked and
dangerous men. (Frederick H. Bair, Jr[1])

The importance of remembering

There are signs of fundamental change in American planning. These
changes are moving the field in two dramatically different directions. On
the one hand, for example, Princeton, Harvard, and the University of
Pennsylvania, three of our most prestigious institutions, have moved
their programs in planning out of schools of design and into schools of
public policy. In contrast, other universities and professional institutions
are renewing their traditional emphasis in physical planning and urban
design. Which of these initiatives is most appropriate for urban planning
is not entirely clear.

   Two recent book reviews are indicative of the search for guiding
principles. The writers of these reviews, Richard Bolan of Boston College
and Allan Jacobs of the University of California-Berkeley, are two of
America's foremost thinkers and practitioners of urban planning. Bolan's
review of *History and Human Existence: From Marx to Merleau-Ponty*, by
James Miller, and Jacobs' review of *A Theory of Good City Form* by Kevin
Lynch, are remarkable because of what they share.[2] These two quite different books, read by two distant people, elicited a deep and singular
response. Each found a book that caused him to remember why he
wanted to become a planner "in the first place." Perhaps, you might say,
they had different reasons. No. Each remembered the same, that he
became a planner to pursue "a humanistic vision" and "a worthwhile
utopia."

   Something is happening to American planners. We are all devoting a lot of time to remembering who we are and where we have come from. In a time of decreased activity, there is a search for new direction. There is a desire to make new commitments. Veterans and students alike are reassessing what it is possible to achieve in a lifetime of planning.

Laurence Gerckens has defined our position. We are at a juncture in American planning. The phenomenon is fairly obvious once it has been pointed out.

The period from 1948 to 1975 was a very abnormal period. We were all the "brave new world" and the past didn't matter. The future was going to be better no matter what happened. Suddenly, there was the downturn . . . the Viet Nam War and the riots . . . There's now a sense that maybe the future isn't going to be so good. And, suddenly, instead of discounting the past, I think there is an emerging attitude that says "My God, but they were bold thirty or forty years ago . . . What are (we) doing today which has any of the boldness of the Burnham Plan of 1909? Bettman's political involvement with the Charter Party of 1923? What president of the AIP is making deals with big labor like Olmsted was making with Sam Gompers in 1917?"[3]

We can be lost, so much of the time, in the details of our daily lives that they occupy our entire field of vision. The present pretends it is not just the present, but also the past and the future. We turn to history because it reminds us that the past was often in fact very different from today, not routine. The importance of remembering is that it opens the imagination to things both old and new, and to thinking differently about the future.

Biography personalizes this historical experience. Through it we may build a better understanding of ourselves, in the discovery of a shared birthplace, a common religious training, an idea affirmed, a disappointment repeated. But do not mistake the purpose of this book. It is not a sentimental regret about a lost world. While every man and woman in it may be a hero, the objective is not to diminish the ambitions and achievements of our own time. The purpose is to restore our memories, to review our commitments, and to extend our sense of company.

These lives and recollections

This book is about the lives of people who were, and some who still are, among the leading city and regional planners in the United States. Their lifetimes span a period of more than a hundred years. The greatest concentration of the book is on the first half of the twentieth century, roughly from the beginnings of the modern planning movement at the turn of the century to the end of the Second World War. The period, broad and richly textured as it may be, represents a special experience. Before the turn of the century there was no visible organized planning movement in this country. Between 1890 and 1910 it emerged with around forty individuals at its center. They maintained leadership, generated ideas, and established new institutions. By the advent of the Second World War there were only a few hundred more. But after 1945, as we shall see later, their growth was exponential, to nearly 10,000 by 1970, and perhaps 25,000 by 1980.

The product of that earlier era was a new profession devoted to the unified and comprehensive planning of cities and regions to satisfy human needs with both beauty and efficiency. Like the larger society from which it grew, the planning movement contained numerous differences of emphasis and contradictions. Yet this powerful idea had its basis in the faith that reason, honesty, and technical skills could be combined to guide the growth of the nation's cities into the twentieth century and toward a better way of life.

The people presented in the biographies and recollections that follow have been divided into three groups representing three general phases of development. The first group are *pioneers* of city planning in the era of municipal reform: John Nolen, landscape architect; Benjamin C. Marsh, political organizer; Walter Moody, promoter and professional booster; Edward M. Bassett, New York zoning lawyer; Alfred Bettman, Cincinnati lawyer and civic reform leader; and Edith Elmer Wood and Catherine Bauer, housing reformers.

The second group are the synthesizers, who integrated interests in regional planning, the natural environment, and new towns. These *regionalists* emerged in the 1920s and expanded their interests throughout the New Deal period. They include: Charles Dyer Norton, a civic leader behind the landmark Regional Plan of New York and Environs; Benton MacKaye, the naturalist; Henry Wright, architect and landscape architect; Rexford Tugwell, agricultural economist; and Lewis Mumford, writer and social critic.

The third group of planners represent the *new professionals*. They spanned the interests of the reformers and the regionalists. Unlike their forebears, they were the first generation to make the new profession a primary career. Harland Bartholomew and Ladislas Segoe, trained in engineering, established major planning firms in St Louis and Cincinnati, respectively; Coleman Woodbury, an economist, integrated housing and planning; Charles W. Eliot, 2nd, a landscape architect, was the executive director of the National Resources Planning Board and later engaged in private practice and teaching; Charles Abrams, a lawyer, focused on real estate, housing reform, and planning in New York. Finally, while societal constraints and barriers to professional training barred women in general from planning, nevertheless many women exerted a significant impact on the development of the field through their participation in auxiliary and peripheral professions. Opportunities expanded for women in planning after the Second World War. This history is presented in the final chapter on women in American planning.

Interesting people do not fit neatly into categories, and these three broad groups of pioneers, regionalists, and professionals may lose some of their clarity after careful reading. A chronological chart of the subjects of each chapter is presented in Figure 1.1 to illustrate the temporal relationships among the groups and their members. Each horizontal bar spans the life-time of a subject. The darkened portion of each bar indicates the period which is the focus of the chapter. In most cases these biographies and recollections have been previously published elsewhere. The last chapter on women in planning was written especially for this volume, and the chapter on Bettman also appears here for the first time. The recollections of Bassett, Segoe, and Woodbury were also specially edited for this collection. The selections were chosen because they represent the best short biographical materials available on these American planners. There are many significant figures for whom little or no biographical material exists. I hope this collection will stimulate interest in adding to that body of literature.

I have purposely omitted two nineteenth-century figures, Frederick Law Olmsted and Daniel Burnham. They are characters of an earlier era who, to be properly treated, would introduce a whole group of individuals not easily incorporated within the perimeters of this book. They did not play a direct role in the development of the planning profession, which of course is indebted to them for their intellectual contributions and practical examples. They have been extensively studied in two lengthy biographies of Burnham and several of Olmsted.[4] I will, nonetheless summarize their contributions later in this introduction.

The rise of the American planner cannot be understood in a vacuum. He is as much a product of his environment as any other emerging modern figure – the architect, the social worker, the civil engineer, etc. He was influenced by the social and economic currents of his lifetime just as is contemporary man. Therefore we turn in the balance of this introduction, first, to review the major factors of the nineteenth-century urban and industrial revolution out of which the planning movement grew. Second, we will consider the contributions of Olmsted, Burnham, and Charles Mulford Robinson toward the formal emergence of the planning movement at the turn of the century. We will then look at the major periods of the development of planning from the age of progressive municipal reform, through the growth of regionalism, to the rise of professionalism, and finally the post Second World War era of metropolitan expansion. We will conclude with some reflections on the future of American planning.

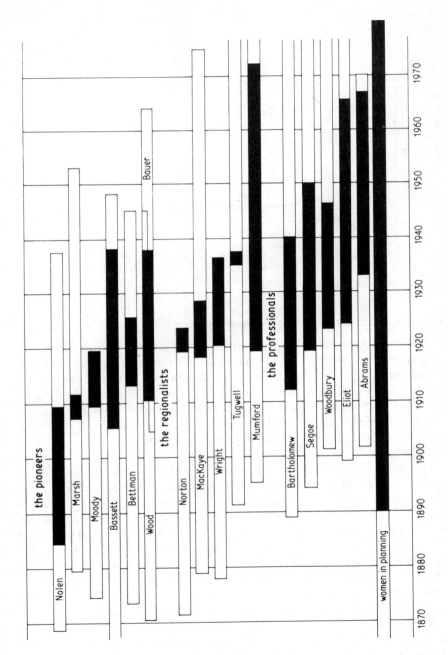

Figure 1.1 A chronological chart of chapter subjects.

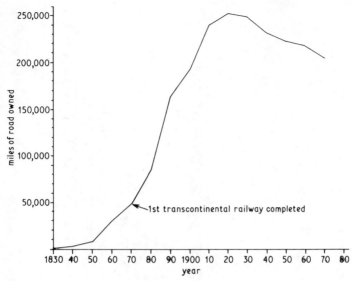

Figure 1.2 Railway mileage in the US.

The nineteenth-century environment

The modern American planning movement began in the progressive era, roughly falling between 1890 and 1910. Although many planning historians have regarded the Chicago World's Fair of 1893 as a convenient symbol of its origin, its roots are older. Three interrelated phenomena occurred in the nineteenth century that transformed American life into the environment from which the planning movement arose: (1) a revolution in the technology of production and transportation, (2) an explosion of population, (3) the development and congestion of cities.

The industrial revolution in nineteenth-century America transformed both the urban and the rural landscapes through massive technological change. "To see the nineteenth century pure and undefiled," Catherine Bauer advises, "we must go to the railroad station."[5] The rise of the railroad is a powerful and dramatic barometer of the technological growth of the century. There were fewer than forty miles of road owned in the United States prior to 1830. By 1840 there were 3000 miles. These tripled in the next decade, tripled again in the next, and increased on the average more than 75 per cent in each of the next three decades. The growth of railroad mileage in the United States is shown in Figure 1.2.[6]

Railroads, of course, were only one of many technical innovations in transportation, industry, and building methods that altered the structure of American cities. In the field of transportation came turnpikes, steamboats,

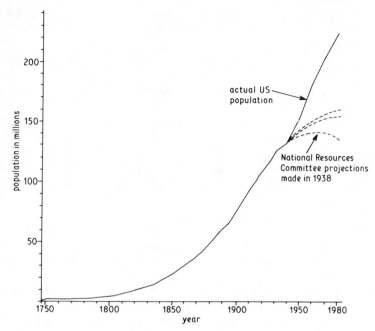

Figure 1.3 Population of the US with forecasts made in 1938 by the National Resources Committee.

canals, steel bridges, subways, and electric trolleys. In industry came large water and steam-power mills, gas lights, electric lights, telegraphs, telephones, and business machines. In building structures came the balloon-frame, tenements, department stores, cast iron and steel construction, elevators, skyscrapers, and the consolidated railroad terminal; all of the building blocks of the modern city but one – the people.

Transportation was an important facilitator of the dramatic increase of population experienced during the nineteenth century. The westward limit of territories was completely transformed by 1860, like a beach in a storm; as wave upon wave of immigrants came to the eastern shores and worked their way inland. The annual number of immigrants did not surpass 50,000 until after 1830, reached 100,000 before 1850, and then in a pattern of pulsating crests, rose to 400,000 in the 1850s and again in the 1870s, to nearly 800,000 in the 1880s and to its apogee in 1908 of over one and one-quarter million.[7] The resultant curve of population growth in the United States is shown in Figure 1.3.[8] (The projections shown in Figure 1.3 will be discussed later.)

The effort to accommodate this abundance of people with the new technology of city-building resulted in terrible congestion. Catherine Bauer describes the view from the railroad station:

A foreground of noise, dirt, beggars, souvenirs and shrill competitive advertising, of tangled street-car lines and tortuous traffic. A middle-ground of warehouses, gilded theaters, competing shop-fronts and commercial hotels with gruesome ornament and unconvincing marble entrances. A background of smokestacks and tall crowded tenements. "Down by the railroad tracks" or "Back of the station" means "slum" in any language.[9]

The sheer magnitude of urban growth is difficult to grasp. The multiplication of towns and cities is shown in Figure 1.4, an illustration from the National Resources Committee's famous 1938 report, *Our Cities: Their Role in the National Economy.*[10] In 1790 there were *twenty-eight* cities of between 2,500 and 10,000 population. By 1930 there were *2,183.* There were *seven* between 10,000 and 100,000 in the year 1790; in 1930 there were *889.* There were *none* over 100,000 in 1790; by 1930 there were *ninety-three.* Consider, for the sake of comparison, a nation that might today commit its resources to the building of twenty-two new towns in one year, and then commit itself to maintaining this rate of building for the next 140 years, stipulating further that in two out of every three years one of the twenty-two cities would be of 100,000 population or larger. The idea of such a choice is preposterous. Yet, in effect, that is what happened.

Now there must have been some planning for all of this growth; and there was. But it was not planning in the sense of public deliberation and governmental regulation that we call planning today. The planning was private, entrepreneurial, and atomistic; the work of land surveyors, real estate developers, industrial managers, and transport companies. As physical city planning it usually consisted of the layout of a grid of streets, the subdivision of land into lots, and the location of a few key public buildings.[11] Later, professional planners would develop a city plan that was qualitatively different, the result of a process of community research and study and a rational differentiation between problems and solutions. The elements of the early modern plan related streets and lots to functions and topography, included railroads and their terminals, waterfronts, municipal buildings and their grouping. It also covered housing conditions, landscaping and parks, water and sewerage, schools and industry, and legal controls on future development, to be administered by commissions of citizens. But like the whole progressive movement and its battery of urban reforms, this new planning developed slowly and was reactive to the flow of events. It came late in the development of the railroad and technology. It came late in the flow of immigration and late in the growth of cities.

Amid these other plans, the nineteenth century had no shortage of

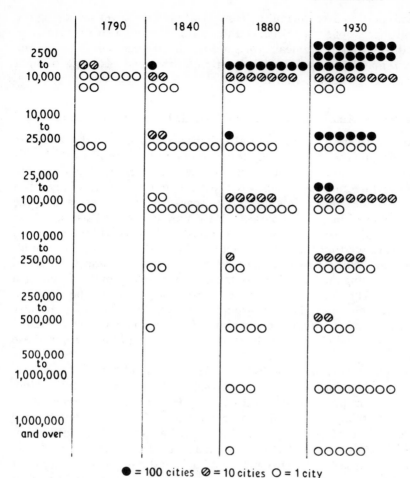

Figure 1.4 Number of cities by size groups.

utopian ideas and experiments that eventually had their influences on the planning movement. They took on a great variety of political, religious, industrial, and philanthropic forms. For example, in America Edward Bellamy's utopian novel *Looking Backward: 2000–1887* (1887) presented a complex urban commercial–industrial city, imagined in the year 2000, that captured the imagination of a very large public. Bellamy's work, as well as others, marked the thought of a London clerk, Ebenezer Howard, whose short treatise *Tomorrow: A Peaceful Path to Real Reform* (1898) sparked the British garden city movement.[12] Howard's work and that of his followers, Sir Raymond Unwin and Barry Parker evolved into the British New Towns program. Similar ideas were experimented with in

America, particularly during the New Deal period. Never achieving the political success of their British counterparts, American efforts remained philanthropic and piecemeal. Nonetheless, the utopian philosophy of the British remained a basic underpinning of American planning thought until the mid-twentieth century.

Pathfinders of American planning: Olmsted, Burnham, and Robinson

In addition to the entrepreneurial efforts of industrial and real estate developers and the examples of utopian community schemes, other roots of American planning in the nineteenth century included the contributions of architecture, landscape architecture, and a network of organizations for civic improvement. In landscape architecture we see the development of major city parks – New York's Central Park being the forerunner of these – the college campus, and the modern suburb. In architecture we find the development of planned groups of civic buildings – the "White City" of the Chicago World's Fair and Columbian Exposition being the forerunner of these – and the rise of the downtown skyscraper. The movement for civic improvement fostered the organization of hundreds of local reform groups and clubs devoted to civic art, city betterment, and eventually to city plans. Frederick Law Olmsted, Daniel H. Burnham, and Charles Mulford Robinson were pathfinders in these efforts.

Frederick Law Olmsted, the father of American landscape architecture, was born in Hartford, Connecticut in 1822, a city founded by his Puritan ancestors from the Massachusetts colony. His childhood, largely spent under the tutelage of several Congregational ministers, concluded more happily with three years of study with a civil engineer. This out-of-door occupation fitted Olmsted's love of the natural countryside, but he moved on to try life at sea, sailing to China and back, and then settled on a career of scientific farming. His appreciation of scenic beauty was heightened on a walking tour of England with his brother and a friend, recounted in his book, *Walks and Talks of an American Farmer in England*; this revealed his first exposure to English parks. Returning to his farm on Staten Island, Olmsted's literary reputation got him a commission to travel throughout the South for the *New York (Daily) Times* to investigate the slavery question. This resulted in his published articles and journals on the seaboard slave states and Texas. In 1852, he made his often noted visit to the utopian farm in Red Bank, New Jersey, a cooperative experiment in communal living based on the theories of the French utopianist, Fourier. While he did not find it faultless – it was too innocent, and caring "little, too little, about the world outside" – he concluded that "the conglomeration of families even works better than I was willing to believe. Nevertheless I am not a Fourierist for myself; but for many, a large part of even an American community I am."[13]

In 1857 he achieved appointment as supervisor of construction of Central Park in New York and collaborated with the young English architect Calvert Vaux on its design. It is considered today to be one of the world's greatest achievements in civic design. Olmsted's extraordinary administrative skills, demonstrated in the Central Park work, led to his appointment during the Civil War as General Secretary of the US Sanitary Commission, precursor of the American Red Cross. He began his career as a landscape architect shortly after the war. In 1865 he rejoined Vaux in New York. They produced numerous park designs throughout the country. Olmsted's suburban design for Riverside, Illinois, in 1869 is among the earliest of the curvilinear street pattern suburbs that comprise the modern subdivision.

His address on "Public Parks and the Enlargement of Towns" presented to the American Social Science Association at the Lowell Institute in 1870 is an immensely intelligent discussion of planning, politics, and human behavior.[14] His other projects include Stanford University's campus, the National Capital site, and the Boston park system. His finale as site planner for the Chicago World's Fair of 1893, under Daniel Burnham's supervision, is shadowed by his declining energies.

He died in 1903, but he had already turned the firm and the new profession over to his successors. The firm was continued by his three junior partners: his stepson John Olmsted, his son Frederick Law Olmsted, Jr, and Charles Eliot, landscape architect, son of the President of Harvard and uncle of Charles W. Eliot, 2nd.

In 1900 President Eliot of Harvard appointed Frederick Law Olmsted, Jr head of the first university curriculum for training in the profession of landscape architecture. He went on to become chairman of the National Conference on City Planning in 1911 and the first president of the American City Planning Institute in 1917.

Daniel Burnham, chief architect of the Chicago World's Fair of 1893, was also of New England Puritan stock. His maternal grandfather held a Congregational pulpit until he was excommunicated for his support of the liberal, almost unitarian teachings of the philosopher–theologian Emanuel Swedenborg. Those teachings were a source of religious inspiration throughout Daniel Burnham's life. While he was still a young boy the family moved to Chicago where his uncle had a law practice. Through good preparatory schools there, and later back East, his exceptional talents as an artist and a social leader outran his scholastic achievements and he failed to achieve admission to Harvard, one of the nagging disappointments of his otherwise very successful career.

After a few false starts, including work in a mining camp in Colorado, he returned to Chicago to apprentice in an architectural firm where he met John Root. With Root he formed the great partnership, in 1873, of Burnham and Root. Root died young, in 1891, by which time they had designed more than 40 million dollars' worth of construction. The firm, which then became D. H. Burnham and Company, led architectural practice into the era of the large firm and the business of skyscraper design. His practice was truly national and included Union Station in the nation's capital, Filene's of Boston, Gimbel's in New York, Wanamaker's of Philadelphia, Marshall Field's of Chicago, and New York's "flatiron" building.

In 1890 President Harrison signed an act designating Chicago as site of the World's Columbian Exposition (opened in 1893). There was disagreement as to where in Chicago it would best be placed, so the famous landscape architect Frederick Law Olmsted was brought in to study the problem and make a recommendation. He surveyed the alternatives with the assistance of Daniel Burnham, who had also been retained to advise the local committee, and they put it, finally, on the lakeshore. Burnham, known for his dynamic leadership and organizational skill, was placed in charge of a team of internationally ranked artists, designers, and architects, with Olmsted as site planner. They designed and built the complex of buildings and public spaces that came to be known as the "White City". It was an inspiration to intellectuals and common folk alike, and marks the beginning of what historians have labelled the City Beautiful movement, the first era in the rise of modern American urban planning.

From the experience of the fair came a national image of planned city grandeur that earned for Burnham a series of commissions for city plans that slowly became a stream of planning work involving the Olmsteds and many others as well. Burnham's first call was to San Francisco in 1903. His characteristic response would be considered extreme today. His own labor, as always in his planning work, was given free of charge to the City of San Francisco, on the condition that his expenses were paid. His expenses included a study trip to Europe and especially the Mediterranean hill-towns, plus the construction of a special studio for his work, high in the hills above San Francisco, complete with a Chinese servant and cook. Only thus, he felt, might a proper perspective on the problem be achieved.

Burnham's planning career took him from the World's Fair, through the National Capital Plan of 1902, plans of Cleveland (1903), San Francisco, and the Philippines (1905) and culminated in the *Plan of Chicago* of 1909, a truly magnificent piece of work. He died in 1912. The efforts of Burnham and Olmsted might never have achieved more than an extension of the definitions of architecture and landscape architecture had it not been for a third force, the broad-based support of planning by civic improvement associations that were inspired and led by the works of Charles Mulford Robinson.

Charles Mulford Robinson, whose first book became the bible of local improvement societies, was born in 1869. A graduate of the University of Rochester, his first career was as a journalist. He edited newspapers, first in Rochester, then in Philadelphia, and finally in New York, and contributed regularly to leading journals of the day. In 1899 he published a series of three articles in *The Atlantic Monthly* on the subject of municipal improvement in the United States. Shortly thereafter he was commissioned by *Harper's Magazine* to travel abroad and write a similar series on municipal development in Europe.

In contrast to Burnham, whose most quoted remark was "Make no little plans, they have no magic to stir men's blood," Robinson was a believer in little plans. His first book on planning, *The Improvement of Towns and Cities,* went through eleven editions.[15] The more than 1200 local organizations using it ranged, he reported, "from the club in that village which has wisely substituted a wish to be attractive and beautiful for the old vain dream of bigness, to a society in one of the second class cities that has 3000 members."[16] His second major text, *Modern Civic Art,* devoted an entire chapter to the topic of "comprehensive planning" that predated Burnham's *Plan of Chicago* by six years. In 1904 he was instrumental in the merger of the American League for Civic Improvement and the American Park and Outdoor Art Association to form the American Civic Association, which he served briefly as secretary.

While his writings on city beautification and improvement propelled him into work on many American cities as a city planner, Robinson took time out of his very successful new career to go to Harvard, as a guest of the University, to study formally landscape architecture and planning as a special student in 1910. In 1913 he was appointed Professor of Civic Design at the University of Illinois, the first such chair in an American university, and his course became a required element in the curriculum in landscape architecture, then called landscape gardening. He died in 1917.

Robinson is of pivotal significance for the emergence of modern city planning for three reasons. First, the breadth of the popular movement he was so instrumental in fostering was essential to the building of a national constituency for the ideas of city planning. The predominantly private, commercial, and institutional sponsors of the work of Olmsted, Burnham, and their peers would likely not have been sufficient to keep the planning movement afloat.

Secondly, Robinson's writings, professional activities, and artistic bent were all supportive of landscape architecture as the progenitor profession and technical base on which planning practice was built. The importance of this factor in the development of planning will be discussed more fully later.

Thirdly, Robinson is the only one of our three pathfinders to have made the intellectual transition from the age of "The City Beautiful" to "The City Practical."

"We have now a large city, a crowded city, and a miserable one," Robinson wrote in 1903.

Out of misery came corruption, debauch of the popular conscience, and – from such favorable conditions – political bravery. These, swiftly, are the steps of the downward course. But all the time there were forces at work for good. The very evil into which affairs had passed created a disgust that vastly aided the reform endeavors.[17]

The progressive reform movement came in on the wave of a new social gospel and faith in progress, and Robinson offered more than a barrel full of sermons, as his work after 1910 clearly reveals.

The second era of modern American city planning is called "The City Practical." Its ideas were fully in place by the end of the first decade, even while Burnham was still gathering steam toward his Chicago report. What changed? The vehicle was still the idea of a plan. But where beauty had been the chief cargo, to it now were added heavy measures of engineering, economy, sociology, and law. "City planning is not tying pink ribbons to the lamp posts!" became the epithet. It was becoming clear that concerted action and tough implementation were required to deal with the great evils of municipal congestion and corruption.[18]

Phases of "The City Practical"

The spread of planning across American cities took place rapidly over the first few decades of the twentieth century. This growth was simultaneous with the technical expansion of the scope of planning concerns, encompassing increasingly sophisticated attention to matters of transportation, housing, sanitary conditions, land use law, and governmental organization, in addition to the continued attention to matters of aesthetics and civic design. Data on the growth of planning in the early decades of the movement were meticulously documented by John Nolen in his presidential address to the National Conference on City Planning in 1925. Before introducing Nolen and our other "pioneers" of this era, we will briefly analyze his data.

There were, according to Nolen, 176 comprehensive planning reports produced for US cities between 1905 and 1926. Of these 176 reports, 93 per cent were done by forty-three different outside consultants. Since a few of them occasionally formed temporary partnerships for some projects, the number of firms is difficult to enumerate exactly. Nonetheless,

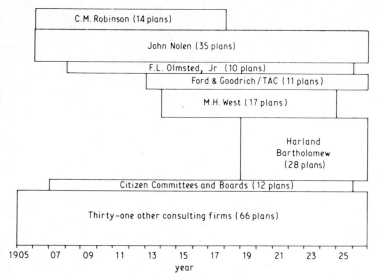

Figure 1.5 The producers of comprehensive planning reports for US cities, 1905–26.

a few leaders were clearly prominent in these early years: the firms of Robinson, Nolen, Olmsted, Ford and Goodrich (who were the Technical Advisory Corporation–TAC), West, and Bartholomew accounted for 70 per cent of the production. The distribution of work among firms, for the period, is illustrated in Figure 1.5.[19]

The comprehensive plan, however, was only one manifestation of the movement. Nolen's data have been combined with other sources, in Figure 1.6, to show the cumulative number of places with comprehensive plans, official planning commissions, adopted zoning ordinances, and later regional and county planning agencies.[20] Four distinct phases of development can be seen.

The first phase runs from 1905 to 1915, when the dominant instrument was the comprehensive plan. Sixty-six plans were produced in this period. In the second phase, from 1915 to 1922, the establishment of official city planning commissions dominated the cities, institutionalizing the planning process in local government. While the production of comprehensive plan reports continued to rise steadily, the infant zoning began its takeoff about 1918. After 1922, zoning ordinances led the third phase of the period. They were stimulated, at least in part, by the national model state enabling act of 1924. Later, we see the emerging organization of regional planning agencies take off between 1930 and 1936.

The planning literature contains striking parallels, as it no doubt should, to these shifting phases of planning practice. The American City

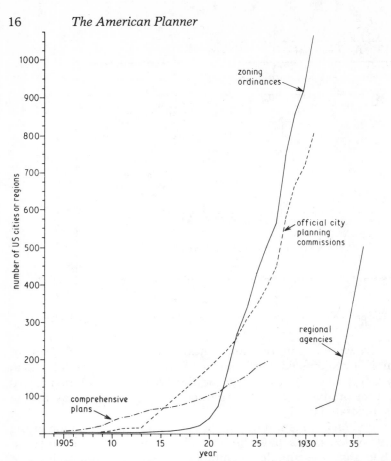

Figure 1.6 Cumulative total number of US cities with comprehensive plans, official planning commissions, adopted zoning ordinances; and cumulative total number of regional planning agencies.

Planning Institute began publishing their first journal in 1915 under the title, *The City Plan*, precisely at the end of the period during which the city plan dominated practice. The journal changed its name to *City Planning*, putting greater emphasis on the process of planning, in 1925, immediately after the official city planning commission's period of domination. The name was changed again, in 1935, to *The Planners' Journal*, in recognition of the expanding constituency of regional and national planners.

We turn now to brief introductions to the pioneers of this period whose lives and works are presented in chapters 2 through 7.

John Nolen (1869–1937) was the most productive city planner of his time. He was born in Philadelphia and educated at Girard College, a school for poor, fatherless boys. He entered the University of Pennsylvania in 1891.

His senior thesis on the Philadelphia Gas Works applied his learning in law, economics and management to its corrupted condition. He expanded his intellectual scope and depth for ten years while executive secretary of the Society for the Extension of University Teaching, a program of adult education. Following his third visit to Europe in 1902, he enrolled in the School of Landscape Architecture at Harvard. His professional practice, which began in Cambridge, soon grew to national prominence. His intellect and leadership were enormously important to the growth of the field.

Benjamin C. Marsh (1879–1953) was the energetic organizer of the first National Conference on City Planning. The son of New England Congregational missionaries, he spent much of his youth in Bulgaria. From Grinnell College in Iowa he went to the University of Pennsylvania in 1902, to study social philosophy. In 1907 he joined the Committee on Congestion of Population in New York City, through which he was instrumental in founding the National Conference on City Planning. He did not stay with the movement much beyond 1910. His unified view of city planning was split by Robert W. DeForest and Lawrence Veiller when they established their separate National Housing Association. None the less, his radical, iconoclastic, and energetic leadership fill an important early chapter in planning history.

Walter D. Moody (1874–1920) was the hired promoter of the *Plan of Chicago* and no one has ever done such a job better than he did. His name is easily confused with the popular Christian evangelist of the period, Dwight L. Moody. But Walter D. Moody was a salesman, drummer, and promoter of the planning gospel. He was hired by the Chicago Plan Commission in 1909 to organize a campaign to promote the Burnham and Bennett plan. To do this, in part, he wrote a textbook entitled *Wacker's Manual of the Plan of Chicago: Municipal Economy* which was used throughout the city's public schools to educate the future citizens of the city. His second book, *What of the City?*, is probably the first book that was genuinely critical of the methods of the modern planning movement in America.

Edward M. Bassett (1863–1948) and *Alfred Bettman* (1873–1945) are the pioneers of planning law. Bassett's family line was drawn from Plymouth Plantation in 1621 to the Flatbush Congregational Church of Brooklyn where he was chairman of the Board of Trustees for over twenty years. He worked his way through Columbia Law School as a teacher of Greek and Latin. He was elected to the US Congress in 1902. Known as the father of American zoning, his contributions to zoning and planning were possibly exceeded only by the younger Cincinnati lawyer, Alfred Bettman. Son of an immigrant German clothing manufacturer, Bettman grew up at the center of progressive reform Judaism in a city incontestably the most corruptly governed in America. After Harvard Law School his local leadership in the reform of Cincinnati grew to national service of high order in the development of planning. Among his greatest achievements was surely the winning brief before the US Supreme Court in the classic test of zoning, *Village of Euclid* v. *Ambler Realty Co.*, 1926.

Edith Elmer Wood (1871–1945) and *Catherine Bauer* (1905–1964) envisioned the linkage between housing and planning before most planners. Wood, the daughter of a naval officer, graduated with honors from Smith College at the age of eighteen. After achieving literary recognition as a novelist and raising four sons, she began a new career in reform by first taking a doctorate from Columbia University in political economy. Her applications of survey research to housing conditions were recognized, by 1919, as the first scientific analysis of the housing problem. Her young collaborator in the drive for public housing policy, Catherine Bauer, was the daughter of New Jersey's chief highway engineer. A graduate of Vassar, with strong interests in architecture, she brought Wood into the orbit of Lewis Mumford and the Regional Planning Association of America. Bauer's skill in political strategy and organization were based in a fiery moral passion for improving the urban condition that leaps from the pages of her famous book, *Modern Housing* (1934).

Nolen, Marsh, Moody, Bassett, Bettman, Wood, and Bauer are representative of the diverse disciplines and interests that converged in the early decades of the twentieth century to form the modern planning movement. They wrote the early formulas for making plans and promoting them, they wrote important textbooks, they provided leadership in local plan development and national organization, they formulated national, state, and local laws to implement the planning process. But the full-fledged expansion of the planning process to the level of the region came later – from a new set of ideas, a new set of conditions, and a new set of planners.

The rise of regionalism

There is an adage about the nature of the region and the problem of planning that is passed down among planners in the form of a question and answer:

Q.   What is the region?
A.   The region is the next level above the one on which we have been working but cannot find a solution.

The idea of regional planning arose because it was needed. And as it came, between the two world wars, it meant different things to different people.

One view of the region was from the metropolis. Its archetype and epitome was in *The Regional Plan of New York and Its Environs* prepared under the general direction of the great British town planner Thomas Adams. Sponsored by the Russell Sage Foundation, the greatest assemblage of planning studies ever focused on an American city filled the plan's ten volumes of research and recommendations published between 1929 and 1931. The work was begun in 1921 under the Foundation's Committee on the Regional Plan of New York and Its Environs, chaired by Charles Dyer Norton. At about the same time regional planning organizations were also formed in Chicago, under private auspices, and officially in the Los Angeles County Regional Planning Commission.

A second view of the region was established, at the other extreme position, on the mountaintop. This was the view of the decentralists. Their real point was not to abandon the city, but to achieve a more balanced form of development in harmony with the natural resources of the region. This view was most eloquently articulated by a group of influential intellectuals in and near New York City who formed the Regional Planning Association of America (RPAA). The core included Clarence Stein and Henry Wright, the architects and planners of the famous Radburn, New Jersey suburb; Lewis Mumford, the brilliant young social critic; Catherine Bauer and Edith Elmer Wood, the housers; Benton MacKaye, the naturalist; Stuart Chase the economist; and Charles Harris Whitaker, editor of the *Journal of the American Institute of Architects*.

Of the several causes advocated by the members of the RPAA, a new town program for America and urban deconcentration, in the spirit of the British movement, were high on the list. Their reputation was equally earned in what they were against. Their well-earned reputation as critics of the establishment was probably no better demonstrated than in their blistering public battle with Thomas Adams and The Regional Plan of New York over issues of housing and centralization.[21] They felt housing for the poor had been ignored and there was too much centralization. Adams thought them impractical.

The third strain of regional planning to emerge between the wars came from Roosevelt's New Deal, and its National Planning Board established in 1933, successively renamed the National Resources Board, National Resources Committee, and the National Resources Planning Board. While city planning agencies generally atrophied as a result of the Depression and the building slump that followed, the New Deal expanded the horizons of the planning vision through the vigorous promotion of state planning activities, regional development, as in the establishment of the Tennessee Valley Authority, and a program of Greenbelt New Towns under the direction of Rexford Tugwell.[22]

The people we have labelled as regionalists and who are presented in chapters 8 through 12 would be treated unfairly if their contributions were considered to be limited to ideas about regions. They most certainly were not. They were also pioneers in the promotion of planning, in recreation, in economics, in design, in the philosophy of planning, and numerous other important categories of endeavor.

Charles Dyer Norton (1871–1923) was the organizing force behind *The Regional Plan of New York and Its Environs*. His father-in-law, the famous architect Charles Follen McKim, stirred his original interest in planning which probably led to Norton's role in obtaining Daniel Burnham's services for Chicago. After serving as personal secretary to President Taft, Norton settled in New York City as vice-president of The First National Bank and became involved in local planning interests there. These led ultimately to his Trusteeship on the Russell Sage Foundation and his vision and establishment of the Committee on the Regional Plan. After his untimely death in 1923 the leadership of the committee passed to Norton's close associate, an engineer, Frederic A. Delano. A decade later Delano followed his nephew, Franklin Delano Roosevelt, to Washington as part of the famous New Deal "brain trust" that blanketed the nation with regional plans.

Benton MacKaye (1879–1975) was the founder of the Appalachian Trail. Born in Shirley, Massachusetts, he was a lover of the wilderness. As some men yearn "to run away to sea,' he confessed, his great desire was "to run away to land." He was educated at Harvard. After thirteen years with the National Forest Service he went into the US Department of Labor. He was a rare individual – a utopian in government. His proposal for the Appalachian Trail gained the support of Charles Harris Whitaker, editor of the *Journal of the American Institute of Architects*, through whom MacKaye entered the fold of the Regional Planning Association of America. There his philosophy of regional planning was nourished and grew. He was ahead of his time, but he lived to see the environmental movement reemerge in the 1970s and his book, *The New Exploration*, revived.

Henry Wright (1877–1938) created, with Clarence Stein, possibly the most famous suburban design in the world – Radburn, New Jersey. He was both a landscape architect and an architect, and was also in the inner circle of the RPAA. That Wright was a very unusual person is uniquely illustrated in the following recollection of Frederick J. Adams, the son of Thomas Adams. After finishing his degree in architecture at Columbia in 1928, Adams briefly went into the offices of Stein and Wright.

Henry took me over into his office and I worked laying out sidewalks and super-blocks. The thing was I had ten months of association with him which was absolutely remarkable. I mean, he was really a wonderful person – very intro-verted and very aggressive at times, but intellectually very stimulating. He took me over to Sunnyside the first time I met Lewis Mumford. I think the same day he took me up to somewhere on Central Park to meet Catherine Bauer who was working there. I had no intention of going into planning until then. Everybody would assume that I did it because of my father. If I'd gone back to England and worked (as an architect) in his office I probably wouldn't have. But I stuck.[23]

Wright also did pioneering work in the economic analysis of housing development, and served on the design team for Greenbrook, New Jersey, one of Tugwell's Greenbelt New Towns.

Rexford Guy Tugwell (1891–1979) had been an agricultural economist at Columbia University until Roosevelt put him in charge of the Resettlement Administration in 1935. From Sinclairsville, New York, son of a farmer and cannery owner, he went to college at the University of Pennsylvania. There he earned a doctorate from the Wharton School of Finance and Commerce and developed a passion for what he called "the magnificence of planning" as a route to social betterment. After the New Deal and his management of the Greenbelt New Towns program, he became the first chairman of the New York City Planning Commission in 1938. Roosevelt appointed him chancellor of the University of Puerto Rico in 1941 and later that year governor of the island. In 1945 he went to the University of Chicago as head of its Planning Program. Through that program's faculty and student body passed many of the postwar giants of the field: Edward C. Banfield, Melville C. Branch, Julius Margolis, Richard L. Meier, Martin Meyerson, Harvey S. Perloff, John Friedmann, John Dyckman, Britton Harris, and others.

Lewis Mumford never formally studied planning, but it is probably safe to claim that no one who did, in the last forty years, did so without studying his work. He was born in 1895 and grew up on New York City's Upper West Side. While still attending college he established a correspondence with Patrick Geddes, the great Scottish biologist, social theorist, and planner. Mumford's own career is phenomenally broad and humanistic. Proud that the great American architect Frank Lloyd Wright saluted him as "the real successor to Emerson," Mumford was a central actor in the RPAA. He was a harsh critic of Adams' Regional Plan of New York, and most of modern architecture and city building since. Regionalism, decentralism, city forms at a human scale for human ends, these are central to his creed and his more than twenty passionate books. Perhaps the most influential of them for its time was his classic, *The Culture of Cities* (1938). It is hard to say: there have been so many and he is, of course, still writing.

These regionalists – Norton, MacKaye, Wright, Tugwell, and Mumford – represent an important expansion of the intellectual and physical territory of the planning domain. They are more like the pioneers of the preceding group than the professionals that follow, in that they were heavily involved in careers and identities not solely that of city and regional planning, with the exception of John Nolen, Catherine Bauer and possibly Henry Wright. But what sets apart the professionals who follow is their experiences of planning as a primary career extending into the post Second World War period and their comprehensive involvement in the affairs and development of the field.

The professionals

While the term "professional" is carelessly applied to almost any identifiable occupation today, the special meaning it has had in the history of American planning is directly tied to the only slightly older profession of landscape architecture. Frederick J. Adams, reflecting again on the development of American planning, credited the landscape architects with the development of a distinctly American style.

I think the fact that planning here, as we know it, came from landscape architecture was really better than having come from the architects or the engineers. They, in the early days, did try to take over, if not the Institute, at least the claim that they were the logical planners; the architects because they knew about three dimensional design, and the engineers because they knew how to lay out streets and sewers. But the landscape architects had a better conception of it.[24]

Adams, who had built the planning department at the Massachusetts Institute of Technology into one of the foremost programs in the world, was considered the dean of American planning education, but he was not a landscape architect. Neither was his father, the famous British planner, Thomas Adams. The tradition, for which he had such great respect, reaches back to Frederick Law Olmsted and his successors.

Olmsted was a purist in art: he abhorred the mixing of styles, but he fathered a profession that was highly synthetic. On the one hand were the tools of science: the empirical knowledge of plants and materials, the systematic analysis of land forms and site characteristics. On the other hand was the art of design: the power of the creative idea and the process of developing a concept into a plan. These processes of scientific investigation and artistic design were molded into a professional service for clients whose problems ranged, in the words of Charles W. Eliot, 2nd, "from the backyard garden to the whole USA." This method, passed on through Eliot's sons and his students, permeated the study of landscape architecture at Harvard, through which a whole generation of students graduated, and then went on to dominate American colleges and universities in the teaching of more American planners.

The powerful role of landscape architecture in the development of American planning can scarcely be exaggerated. Its influence becomes overpoweringly clear when one looks at the college departments in which instruction in city planning was offered between 1910 and 1930. As

Table 1.1 College departments in which instruction in city planning was offered in the US 1910–30

Department	1910	1915	1920	1925	1930
Other	—	—	—	1	4
Art	—	—	—	2	3
Architecture	—	—	—	2	3
Civil Engineering	1	3	4	8	11
Landscape architecture	2	8	10	12	12
	3	11	14	25	33

shown in Table 1.1, landscape architects dominated the instruction throughout the entire period, as engineering, architecture, art, and other departments more gradually accumulated interest.[25]

Henry Hubbard of Harvard University, a founding editor of the most important professional journals of both landscape architecture and city planning, often wrote in defense of the new planning profession. One of these editorials, published in *City Planning* in 1926, was in response to an architect who after chauvinistically complaining about the quality of articles in planning journals, made the following claim.

If things in this world might take their normal and proper course, and the curse of "Specialists" might cease to appear to be a necessary evil – there would be no need for City Planners at all. All Cities, Towns, Villages, and other groups of buildings and open spaces, would be designed by the Architects. Once upon a time it was thus – and some day, if the number of Architects interested in City Planning continues to increase, it may be thus again.[26]

In contrast, Hubbard's cool and firm response is characteristically free of any guild mentality or proprietary claims over the planning field. He answered, in part, by saying:

City Planning is cooperation – cooperation of fallible humans each contributing what he can. And only a small part of the required total is to be found in the bounds of any one profession. The city planner is a recorder of the decisions of many men; he is not in himself the Olympian decider of human destinies.

Architects are doing much in city planning. The President of the American Institute of Architects says that they have the power and therefore the duty to do more. Surely this attitude is more likely to bring results than the attitude that through some unexplained God-given right they should wave aside the rest of the world while they do it all.[27]

Given the development of a field in which Hubbard's catholic attitude prevails, it should come as no surprise that there are a few, but only a few landscape architects among the professionals we now introduce.

Harland Bartholomew perhaps the nation's first full time employee of a city planning commission, in Newark, New Jersey, also built one of the largest and most successful consulting firms in the country. He was born near Boston in 1889. After high school in Brooklyn, New York, he studied civil engineering at Rutgers University for two years. He left college to go to work for E. P. Goodrich, a civil engineer in New York City. He was put in charge of the Technical Advisory Corporation's plan for Newark, and in 1914 left the firm to work full time for the city. In 1916 he moved to St Louis where he established the home base of his consulting firm and colonized the nation with his plans and his planners. In more than fifty years of practice he also conducted and published seminal research on urban land use, taught planning at the University of Illinois for thirty-seven years, and was a national leader in professional organizations.

Ladislas Segoe was the chief planner for the 1925 plan for Cincinnati, the first city plan to be officially adopted by a major American city. Born in Hungary in 1894, he discovered the field of planning while taking his degree in engineering in Budapest. After serving in the First World War, he worked briefly in Yugoslavia as a planner before coming to the United States in 1922. His first position here was also with Goodrich and Ford at TAC in New York, who sent him to Cincinnati where he followed the Bartholomew plan – took a job with the city and then set up his own consulting practice. He was a close associate and friend of Alfred Bettman. Segoe also taught planning, mainly at the University of Cincinnati, authored one of the most important textbooks in the field, and was a major figure in the leadership of the profession. He spent fifty-two years in the practice of planning in America.

Coleman Woodbury was the first executive director of the National Association of Housing Officials (NAHO) and a major link between the housing and planning professions. He was born in Illinois in 1903, educated at Northwestern University where he received his Ph.D in economics under Richard T. Ely, one of the most important academic pioneers of social reform in American history. Woodbury's interests in planning and housing led him into numerous official posts in government. He served NAHO from 1934 to 1942, was assistant administrator of the National Housing Agency from 1942 to 1946, and had a long association with the University of Wisconsin's teaching and research programs in urban planning.

Charles W. Eliot, 2nd, was the top ranking professional planner in Roosevelt's New Deal administration. Born in 1899, his roots in America go down to seventeenth-century New England and come up through his great-grandfather, Mayor of Boston, his grandfather, hailed as the most influential leader in the educational activities of the country, and his father, minister and president of the American Unitarian Association for twenty-seven years. Charles extended these traditions of leadership, intellect, and vision with ease through his practice and teaching of planning. His career in public service began at the National Capital Park and Planning Commission in 1926. He left Washington for California in 1944 after ten years of service to the Roosevelt administration. Later he returned to Massachusetts to establish his practice there and to teach at Harvard. His wise and sensitive ''Thoughts on Planning,'' included in chapter 16, would be fittingly compared with Daniel Burnham's epic creed.

Charles Abrams (1902–1970), lawyer, educator, and international authority on planning, is the storybook New Yorker. His father sold herrings and pickles from a stand on the sidewalk, across the street from their tenement in the Williamsburg district of Brooklyn. His was not the stream of progressive New York and Cincinnati Jews who could look forward to sending their sons to Harvard Law School. This was the orthodox community from Poland and Eastern Europe, of six-story walk ups and three-room flats. For Charles Abrams it was evening classes at Brooklyn Law School. After a short and very profitable career in law and real estate speculation, his earnings and holdings of Greenwich Village properties, and the lessons he learned in the marketplace, supported his subsequent career in planning and housing law.

Women have contributed greatly to American planning; through grass roots organizations and key national leadership roles in the first half of the century and in recent decades through leadership in professional practice. This history is reviewed in chapter 18 through the lives of several prominent figures: *Theodora Kimball Hubbard* (1897–1935), Harvard librarian and author; *Charlotte Rumbold* (1865–1960), activist in Cleveland; *Elisabeth Herlihy* (1880–1953), Massachusetts planning official for thirty-seven years; *Harlean James* (b. 1877), author and executive secretary to the American Civic Association for thirty-seven years; and many others. The first women to receive planning degrees from American universities earned them during the New Deal era. By 1976, 28 per cent of the planning degrees being awarded were earned by women. In 1978 Constance Lieder, of Baltimore, became the first woman president of the American Institute of Planners.

The most striking characteristic of this group of planners is their diversity – of origins, of training, of skills, and experience. And this characteristic dominates not only this group, but the previous groups as well. That a profession might grow from such a rich variety of talents to be characterized as ''cooperative'' is a truly remarkable accomplishment. And it is to these qualities of professionalism that we can attribute in large measure the postwar success of urban planning.

The postwar expansion of planning

If the planners at the National Resources Board had correctly forecast national growth, the story of the development of city and regional planning might have ended forty years ago. You will recall from our graph of US population growth in Figure 1.3 that the several forecasts made by the NRB in 1938 assumed that the great age of expansion was over. There were several events in the succeeding few years that encouraged this view. The most monstrous surprise, of course, was the war. Many of the younger planners entered the armed services, decimating the ranks of the profession. Those who were not sent to fight abroad found themselves fighting different battles at home.

The great domestic issue was planning for postwar recovery and the expansion and redevelopment of cities after the war. Britain took bold and decisive steps toward centralized national control of these matters. The debate in America was bitter, with many planners caught in the middle. The left was critical because we did not think boldly enough, along the lines of the British. The right considered planning as fundamentally communistic and inherently unAmerican. There were practical as well as ideological implications of the debate. The middle ground was a postwar agenda for urban redevelopment and public works that would bridge the anticipated valleys of unemployment and housing shortage immediately after the war. The big political question was who was going to control these jobs and expenditures. It was the classic question of local versus centralized control. Robert Moses of New York, who probably controlled more local public works than any other single individual in America, led a vulgar campaign against his enemies, the "long-haired planners."[28] After the war these issues of ideology were slowly submerged in the flood of new realities.

Housing mushroomed after the war. From 1930 to 1945 the number of housing starts in the nation had been averaging less than one-half million per year. After the war this figure leaped to 2,000,000 units per year. The other great force in urbanization was the ubiquitous spread of the automobile. The suburban housing phenomenon and its complement of private automobile consumption are shown in Figure 1.7.[29]

The expenditure of public dollars on domestic development programs also exhibited a takeoff after the war. Direct federal expenditures plus state and local expenditures on highways, housing, and urban renewal are shown in Figure 1.8.[30] The planning profession thrived on the cumulative growth of successive waves of federal programs. The various housing construction, loan, and mortgage insurance programs, the urban renewal program, the comprehensive planning assistance program, and the interstate highway program – these filled the agenda of the 1950s.

The early 1960s revealed reactions to the postwar building boom. There were unintended side-effects of urban renewal that aggravated racial and class inequalities and destroyed social neighborhoods. The highway program that drove people to the suburbs fostered suburban shopping

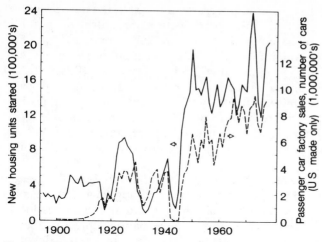

Figure 1.7 Housing starts and car sales, 1900–70+.

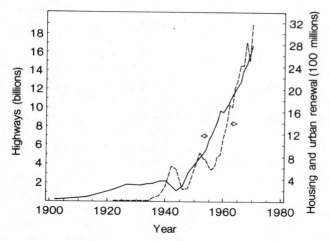

Note: Highway expenditures given in billions of dollars; housing and urban renewal given in 100 millions of dollars.

Figure 1.8 Federal, direct, plus state and local expenditures on highways and housing and urban renewal, 1902–70.

malls that undermined the economies of older downtowns and further reduced both the quantity and quality of inner city living space. In the face of all this there was some loss of confidence in the comprehensive plan, which was too often of little protective or directive assistance.

The ranks of the planning profession, however, grew by leaps and bounds. The later 1960s brought the programs of "the great society," "model cities," and the "war on poverty." Integral to the new programs was the extension of community participation in control over public expenditures. One characteristic "solution" that emerged was an improbable fusion of communitarian and Department of Defense ideas, known as the Planning, Programming, Budgeting System (PPBS). It had something to offer almost everyone: a political promise of popular control, the uncompromised efficiency of rational economic allocation, and a handbook of procedures requiring minimal technical knowledge. It was a simple idea but difficult in practice. It gave way in the following decade to more workable notions of program evaluation and policy analysis.

The federal grants economy developed. The 1960s brought greater involvement of the federal government in providing local revenues. In the 1970s, block grants and revenue sharing attempted to reallocate control over these federal expenditures. New national priorities arose again, first in environmental protection and then in energy development and conservation. As each of these initiatives grew, more diverse planners joined the pool of sociologists, geographers, engineers, economists, political scientists, and lawyers assembled to tackle these problems.

The postwar era was also a period of great intellectual ferment and change within planning and the allied disciplines. The social sciences were slow to give up their traditional priorities to the applied problems of urban affairs. Sociology and geography were among the first and more successful to develop recognized urban subdisciplines. Regional science, established about 1955, attempted to recast geographic analysis, economic theory, and urban and regional planning problems in the language of statistics and mathematics. It fueled the hopes for a science of planning and transformed permanently the analytic capacity of the field. The broader interests of mainstream economists were more slowly attracted to urban problems, stimulated by conflicts in the environmental movement between economic development and environmental protection and the increasing concern for regional growth and social equity.

The prewar dominance of the design professions, architecture and landscape architecture, has diminished. While imaginative new university programs in urban design, regional land use planning, and behavioral aspects of environmental design have developed, the limelight of planning has been dominated by the greater interest in so-called non-physical solutions. The shifting balance of the field was felt by Hegemann and Peets as early as 1922:

The young profession of city planning is drifting too strongly in the directions of engineering and applied sociology. This is perhaps natural, for there are problems of such tremendous importance in these fields, problems of a practical importance

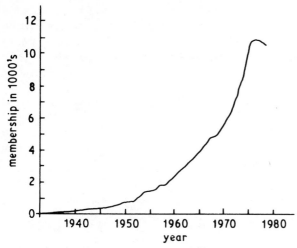

Figure 1.9 Growth in the American Institute of Planners, 1935–78.

which newspapers and public officials can appreciate and even property rights can be induced to recognize, that men in the profession are attracted in that direction. Besides, it is much easier and more respectable to be an engineer, an "uplifter," or a business man, than it is to be an artist.[31]

Reflecting on the future of American planning

The impact of the postwar era was little short of life-saving. At its inception in 1917 the American Institute of City Planning had twenty-one members. By 1940 there were eighty-nine full members, seventeen associates and forty-three junior members (plus nine honorary and eleven affiliates). During the war the Institute had nearly ceased existence. The *Journal* suspended publication. Organizational and professional prospects were grim. The postwar transformation of the Institute to nearly 5000 planners by 1970 and more than twice that number by 1978, is shown in Figure 1.9.[32] The counting of planners is confounded by the changing historical structure of organizations, such as the merger of the American Institute of Planners and the American Society of Planning Officials in 1978, whose joint membership, in the American Planning Association, now approaches 20,000. The historical trace of planning's organizations is portrayed in Figure 1.10.

Characteristic of the idea of cooperation, the first national conference on city planning, in 1909, was a joint effort among the architects, landscape architects, the Committee on Congestion of Population, the League of American Municipalities, the National Conference of Charities and Corrections, and the American Civic Association. In 1910 the National

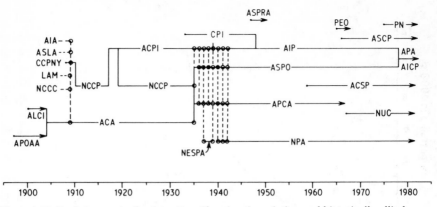

Figure 1.10 Predecessors to the American Planning Association and historically allied organizations.

AIA, American Institute of Architects (1857–)
ASLA, American Society of Landscape Architects (1899–)
CCPNY, Committee on Congestion of Population in New York
LAM, League of American Municipalities
NCCC, National Conference of Charities and Corrections
ALCI, American League for Civic Improvement (1900–4)
APOAA, American Park and Outdoor Art Association (1897–1904)
ACA, American Civic Association (1904–35)
NCCP, National Conference on City Planning (1910–17, 19–35)
ACPI, American City Planning Institute (1917–39)
CPI, California Planner's Institute (1933–48)

ASPRA, American Society for Planning Research & Action (1947–?)
AIP, American Institute of Planners (1939–78)
ASPO, American Society of Planning Officials (1935–78)
APCA, American Planning & Civic Association (1935–67)
NESPA, National Economic & Social Planning Association (1937–39)
NPA, National Planning Association (1940–)
PEO, Planners for Equal Opportunity (196?–?)
PN, Planners Network (1975–)
ACSP, Association of Collegiate Schools of Planning (1959–)
NUC, National Urban Coalition (1967–)
ASCP, American Society of Consulting Planners (1966–)

APA/AICP, American Planning Association/American Institute of Certified Planners (1978–)

Conference on City Planning was formed, and interrupted briefly in 1917 by the American City Planning Institute. Two years later the NCCP was revived to continue the conference.

The period between the Depression and the end of the Second World War saw some convergence of interests. From 1935 to 1943 was a highly interactive period among mutually supportive institutions, including interests in national planning and the newly formed American Society of Planning Officials, established in Chicago at the Public Administration Clearing House. After the war the California Planning Institute merged with AIP, whose new name had been taken in 1939, to form a truly national professional organization.

Subsequent trends seem more sectarian. The American Society for Planning Research and Action was a short-lived group, centered around the Chicago School's interest in social science, that was soon informally absorbed into the mainstream of AIP. The Association of Collegiate Schools of Planning formed an academic wing for the profession in 1959. A separate American Society of Consulting Planners was formed in 1966 to serve their special interests. Planners for Equal Opportunity rose on the crest of the advocacy and civil rights movements and thrived for a few years, centered in New York City. Similar interests in radical analysis were revitalized in the Planners Network in 1975. In 1978 AIP and ASPO merged to form the American Planning Association, having within it the semi-independent institute for professional certification, the American Institute of Certified Planners, the extension of the former AIP.

While it is not graphically obvious, and it is certainly highly debatable, there are a number of observers of planning who suggest that we have completed a circle. Beyond the endurance of acronyms that has turned ACPI into ACIP, there is an undeniable pluralism of professional interests today that is reminiscent of the days of the planning pioneers. Critics and detractors have misinterpreted this development, accusing planners of having too many interests, with the diagnosis of "rampant schizophrenia," and the conclusion that "if planning is everything, maybe it's nothing."[33]

Rapid growth and change of the magnitude of the past three decades would be stressful to the definition and identity of any responsive profession. The planning movement brought with it much of the technical and intellectual baggage that American society wanted and needed for its trip from the 1940s to the 1980s: a commitment to urbanism as a way of life, a public process for setting goals and guiding change, workable techniques of social research and forecasting, a tradition of real concern for the poor and the environment, enough knowledge of the law to be inventive in its applications, enough skill in design to offer tangible solutions to physical problems, and a genuine commitment to democracy. It should have come as no surprise that the postwar urban explosion, spurred by the civil rights movement of the 1960s, and the environmental movement of the 1970s found planning a convenient vehicle for the advancement of societal reforms. It is clear that the age from 1900, or thereabouts, to the Second World War was of a piece. And it is also clear that a second great era in American planning is near its close. National political shifts and international developments are signalling redirection. To mark precisely the end and measure the new beginning is not our objective here and even may be premature. But change is in the air and there is a growing hope for the new beginning. It is a good time for remembering why we chose to become planners in the first place. It is why we look back at the lives and recollections that follow.

Exactly where we go from here is not as important now as to affirm just how and why we will proceed. We would do well to follow the advice of that great American planner and sociologist Louis Wirth who gave to the National Planning Conference, on the threshold of our time, this "planner's creed."

A planner's creed

If we are to plan on a scale and of a quality that will meet the problems of our time we must have planners who are equal to the magnitude and complexity of the task. I shall merely record my conception of what it takes:

1   The planner must, of course, have technical competence. He must know the facts of life and he must have mastered the techniques of analysis and synthesis.
2   He must have courage and steadfastness of purpose.
3   He must have personal integrity and be able to resist the temptation to prostitute himself by the lure of gold or fame or power to the wiles of those who happen to possess gold or fame or power.
4   He must be responsible to himself, to his profession and to the community.
5   He must love his fellow men – not merely the rich and the great, but all his fellow men regardless of race, creed or station in life – and he must consider the equal claims of all.
6   He must cultivate humility and be willing to acknowledge what he doesn't know and let others take credit for what he does.
7   He must believe in progress. He must be a conservative in the sense of seeking to conserve the best of what is; a radical in the sense of daring to transcend the limitations and frustrations of the present.
8   He must be patient without being supine. He must have an appreciation of social values without blithely accepting established dogmas.
9   He must have a disciplined imagination which leads him continuously to push out the frontiers of the possible without losing himself in the pursuit of the end of the rainbow.
10 He must learn to see farther and deeper than those who have not presumed, as he has, to play the responsible and dangerous role of counsellor of men, of communities, of states and nations, and he must see things in their together-ness. He must sense and be willing and able to trace the longer-range and less obvious implications of trends and of actions and he must be constantly aware that a change in any part of this complex world will have repercussions upon the whole.[34]

Notes

1   Perry L. Norton (ed.) (1960) *Bair Facts: The Writings of Frederick H. Bair, Jr.*, West Trenton, New Jersey, Chandler-Davis, pp. 37–8.
2   These two reviews were published back-to-back in the *Journal of the American Planning Association* (1981) 47, 3, 356–9.
3   Quoted in "The cultivation of judgement and wisdom," by Eugenie Ladner Birch, October 1, 1979.
4   See, for example: Thomas S. Hines (1974) *Burnham of Chicago: Architect and Planner*, New York, Oxford University Press; and Laura Wood Roper (1973)

FLO: A Biography of Frederick Law Olmsted, Baltimore, The Johns Hopkins University Press.

5 Catherine Bauer (1934) *Modern Housing*, Boston, Houghton Mifflin Company, p. 5.

6 Data source: US Bureau of the Census (1975) *Historical Statistics of the United States, Colonial Times to 1970*, part 2, Washington, D.C., US Government Printing Office, Series Q 284–312, pp. 727–30.

7 Data source: US Bureau of Census (1975) *Historical Statistics of the United States, Colonial Times to 1970*, part 1, Washington, D.C., US Government Printing Office, Series C 89–119, pp. 105–9.

8 National Resources Committee (1938) *The Problems of a Changing Population*, Washington, D.C., US Government Printing Office, p. 24; and US Bureau of the Census (1977) *Statistical Abstract of the United States: 1977* (98th edn), Washington, D.C.

9 See n. 5.

10 National Resources Committee (1937) *Our Cities: Their Role in the National Economy*, Washington, D.C., US Government Printing Office, p. 1.

11 Planning of this type is magnificently analyzed in two books by John Reps: (1965) *The Making of Urban America: A History of City Planning in the United States*, Princeton, Princeton University Press, and (1979) *Cities of the American West: A History of Frontier Urban Planning*, Princeton, Princeton University Press.

12 A good comparative introduction to Howard is Robert Fishman (1977) *Urban Utopias in the Twentieth Century: Ebenezer Howard, Frank Lloyd Wright, and Le Corbusier*, New York, Basic Books. A fascinating perspective on Howard's success can be gained from Barbara W. Tuchman (1966) *The Proud Tower*, New York, The Macmillan Company, esp. ch. 2.

13 Charles Capen McLaughlin and Charles E. Beveridge, eds (1977) *The Papers of Frederick Law Olmsted*: volume 1, *The Formative Years 1822–1852*, Baltimore, The Johns Hopkins University Press; letter to Charles Loring Brace, July 26, 1852, pp. 375–87.

14 Frederick Law Olmsted (1870) *Public Parks and the Enlargement of Towns*, Cambridge, Mass., American Social Science Association. Reprinted edn 1970 by Arno Press, Inc.

15 Charles Mulford Robinson (1901) *The Improvement of Towns and Cities; or, The Practical Basis of Civic Aesthetics*, New York, G. P. Putnam's Sons.

16 Charles Mulford Robinson (1903) *Modern Civic Art; or The City Made Beautiful*, New York, G. P. Putnam's Sons, p. iii.

17 ibid., p. 15.

18 An excellent general history, relied upon throughout the period since 1890, is Mel Scott (1971) *American City Planning since 1890*, Berkeley, University of California Press. Two excellent works on the reform period are by Roy Lubove: (1962) *The Progressives and the Slums*, Pittsburgh, University of Pittsburgh Press, and (1967) *The Urban Community: Housing and Planning in the Progressive Era*, Englewood Cliffs, N.J., Prentice-Hall. Also see Jon A. Peterson (1976) "The City Beautiful movement: forgotten origins and lost meanings," *Journal of Urban History*, 2 (4), 415–34.

19 Composed from data in John Nolen (1927) "Twenty years of city planning progress in the United States," *Planning Problems of Town, City, and Region*, Philadelphia, National Conference on City Planning, pp. 1–44.

20 Sources of data include: ibid.; the annual surveys of city and regional planning in the United States, published in *City Planning* by Theodora Kimball Hubbard

from 1926 to 1930 and by Harold S. Buttenheim in 1931 and 1932; and Harvey S. Perloff (1957) *Education for Planning: City, State, and Region*, Baltimore, The Johns Hopkins Press.

21 Excellent studies of the RPAA are found in: Roy Lubove (1963) *Community Planning in the 1920's: The Contribution of the Regional Plan Association of America*, Pittsburgh, University of Pittsburgh Press; and in Carl Sussman (ed.) (1976) *Planning the Fourth Migration: The Neglected Vision of the Regional Planning Association of America*, Cambridge, Mass., The MIT Press.

22 New Deal planning is treated extensively in: Otis L. Graham, Jr (1976) *Toward a Planned Society: From Roosevelt to Nixon*, New York, Oxford University Press; and in Marion Clawson (1981) *New Deal Planning*, Baltimore, The Johns Hopkins University Press.

23 Unpublished interview of Frederick J. Adams, January 4, 1979.

24 ibid.

25 Adapted from table III in Frederick J. Adams and Gerald Hodge (1965) "City planning instruction in the United States: the pioneering days, 1900–1930," *Journal of the American Institute of Planners*, 31 (1), 43–50.

26 Henry Hubbard (1926) "Editorial," *City Planning*, II (3), 198–9.

27 ibid.

28 For a good treatment of this period see Phillip J. Funigiello (1978) *The Challenge to Urban Liberalism: Federal–City Relations during World War II*, Knoxville, The University of Tennessee Press.

29 The sources for the data in Fig. 1.9 are: US Bureau of the Census (1975) *Historical Statistics of the United States, Colonial Times to 1970*, part 2, Washington, D.C., US Government Printing Office, Series N 156–69 and Q 148–62; US Bureau of Census, Department of Commerce Construction Reports (December 1978) "Housing starts," C20–78–10, Washington, D.C., US Government Printing Office; also C20–79–2, February 1979; and Motor Vehicle Manufacturers Association (1978) *Motor Vehicles Facts and Figures*, Detroit, MVMA, p. 9.

30 Sources for Fig. 1.10 are: US Bureau of the Census, *Historical Statistics of the United States, Colonial Times to 1970*, Series Y 605–37 and Y 682–709.

31 Werner Hegemann and Elbert Peets (1922) *The American Vitruvius: An Architect's Handbook of Civic Art*, New York, The Architectural Book Publishing Co., p. 4.

32 See Donald A. Krueckeberg (1980) "The story of the Planner's Journal 1915–1980," *Journal of the American Planning Association*, 46 (1), p. 18. Also see Eugenie Ladner Birch (1980) "Advancing the art and science of planning: planners and their organizations, 1909–1980," *Journal of the American Planning Association*, 26 (1).

33 The parenthetical expressions are from John F. Kain (1970) "Rampant schizophrenia: the case of city and regional planning," *Journal of the American Institute of Planners*, 36 (4), 221–3; and Aaron Wildavsky (1973) "If planning is everything, maybe it's nothing," *Policy Sciences*, 4, 127–53.

34 Louis Wirth was largely responsible for establishing the planning program at the University of Chicago, of which Tugwell was the first head. Wirth delivered the keynote address at the National Planning Conference held in Cincinnati in 1947. He titled it, "Planning means freedom." When he died on May 3, 1952, this excerpt from his address was published, in memoriam, on the front page of the *ASPO Newsletter*, June 1952.

Part 1 The pioneers

2 John Nolen:
the background of a pioneer planner

John Hancock*

The early development of modern physical planning as a separate
profession in the United States coincides with the reform period in
our political history known as the "progressive era." Both
phenomena were new attempts at dealing with a changed condition
– the emergence of America as a culture whose traditional lifeways
had become increasingly depersonal, thoroughly industrialized, and
predominantly urban. Of the planners, few seem to have been better
prepared to deal with the demands of a rapidly changing order than
John Nolen, whose background prior to his first major works in 1909
exemplifies that mixture of ongoing attitudes and innovations
necessary to meet changing cultural conditions.

In the fall of 1908 a group of prominent business and professional men
formed the Civic Association of Reading, Pennsylvania, for the singular
purpose of promoting their city's better physical development. Officially
a non-political body, their aim was to influence key local power groups by
making an extended survey of Reading's problems and then to use its
results in pressuring for improvements through concerted municipal
action. Later the Association members were to indicate, individually,
some strong ideas about the nature and solution of civic problems in
Reading; but they did not specify any particular course of improvement
during the period of organization. Instead their first act as an organized
body was to seek the advice of an "expert" who, coming from outside the
city, could analyze its physical problems, forecast future needs, and then
"form a general programme of city making."[1]

* *Author's note:* This essay originally was written as part of a case study of city planning as
an agent for cultural change in Reading, Pennsylvania, 1908–16. It is *not* a definitive statement of Nolen's total life or works; instead, it seeks to define the societal and intellectual
milieu of Nolen *up to* the eve of his first major planning efforts.
  For their helpful reading of this text, I wish to express my appreciation to members of
the City Planning Department at the University of Pennsylvania, to Wallace E. Davies of
the History Department, for whom this was first written, and to Barbara Nolen Strong, Mr
Nolen's daughter. For their intellectual support and incisive critical perceptions, I am
indebted above all to William L. C. Wheaton, of the University's Institute for Urban
Studies, and to planning consultant John Nolen, Jr, who also has made his father's papers
available to me. Judgments expressed in this paper are the sole responsibility of the
author.

The "expert" they selected was John Nolen of Cambridge, Massachusetts, a man whose professional title was "landscape architect," although he had been working extensively with the replanning of cities for three years and had been interested in municipal problems since his undergraduate days in the 1890s. The choice of the Association was a fortunate one for both parties. For the Association, Nolen was an unbiased specialist whose presence in Reading could not offend anyone. It was announced in the newspapers that Nolen, a man who "beautified cities," had come to Reading to advise its citizens on the means of making it a more attractive place, particularly to outside businessmen looking for new industrial locations.[2] To Nolen, the Association represented a body of intelligent leading citizens seriously interested in civic betterment who could be taught, should they not realize it already, that city planning meant not just beautification but also provision for environmental needs of all Reading's citizenry – that planning for the health and welfare of her people was sound business sense as well as the ultimate purpose of "city making."[3]

In interests and background, Nolen had much in common with these men. Born in Philadelphia in 1869, he remained an urban Easterner all his life. College-educated, he was able and eager to give expression to his concerns. Although never a businessman in the limited sense, he was a professional in business for himself, whose work consisted of selling services – ideas and plans – to others. His office undertook the planning of large-scale municipal projects on a contract basis throughout the United States without ever being an official part of any government, as are so many planning services today. His success, like that of the commercial and civic organizations who first employed him, depended in large measure upon his persuasive abilities. At the same time, his early life was more thoroughly illustrative of mobility and success in the traditional American ideology than that of his sponsors and emphatically unlike that of his predecessors in the field of large-scale planning:[4] he was of obscure lower-middle-class parentage; he had to make his own way from early adolescence; he had not set out to be an artist, architect, or engineer as an undergraduate – he did not even become a landscape architect until he was thirty-five; his interests at college were in economics, history (especially near-contemporary American history), philosophy, and public administration; although widely traveled, he never studied in any of the European art schools; he had very few personal contacts with members of the social register or with the well-known late-nineteenth- and early twentieth-century artists then admired, such as Charles McKim, Stanford White, the Hunts, Saint-Gaudens, the elder Olmsted, and D. H. Burnham, although he had met these men and soon acquired many prominent, powerful friends among the newly and the almost wealthy. In brief, his

Plate 2.1 John Nolen, 1895.

background equipped him with a point of view as a planner, more characteristic of the young militant, middle-class reformers of the twentieth century than of the more established, paternalistic stewards of wealth and their retinue of the late nineteenth. From both groups, however, he inherited the common legacy of a sense of responsible leadership and an adherence to the main tenets of the American value system.

Early education in laissez-faire America

Hard work, sympathetic awareness of man's needs at several levels, and continuous education were the main foundations of Nolen's development in professional planning. He came by these characteristics early and almost instinctively. His father, a carpenter, died when the boy was less than two years old; his mother, long an influence on his ambitions, cared for him until the age of nine when she was able to take him out of the Philadelphia public schools and enroll him in Girard College, where he graduated in 1884. The training young Nolen received at this school for fatherless, poor, white boys was to be recalled vividly in his later ideas and activities. In accordance with its founder's firm views on education, Girard College sought to develop, or redevelop if you will, every aspect of a boy's character. Nolen and others like him received closely supervised training in academic, vocational, physical, and moral subjects. At Girard, Nolen, who graduated first in his class, acquired his lifelong love for literature, was exposed to European history and the modern romantic languages, demonstrated an unusual capacity for public speaking on contemporary issues, learned the Bible thoroughly from a non-sectarian but basically Protestant point of view, and was trained unceasingly in the rudimentary duties of responsible citizenship. In addition he learned to use industrial machinery, should the future require his employment as a workingman; and, finally, he was imbued with the concept of regular daily exercise in the out-of-doors and the need to be proficient in at least one sport throughout life.[5]

Girard College's rigorous curriculum was based upon the activist, somewhat Calvinistic, notion that men succeeded in life only through individual hard work, self-discipline, clean living, and service to others. In fulfilling Stephen Girard's dictum that "No man shall be a gentleman on my money," idleness was never tolerated.[6] But the training was also extremely practical when one considers how closely it paralleled the ethic of success in New Testament America – if one did not become a Captain of Industry he would at least acquire skills enough to be satisfied with the existing system of mobility, just as he would understand he had been the one poor orphan Alger out of five or six fortunate enough to have been snatched away from a probable life of degradation and misery in the streets. Furthermore, the training had the real merit of being very progressive for its time, thanks to frequent reinterpretations of Girard's liberal, if non-permissive, will. Cheesman Herrick, a Nolen classmate at the University of Pennsylvania and a later president of Girard, has summarized the school's close kinship to the changing world outside:

In the last analysis, Girard College is a little world . . . [boys] are getting their equipment for the life they will later go to, and they are fitted for the real world just so far as the elements and features of this world are brought into their training . . . the school is more than preparation for life; it is life.[7]

Thus, Nolen finished his early education equipped with the basic tools for success in late nineteenth-century America and supplied with a headful of moral rationalizations of the status quo in the very possible event that the tools were not enough.[8]

Most of Nolen's worldly experience before 1904 was acquired in administrative and educational positions. After Girard, he clerked in a grocery store for a year and then returned to the school at sixteen to serve as a minor secretary of the Girard Estate Trust Fund for the next five years. These jobs enabled him to accumulate money enough to enter the University of Pennsylvania's Wharton School as an economics and public administration major in 1891. Upon examination, he entered as a junior, and in 1893, at the age of twenty-four, he was graduated with a Bachelor of Philosophy degree. Thus, although he had come comparatively late to college, he already had accumulated five years of administrative experience and several more of constant employment. In three summers away from the University he also served as director of Onteora Park, a New York State resort; and before his graduation, he undertook a full-time job with the newly formed Society for the Extension of University Teaching.

Learning to challenge the older order in a changing society

At Pennsylvania he combined several of his former interests with formal training in administrative work. He was a member of the Wharton Congress, a debating group; he won third prize in the University oratorical contest in his senior year; together with Franklin Spencer Edmunds, he founded and wrote for the Wharton *Bulletin*; continuing his progress as a distinguished student (he graduated "with distinction" in a class that included Thomas Soverign Gates, who became president of the University in 1930), Nolen was deemed certain to attain success and renown.[9]

His formal course work reflected his interests in contemporary affairs and it was also an index to the near-vocational fields then opening up on the edge of the traditional humanities. He took courses in "money management," "constitutional law and politics," the "sociology" of the state, "finance and administration." From liberal economist Simon N. Patten (who along with Richard Ely and others led the revolt against classical economic theories and spearheaded the modern interest in national economic planning), he learned the rudiments of "political economy." Patten was also the source for many of the concepts on national planning held by Rexford G. Tugwell, head of the Resettlement Administration during the New Deal; and Patten's ideas appear nearly unadulterated in the writings of Walter Weyl (*The New Democracy*), one of the theorists of the progressive movement.[10] Strikingly close as thinkers although not contemporaries as students, Nolen, Weyl, and Tugwell all studied under Patten at Pennsylvania.

In contrast, Nolen also had a course from Francis Moore on the new "science" of sociology; his handwritten notes reveal Moore's view that the function of the state was to govern as little as possible and that Socialist "theory" was based on obtaining control of industrial affairs. Professor Robert Ellis Thompson (who also taught Nolen's course in American church history) lectured optimistically on American industrial history, but warned his students that, despite the general correctness of the stewardship doctrines of wealth, competition in some fields was insufficient protection to the public interests and in a few cases (he mentioned the railroads) even required government regulation. For pioneer social historian John MacMaster's course on the "political history of the United States," Nolen wrote a factual, historical essay on private acquisition of the public domain. He was also in James Harvey Robinson's first class on European history – Robinson later remembered Nolen as his most outstanding student at Pennsylvania. Nolen also wrote papers in the history of philosophy – on Descartes because he was, said Nolen, "the father of modern philosophy," and on John Stuart Mill, the political theorist.[11]

For his senior thesis and first real published work, Nolen characteristically wrote of a contemporary problem: municipal mishandling of the Philadelphia Gas Works and the steps which should be taken to correct the corruption. His conclusion was that the early mismanagement was "not chargeable to public ownership; it was inherent in the system adopted." He suggested that instead of granting a public lease to private corporations there should be outright public ownership, development, and maintenance of gas facilities. He also pointed out that *city* departmental "waste" of gas could be prevented by deducting the cost of gas used from their budget appropriations, and that the price of gas to the consumer should be little more than the cost of its manufacture plus a small amount set aside for its future improvement: "Otherwise a portion of the gas rate becomes a tax upon the consumers of gas, and [since the 'wealthy classes' use, proportionally, less than the 'poorer classes'] . . . this tax is an unfair burden upon the latter."[12] This paper was written under the general supervision of Dean Edmund James, of the Wharton School, who, with Patten, Ely, and other rebels against the laissez-faire school, had formed the American Economic Association in 1885.[13]

A "Municipal Statesman" foreshadowed

There is no doubt that Nolen considered the administrative problems of city government the most pressing domestic issues of the day. In the next few years, he would turn to them again and again – foreshadowing his later, immediate shift from landscape architecture to cooperative municipal action in planning. Addressing the Girard College class of 1895, he spoke of the city's new role in American life and the need for a new type of local leader to cope with its problems.

> The problems of the day . . . which demand our attention are not so much *national* as *municipal*. Life, in its most complex relations, is now in the cities, the vilest criminals, the purest saints are to be found in the great centres of population. Public spirit is not so much needed in Washington as in Philadelphia. On every side we hear the cry for *Municipal Statesmen*.
>
> Who is the man, then, that we should honor? Who is it that deserves our praise? It is he, who lives the fullest civic life. It is he who works for his city with a confidence born of faith. . . . He keeps ever before him an ideal, and strives to make it a reality. Citizenship to him does not merely mean good government and politics, but includes all that effects the happiness, usefulness and virtue of any individual.[14]

Overtly he was leading up to a few words of praise for Stephen Girard, but in fact he was describing his own deepest beliefs, beliefs which in ten years were to make city planning almost a religion with him. His eventual move into that field occurred precisely because he visualized city planning as a profession which must consider "all that effects the happiness, usefulness and virtue" of men. Nolen aspired to be a "Municipal Statesman" himself because, in his eyes, it offered the chance for service, hard work, and self-sacrifice to community goals he had learned to believe in. Nolen was seeking for some kind of total commitment to his society's basic ideals. He did not stop to find it either in political or aesthetic reform but went beyond these to something that might include them and more – the challenge of "comprehensive" (his favorite word) city planning, the opportunity to redesign man's whole environment.

"The People's University"

But professional city planning in America had not yet developed, just as urban reform had not yet found the broad public support necessary for sustained action. So for the next ten years after college, Nolen's education continued, as he accumulated administrative experience in Philadelphia as executive secretary of the Society for the Extension of University Teaching. He had been recommended for the post by Dean James, a founder of the Extension.

The Extension is an example of the rising popularity of adult education in late nineteenth-century America and the attempt by men like James to devise a means for the further development of an informed citizenry in a rapidly concentrating democratic society. Somewhat like the old Lyceum, Chatauqua, and Redpath Bureau lectures, it brought a series of public lectures to Philadelphia and other eastern cities – usually to give a "course" consisting of six evening talks on a single subject. Like the winter Chatauqua correspondence program and the newly created night schools for workingmen and immigrants, papers were graded and certificates were awarded those who paid fees and completed the "course." Unlike all the others, it also offered the prestige of association with a university-level, adult educational movement which had its beginning at Oxford. And, most importantly, this early experiment in university extension schooling provided lecture discussion by outstanding figures on some of the most stimulating issues of the day. Besides the usual presentations on literature, art, and the sacred trinity of mother–home–God, the Extension (from 1890 to 1903) offered college credit in most of the humanities and sciences. It introduced lectures on unionism, socialism, social reform, psychology, evolution, heredity and environment, conservation, the American negro, and Philadelphia municipal government – to name but a very few current topics and new intellectual interests of that day.[15]

These ten years of working for the "People's University," as it was sometimes called, were heady stimulus to Nolen's own intellectual development. He attended almost every lecture given in Philadelphia; he participated as moderator or devil's advocate in the open questioning which followed each talk; he edited most of the Extension's annual reports and campaigned throughout the mid-Atlantic area for the idea of education beyond the formal school years; and for a short time he helped found and edit the Society's short-lived bulletin, *The Citizen.*

Always a prolific reader, Nolen also began to develop his extensive personal library in this period, collecting books by men who remained favorites throughout his life – Emerson, Whitman (then considered a major writer by sociologists if not by English professors), Franklin, Veblen, Bellamy, Twain (whom he knew), Sir Thomas More, Dickens, Arnold, Ruskin, Mill, Goethe, Barrie, and Stevenson among many. All had been subjects of Extension lectures; all were representative of Nolen's general, non-professional reading habits. Self-made men, social critics and utopians, and writers of the whimsical world of children were the authors he preferred.[16]

Conspicuous by their absence in his library were the works of such important modern intellectual giants as Marx, Darwin, Freud, and other determinists who challenged, effectively if indirectly, his optimistic American belief in a society growing out of individual free will, hard work, and voluntary self-sacrifice to commonly agreed upon goals. For Nolen, never an angry man although often a zealous one in quest of his beliefs, anything was possible; the pursuit of the grandest schemes was preferable to patchwork adjustments of reality. In the height of the progressive era he had said: "we have given, heretofore, too much attention to caring for the mere wreckage of society, and too little toward establishing a better social order that would permanently reduce the amount of wreckage."[17] Not a utopian believer in overnight millenniums, he nevertheless sought a broader social order which, although achieved in the future, could be prepared by continuous replanning in the present. His own early mobility had only substantiated his beliefs, only reinforced what had been held up to him as true. His early reading choices confirmed them. Yet he was not a formalist either, in life values or in his art and behavior. To the end of his life he never stopped expanding his intellectual horizons, never ceased looking for new ways of solving both his own and his culture's larger problems. Ever the pragmatist and innovator, John Nolen's core values, derived largely from his early experiences, were quite sufficient to help direct him successfully through the changing dimensions of twentieth-century America. Later compromises, however necessary, would not dissuade him of their general validity.

Landscape architecture

In 1903 Nolen left Extension service and entered the School of Landscape Architecture at Harvard University. From the available evidence, his decision seems a sudden one, but it is not surprising given his earlier orientation.

In the first place, there was the importance of his working background – more than fifteen years of administrative experience in service fields plus two more of formal training for such work – all of it in areas more idealistically than financially remunerative. In landscape architecture, his already practiced ability at popularizing and selling services would go far in determining his success. Skill at oratory and writing would underscore that ability. The friendship of many people associated with his work and early life gave him contacts throughout the United States and Europe. Among other things on his application for the degree in landscape architecture, he stated specifically that he wanted his work to "consist in writing and speaking upon the subject, as well as in professional practice."[18]

In the second place, there were the always-present influences of his beliefs in a well-managed, free society, in an environment which could provide opportunity for all people, and in the satisfaction of meeting new challenges, all combined, most importantly, with a love for life out-of-doors. Girard College's emphasis upon a healthy life as a happy one, three pleasant summers as superintendent in charge of landscape work at Onteora Park, a move (in 1896) away from the city's closeness to his own piece of wooded land in Ardmore, where he could, and did, practice the art of landscaping his property – all were forms of preparation for the apparently sudden move.[19]

In the third place, Nolen now had a wife and two children who required adequate means of support. He needed to find a professional or business field with a promising future. Realistic about family needs and idealistic about personal ones, he had too much of the creative instinct to be content with merely administering forever the ideas of other men. Having already worked seventeen years for the things he wanted, ready to sell his Ardmore house to obtain the money for a return to school, he surely believed that landscape architecture not only would challenge his ideals but also could offer reasonable opportunity for economic self-sufficiency.

The lessons of Europe

Finally, there is evidence to suggest that, after a year-long visit to Europe in 1901–2, Nolen decided to study landscape architecture as a means of redesigning the city. During this visit, his third and most extensive in six years, he saw most of the great cities and architectural complexes of western Europe. The cities of Germany and Switzerland impressed him the most – Switzerland because of the beauty its natural environment gave its urban environment, and Germany (which he always loved above all the foreign countries he visited) because of the forest conservation and urban relandscaping projects underway through the stimulus of state law and municipal planning commissions. He informally attended courses at the University of Munich on German law, economics, the history of Italian painting, German architecture and plastics, and the cultural history of the Renaissance, and while there he visited in the homes of his professors.[20]

His scrapbooks and notes on this period did not reveal his attitude about such well-known examples of landscaping as England's formal gardens, Italy's terraced estates, the great boulevards of Baron Haussmann in Paris, and the vast expanse of gardens at Versailles. Apparently even during this first flirtation with the landscape arts, Nolen shied away from the sculptural monumentality and aesthetic impact of large design. From his later writing on the subject, one gathers that, instead, he sought landscaping techniques which were inclusive but adaptable to a more modest, more natural, above all less wasteful, scale of human existence.[21]

He was probably one the few Americans more overwhelmed by the industrial city of Dusseldorf than by the famed gardens of Versailles. The former represented what was possible in the campaign against human and natural waste so important to Nolen; without disparaging the latter, he merely said that in borrowing from Europe one took what one could use in his own country. He believed that Dusseldorf's parks, fountains, playgrounds, belt lines, and zoning system – in a city otherwise so comparable to Pittsburgh – were stimulating examples of what could be done inexpensively yet at great savings of human lives in America.[22] Thus Nolen stood some distance from the many American landscape architects at the century's end who were still concentrating upon grandiose appearance rather than everyday utility in the practice of their profession.

Probably there was no *exact* moment when he decided to study landscape architecture. In any case, this decision and his later use of that training come as no surprise. The earliest record of his decision that is available to me, was in a letter to his wife, September 17, 1902, after the return from Europe and written just after a visit to Central Park to study the "effects of Landscape Architecture, in which my interest now is naturally very keen." And again in a letter to his wife the same week, he spoke at length of his decision:

In the intervals of work, I have naturally thought some of the future possibility of "John Nolen: Landscape Architect." And I must say I have only satisfaction in the thought – in spite of obstacles ahead. In one respect my experience in selecting the profession is not unlike Charles Eliot's. Once the decision is made or even seriously considered, so many things in the past seem to point to it. For example, out of last year (European trip), when I was away from the things that ordinarily engross me, come three convictions: (1) that art had permanent interest for me and that I must try to do something in it myself; (2) that I love to be out of doors, especially in the open country; (3) but in spite of that fact I doubted any high satisfaction in forming at this time of my life [sic], because it would cut me off so from intellectual contact and afford no large and constant opportunity for public good. Now this new career fits in these [sic] like a ball in a socket.[23]

The "now" of that last sentence apparently stems directly from his reading of Charles William Eliot's book about his son, *Charles Eliot, Landscape Architect*, which had just been published. Although he did not always agree with the ideas of the younger Eliot, his later career shows how fundamentally he took to the idea "what must be fair, must be fit." Moreover, it was the Eliot book which confirmed Nolen in the beliefs that "I have a fundamental fitness for such a career" and "that it is a career that I would find congenial and useful."[24]

In these earliest days of defining what would later become his lifelong professional interests, Nolen knew of but apparently was not heavily influenced by the English garden city movement – a movement which vitally affected his work after 1909. But although the direct early evidence of cross-cultural influence is not yet known to me with any completeness, it seems clear that Nolen was but one of several men in the western world, impelled by idealism and the press of modern, urban industrial life, to turn to the physical replanning of society. One of them, an English court stenographer named Ebenezer Howard, had already published a widely popular book, *Tomorrow: A Peaceful Path to Real*

Reform (1898), better known later (1902) as *Garden Cities of Tomorrow*, which described, as one historian put it, his plan for the "healthy, natural and economic combination of town and country life."[25] Howard, who had lived in the United States and had participated in two earlier social experiments, states flatly that his book was born from an enthusiastic reading of the American Edward Bellamy's *Looking Backward* and from his subsequent decision to test the practicality of Bellamy's cooperative principles in action.[26]

Howard's first Garden City, Letchworth, was dedicated in October 1903, just as Nolen entered Harvard. The new town proved a landmark in city planning's professional development – much more indicative of the field's future directions in comprehensive community planning than the so-called "City Beautiful" movement associated with Burnham and Olmsted's plan for the Chicago World's Fair; and it remains today a living symbol of early twentieth-century English social reform. By no means utopian, it attempted a workable combination of rural land ownership and diversified urban services through public control of land use, landscaping of individual homes, and the creation of green-belt barriers to separate the town's several functions. Nolen, who formed a close, lifelong friendship with Raymond Unwin after 1909 and who succeeded Howard in 1931 as president of the International Federation of Housing and Town Planning, incorporated many of the pioneering Englishman's ideas into his own distinct contributions to new town and other city design – including a stress upon public ownership and control of land, although the American economic system and cultural pattern would modify its application.[27]

Toward a professional point of view

Nolen hurried through his courses at Harvard's new school of landscape architecture. By virtue of his graduation "with distinction" from Pennsylvania, his long work and independent study period from 1893 to 1903, and his year of informal study in Europe, he was admitted to the second-year class in 1903 and immediately entered the summer school to pick up a course in architectural drawing, which he never had as an undergraduate.[28]

At Harvard the curriculum was dominated by an accent on nature's beauty and vicarious uses despite many deferences to the "utility" of open spaces. Nolen studied under several of the most important figures in the American field of landscape architecture, including the younger Olmsted, who were then teaching, as Charles Eliot once put it, a version of the fine arts:

Landscape Architecture is primarily a fine art, and as such its most important function is to create beauty in the surroundings of human habitation . . . but it is also concerned with promoting the comfort, convenience, and health of urban populations, which have scanty access to natural scenery, and urgently need to have their work-a-day lives refreshed and calmed by the beautiful and reposeful sights and sounds of which Nature, aided by the landscape art, can abundantly provide.[29]

No one would deny landscape design the status of an art, of course, nor that it should help promote man's "comfort, convenience, and health." These indeed were Nolen's aims also. However, he did not agree they were achieved by merely tickling the "work-a-day" individual's sense of "sight and sound," as he rushed by to and from the factory. Nature's beauty, said Nolen, was meant to be enjoyed physically too, not just stared at as though it were only a highly valued pastoral painting:

It is a grave mistake to look upon civic improvement as concerned mainly, or evenly primarily, with beauty; at least if by beauty is meant an agreeable and pleasing appearance. "What is fair must be fit." Serviceableness as well as charm, use as well as beauty, must always be secured. Without serviceableness city life is inefficient, without beauty, sordid and commonplace.[30]

As for the "uses" of nature, these should be in the form of large, free, out-of-the-city parks which "people of small means" and "worn out workers" could periodically vacation in.[31] The city had a further responsibility to provide for landscaped open spaces, playgrounds, and small parks within its confines sufficient to "guarantee" daily recreation, rest and fresh air "to every child and citizen of the town."[32]

Early work

Once in the field of landscape architecture as a professional, John Nolen moved quickly from landscaping private estates to planning complete park systems and other large-scale civic improvements – his original goal – and to city planning – its ultimate result. In 1904, almost a year before his graduation from Harvard, he opened an office on the Square in Cambridge and immediately began to practice, landscaping several private homes in Ardmore and a West Philadelphia factory grounds for Joseph Fels (the famed soap tycoon associated with the progressive movement who, like Thomas Lawson and Tom Johnson, underwent a change of conscience about the manner in which his money had been accumulated). By 1905 and his graduation from Harvard with a Master of Arts degree, the thirty-six-year-old landscape architect had small projects underway in several states.

His first real breakthrough to civic work came that June when President Eliot and several of his instructors at Harvard recommended him for the job of advisor to the Park and Tree Commission of Charlotte, North Carolina.[33] Within two years, thanks to his ceaseless plugging for unified civic design, the scope of his work broadened from advising individual home owners about shrubs and grass to drafting a complete city plan and report. This report, and a park plan for Savannah, Georgia, about the same time, was as close as Nolen would ever get to the "City Beautiful" movement. Its recommendations included all the exterior trappings then in vogue among the civic minded – a park, a public square with pseudo-classical buildings facing on it, and tree-lined streets. These things were not objectionable in themselves – Charlotte undoubtedly would have looked better had all of them been carried out. But compared with his later work, including that in the Myer's Park subdivision of Charlotte (1912), they were not enough. The recommendations lacked any real human relevance or scale; they appeared imposed from without and lacked a sure grasp of broad local needs.[34] They were almost certainly among the last vestiges of a purely textbook approach to local community needs. But at least he had made the big step, if cautiously, into city planning. Once there he never turned back to the comforts of smaller triumphs. His work now took him to planning cities, and laying out large-scale park and street systems, and residential areas throughout the United States, Cuba, and Canada.

As more work was obtained, Nolen increased the range of his recommendations and the intensity of his criticisms. The main recommendations still included the nature and disposition of parks, playgrounds, and civic squares. But now more space was devoted in his reports and surveys to recognizing and easing such urban irritants as traffic patterns, indiscriminate overlapping of industrial and residential areas, poor railroad and streetcar routings, the conflicting role of business and government in the community, the city's responsibility for the rights of children, and other ideas about government's share in promoting human welfare, and, in advance of other planners, the need to eliminate submarginal housing.[35]

Although he did not always succeed in obtaining the city's follow-through on a plan, he generally had the enthusiastic support of his sponsors, many of whom were, like himself, advocating municipal reform. They included well-to-do private individuals (novelist Zona Gale, paper manufacturer Charles S. Bird, department store merchant George S. Marston – extremely significant social reformers in their own regions); civic, commercial, and art associations – generally in cities with newly elected, liberal governments (San Diego, 1908; La Crosse, 1908; Montclair, 1908; Madison, 1909); and large business corporations (Pabst Brewing Company, 1910; American Brass Company, 1916; American Cast Iron Pipe Company, 1915; General Electric Company, 1916).[36]

Growth of the social conscience

Thus working together, the city planner and civic reformer slowly pushed long-range planning and physical development of the city to the fore as an approach to solving America's rapidly multiplying domestic problems. Playgrounds were urged as a means of fighting vice and promoting team-work, parks were offered as essential to the requirements for fresh air and health of those who could not afford their own piece of land, and so on. Planning was visualized as a way of bringing "vitality" back to the public body; and vitality, as everyone was told, was one-half of "efficiency and happiness."[37] "What is needed in American city planning?" asked Nolen at the first National Conference on City Planning in May 1909. "Everything," was his conclusion, paralleling Lincoln Steffens' assessment of the corrupt municipal government situation uncovered by his muckrake (e.g. *The Shame of the Cities*). More optimistic about solutions than Steffens, Nolen, in the language of the progressives, went on to suggest:

We need (1) to make recreation more democratic; (2) to develop the individuality of our cities; (3) to stop waste. First, then, we need to make many improvements which are for the benefit and enjoyment of everybody, for the common good. . . . [Here he cites things that are free in Germany which are accessible only to the wealthiest in America.] We should no longer be content with mere increase in population and wealth. We should insist upon asking, How do the people live, where do they work, what do they play . . . there is a close relation between moral reform and material progress. A more honest, economical and wiser expenditure is indeed sorely needed, and, ultimately the change of (civic) policy would lead there. . . . The main sources of this new wealth . . . is in a wiser husbanding of our aesthetic and human as well as our national resources, in the promoting of physical health, legislation that meets more successfully the needs of twentieth century city life, in doing things at the right time . . . in the right way, using to our advantage science, art, skill, and experience. . . . By saving waste in these ways and by the timely investing (not spending) of public money in great enterprises. . . . [we shall obtain the improvements we want but thought we couldn't afford].[38]

The importance of this quote is its general philosophic position; Nolen was critical of the present, yet not discouraged about the future. If the senses were open and clear, man *could* plan a better future using many of the basic stuffs of the present. There was no need for the fatalism or pessimism being prophesied by some men.

A case in point is the difference between the positions of Nolen and Steffens (1866–1936), contemporaries in their life spans and sharing a common concern for reform. In his understanding of the world and hence of its future, Nolen was much the more optimistic, essentially because he never really had learned to mistrust it or himself in it. With some small measure of outside assistance, he had helped himself steadily up from near the bottom of the socio-economic ladder. Although not at the top nor particularly aspiring to many of the badges and awards of success, he was still the gainer as he moved on up; and, almost certainly, there was little opportunity in these early ambitious years to establish sufficient position from which to experience the steady and disillusioning falls from idealism that Steffens suffered. What had Nolen to fall from, coming out of nowhere and working in a field whose theoretical bases were barely outlined as yet? Never doubting the need for planning, he campaigned strenuously for broad planning's acceptance and sometimes found success.

But Steffens, the journalist from a comfortable, upper-middle-class home, suffered from the unsettling mixture of an overly romanticized but nevertheless workable childhood idealism diluted by his deeply sensitive awareness and gradual initiation into its opposite, the world of reality – which he found to be a greedy, rather ugly, entirely adult world. He found that

cities and states are jelly-fish now. They have a life of their own but no mind. The people in them have minds, but the people *as a community* have no conscious purpose as communities. Nothing but instinct guides them, or at best, a few bum politicians who live off the flabby, hog-selfish people.[39]

In Steffens' lifelong search for some hint of a better world he did not find conditions anywhere permanently otherwise, from reform capitalism to Russian communism, and thus he trusted finally to love alone, as shared by two people amid the world's growing, chaotic forces.[40] Nolen's equally sensitive but more realistic and (perforce) active idealism, on the other hand, developed, as we have already seen, out of early chaos and uncertainty into an enthusiasm for society's future. He understood Steffens but was incapable of sharing his pessimism, except as a warning of what *could* happen if man lost faith in working for the future. Although a cluster of divergent circumstances fell into a satisfactory pattern for Nolen's ambition and of course had much to do with his beliefs, he was still accurate in assuming from the evidence of his own life and of the lives of men he had learned to admire that the requisites for *his* better world were good fortune, an open society, hard work, and seriousness of purpose. Like the progressives, if not like Steffens, he intended to work at expanding the opportunities already existent in American culture. And unlike both the general run of progressives and Steffens, the circumstances of Nolen's beginnings continued to play a major role in his successful transition and growth through several periods of civic reform, planning, and change, until his death in 1937.[41]

Almost all his early life had been preparation for guiding the "civic spirit" he so much believed in. "The first and last need of a city, the one that outweighs all others," civic spirit, was to Nolen "the main end of reforms," the *raison d'être* of planning. In an era of reformers agitating for "good," "honest" government, for the elimination of "waste", and for restrictions on the "evils" of the competive system, Nolen, like his peers in the political arena, rededicated himself to the highest aspirations offered by the existing culture. Thus Nolen went to the communities which sought his services to activate their civic ideals, believing that "comprehensive" city planning was "one of the best means for expressing this awakened consciousness, this stirred conscience" whose stimulus had in large part been a too sudden human and technological growth.[42]

Notes*

* The unpublished "Nolen Papers" cited below at the University of Pennsylvania were acquired by Cornell University in 1969. For the published work and reports see John Hancock (1976) *John Nolen: Bibliographic Record of Achievement*, Cornell University, Program in Urban & Regional Studies. For an expanded version of this article see chapter 1 in John Hancock (1964) "John Nolen and the American city planning movement: a history of cultural change and community response, 1900–1940," Ph.D. dissertation in American Civilization, University of Pennsylvania.

1 H. J. Potts to John Nolen, January 13, 1909; Nolen to Potts, January 15, 1909 and January 21, 1909; all in office correspondence, Reading folder, Nolen Papers (hereafter cited as IV NP), Fine Arts Library of the University of Pennsylvania; and Nolen (1910) *Replanning Reading: An Industrial City of a Hundred Thousand*, Boston, George Ellis Co. p. iii. The roman numeral system used here to designate sources is arranged as follows: I or Box I is used to denote all primary material of an autobiographical or biographical nature and all articles on Mr Nolen. II indicates citations from the library holdings of Nolen, both personal and professional, and all papers written or accumulated by him on non-planning matters. III refers to all his unpublished essays, lectures, and speeches on planning. IV is the source of all project folders, plans, survey data, office records and correspondence. V contains his collection of photographs.

2 Announcement of a Nolen slide lecture, Reading *Eagle*, March 14, 1910.

3 Nolen, op. cit., pp. 87–90.

4 For recent historical treatment of municipal reform in this period see George E. Mowrey (1958) *The Era of Theodore Roosevelt*, New York, Harper Bros., pp. 1–105; information on Nolen's sponsors in Reading was drawn from city directories, wills, and letters and is discussed at length in my unpublished paper (1958) "City planning in the progressive period: a case study of John Nolen's plans for Reading, Pennsylvania." This information correlates closely with that found in Mowrey's study (1952) of the life histories of select individuals connected with municipal reform in one state, *The California Progressives*, Berkeley, University of California Press.

5 Autobiographical notes, Box II, NP; Nolen's student notebooks, Box IV, NP; both in temporary possession of the author. Unless otherwise noted all Nolen biographical information is taken from his private papers and published works. Girard College aims and values taken from Cheesman A. Herrick (1927) *History of Girard College*, Phila., Girard College, pp. 201–47.

6 Quoted in Herrick, op. cit., pp. 228–9.

7 ibid., p. 228. Nolen owned a copy of this book and underlined the sections stressing mental, moral, and physical development.

8 In his last several years as a student at Girard, Nolen had been the president's office boy. In two alumni addresses at Girard, forty years apart, Nolen characteristically stressed Stephen Girard's own personality development and expressed his belief that this personality above all was Girard's bequest to the future. See 1895 Alumni Address, II NP; and 1936 Anniversary Address (1936) reprinted in *Steel and Garnet* XXX, x, 70. It is hardly strange after such training that Nolen's earliest American heroes were the adaptable and supposedly "self-made" Benjamin Franklin, Stephen Girard, Samuel F. B. Morse, William Cullen Bryant, and Mark Twain. See his personal notebook of great men and events in history, compiled 1884, I NP.

9 University of Pennsylvania, *Class Record of '93* and additional *Records of the Class of '93* in 1898, 1903, and 1930.

10 Sidney Fine (1956) *Laissez Faire and the General-Welfare State*, Ann Arbor, University of Michigan Press, pp. 241–7. Patten's best early statements are found in *The Premises of Political Economy* (Philadelphia, 1885), and *The Theory of Dynamic Economics* (Philadelphia, 1892), both known to Nolen. For a recent perceptive treatment of Tugwell, Patten, and the national planning people see Paul K. Conkin (1959) *Tomorrow A New World: The New Deal Community Program*, Ithaca, Cornell University Press, pp. 73–92.

11 Information on Nolen's class work is taken from his class notebooks, inscribed texts, and essays. The Robinson reference is found in Robinson to Nolen, January 1, 1931, I and II NP.

12 This senior thesis was printed along with others by members of the senior class in *The City Government of Philadelphia: A Study in Municipal Administration* (1893) introduction by Edmund J. James, Philadelphia, Wharton School of Finance and Economy, pp. 99–110.

13 Fine, op. cit., pp. 216–19; Richard T. Ely (1886) "Report of the organization of the American Economic Association," *AEA Publications*, I, 5–16; and Ely (1910) "The American Economic Association 1885–1909," *AEA Publications*, XI, 47–92.

14 From the original notebook draft of his Alumni Address to the Girard College Class of 1895, Box IV, NP.

15 The records of this Society are quite complete and an index of them in the Nolen Papers alone, as catalogued by the author, covers four pages. The Society's publication of "Syllabi" are a treasure of information for students of intellectual and cultural history in the period. They have not been expanded upon here because of space limitations, but they include talks by Charles Andrew, John Fiske, W. E. B. DuBois, MacMaster, Patten, Robinson, Woodrow Wilson, Lyman Powell, Brander Matthews, Arthur T. Hadley, Bliss Perry, Hillaire Belloc, Graham Wallas, W. Hudson Shaw, and Michael Sadler – many of whom became longtime friends of and correspondents with Nolen; *Syllabi of the ASEUT for the Academic Years 1901–1902, 1902–1903*, Philadelphia, American Society for the Extension of University Teaching, 1903, and *Records, Reports, Lecture Syllabi, 1890–1900*, Philadelphia, 1899, 5 vols. The Society grew out of the Oxford experiment and an early series of University of Pennsylvania "afternoon" extension lectures begun in 1887. From 1893 to 1903, the years of Nolen's association with it, the Society brought in over a hundred lecturers per year for six talks each before audiences of up to as many as two hundred interested townspeople, many of whom took the courses for college credit, at a small fee. Information in the text above is taken from the reports just noted and from the Board of Directors (1901) *Ten Years' Report of the American Society for the Extension of University Teaching,*

1890–1900, Philadelphia, ASEUT; Secretary of the Extension (Nolen), *Annual Reports*, 1890–1900; and annual *Syllabus*, 1890–1900. Anonymous (1899) *Concerning University Extension: Its Significance, Method and Results*, Philadelphia, ASEUT; a more recent, brief account by Franklin Spencer Edmonds also sheds light on this group (Nov. 1943) "The beginnings of University Extension in Philadelphia," *Phila. Forum*, pp. 12–14. Nolen edited all the secretary's reports after 1896.

16 Unpublished lists of "The personal library of John Nolen"; "Catalogue of books (professional), library of John Nolen"; Box II, NP. Many of the latter are part of the John Nolen City Planning Collection, University of North Carolina Library. Manuscript of all unpublished reports and printed copy of all published reports and books are on temporary loan to the Fine Arts Library, University of Pennsylvania.

17 John Nolen (1912) *Replanning Small Cities*, New York, B. W. Huebsch, 1912, p. 2; for an early statement of the importance of constant and "comprehensive" replanning see Nolen (1908) *San Diego, A Comprehensive Plan for its Improvement*, Boston, George H. Ellis, 1908, pp. iii and 10.

18 Nolen to the Administrative Board of the Graduate School, Harvard University, March 14, 1904, Box I, NP.

19 Description of the Ardmore property in "John Nolen, miscellaneous papers," 1895–1903, Box I, NP.

20 Unpublished "Scrapbook, record of European trip, 1901–1902"; Ex-Matriculation certificate, "Universität München," Oct. 19, 1901 to March 4, 1902 (winter semester) in "Miscellaneous papers"; record of courses taken at Munich in Nolen to Administrative Board, ibid. (March 14, 1904); all Box I, NP.

21 See the following, all by Nolen: *San Diego*, 13, 29–40; *State Parks for Wisconsin*, Madison, State Park Board, 1909, p. 41; *Re-Planning Reading*, pp. 81–4; *Replanning Small Cities*, p. 13; offprint of Address to the First National Conference on City Planning, "What is needed in American city planning?" May 21, 1909, and unpublished report to the Boston Municipal Planning Commission, "Public hospitality in Europe," Sept. 1911, III, NP.

22 Interview, John S. Gregory (1913) "The coming city," *The World's Work*, pp. 82–4.

23 Nolen to Barbara S. Nolen, Sept. 17, 1902; for long quote Nolen to Barbara S. Nolen, Sept. 19, 1902; both extracted from letters in possession of John Nolen, Jr, forwarded to the author June 3, 1960.

24 ibid., for reference to an inquiry made before the European trip in September 1901, about studying at the Lawrence School, see Nolen to J. L. Love, Sept. 12, 1902, I, NP.

25 Ebenezer Howard (1902) *Garden Cities of Tomorrow*, London, Faber & Faber. The quote is from Dugald Macfadyen (1933) *Sir Ebenezer Howard and Town Planning*, Manchester, Manchester University Press, p. 27.

26 Howard also rejected Bellamy's "most outstanding" contention that change of this scale could be effected "overnight," ibid., pp. 20–1.

27 John Nolen (1927) *New Towns for Old*, Boston, Marshall Jones Co. Although better known for his work in such new towns as Kingsport, Tennessee and Mariemont, Ohio, Nolen's use of the garden city scheme as applied to a cooperative system of land ownership is seen as early as 1912–13 in his plan for Neponset Village, East Walpole, Mass. The whole question of cultural modifications to Nolen's American planning schemes is the subject of a longer paper I now have in progress.

28 Nolen to the Lawrence Scientific School, Sept. 11, 1902; Nolen to J. L. Love, May 3, 1903; Love to Nolen, May 19, 1903; Nolen to Administrative Board, March 14, 1904; John G. Hart to Nolen, May 3 and July 7, 1904 (receives Austin Scholarship for 1904–5); all in Box I, NP.

29 Quoted in T. A. Mawson (1927) *The Life and Work of an English Landscape Architect: An Autobiography*, New York, Charles Scribner's Sons, p. xii. For further expressions of this point of view see Charles Wm Eliot's book about his son (1902) *Charles Eliot, Landscape Architect*, Boston, Houghton, Mifflin & Co., pp. 551–5, 592–601, and other direct statements by the younger Eliot. It should be added here that no attempt is being made by the author to disparage the many contributions of men like Olmsted and Eliot to landscape architecture, nor to underscore the importance of beauty to Nolen. The influence of both on Nolen's work is obvious, *but* so are his own innovations on accepted ideas in the fields of landscape architecture and large-scale planning which developed out of his personal orientation.

30 John Nolen (1907) *Roanoke: A Small City of the New South*, Roanoke, Roanoke Civic Improvement Association, p. 13. Despite this clear point of view, the report has been considered by one writer as an example of the strong "City Beautiful" bent of planners before the First World War (Robert A. Walker [1930] *The Planning Function in Urban Government*, revised edition [Chicago, University of Chicago Press] pp. 14–15). Actually no ongoing society switches so abruptly from one viewpoint to another in just a year or two. The Nolen quote above for example is merely an early reference to the "City Efficient" point of view which the progressively inclined pioneer planner was expressing long before the First World War.

31 Nolen, *State Parks for Wisconsin*, p. 41.

32 John Nolen (1909) *Montclair: The Preservation of its Natural Beauty and Its Improvements As a Residential Town*, Montclair, Municipal Art Commission, p. 63.

33 Conversation with John Nolen, Jr, May 28, 1959.

34 Unpublished report, project folder, "Charlotte, N. C.," Box V, NP; for a published report of Meyer's Park see Alfred F. Muller (Spring, 1915) "Meyer's Park, Charlotte, N. C.," *The Wildwood Magazine*, pp. 8ff.

35 Nolen, *San Diego*, pp. 58–61; *Madison: A Model City*, Boston and Madison, The Madison Park and Pleasure Drive Assn, 1911, pp. 35–150; *Montclair*, pp. 59–72; *Replanning Small Cities*, pp. 1–21; John Nolen (1910) "The parks and recreation facilities in the US," The *Annals* of the Amer. Academy of Political and Social Science, p. 217; anonymous (1937) "John Nolen," *Newsletter*, Amer. Soc. of Planning Officials, III, 3.

36 See project folders indicated by name, as above, in Box V, NP. See also project folders "Portage, Wisconsin"; "Erie, Penna."; and "Waterbury, Conn."; *San Diego*, p. iii; the La Crosse *Tribune* and La Crosse *Leader-Press*, both November 11, 1908; *Montclair*, pp. 9–12; *Madison*, "Explanatory"; this last report, in the city Nolen admired above all others before the First World War, also contains some early ideas on regional planning, see the Montclair–Glen Ridge reports for same. In the project folder "High Shoals Village, N. C.," Box V, NP, is a preliminary plan for a new town, one of the earliest in America in this century and foreshadowing, like Neponset, Nolen's eventual great interest – creating a new town from the ground up – and that of his later associates Hale J. Walker (Greenbelt town planner) and Justin R. Hartzog (Greenhills town planner).

37 Nolen, "Parks and recreation facilities," The *Annals*, pp. 217–18.

38 Offprint of Address to the NCCP (May 21, 1909), Box I, NP.
39 Original source unknown, quoted in John Nolen (1915) unpublished "Address on the Boston Community Planning Project", Boston, A Program for 1911, III, NP.
40 Consult the general divisions and especially the last section of Steffens (1931) *Autobiography*, New York, Harcourt, Brace, 1931.
41 The best study of class, mobility, and role of the progressives is Mowrey's discussion of forty-seven life histories in *The California Progressives*, pp. 86–104. With an occasional major exception like Harold Ickes, it is clear the progressives were definitely out of political favor by the period of the New Deal which enacted so much of the legislation they had demanded twenty years earlier. While the reasons for their demise are not yet clear, it may be suggested that the answer lies partly in their strong individualistic beliefs, their emphasis on *restrictive* legislation and their refusals to admit, even privately, that there were *traditional* class divisions in America. See Mowrey, ibid. and his more recent summary, *Theodore Roosevelt and the Progressive Era*, pp. 1–105. In contrast, Nolen was never a dogmatist, welcomed the passing of an older order, served as consultant to the Division of Subsistence Homesteads and the National Resources Board, and remained an enthusiastic New Dealer to his death.
42 Nolen, unpublished "Address on the Boston Community Planning Project," 1911, Box I, NP.

3 Benjamin C. Marsh and the fight over population congestion

Harvey A. Kantor

Benjamin C. Marsh, a vigorous young social worker in the early
years of the twentieth century, attacked the extreme congestion of
poor people in the nation's largest cities. In his analysis of the causes
of congestion, Marsh identified the basic dynamics of large-scale
crowding and offered some of the most radical solutions of taxation,
land use, and planning proposed during his day. As an early leader
against the overcrowding of land, the author of the first book
devoted entirely to city planning, and the founder of the first
National Conference on City Planning, Marsh's career points up the
diversity of style and ideology that characterized the pioneers of the
planning profession.

In the early years of the twentieth century, city planning existed less as
a profession than as a mélange of experiments and untested ideas.
Engineers, housing reformers, municipal officials, and journalists all
claimed solutions to the disorders of unrestrained urban growth.
Throughout this embryonic stage speculative thinking flourished. The
success of a particular scheme usually depended upon the passion of its
promoters; and unsupported proposals were quickly dropped and replaced by new ones.

One of the most radical of these programs struck at the heart of urban
dynamics. Known as the "congestion movement" and headed by an energetic reformer named Benjamin C. Marsh, it attacked the overcrowding
of population as the single most important cause of big city ills. Focusing
on real estate speculation and unplanned development, Marsh and other
leaders of the congestion movement fought for land and tax reform,
public control of undeveloped real estate, and planned communities to
decentralize inner city population. These programs for guiding future
urban growth were the most original and far-reaching programs of the
time and helped to catalyze the disparate planning movement into a
national organization.

The anti-congestion campaign began in the nation's largest urban
center, New York City, under the leadership of that city's active social
settlement workers. Wrestling with the day-to-day problems of aiding the
poor of the slums, social workers astutely analyzed the problems of urban

poverty. So forceful were they in their pursuit of remedies that they constituted one of the most vital elements in the national progressive drive for reform (Davis, 1967; Kraus, 1970). In searching for ways to ease the burdens of the poor, the settlement workers recognized that alleviation of the crowded conditions of the slums had to be a major goal.

CCP established

In early winter, 1907, Florence Kelley, an influential social worker and secretary of the National Consumers' League, became convinced that congestion of population, so apparent on the Lower East Side of New York, stood as the chief affliction of thousands of poor people in large cities throughout the United States. "Instead of assenting to the belief that people who are poor must be crowded," Kelley argued, "why did we not see years ago that people who are crowded must remain poor?" (Davis, p. 70). In discussing her views on this problem, she found that others had come to the same conclusion. She then joined with Mary Simkhovitch, director of Greenwich House; Lillian D. Wald, head of the Nurses Settlement; Reverend Gaylord S. White of Union Theological Seminary and Union Settlement; Dr Herman C. Bumpus, director of the American Museum of Natural History, and others, in 1907, to form in New York an organization called the Committee on Congestion of Population (CCP).[1] The committee's purpose was to collect data on the population question and to present it to the public in hopes of arousing concern (Lubove, pp. 231–8; Toll, pp. 122–4; Scott, pp. 84–8).

Marsh joins Committee

In February 1907, the CCP retained Benjamin C. Marsh as its first executive secretary. Marsh was a wiry young man with a tremendous capacity for work. Associated with a variety of reform issues during his lifetime, he gained a reputation as one of the nation's most effective lobbyists for reform causes. A combination I. F. Stone and Ralph Nader, Marsh brought an equal degree of ardor to each of his projects and infused all of his activities with a missionary zeal. He was a feisty infighter; a bantam rooster who poked at the shibboleths of the establishment with obvious relish. Described as a "character," a "charlatan," and a "radical," Marsh cluttered numerous offices throughout his Washington career with propaganda supporting his causes of peace, consumer protection, and trust-busting (Marsh, 1953, pp. vii–xii).

When he came to the Congestion Committee in 1907, Marsh was only a budding, young "people's lobbyist." Yet his alertness, his restless energy, and the originality of his ideas impressed his colleagues. So brash was the young Marsh, however, that his early rantings quickly drew the warning from patrician reformer Robert W. DeForest that "if you touch the land problem in New York, you probably won't last here two years" (ibid., p. 35).

Marsh's iconoclastic ways were molded both by his parents and by his teachers and stayed with him throughout his long life from 1879 to 1953. The son of New England Congregational missionaries, he spent much of his youth in Bulgaria observing his parents' methods in spreading the gospel. Back in the States he graduated Phi Beta Kappa from Grinnell College, a small liberal arts school in Iowa, attended the University of Chicago, took a job with the YMCA, and became a fundraiser for overseas church missions. In 1902 he won a fellowship to the University of Pennsylvania which enabled him to refine his social philosophy (*New York Times*, 1953).

As an undergraduate Marsh had absorbed some of the doctrines of Fabian socialism and also became enamored of the single-tax thinking of Henry George. Now in graduate school at Penn he naturally gravitated toward the progressive economist Simon Patten. Patten, a captivating professor, stressed the notion that industrialism had rendered scarcity obsolete and that abundance, the new order of the day, wiped out the necessity of poverty. Patten infused Marsh with the ideal of a society that could provide for the basic needs of its citizens. Fresh from these heady theories, Marsh tried out his ideas in his position as secretary of the Pennsylvania Society to Protect Children from Cruelty. Advocating better housing, Marsh offended some of the slumlord members of the society's board and his tenure came to an abrupt end. It was with this intellectual baggage and experience that Marsh came to New York in 1907 to tackle the problems of population overcrowding.

To prepare for his work, Marsh spent the summer of 1907 in Britain, France, and Germany collecting material on housing and city planning for the CCP. His visits to Europe's major cities impressed him, but the highlight of the trip occurred at the International Housing Congress in London. Here the major question of congestion drew a great deal of attention and the conferees concluded that "the creation of new congested districts without the necessaries of healthy life now going on in large cities, can only be prevented by obtaining power to forbid the erection of any new buildings except in accordance with a general plan for developing all uncovered land within the city boundaries." The emphasis on state planning laced neatly with Marsh's own notions of social responsibility (Marsh, 1908, p. 1515).

The Congestion Exhibition

Marsh and his colleagues in the CCP launched their anti-congestion campaign with an exhibition held from March 9 to March 28, 1908, at the American Museum of Natural History. Governor Charles Evans Hughes opened the show and generated much publicity with a speech expressing his basic sympathy with the aims of the Congestion Committee (Simkovitch, 1938, pp. 160–1; "Congestion," 1908, pp. 1730–40). According to the catalogue, the show aimed to "depict some of the causes, the conditions and the evils of the massing of people in New York and in limited areas; and present methods of dealing with the problems involved and the methods, legislative and others, which should be adopted to remedy such congestion" (*Catalogue* 1908). Maps, diagrams, charts (one of which read, "The population of the world could be contained in Delaware if they were as congested as the people in eleven New York City blocks, at the rate of twelve hundred per acre"), statistics, models, photographs, and pictures all presented the image of congestion as New York's most urgent social problem ("Problems," 1908; "Main," 1908).

Various civic and social agencies in the city – such as the Charity Organization Society, Tenement House Department, and the National Consumers' League – sponsored booths at the exhibition to display graphically contemporary living conditions in New York City. The show emphasized the vast increase in the numbers of people that crowded all aspects of New York's life, and maintained that if anything were to be done about substandard housing, spreading tuberculosis, poverty, and crime, the crowding would have to cease.

The displays reflected the general philosophy of the Committee on Congestion of Population. They showed that concentration of land ownership, high rents, and an imperfect system of taxation aggravated the evils already caused by economic growth and immigration. Oppressive rents charged by owners who made huge profits from skyrocketing land values were the crux of the issue. Tenement house reform and tax adjustments seemed logical, though conservative, cures. But the Congestion Exhibition offered far more creative solutions, in the most original discussion of land use to which New Yorkers had ever been exposed.

Suggested solutions to overcrowding

The first of these solutions recognized that expansion of the transportation network could not relieve congestion. More subways only caused more concentration of tenements, and the original purpose of the track extension inevitably became subverted. Instead, factories needed to be evenly distributed with a zone of working-class housing near each new industrial site. Workers could then walk to work, and to the park and recreational facilities also provided nearby. The scheme, originally proposed by the City Club of New York, ranked as one of the first that understood the limited value of subway extension as a means of easing congestion and offered an alternative.

A second more drastic solution suggested bodily removal of individuals and families to less densely populated areas of the country. Citing the work of the Industrial Removal Office, the Jewish Agricultural and Industrial Aid Society, and the Children's Aid Society, the Exhibition hailed the benefits of a back-to-the-land movement. The New York State Department of Agriculture featured its own program which attempted to convince recent immigrants of the value of fresh air in a rural locale.

A model village plan suggested a third possible solution. Unsettled parts of the city, with cheap land still available, could be chosen as sites for new communities. A plan was shown by which 900 persons could live in individual houses with plenty of open spaces and pay only $2.00 to $2.25 a month rent. Private developers could still make a profit, and the slums could be somewhat eased by allowing workers to move out of the city into these prototype communities.

Besides these innovative suggestions of factory distribution, removal to the farm, and model villages, the exhibition stressed planning within the city itself as an urgent necessity. The Cologne, Germany, example of zones set up for specific land uses was displayed. And Charles Robinson, a leading author on city planning, speaking during the exhibition, made the point that "deliberate planning secures an enlargement of the habitable area available for the least paid workers by improving the means of circulation and the removal of factories to the suburbs" (Martin, pp. 29–38).

But perhaps the Congestion Exhibition was too successful in drawing public attention to the problems of urban overcrowding. According to Mary Simkovitch, reflecting several years later on the effects of the presentation, "many superficial observers horrified at the evils of overcrowding felt that the problem was of such magnitude that it was hardly worthwhile to have brought the public to a realization of evils which in the nature of the case could be remedied or prevented only in the course of years and after a prolonged struggle" (Simkhovitch, 1910). Marsh, in his usual direct manner, maintained that the exhibit "was a distinct success from every point of view – except producing action to remedy the condition shown!" (Marsh, 1953, p. 18).

Nevertheless, after the exhibition, the CCP continued its work, beginning further investigations and accumulating more data to aid its cause. Several smaller exhibits were held in Brooklyn (Marsh, 1908b) and at the National Conference of Charities and Correction; speech-making continued at a furious pace; and then Marsh took off to spend his second consecutive summer in Europe. This 1908 trip motivated him to collect his

New York and European experience into a small book which became the first volume published by an American dealing exclusively with city planning.

Marsh's book

Supremely confident in his cause, Marsh published privately in 1909 his *An Introduction to City Planning: Democracy's Challenge and the American City*. This 158-page paperback attempted to catalogue the achievements of foreign cities and to review the status of planning in America. But Marsh, of course, was no simple list-maker. The main purpose of the work prompted action. "A city without a plan is like a ship without a rudder" blared the opening headline and Marsh intended civic activists to heed his pleas for planning to "prevent the direful conditions of congestion, maladjustment and pre-eminently land speculation which have reached their horrible limit in Manhattan." For guidance he included a chapter on the "Methods of securing a city plan in some cities," model statutes for planning commissions in Hartford and cities in Wisconsin, a list of steps to follow in establishing a city plan, and a bibliography of "some good books on city planning."

Marsh ranked Frankfurt, Germany as the ideal model and concluded from his observations there that "the most important part of City Planning, as far as the future health of the city is concerned, is the districting of the city into zones" (Marsh, 1909, p. 28). Frankfurt's additional policies of taxing the increased land values after each title change and purchasing land on its own for future development greatly appealed to Marsh. In comparison, he found American cities woefully lacking and a public that "has not been trained to demand such a farseeing outlook and plan for the city as a whole" (ibid., p. 98).

Marsh's little book provides an interesting glimpse not only of his own thinking but of the state of city planning in general in 1909. The first manual on the subject came from a social worker, a supporter of reform causes. The technical aspects of the field were only touched upon briefly in a separate chapter by Marsh's architect friend George B. Ford. The primary examples of good planning drew on European, particularly German, models. Reflecting Marsh's own proclivities, the work emphasized zoning, land taxes, and municipal control of undeveloped property. *An Introduction to City Planning*, activist in overtone, strongly carried the message of the city's responsibilities in land development, and Marsh clearly challenged the dominant urban trend of unrestricted growth.

Having pioneered in the textbook field, Marsh moved to present the first City Planning Exhibition ever held in the United States. In early 1909, the CCP joined with the Municipal Art Society in providing an exhibition stressing the need for planning. The joint sponsorship of the program signified that these two private groups, one concerned with social problems and the other primarily with aesthetic ones, had come to the same conclusion – planning could solve the major questions with which each was concerned. Charles Robinson, describing the value of the exhibition, said, "No loyal New Yorker, or, indeed, American, could leave the hall with a smug and comfortable feeling as to the future of urban life under the conditions now usual" (Robinson, 1909).

City Commission established

The agitation by the Congestion Committee finally caused city officials to act (Kelley, 1909; Goodnow, 1910). On April 12, 1910, the Board of Aldermen authorized the appointment of a commission to investigate the issue of population congestion and to make recommendations. From the start, however, skepticism greeted the city's efforts. CCP members Gaylord White and Edward T. Devine wrote to the president of the Board beseeching him to set up immediately a city planning body within the government, rather than merely appointing an investigative group (Board, 1910a). The New York City chapter of the American Institute of Architects also thought that nothing would happen if a temporary commission were established. The group maintained that "the history of every such commission in the past is the production of many schemes, beautiful to look at and admirable in themselves were they possible of execution, but the actual result of the work of these previous commissions has been almost nil" (Board, 1910b). Brushing aside such pleas, the Board of Aldermen created in May the City Commission on Congestion of Population to investigate the problem of overcrowding.

   The *New York Times* endorsed the new group, but urged the Aldermen to stay off the Commission and appoint only qualified experts (*New York Times*, 1910). This advice, too, was rejected and when, on May 17, 1910, the nineteen members of the commission were appointed, ten of them were Aldermen. Chosen to head the Congestion Commission, however, was Jacob Cantor, the former Manhattan Borough President and early advocate of city planning. Cantor had retained his political connections and was a close associate of the new Tammany mayor, William J. Gaynor (*New York Times*, 1912). Frank J. Goodnow, of Columbia University, sat as the resident municipal expert on the staff; and Benjamin Marsh, because of his knowledge of overcrowding, was appointed secretary. The remaining places on the Commission were filled primarily by real estate men. After eleven months of investigation and public hearings, the group presented its extensive report to its fellow Aldermen and Mayor Gaynor on February 28, 1911 (*Report*, 1911).

City Commission's Report

The most significant finding of these investigations held that the congestion situation now appeared worse than it had been when the issue was
first raised (McAneny, 1910). Density figures in Manhattan had jumped
15 per cent, from 131.8 persons per acre in 1900 to 166.1 in 1910, and the
Commission concurred with housing expert Lawrence Veiller's appraisal
that "the limits [of congestion] have not only been reached but have long
been past" (*Report*, 1911, p. 1830). The Committee attributed the congestion to a variety of causes: poverty, concentration of factories and offices,
consolidation of the Greater City, intensive use and high cost of land, lack
of control over aliens and immigration, long hours of work, cost of transit
and general transportation conditions, lack of a definite city plan,
inadequate taxation, failure to prepare land for housing purposes,
methods of administering charity, and failure of the city to adopt a policy
that would attract people to outlying boroughs. All aspects of these causes
and their effects were exhaustively treated in the final 270-page report.

On the subject of city planning, the Commission believed that "the
failure to provide a City plan determining the way in which various
sections of the City are to be developed is also largely responsible for the
congestion through intensive use of land." "Intensive congestion has
been perfectly natural," the Commission felt, because "private interest"
rather than "the public welfare" had been "permitted to control the
development not only of Manhattan but of the other Boroughs" (*Report*,
1911, pp. 1830–4).

The findings were a severe indictment of the city's role in dealing with
the physical well-being of its citizens. The various subcommittees of the
Commission made remedial suggestions, but none of the recommendations was drastic enough to counteract the impressive physical forces and
the governmental inertia responsible for the condition. The most con-
troversial of the proposals, however, dealt with the question of taxation of
land.

Not surprisingly, Marsh pushed land tax issues to the forefront of the
report. Some members of the Commission agreed with the more doctri-
naire single-taxer, Frederic C. Howe, that "the housing question is the
land question" and that "an ounce of land taxation will do more than a
pound of regulation" (Howe, p. 1067). Therefore the Commission,
although it did not directly advocate a land tax, strongly urged that the
municipal government seriously study the possibility of its enactment.
Also the Commission recommended that land be taxed at a higher rate
than the structure built upon it. Thus taxes on buildings would be halved
while taxes on land would be doubled (*Report*, 1911, p. 979).

Another even more innovative proposal in the Congestion Commission's

Report dealt with public incentives for improvement of private land. This scheme would have changed the manner of apportioning tax on real property. Instead of taxing at an equal rate the value of improvement and land, the rate for improvements would be only half the rate on unimproved land. The landholder would therefore be given a tax break if he did something constructive with his property. Although the idea did not gain acceptance at the time, it stands as one of the earliest expressions of municipalities giving tax incentives to property owners for improvements carried out at their own expense.

Reaction to Report

The New York Commission's Report was on the whole a valuable document – hailed by some as "epoch-making." ("Overcrowding," 1911). Unfortunately it went the way of so many city reports, to obscurity in a file cabinet. Although it contained nothing extreme, even the mere use of phrases like "land tax" and "keeping land cheap" scared people. Its mere implications for restructuring the tax system on property infuriated its critics more than the actual measures it proposed. For instance, Grosvenor Atterbury, an architect and original member of the Committee on Congestion of Population, latched onto the ideal stated in the report for keeping land cheap. Although nothing specific was advocated to accomplish this goal, Atterbury attacked the Report for merely alluding to the proposition. In reviewing the final Congestion Commission's Report, Atterbury stated that making land cheap enough for anyone was not "true economics" and was therefore inappropriate. He wrote:

The Report recommends "keep land cheap." This, of course, can be done only by limiting its usefulness. Is it certain that we want that? Cheap land, like labor, may be the most expensive from the point of view of true economy. Would the effect of the restriction of the price of land (even if feasible) be true economy? What we want in this matter is the most economical use of land compatible with hygienic and social standards, a situation not necessarily synonymous with "cheap" or low price land (Atterbury, 1911, p. 1070).

Thus even though the Commission only talked about the ideal of keeping land cheap, and stopped short of making concrete recommendations, still it drew heavy attack. Even though it never definitely advocated a single tax, but only requested a study of its effects, it was attacked as radical. The Board of Aldermen refused to allocate funds to press for enactment of any of the proposals, and with this lack of official support for the Congestion Commission's proposals, the entire effort failed. Governor Hughes appointed a State Commission on the same matter with Marsh at its unpaid head, but the damage had been done on the local level (Hebberd, 1910). Municipal officials had rendered their verdict – massive urban crowding would somehow have to dissipate on its own.

Mary Simkhovitch analyzed the congestion campaign's failure on the grounds of the public's reluctance to act. "It needs far more than five years work to effect so radical a change" (Simkhovitch, 1910). But fundamentally it was a question of more than time. For beneath all the agitation dealing with problems of congestion lay a basic need to reorder the prevailing economic structure. In Marsh's words, congestion resulted primarily from "protected privilege and exploitation," and "with expensive land no remedy for congestion among unskilled workers can permanently be found" (*The True Story*, 1910, p. 14). The high cost of land, low rate of wages, congestion of factories, and speculation in real estate sales all had to be drastically rectified. Such conditions, he thought, were "largely the outcome of a system of laissez-faire . . . and the police power of the state must be extended and enlarged to deal with it" (Marsh, 1910a). Marsh clearly believed something more than time was necessary for change to take place. He vociferously attacked land owners who benefited from increased value of unimproved land, and his views painted the congestion movement with a hue of radicalism which retarded immediate action.

Marsh and the single-tax

Marsh's brand of Henry George single-taxation clearly unnerved people. He advocated a sharp departure from traditional tax systems called the differential or graded tax. Besides the regular tax on land, a progressive levy would be charged on increases in land values. This differential tax would tax land at a much higher rate than buildings, and the "unearned increment" derived from merely holding property while it rose in value would be partially returned to the community. Such a tax therefore would make it far less profitable for the speculator to hoard unimproved land (Lubove, p. 236).

In true Henry George fashion Marsh argued that no individual should benefit merely from the increased value of his land when that increase usually stemmed from improvements in the community as a whole. High land values inevitably led to landholders making the most use of their property and congestion always resulted. The differential tax promised to keep land cheap and therefore lower building costs as well as rents. In addition, the increased tax revenues could fill the growing "social needs" of the city.

Marsh's critics

Such a dramatic shift in taxation, of course, did not sit well with the financial community. An example of the hostility Marsh engendered was the reaction of Charles Pratt, the treasurer of Standard Oil, who declined an invitation of Frank Goodnow to appear before the Congestion Commission. He wrote: "I don't believe you know how radical that man Marsh is, or you wouldn't have anything to do with him." Goodnow, in turn, remarked to Marsh: "I'm backing you, but I suppose we can't expect people to contribute to the cutting of their financial throats" (Marsh, 1953, p. 24).

Marsh's views also ran against the grain of the professional economic thinking of the day. When he wrote to the Department of Economics at Harvard University, hoping to obtain expert opinion on the reasons behind congestion, he received the following caustic reply: "We must reckon with the fact that people flock to the congested districts because they want to be there; just as, for instance, single taxers flock to membership in congestion committees because they want to be there" (Bullock, 1913).

However, irritating established financial or educational interests was perhaps not as significant as dividing the small band of planning supporters themselves. This apparently is what Marsh also had done. The breach is evident in a confidential letter from Robert DeForest to Jacob Riis. DeForest, president of the Metropolitan Museum of Art and a member since 1906 of the Municipal Art Commission, was one of the leading planning spokesmen in New York ("DeForest," p. 61). He was perhaps the prototype of the cultivated supporter of City Beautiful programs, and according to some, let his upper-class background keep him "a little distant with commonplace people and affairs" (Reynolds, n.d.). Yet DeForest did advocate city planning, and his support for the Congestion Commission could have been crucial. On this occasion his support was not forthcoming, as he wrote to Riis: "The leader of this movement [Congestion] is I think Mr Benjamin C. Marsh, who has lots of enthusiasm, lots of go, lots of good intentions, but as to whose practical judgment I have serious doubts. Some of my friends who have been more or less associated with him have found it desirable to withdraw and I should not look for practical results from a Commission, the leadership of which rested in some of our Aldermen and Mr Marsh" (DeForest, 1910).

Even Charles Mulford Robinson, publicist of civic improvement and enthusiast of almost everything having to do with planning, criticized Marsh and his methods. Robinson believed it "a questionable policy for city planners to appeal as yet – though one may eventually come to it – for a radical change in methods of taxation" (Robinson, 1909).

Although obviously not seeing eye to eye with everyone who supported planning in general, Marsh worked to coalesce the fledgling profession into a single national organization in hopes of enlarging the forum for his views and advancing the cause of city planning in general. His efforts in early 1909 to form such a group were further evidence of his capacity for work. For while involved in the establishment of the national organization, Marsh still retained his position with the New York CCP, served as the unpaid secretary of a new Society to Lower Rents and Reduce Taxes on Homes in New York, lobbied for the creation of the City Commission on Congestion of Population, delivered numerous speeches and wrote many articles as well as his *An Introduction to City Planning*, and co-ordinated the city planning exhibition with the Municipal Art Society. As the author of the first text, designer for the first exhibition, and founder of the first national organization of city planning in 1909, Marsh clearly ranked as a prime mover in the evolution of this young field.

The first National Conference on Planning

Henry Morgenthau, the chairman of the New York CCP, worked closest with Marsh in setting up the national conference. A director of several banks and real estate firms and owner of large amounts of undeveloped New York property, Morgenthau was a curious champion of anti-congestion. Nonetheless, eager for civic responsibility, he pledged $1500 to the CCP, donated office space for its use, and served as its chairman. Morgenthau and Marsh formed that special kind of partnership (similar to Robert DeForest and Lawrence Veiller in the housing field) that existed in many reform causes, that of the well-bred civic promoter listed on the organization's masthead allied with the energetic social reformer who did most of the work. During the period of American progressivism this union usually resulted in the conservative tempering the reformer's ardor. No one could do this to Marsh and this alliance soon withered. But not until it bore the fruit of the first National Conference on City Planning and Congestion.

Morgenthau and Marsh approached President William Howard Taft to preside at a national meeting of city planning. Taft, fearing reprimand from the Congress for usurping initiative, begged off, but suggested Secretary of the Interior Richard A. Ballinger as an appropriate alternative. With Ballinger, Speaker Joseph Cannon, and Senator Francis Newlands in attendance, the National Conference on City Planning and Congestion met in Washington, D.C., on May 21 and 22, 1909, to discuss the multifaceted problems of housing, transportation, recreation, and planning in the cities (US Congress, 1910).

The forty-three conferees met in an air of excitement and hope. Many of the nation's leaders in urban affairs attended, including Frederic Howe, Jane Addams, Mary Simkhovitch, George Ford, John Nolen, Frederick Law Olmsted, Jr, and Herbert Croly, the editor of the *Architectural Record* and author of the recently completed *The Promise of American Life*. Representatives of municipal art, social work, architectural, civil engineering, and conservationist groups also attended. The meeting vividly reflected the many interest groups concerned with city planning at the time.

Henry Morgenthau displayed his upper-class social morality and Darwinistic economics in his address before the group on the evening of May 21 at the Masonic Temple in Washington. "We are all proud of our country, its achievements, and the opportunities it has offered us and is offering others," the financier pronounced. But, he warned,

we will not permit anything to mar its onward and upward progress, if we can help it. There is an evil [congestion] which is gnawing at the vitals of the country, to remedy which we have come together – an evil that breeds physical disease, moral depravity, discontent, and socialism – and all these must be cured and eradicated or else our great body politic will be weakened. This Community can only hold its pre-eminence if the masses that compose it are given a chance to be healthy, moral and self-respecting. If they are forced to live like swine they will lose their vigor. (US Congress, 1910, 59).

Marsh, on the other hand, struck a more pragmatic chord in his remarks before the conference. Taking the themes developed in his book, Marsh outlined the steps necessary to advance a meaningful city plan – a survey, publicity, and legislation allowing cities to plan. This outline fit squarely with Marsh's modus operandi of gathering "facts" to be used as weapons "against which corporate interests cannot contend" and publicity, similar to the Congestion Exhibition, "to make possible the awakening of the public interest" (US Congress, 1910, p. 61). Marsh's speech bristled with his own personal vigor, and Mel Scott observed: "If some delegates had the impression that city planning was for Marsh a holy war against predatory forces, especially real estate speculators, they were perhaps not mistaken" (Scott, p. 99).

As one of the principal organizers of the group Marsh stayed on in Washington after the two-day meeting ended and testified before the Committee on the District of Columbia. The Conference proceedings and Marsh's testimony were then published by the federal government. The history of the first National Conference on City Planning is therefore recorded as a Senate Document.

The 1909 meeting in Washington began a long and fruitful existence for the city planning profession as a national movement. It remains, however, the only significant juncture where Marsh and the national urban planning drive stood together. The reasons for the subsequent division are as varied as Marsh's personality and interests and as discordant as the numerous elements of early city planning.

Division in the planning movement

After the national conference Marsh returned to New York to continue his anti-congestion campaign on the local level. The City Commission began its work and it was then that Marsh began engendering the opposition of powerful financial groups against his single-tax schemes. The fire got hot and even housing reformer Robert DeForest attacked him. Worse still, the financial support and backing of the CCP by Henry Morgenthau ended. Morgenthau, worried that adoption of the single-tax would hurt his investments, could not convince Marsh to drop the proposal from the CCP's platform. He therefore resigned his chairmanship, reneged on his financial pledge, and kicked the group out of the office he had been providing. Marsh's uncompromising advocacy of taxing land higher than buildings struck the majority of New Yorkers of the day as radical. He could not budge the powerful financial interests arrayed against him and even his potential allies dropped support (Marsh, 1953, pp. 27–9).

The national picture appeared equally dismal. Marsh's hopes for a single national organization devoted to city planning shattered in 1910 when Robert DeForest and Lawrence Veiller formed the National Housing Association. Although the NHA worked closely with the National Conference on City Planning and speakers at each group's conventions frequently overlapped, the division remained essentially damaging. Housing and planning were inextricably bound and a national organization for each served neither's best interests. Also, since DeForest served as president of the National Housing Association, Marsh could hardly expect a sympathetic forum within that group (Walker, p. 12).

The winds rapidly changed within the national planning conference also and worked against Marsh's prime interests. At the second meeting in Rochester, New York, in 1910, the group dropped "Congestion" from its title and became the National Conference on City Planning. The name change was significant. The NCCP, beginning in 1910, concerned itself far more with the techniques of professionalism than with broad social problems. Fewer social workers and civic reformers attended, and increasingly the NCCP revealed itself as a "professional" organization concerned with data, statistics, techniques, management, standards, efficiency, and evaluation.

One of the principal movers in this regard, George B. Ford, had written the technical chapter in Marsh's textbook. In part reacting to the overly aesthetic City Beautiful mode of planning, Ford stressed "scientific management" applied to urban planning. Planning must become systematized, Ford and others argued, in order to develop as a meaningful profession and gain the support of the businessman "who has to pay the bills." Obviously, Marsh fumed at planners' desires to dovetail with business interests (Hancock, 1967).

Zoning emerged as the tool the scientific planners latched onto, and increasingly zoning became the major preoccupation of the planning profession. Supported by Marsh, zoning initially had the same radical connotations that Marsh's land tax proposals had. But when the first comprehensive zoning law was passed by New York City in 1916, real estate men supported it. That city's large businessmen realized that zoning could stabilize the uncertain real estate market while placating those concerned with overcrowding. Zoning therefore outflanked its radical predecessor, the anti-congestion fight, because it bolstered the real estate market while purporting to do something about easing congestion. Zoning became the conservative's tool to temper the reformer's ardor – something that Marsh's single-tax would never have done (Kantor, pp. 165–229).

Marsh abandons planning

Marsh continued his lonely advocacy for his differential tax and appeared briefly before the zoning Commission's hearing (Marsh, 1910b, 1914). But by 1917 his isolation from the new mainstream of city planning was complete. In that year the American Institute of Planners formed to serve even more closely defined professional interests than the NCCP. Two years' experience in city planning activities were required for membership. Benjamin Marsh, although meeting the requirements easily, failed to appear on the list of charter members (Scott, p. 164).

The absence signified as much an interest in new fields as an isolation from professional planning. The Balkan War had taken him away from New York as early as 1912 and he served as a correspondent there for two years. Upon his return he worked with the Farmer's National Council and beginning in 1918 with the People's Reconstruction League. Marsh beame a familiar figure in Washington during the Hoover Administration and led his People's Lobby of over 1000 members in numerous reform causes. He constantly appeared before Congressional Committees and orchestrated press releases on depression relief, social control of industries, and a myriad other popular causes. Under a new law in 1946 Marsh became the first lobbyist to register with the federal government. Characteristically, when sent the form to register income and expenditures. Marsh replied on his own stationery and not on the newly printed government form (*New York Times*, 1953).

Marsh himself did not slow up at all on his exit from the planning field he had so visibly affected. One wonders, however, if his absence did not reduce the vitality of his jilted profession. To be sure, his restless energy could never have been restrained by the confines of a single interest. But the growing professionalism of city planning which offended Marsh the reformer and the propagandist could surely have used a bit of his inconoclastic verve in its efforts to guide the future of the metropolitan leviathan.

Notes

1 Other original members in the Committee on Congestion of Population included Grosvenor Atterbury, Edward T. Devine, Charles Ingersoll, Paul V. Kellogg, John Martin, and Carola Woerishoffer.

References

Atterbury, Grosvenor (1911) "City planning and congestion," *Survey*, 25 (March 25), pp. 1069–70.
Board of Aldermen (1910a) *Proceedings* (April 12), pp. 135–7.
____ (1910b) *Proceedings* (February 4), p. 3.
Bullock, C. J. (1913) Bullock to Marsh, March 27, Benjamin C. Marsh Papers, Library of Congress.
Catalogue of Exhibit of Congestion of Population in New York (1908).
"Congestion of population" (1908) *Charities and the Commons*, 19 (March 21), pp. 1739–40.
"Congestion and its relief" (1910) *American City*, 3 (December), pp. 285–8.
Davis, Allen F. (1967) *Spearheads for Reform*, New York, Oxford University Press.
DeForest, Robert W. (1910) DeForest to Riis, April 5, 1910, Jacob Riis Papers, New York Public LIbrary.
"DeForest, Robert W." (1967), p. 15 in *National Cyclopaedia of American Biography*, vol. XLII, Ann Arbor, Mich., University Microfilms.
Goodnow, Frank J. (1910) "Reasons for a Commission on Congestion," *Survey*, 24 (April), pp. 77–8.
Hancock, John L. (1967) "Planners in the changing American city, 1900–1940," *Journal of the American Institute of Planners*, 33 (September), pp. 290–304.
Hebbard, Robert W. (1910) "The work of the State Commission on Distribution of Population," in New York State Board of Charities, *Report*, 1, pp. 907–15.
Howe, Frederic C. (1911) "Land values and congestion," *Survey*, 25 (March), p. 1067.
Kantor, Harvey A. (1971) "Modern urban planning: origins and evolution in New York City, 1890–1933," Ph.D. dissertation, New York University.
Kelley, Florence (1909) Kelley to George McClellan, June 22, Mayoral Papers, New York City Municipal Archives.
Kraus, Harry P. (1970) "The Settlement House movement in New York City, 1806–1914," Ph.D. dissertation, New York University.
Lubove, Roy (1960) *The Progressives and the Slums: Tenement House Reform in New York City, 1890–1917*, Pittsburgh, University of Pittsburgh Press.
"Main charts contributed to the Congestion Exhibit" (1908) *Federation*, 5 (May), pp. 19–48.
Marsh, Benjamin C. (1908a) "City planning in justice to the working population," *Charities and The Commons*, 19 (February), pp. 1514–18.
____ (1908b) "Congestion Exhibit in Brooklyn," *Charities and The Commons*, 20 (May), pp. 209–11.
____ (1909) *An Introduction to City Planning*, New York: privately published.
____ (1910a) "Causes of congestion of population," Second National Conference on City Planning, *Proceedings* (1910), pp. 35–9.
____ (1910b) "Taxation and the improvement of living conditions in American cities," *Survey*, 24 (July) pp. 605–9.
____ (1914) "Can land be overloaded?" *Annals*, 51 (January), pp. 54–8.

_____ (1953) *Lobbyist for the People*. Washington, D.C., Public Affairs Press.

Martin, John (1908) "The Exhibit of Congestion interpreted," *Charities and The Commons*, 20 (April), pp. 27–39.

McAneny, George (1910) "Bulletin for press release on congestion, February 26, 1910," George McAneny Papers, Princeton University.

New York Times, April 13, 1910.

_____ January 20, 1912.

_____ January 1, 1953.

"Overcrowding must stop" (1917) *Survey*, 25 (March), p. 989.

"Problems of overcrowding" (1908) *Outlook*, 88 (March), p. 615.

"Report of New York Congestion Commission" (1911) *Survey*, 25 (March), pp. 977–9.

Report: New York City Congestion Commission (1911) in *The City Record*, 40 (March 7), pp. 1830–1903.

Reynolds, Jackson (n.d.) "Reminiscences," Columbia Oral History Project, Columbia University.

Robinson, Charles M. (1909) "The City Plan Exhibition," *Survey*, 22 (July), p. 317.

Scott, Mel (1969) *American City Planning since 1890*, Berkeley and Los Angeles, University of California Press.

Simkhovitch, Mary (1910) "Speech of November 16, 1910," Mary Simkhovitch Papers, Schlesinger Library, Radcliffe Library.

_____ (1938) *Neighborhood: My Story at Greenwich House*, New York, W. W. Norton.

The True Story of the Worst Congestion in any Civilized City (1910).

Toll, Seymour I. (1969) *Zoned American*, New York, Grossman.

US Congress (1910) "City planning," 61st Congress, 2nd Sess., 422 Senate Documents, LIX, 57–105.

Walker, Robert A. (1950) *The Planning Function in Urban Government*, Chicago, The University of Chicago Press.

4 Burnham's *Plan* and Moody's *Manual*: city planning as progressive reform

Thomas J. Schlereth

Using Walter D. Moody's *Wacker's Manual of the Plan of Chicago* (1911) as an early classic in the history of American planning promotional literature, this chapter explores the relations of Daniel Burnham's 1909 *Plan of Chicago*, as translated by Moody into a more democratic medium, with the intellectual concerns of progressive reformers at the turn of the twentieth century. Special emphasis is given to the emerging profession of the civic promoter and his impact on urban planning.

Moody's *Manual* provides the primary documentation for this study; the book's key ideas (e.g. belief in mass education, the efficiency movement, the efficacy of public relations in implementing public planning, the influence of the urban environment upon human behavior), as well as its deficiencies and legacies, are analyzed within the context of the intellectual history of the American city planning movement and in the history of the reform movement known as progressivism.

To Chicagoan Walter Dwight Moody, "the completion of the *Plan of Chicago* was the most important civic event in the history of the city." Moody maintained that if implemented, the 1909 metropolitan plan prepared by Daniel H. Burnham and Edward H. Bennett[1] would enable Chicago to become nothing less than "the center of the modern world." No small claim for a city hardly seven decades old, but not atypical braggadocio for a midwestern metropolis already notorious for its special brand of civic and architectural boosterism.

Moody, a former general manager of the Chicago Association of Commerce and the first managing director of the Chicago Plan Commission (CPC), made his boast in a strangely titled, now largely unread work called *Wacker's Manual of the Plan of Chicago: Municipal Economy*.[2] First published in 1911, this curious volume in the history of American city planning literature went through several editions during the decade (1911–21) that Moody superintended the promotion of the Burnham/Bennett *Plan*. The book's misleading title prompted contemporaries as well as a few modern scholars mistakenly to attribute the work's authorship to Charles Wacker, prominent Chicago brewer turned real estate developer, financier, civic leader, and first chairman of the CPC.

Moody's middle and surname also occasionally prompted confusion with that of the popular Chicago evangelist Dwight L. Moody whose tabernacle and ancillary structures (bible college and institute, bookstore, radio station, etc.) still dot Chicago's near northside cityscape.[3]

The *Manual's* author

Who was Walter Dwight Moody? Why did he write a bestseller and ascribe it to another man? What were the work's principal ideas? What might such ideas reveal about the philosophy and the practice of turn-of-the-century urban planning in Chicago and the nation? What might the intellectual history of this segment of the American city planning movement add to our understanding of the main currents of American intellectual history?

This chapter attempts to explore these questions through a textual analysis of Moody's widely promulgated book as an early classic in city planning promotional literature. While other historical data (e.g. correspondence, municipal archives, Chicago Planning Commission minutes) has also been consulted, the *Manual* itself stands as the principal documentation that informs this study. Thus the *Manual's* ideas – belief in mass education, progressivism, the efficiency movement, and environmentalism – are the focus of the analysis that follows. Concentrating primarily on Moody's text rather than his context, on what he wrote rather than what he did, this study interprets the *Manual* as an important document both in the intellectual history of the American city planning movement and in the history of the many-faceted reform movement known as progressivism.

The occasional mistaken identity of Walter Dwight Moody with Dwight Lyman Moody contains one clue to the former's character. In his efforts in "putting the *Plan* across," W. D. Moody openly acknowledged that he did so with all the zealotry of "the clergyman and the pedagogue."[4] In an era when many reformers had clerical backgrounds (e.g. Richard Ely or Graham Taylor) or personal religious motivations (e.g. John Bates Clark or Charles H. Cooley) behind their attempts to bring about social and political change,[5] his evangelical fervor to promote urban planning as the redemption of American cities seems to put Moody perfectly in step with many of his fellow progressives.

Moody's career began, however, not in salvation but in sales. The title of one of his early publications can serve as a capsule biography. On a 1907 book cover, he proudly proclaimed himself as one of those "men who sell things," the book being the *Observations and Experiences of Over Twenty Years as a Travelling Salesman, European Buyer, Sales Manager,*

Employer.[6] Drummer, promoter, ad-man, business college teacher, show-man, Moody personified the late nineteenth-century American whom Daniel Boorstin has symbolized as "the go-getter," and whom both Burn-ham and Wacker saw as "a hustler, a man who knows how to do things and to get the greatest amount of publicity out of a movement."[7]

To such a man the CPC entrusted the monumental task of making every Chicagoan fully plan conscious. The objective was to reach the one and one-half million citizens who could not afford the prohibitively expensive ($25.00), lavish, limited first edition of two thousand copies of the *Plan* published by the Commercial Club.[8] Handsome though it was, filled with evocative sketches in both color and black and white by Jules Guerin and Jules Janin, Burnham and his Commercial Club associates recognized that the *Plan of Chicago* was little more than sagacious advice from people with no official power. In accepting one of the limited edition copies, Mayor Fred Busse, who would later create the CPC, was careful to note that the *Plan's* proposals were not "hard and fast" and would not neces-sarily result in immediate changes.[9] The unofficial nature of the venture, however, inspired Charles Eliot, the retired president of Harvard, to write:

That a club of businessmen should have engaged in such an undertaking, and have brought it successfully to its present stage, affords a favorable illustration of the workings of American democracy. The democracy is not going to be dependent on the rare appearance of a Pericles, an Augustus, a Colbert, or a Christopher Wren. It will be able to work toward the best ideals through the agency of groups of intel-ligent and public spirited citizens who know how to employ experts to advantage.[10]

To promote the *Plan* that they had had experts produce, the Com-mercial Club members, through their control of the CPC,[11] employed another expert. Walter Moody, a professional organizer and one of the new breed of public executives who made careers out of managing civic organizations, assumed this responsibility. As early as 1909 Moody had been approached by Charles D. Norton (later Assistant Secretary of the Treasury under William Howard Taft) to publicize the *Plan* as the exclusive promotional property of the Commercial Club. When the *Plan* was presented to the city, and The Chicago Plan Commission, a public agency, was created by municipal ordinance, Moody's talent was again solicited – this time by the CPC's first chairman, Charles H. Wacker. Moody accepted the task of mobilizing a comprehensive promotional campaign to match the sweeping metropolitan scope of the *Plan* itself.[12]

Although he never pretended to be a practicing planner like Burnham or Bennett, Moody considered his task of "the scientific promotion of scientific planning" to be equal in importance to whatever was accom-plished on the drafting table or in the architectural office. He defined city planning as "the science of planning the development of cities in a systematic and orderly way." Furthermore, he divided city planning into two distinct and widely separate scientific branches. The first, or technical branch, embraces architecture and engineering. The second, which is promotive, is likewise scientifically professional and could be truthfully termed the dynamic power behind the throne of accomplishment.[13]

The terms "scientifically professional" indicated another characteristic that Moody shared with many other thinkers of his era. As David Noble, Richard Hofstadter, and Charles Forcey have argued, many progressives believed strongly in the efficacy of the scientific method, guided by professional expertise, to achieve social change.[14] Walter Moody shared this assumption, not only in his promulgation of the Chicago plan but also in his promotion of city planning as a profession. The special identity that Herbert Croly claimed for architects, that Frederick Winslow Taylor coveted for industrial engineers, and Louis Brandeis wished firmly established for lawyers and businessmen, Moody sought for city planners.[15] Like Charles Mulford Robinson and John Nolen, his contemporary colleagues in city planning, he endeavored to contribute to what has been called the late nineteenth- and early twentieth-century "culture of professionalism." Moody's decade of work with the CPC, his numerous magazine and newspaper articles, and his two major books all were methods by which he sought to make the profession of city planning a vehicle of urban reform.[16]

The key to Moody's reformism was publicity. In debt to the social scientific advertising techniques he borrowed from the pioneering social psychologist Walter Dill Scott (a fellow Chicagoan who later became president of Northwestern University), Moody made his appeal for implementation of the 1909 *Plan* to each of the assorted interest groups and power blocs in Chicago.

Of the multiple constituencies to be persuaded of the necessity of the *Plan*, Moody felt most confident of the city's capitalists. After all, had it not been an informal competition as to who would actually sponsor a city plan that encouraged the merger of Chicago's Merchants and Commercial Clubs? By the time the Commercial Club produced the Burnham plan, its members had also invested over a half million dollars in the enterprise.[17] Moody was less sure of the general electorate. His first major publication as managing director of the CPC, therefore, sought to reach this citywide, adult audience. A ninety-page, hardbound reference work titled *Chicago's Greatest Issue: An Official Plan* was distributed to over 165,000 Chicago residents; these were property-owners and tenants who paid $25.00 or more per month in rent. The booklet is usually credited with countering the initial critiques of the *Plan* (such as George Eddy Newcomb's caustic *Chicago Replanned* [Chicago: privately printed, 1911] and the protests of

Plate 4.1 McCutcheon, a friend of Moody, drew this cartoon for Moody's use in widening the exposure and appeal of the 1909 *Plan of Chicago.*

the Twelfth Street Property Owners Association), and with securing support for the passage of the first plan bond issue (the widening of Twelfth Street) proposed to the Chicago voters in 1912.[18]

The *Manual's* origins

Within the first six months of administering the CPC, Moody moved to institute a city planning study program in the Chicago schools. Daniel Burnham had suggested this move believing that for comprehensive urban planning to succeed "children must grow up dreaming of a beautiful city." Burnham, who had been extremely disappointed when his 1905 *Plan for San Francisco* failed to be implemented because of inadequate promotion and subsequent citizen apathy, hoped to achieve this educational objective by lectures and the distribution of literature in the city schools.[19] Moody had bigger plans. Believing that "the ultimate solution of all the major problems of American cities lies in the education of our children to their responsibilities as future owners of our municipalities and arbiters of their governmental destiny," he proposed introducing an accredited course on the Chicago plan into the city's public school curriculum. The course would be a part of Moody's program for "scientific citizen making."[20]

To assist in such civic nurture, Moody wrote the first city planning textbook to be used in American schools. He named the text *Wacker's Manual*, because he believed that the people "should come to know intimately the individual who to a large extent held the destiny of the city in his hands." He felt it imperative for the populace to have the same confidence and knowledge about their plan leader, Charles Wacker (chairman on the CPC), as in their plan.

Influenced by the work of German educators who had been instructing children in urban planning since the 1880s, he designed his text and its accompanying teacher's handbook for use in the second semester of a civics course already operating in the final term of Chicago's public grammar schools. The eighth grade was selected because many contemporary educational psychologists contended that at that stage of growth children were most impressionable. Also, after grammar school many would drop out of the system. While writing the *Manual*, Moody sought help from the University of Chicago faculty, the staff at the Chicago Historical Society, and the Art Institute. He persuaded Ella Flagg Young, city superintendent of schools, to have the Board of Education officially adopt and purchase (at 34¢ a hardbound copy) the 1911 first edition for use in the spring of 1912. Eventually over fifty thousand copies of *Wacker's Manual* were printed. They were read not only by Chicago school children but also by their parents.

While by no means as stunning as the *Plan* in terms of diversity of pictorial media or aesthetic quality, the *Manual* aspired to make as powerful a visual impact. The *Manual* included over 150 charts, maps, and pictures – many reproduced from the *Plan*. (The *Plan* had 142 illustrations.) Similar to the parent *Plan*, nearly a third of the *Manual*'s graphics were of foreign urban design. Color renderings in both Burnham's treatise (where they were largely the work of Jules Guerin)[21] and Moody's textbook were hazy, subdued pastels, connoting a tranquil, sunlit, environment for Chicago which corresponds with an equally unreal absence of automobiles, pollution, and congestion in these visual utopias of Chicago's future.

Moody further modeled his 137-page primer along organizational lines roughly parallel to the 164-page, octavo-size *Plan*. He divided the textbook into four major topics: (a) general urban planning philosophy and nomenclature (chapters 1–3); (b) a historical survey of city planning since antiquity (chapters 4–7); (c) Chicago's historical, geographic, economic, and civic development, including the origins of the 1909 *Plan* (chapters 8–10); and, (d) a detailed exegesis of the Plan's main components – transportation network, street system, Michigan Avenue redevelopment, park system, and civic center (chapters 11–16).[22]

Of the four media he produced in advancing the *Plan of Chicago*,[23] Moody considered the *Manual* to have the most long-range influence. Like previous American educational reformers Benjamin Rush, Horace Mann, Henry Barnard, and Francis Parker, he believed that the promise of a more enlighted, public-minded citizenry rested with the current school age generation. Moody had been an educator for several years in Chicago's LaSalle Extension University, and he felt that his text "recognized the need for bringing out in the children of our cities a sharp, clear, vivid interest in those cities, in their history, their growth, in their present and their future."[24] As a consequence, the *Manual* can be considered one of the earliest urban histories for use in the secondary schools. Moreover, given its visual and verbal coverage of the American and European urban built environment, the *Manual* also introduced eighth graders to civic art and public architecture – areas of the fine arts that progressive educators usually found sorely neglected in most American classrooms.

Through his *Manual*, Moody shared with fellow Chicagoans Francis Parker and John Dewey the desire to create a larger classroom by relating school and society. Like Parker and Dewey, Moody sought to adjust education, through the discipline of city planning, to the interests of young people and to tie what he called "civic learning" to the real world outside the classroom.[25] The *Manual's* injunctions to use the city itself as a part of the curriculum were perfectly consonant with Dewey's principles of integrating *The School and Society*. Although in actual practice he exhibited none of the innovative pedagogical techniques that Dewey and his followers advocated,[26] Moody completely agreed in theory with progressive education's concern to adapt schooling to fit the needs of the child rather than to the demands of tradition.

Perhaps the greatest common ground shared by Moody (as a promoter of planning education) and Dewey (as a proponent of progressive education) was the assumption regarding the correlation between education and politics. Just as Dewey in *Education and Democracy* (1916) – a major educational manifesto of progressivism – wrote: "we may produce in the schools a projection in the type of society we should like to realize and by forming minds in accord with it generally modify the larger and more recalcitrant features of adult society;" likewise, Moody, in *Wacker's Manual* (1911) proposed to "prepare the minds of our children to grasp and lay fast hold upon the science of city planning for the future glory of Chicago and the prosperity and happiness of all her people."[27]

The *Manual's* ideas

Along with providing a pioneering pedagogy for disseminating "the principles and practices of scientific planning," Moody also wrote his primer, quite unabashedly, in order to inculcate what he variously termed "community patriotism," united civic interest," "civic patriotism" and "community virtue." In the *Manual* building citizens and planning cities were synonymous since Moody saw the *Plan* and its implementation across the cityscape as the artifactual evidence that "gave the people of Chicago a way to express in solid form their progressive spirit."[28]

In an article in the *Century Magazine*, "White city and capital city," Daniel Burnham specifically identified himself and his city planning with the progressive movement.[29] Architectural historian Thomas Hines has recently pointed out the ramifications of Burnham's reformist liberal Republicanism, particularly its influence on the shape and substance of the 1909 *Plan*.[30] Such progressivism became further pronounced when Moody translated the plan into a manual.

By progressivism, Moody and Burnham meant something more than the Progressive (or Bull Moose) Party formed in Chicago by the Republican insurgents who supported Theodore Roosevelt for the presidency in 1912. As contemporaries such as B.P. DeWitt (*The Progressive Movement*, New York, Macmillan, 1915) almost universally recognized, progressivism was a pervasive, many-sided crusade of uplift and reform, often inconsistent, often naive, and sometimes palpably conservative. This broad impulse toward criticism and change was increasingly conspicuous after 1900 and had quite dissipated by the mid-1920s; as Richard Hofstadter states, progressivism was not so much the movement of any one social class, or coalition of classes, against a particular class or group as it was a rather widespread and remarkably good-natured effort of a significant segment of the urban middle class to achieve within their areas of expertise (e.g. law, academe, politics, social work) a societal self-reformation.[31] Accepting industrialization and urbanization as facts of twentieth-century American life, never seriously doubting the continued possibility of progress and prosperity, the majority of progressives sought the restoration of a type of modified economic individualism within a collective political democracy that was widely believed to have existed earlier in America and to have become threatened by greedy corporations, corrupt political machines, and apathetic citizens.

As representatives of what might be called "mainline progressivism" Moody and Burnham shared this political and social temper that was, paradoxically, innovative and reforming as well as traditional and conserving. Given this brand of progressivism, they understandably had an affinity with local Chicago reformers such as Charles Merriam (political scientist at the University of Chicago) or Mayor Tom L. Johnson (who first enlisted Burnham in comprehensive planning for the city of Cleveland). With moderate social progressives such as George E. Hooker and Jane Addams, Moody and Burnham's cautious reformism had only partial acceptance. More radical social progressives like Graham Taylor or Florence Kelly questioned Moody and Burnham's lack of concern in both *Plan* and *Manual* for adequate neighborhood housing and social welfare. Chicago labor progressives like John Fitzgerald and militant socialists like Lucy Parsons considered almost all progressive reforms, including proposals such as the *Plan* and the *Manual*, as but "band-aid" remedies designed to bolster the city's corporate capitalist interests.[32]

Moody, while basically a supporter of capitalistic individualism (he had been the executive director of the Chicago Association of Commerce before joining the CPC), also saw the need – perhaps in the interest of preserving capitalism – for greater social collectivization and municipal cooperation among individual citizens. Long-range, large-scale city planning would, he admitted, proscribe certain rights and prerogatives of the city dweller. Moody worried, however, that in early twentieth-century American cities such as Chicago, rampant individualism perhaps had gone too far and that the system's inherent atomism was rapidly destroying communal urban life.[33]

To meet this dilemma, Moody advocated major environmental and architectural change as a method by which to infuse his form of progressivism into the American city. Calling for planners to design a "New Metropolis" – an image bearing a striking resemblance to other "new" reform manifestos being issued by fellow progressive publicists (e.g. Walter Lippmann's *New Republic* or Walter Weyl's *New Democracy*) – Moody espoused a politics that wished to conserve what was valuable from the past and also remain cognizant of the new challenges brought on by economic and urban concentration. In short, he argued in both the *Manual* and in his later writings for a greater combination of central planning and voluntary individual cooperation. As his friend Bernard W. Snow summarized it in an address honoring the CPC in 1910: "Every generation has its burdens. To this is given the duty of curbing the individualism and establishing the collectivism of Democracy."[34]

Walter Moody promulgated a political progressivism that historian

Stow Persons has labelled neo-democracy.[35] Non-partisan, believing in the political role of public opinion, anxious to separate electoral politics from public administration, Moody's writings are a perfect case study of an early twentieth-century neo-democrat in action. With his fellow progressives, Moody was willing to revise his original ideal of social progress as achievable solely in individualistic terms and to concede to the state (particularly via a strong executive and numerous public commissions) the rapid expansion of its functions and powers. Moody saw in neo-democracy a political philosophy which did not threaten the prerogatives of the expert. Like Walter Lippman, he did not fear either a big leader (especially if the leader were a Burnham) or bigness in business, labor, or government. The public relations man who translated the philosophy of a business client such as Burnham (who always insisted "Make no little plans") could hardly see bigness as a bogey.[36] Nor could he deny the power of the *word*, especially the printed word, in shaping democratic political thought and action. A reformer who had written a half dozen books, over forty pamphlets, position papers, reports, and newspaper and magazine articles would not think otherwise.[37] Finally, insistent that change would come about by working through the established political system, Moody concurred in the direct democracy principles of reformer Frank Parsons and maintained "that the ballot box always precedes the city planners."[38]

Since the ultimate implementation of the Burnham Plan depended upon widespread voter acceptance of each of its specific proposals, Moody saw his task as identical to that of Frederic C. Howe (1905) who in *The City, The Hope of Democracy* (New York: Charles Scribner's) had argued the necessity of linking all city planning reform with an extensive information and publicity program for adults and a comprehensive educational component for children.[39] Moody's *Wacker's Manual* and his adult primer *What of the City?* served these purposes. They also contain evidence of at least two other important intellectual currents of late nineteenth- and early twentieth-century America: a quest for efficiency and order in personal, commercial, industrial, and political activity, and the belief in the physical environment as a primary determinant of human behavior.

In a work subtitled "Municipal Economy," it comes as no surprise to find repeated pleas for greater centralization, the absolute necessity of eliminating all waste, the commercial value of beauty, and the civic efficacy of "good order, cleanliness, and economy."[40] In fact, many sections of Moody's tract could have been written by any number of Chicagoans – George Pullman, Marshall Field, Gustavus Swift – each of whom sought to impose an entrepreneurial system on the industrial and commercial landscape. This "search for order," as historian Robert Wiebe five feet above the surface in water fifteen feet deep?

25. What is it evident that the city furnishes?
26. How do city officials, Sanitary District contractors all agree they will save money? building contractors
27. How is the total waste of the city divided?
28. What is the number of cubic yards of cinders and ashes produced each year by the city's consumption of coal?
29. How is this moved?
30. What will be the value of the land Chicago can create upon the lake front in five years?
31. What do export engineers say can be created from the city's waste within thirty years?
32. What did the architects take into account in planning the lake front parks?
33. How did they answer this demand in the plans?
34. Beside a wide strip of shore land facing the open lake?
35. What will run along this shore?
36. What will be built beyond the water course to protect it and provide safety and shelter for pleasure craft?
37. What will be located at the northern terminus of the long park at the foot of Twelfth Street?
38. What is to be located on the main shore in the mile of park land between Twenty-second and Twelfth Streets?
39. What will extend northward from the Athletic field on the main shore?
40. What will be situated at the northern extremity of the main harbor?
41. Where are the piers to be built, and how will they be reached?
42. What is to be provided off Jackson Park where the water is quite shallow?
43. How is the lake front to be improved in the district from the mouth of the river north to Chicago Avenue?
44. What steamers will dock at the wharves in the harbor between the Chicago River and Chicago Avenue?
45. How do the lake front plans vary in detail from the south shore plans to the north ward of Chicago Avenue?
46. How will the people benefit from the parks along the lake shore?
47. What does the second element in park development for the future Chicago aim to create?
48. What was decided in the plans after considering the shape of the city, location of its great body of citizens, direction of its growth and all other conditions?
49. Where are the three large new parks to be located and how connected?
50. Why was it decided to pipe the west side the largest single park in Chicago and make that park the center of the future city's park system?
51. What relation does the park system as planned bear to the rest of the future city?
52. Why is the great west side park planned to be located on Congress Street?
53. Describe the proposed Congress Street Park.
54. Describe the south side park as proposed.
55. Describe the north side park as proposed.
56. What have the architects projected to connect the three parks?
57. Describe the curving connecting boulevard, beginning with the great south side park.
58. What is the relation of Western Avenue to this sweeping bow-shaped boulevard?
59. What would the acquisition of these three parks and the bow boulevard add to Chicago's park area and where would it place Chicago in relation to the park area of other cities?
60. What have modern cities learned that they must do to provide recreation areas for their people?
61. What does every European capital have within easy reach of its people but outside of its limits?
62. What do the people of London, Paris, Berlin and Vienna do on Sundays in Summer?
63. Where is New York acquiring outer territory for park purposes?
64. Describe the territory surrounding Chicago procurable for forest parks.
65. Describe the sort of spaces that should be acquired for forest reserve purposes.
66. What has provisional search resulted in?
67. Describe the five proposed forest reserves, in their order.
68. What has modern man learned of city life in a period of less than a century?
69. How is city life different from country life?
70. What is the only way known by which a city may lessen these ills or do away with them?
71. What is necessary to uphold Chicago and enable her to keep her place in commerce and to grow in power in the modern stressful warfare of trade?
72. State the only way for Chicago to increase and maintain the vigor of her people.

CHAPTER XVI

CREATING A CIVIC CENTER

In becoming the second city of the United States in population, Chicago has not until now taken any account of unity, or of centralizing its governmental activities. First there was the settlement about Fort Dear-

cago. Finally Chicago spread out until these villages were swallowed up within the city, giving up their little local governments and becoming districts of Chicago itself.

In this process by which Chicago absorbed its neighboring towns and villages there was no planning for the creation of a center. Instead of creating a great unified

CHICAGO. View, looking west, of the proposed civic center, plan and buildings, showing it as the center of the system of arteries of circulation and of the surrounding country. [Copyrighted by the Commercial Club.]

born, then the extension of the village to cover a square mile or so. While this was in progress at the heart of affairs nearby farm centers grew into little settlements. Township governments were established, and in each township village came into being. Chicago grew toward these villages in all directions, and the villages extended their streets and settlements toward Chi-

city, therefore, we built up one by grouping together numerous adjoining towns. By good fortune, these towns and villages were so laid out that for the most part their streets blended well with the system of Chicago, and so we do not notice, in going about the city, that Chicago is really the result of patching several towns together.

Plate 4.2 Catechetical questions at the end of each chapter illustrate the "primer" nature of Moody's *Manual.* Lavish graphics at chapter beginnings were intended to catch the reader's eye and attention.

labels late nineteenth-century American history,[41] pervades the *Manual*, a work that anticipates Walter Lippmann's *Drift and Mastery* in its demand for a "community patriotism to substitute order for disorder; and reason, common sense and action for negligence, indifference and inertia."[42] Moreover, Moody's incessant arguments for the efficient use of public space strongly parallel Frederick W. Taylor's similar claims (published in the same year as the *Manual*) for *The Scientific Principles of Management* in the organization of industrial space.

Moody took the making of Chicago into a centralized city rather than a group of overcrowded villages to be a basic premise of the Burnham *Plan*. Chicago's street and highway pattern, railroad network, and cultural and civic activities would each have a center and, in turn, be a component of a new central city. The linchpin on this new urban core was a monumental civic center that would be to Chicago what the Acropolis was to Athens, the Forum to Rome, and St Mark's Square to Venice – the very embodiment of the reformed civic life that Burnham and Moody hoped to see come to pass in Chicago. Although we have understandably lost sympathy for neo-classical expressions of institutionalized political power, the progressives felt that neo-classicism's unity, permanence, balance, order, and symmetry best proclaimed both the symbolic role and the functional role of public buildings and communal spaces. A civic center, a unified cluster of "vast civic temples" as Moody called Burnham's proposed building group dominated by a colossal municipal administration building,[43] would typify the permanence of the city, record its history, and express its aspiration for reform. In Moody's estimate, the civic center would "give life to the spirit of unity in the city.[44]

Congestion and waste would be eradicated in the process of centralization. In his *Manual*, Moody warned his young readers that "the *elimination of waste is the World's Greatest Scientific Problem*" (emphasis original); and in his manifesto for adults he suggested various ways by which scientific planning would solve this international dilemma: zoning controls, public health regulations, uniform building codes, and standardized construction materials and designs.[45] A pet Moody project was a proposal he outlined in a pamphlet titled *Fifty Million Dollars for Nothing!* where he discussed how the people of Chicago could obtain thirteen hundred acres of lakefront parks, playgrounds, and watercourses by recycling the city's garbage and waste material – old bricks and mortar, excavation soil, street sweepings, cinders, and ashes. In twelve years, estimated Moody, Chicago taxpayers would have new parklands along the lakefront worth fifty million dollars, at no cost whatsoever.[46]

As both Samuel Haber and Samuel Hays demonstrate in their investigations[47] of the scientific management and conservation movements, progressives like Moody, Burnham, and their associates became enthralled with the principles of rationalization, standardization, and centralization in civic life because they had already attempted to implement such principles in business life. Although they looked to Europe for their aesthetic inspiration – particularly to that of Baron Georges Eugene Haussmann and the French Ecole des Beaux Arts[48] – their planning ideas reflected primarily the order and systematization they prized in their own businesses. For example, Frederic Delano, a Commercial Club Plan Committee member who had made his way up to the presidency of the Wabash Railroad at age twenty-two, maintained that, in his mind, "a comprehensive city plan represented a natural progression from his own idea of centralization of the Chicago passenger railroads."[49]

During a decade that produced studies on waste and scientific management in education, churches, and private homes,[50] it is hardly surprising that Moody should refer to the Chicago *Plan* as an instrument of "the City Practical" as opposed to the City Beautiful with which it was often confused.[51] A rational, unified, efficient, scientific, practical plan, he insisted, was the sole way to order the chaos attendant to rapid urban growth.

To the elements of education and efficiency that have been suggested thus far as crucial to Moody's strategy for civic reform must be added a third feature: environmentalism. Like many of his generation, Walter Moody believed in a modified ecological determinism. He was taken with the emergence of American social science in the latter half of the nineteenth century and confident of its beneficial application to city planning. Thus, he maintained that the "physical conditions which make for good health, good order and good citizenship must be made clear to our children." Moody stated the conviction that "splendid material upbuilding" of the metropolis would yield "a social, intellectual and moral upbuilding of its people" as a simple environmental equation: "city building means man building."[52] Following an evolutionary analog used earlier by Chicago novelist Henry Blake Fuller to explain the progressive development of "a higher type of Chicagoan" in cultural achievements, Moody predicted a parallel social evolution to follow upon the advent of social scientific urban planning in the "prairie city."[53]

Such city planning could not come too soon in Moody's judgment. "The physical condition of people in the cities as compared with the people of the open country is deteriorating," he warned his young readers, because "city life is an intense life, many times more wearing upon the nerves than country life." Quoting various social scientists, he also proposed that the unplanned and unkempt city "saps the energy of men and makes them less efficient in the work of life." Moreover, it was "this strain of city life which increases insanity and brings weaknesses of many kinds to shorten life and deprive people of their vigor."[54] Heady stuff for mere fourteen-year-olds but only one example of the *Manual*'s argument that the physical environment conditions public behavior.

Several of the *Manual*'s proposals to correct physical deterioration of urban dwellers bear a striking resemblance to the theories of American psychiatrist George M. Beard, discoverer of neurasthenia or "nervous weakness." Beard believed that environmental tensions, particularly when exacerbated by the stress of urbanization, modernization, and technological innovation, were the chief causal factors in the etiology of mental illness. In his most famous book, *American Nervousness*, Beard claimed that the incidence of mental disorders was unusually high (and growing even more so) in late nineteenth-century urban America. There had been no nervous exhaustion or physical deterioration, for example, in those cities of ancient Greece or Rome that Burnham and Moody held up as exemplary of ordered, planned, urban design. These ancient civilizations, Beard contended, lacked five characteristics peculiar to nineteenth-century civilization: steam power, the telegraph, the periodical press, the sciences, and the mental activity of women.[55] Beard felt America was a quarter century more advanced than any European country in each of these aspects of modernity.

Since at least the time of Benjamin Rush, American physicians had almost as a matter of course acknowledged that the unique pace of American life (e.g. its competitiveness, its religious pluralism, its lack of stability in social status) was somehow related to America's higher rate of mental illness. After the Civil War, two other ideas – the concept of evolution and the increase in the population and number of American cities – had been added to this traditional belief in the relationship between American civilization and psychological and physical health. Beard accepted and amalgamated both evolution and urbanization into his interpretation of American nervousness. He maintained that the conquest of neurasthenia need involve no change in man himself, just in his environment. The technology which had produced the telegraph, the railroad, and the factory had already begun to provide other technological innovations which helped to reduce the tensions of American experience. Beard cites as specific examples the elevator, the sewing machine, and the Pullman palace car.[56]

Although there is no evidence that he ever met or read Beard, Moody shared Beard's belief in evolution and in urban neurasthenia. Like Beard, he looked to the continued advance of material and technological progress to offset evils of the American urban environment. City planning, in Moody's view, naturally provided one panacea whereby urbanites could overcome, or at least mitigate, ecological determinism. In the school text that he also called "a physical geography," Moody (with an analogy he borrowed from Frederick Law Olmsted) made a special case for how urban parks and forest preserves could be "compared with the lungs of a person, as the means by which the city and its people get the stimulus of fresh air so necessary to normal well-being."[57] Much like Olmsted who argued for orderly park design as a method of social control and urban reform, Moody envisioned the parks of the 1909 *Plan* as crucial components in alleviating stress, overcrowding, and congestion. In the Chicago city parks, the masses supposedly would find an environment conducive both to activity and to contemplation.[58]

The *Manual*'s deficiencies

Critics of Burnham's *Plan* and Moody's *Manual* complained, however, that the *Plan* did not do enough to alleviate the social evils that afflicted numerous Chicagoans: lack of housing, schools, or adequate sanitation. Charges of elitism and lack of concern for public improvements at the neighborhood level were directed at a plan that, admittedly, dealt primarily with elaborate transportation systems, monumental aesthetic centerpieces, and symmetrical street façades. In several respects the Chicago that Burnham had planned and that Moody promoted was a metropolis for businessmen where, ironically, with the exception of the central business district, there were no carefully designated areas for commercial expansion throughout the rest of the city. Nor were there any model tenements for workers, much less model neighborhoods.

Not that Moody was oblivious to Chicago's housing or social problems. Slums were mentioned in both the *Manual* and the *Plan* but only briefly. Once in the *Plan*, for example, it was suggested that "it is no attack on private property to argue that society has the inherent right to protect itself [against] gross evils and known perils" by imposing restrictions on overcrowding, enforcing sanitary regulations, and limiting lot coverage.[59] As Mel Scott has discovered, there is even assertion in the *Plan* that if private enterprise cannot rehouse persons forced out of congested quarters, the city itself may have to do so "in common justice to men and women so degraded by long lives in the slums that they have lost all power of caring for themselves."[60] But this daring idea only appears as an afterthought in the Burnham/Moody philosophy of the city, tucked away surreptitiously, at best a very minor chord in a grand symphony of magnificent boulevards, imposing structures, and splendid parks. The housing concerns of other progressives in other cities (e.g. Lawrence Veiller and Jacob Riis in New York) did not exist in most of their counterparts of the Burnham/Moody persuasion in Chicago.[61]

Moody, as his writings reveal, had many of the myopias of the contemporary neo-democratic mind. He had little notion of the racial changes that were going to sweep over neighborhoods in a city such as

Chicago. He was far too sanguine about the coexistence of the city and the automobile. Furthermore, he tended to exaggerate the beliefs that the conservation of wasted energy and resources alone would solve urban problems, or that ordered civic spaces, efficient circulatory systems, and grandiose natural landscapes would yield contented, prosperous, virtuous citizens. Had social problems been stressed more directly in Moody's translation of Burnham's *Plan*, however, as they were in the St Louis *City Plan* of 1907,[62] perhaps nothing of the Chicago 1909 *Plan* would have been implemented. So argues historian Robert Akeley, who is persuaded that if Moody had not played down the social reform dimension of what would have eventually had to accompany any genuine municipal rejuvenation, the success of the physical proposals and the image of the *Plan* as a comprehensive program of civic renaissance would have been seriously jeopardized. Akeley also feels that "Chicago planning salesmanship was based upon enthusiasm and commitment, rather than on calculated exploitation."[63]

The *Manual*'s legacy

Moody assuredly was an enthusiast. "No one has ever equaled him in promoting city planning, convincing an entire metropolis of its value, and winning support of a particular plan from voters and public officials alike."[64] An ingenious and skillful propagandist, he promulgated the necessity of scientific city planning in ways other than through *Wacker's Manual*. Thousands of pamphlets, mailings, and circulars with titles like "Chicago can get fifty million dollars for nothing!" "Reclaim South Water Street for all the people," "Pull Chicago out of the hole – united action will do it!" and "Economic readjustment from a war to a peace basis" were his work.

As adroit with other communications media as he was with publications, he developed an extensive stereopticon slide library illustrating all aspects of the Burnham Plan and many examples of city planning throughout the world. Over the ten years that he gave slide-lectures on planning all over Chicago and around the country, he estimated he had talked to approximately 175,000 people. Under his direction, the Chicago Plan Commission even made its own movie, *A Tale of One City*, a two-reeler contrasting the existing conditions of Chicago with the 1909 *Plan* proposals. The first documentary film on city planning ever produced, it opened in Chicago (a city that in 1915 still hoped to become the movie capital of the country) to a sell-out crowd at the Majestic Theater. Shown in fifty theaters in the Chicago metropolitan area and then in other US cities, over 150,000 people saw the film during its premier year of 1915.[65]

Finally, in 1919 Moody wrote a 440-page treatise titled *What of the City?*

Plate 4.3 In his last planning treatise, *What of the City?*, Moody included a photograph of Charles H. Wacker for whom the *Manual* had been named.

where much of the history of the Chicago Plan Commission as well as his own history in the planning movement was recounted. Probably his most sophisticated analysis of Chicago city planning within the context of the national urban planning movement, the book's highly autobiographical content also reveals much about Moody the plan promoter; along with the *Manual* it summarizes his main political and planning ideas. Whereas the *Manual* had proselytized on the local level, *What of the City?* sought converts throughout the nation. Moody designed the former publication to reach the generation of the future, still occupying Chicago's class-rooms; he prepared the latter book for the continuing adult education of his own generation throughout the country's cities.

To talk of converts and proselytizing recalls an initial characterization of Walter Moody made earlier in this chapter. W. D. Moody, it will be remembered, was occasionally confused with fellow Chicagoan D. L. Moody. A later historian of American city planning, while not mistaking the two men, aptly calls Moody an "evangelist of planning" whose "bible" was the 1909 *Plan*, and who sought to spread that gospel of municipal reform ''with the aggressiveness of a salesman and the fervor of a religious zealot.''[66]

Within this context Moody might also be compared to William Thomas Stead, editor of the Anglo-American *Review of Reviews*, who a decade earlier had written another municipal reform tract, *If Christ Came to Chicago!* Stead's best-selling exposé of municipal corruption and his program for urban reform included in a final chapter a comprehensive city plan to implement comprehensive civic reform.[67] A detailed comparison of Moody's primer and Stead's intriguing city plan for making Chicago ''the ideal city of the world,'' while pertinent to this discussion, will not be done here; mention is made merely to suggest that Moody's techniques were by no means novel to the Chicago reform effort that sought to improve the city by altering the cityscape.

Moreover, W. T. Stead, a Congregational minister who preached civic and social reform at rallies in the city's Central Music Hall in the wake of the World's Columbian Exposition,[68] could only have smiled with approval at one of Moody's last official acts to promote the Burnham *Plan*. In early 1919, Moody wrote *Seed Thoughts for Sermons*, a seven-page appeal to the city's clergymen to recognize the humanitarian and social value of the *Plan of Chicago* that had been written a decade earlier. Numerous clergy followed Moody's injunction to preach the value of comprehensive planning to their congregations on January 19, 1919, the date chosen as ''*Plan of Chicago* Sunday'' throughout the city. Later that day was alluded to as ''Nehemiah Sunday'' because so many ministers had used Nehemiah's description of the rebuilding of Jerusalem and the temple as their text; many congregations also displayed the Chicago flag on their churches while others sang hymns such as ''Work, for the night is coming!''[69] W. T. Stead would have loved it.

The British reformer would also have endorsed Moody's career as a propagandist, particularly Moody's crucial role in effecting the transition whereby a private plan drawn up by a private club became a public ordinance to be implemented by a public commission which, in turn, hired as its managing director a former publicist for private enterprise who became a public civil servant who wrote a public school textbook. Stead, had he lived to see a copy,[70] would have also approved of Moody's *Manual*, a book that can serve the historian as a tracer element in order to reveal some of the less familiar intellectual history of the vast effort surrounding the 1909 *Plan*.

Thus the legacy of the Burnham *Plan* and Moody's promotion of it is assuredly multiple. Simply in terms of actual alteration of Chicago's cityscape, it has been estimated that over three million dollars in public construction can be directly attributed to the inspiration of the *Plan* and its purpose.[71] Every major subsequent planning enterprise in the city of

Chicago has had to react to its premises and its presence. For example, in the struggle to keep the city's lakefront, "forever, open, clear and free," historian Lois Wille credits Burnham, Wacker, and especially Moody with launching "the most energetic public information effort in the city's history."[72]

While Moody's enthusiastic promotion of the changing, building, regrouping, and restructuring of the face of America's urban landscape on the Chicago model did assume the dimensions of a real reform movement (or at least a significant planning and architectural arm of that movement), his progressivism in planning was not without its inadequacies. For instance, his own myopias (e.g. his overreliance on the premise that structured, orderly, public buildings, circulatory systems, and civic landscapes would result in an enlightened citizenry) and his unquestioned support of Burnham's retreat to the safety of the neo-classical womb as the recommended style for the new urban America reminds us of the strong conservative strain in his progressivism and the high degree of caution in that reform movement generally. This inconsistency, ambiguity, and paradox were also bequeathed to posterity via the 1909 *Plan* and the 1911 *Manual*.

On balance, however, Moody's numerous publications contributed positively to the early literature of the city planning profession. His prolific corpus, but especially the *Manual* and his most mature work (*What of the City?*), sought consciously to provide the professional city planner with personal inspiration for the work in the decades ahead.[73] The *Manual* also prompted an increased demand for the services of city planners in cities all over the nation thereby giving the emerging profession even greater visibility through the actual practice of its craft.[74]

Finally, because of Moody's salesmanship of Burnham's idea, the Burnham *Plan* became the paradigm for the American city planning movement for the next generation, the model of the City Practical that future planners and politicians in Chicago[75] and elsewhere built on, adapted, or rebelled against in their collective task of what Moody called the science of city planning and citizen building.[76]

Notes

1 Daniel H. Burnham and Edward H. Bennett (1909) *Plan of Chicago Prepared Under the Direction of the Commercial Club During the Years 1906, 1907, 1908*, edited by Charles Moore, Chicago, The Commercial Club; hereafter cited as *Plan of Chicago*. A modern edition (1970), with an introduction by W. R. Hasbrouck, has been issued in the DaCapo Press Series in Architecture and Decorative Arts, number 29, New York, DaCapo Press.

2 Walter D. Moody (1911) *Wacker's Manual of the Plan of Chicago: Municipal Economy*, Chicago, Chicago Plan Commission, p. 3; hereafter cited as *Wacker's*

Manual. As an example of a full-blown instance of Moody's proposed economic and cultural hegemony for Chicago, see his essay (1912) "Chicago destined to be the center of the modern world," *Municipal Engineering*, 43(3), 49–61, and also (1912) in *The Bank Man*, 7, 307–24.

3 See James Findlay (1969) *Dwight Moody*, Chicago, University of Chicago Press.

4 Walter D. Moody (1919) *What of the City? America's Greatest Issue – City Planning, What It Is and How To Go About It To Achieve Success*, Chicago, A. C. McClurg & Co., p. 3; hereafter cited as Moody, *What of the City?*

5 Henry May (1949) *The Protestant Churches and Industrial America*, New York, Harper & Row, pp. 182–234.

6 (Chicago, A. C. McClurg & Co., 1907). This handbook of "modern salesman-ship" went through seventeen editions.

7 Daniel Boorstin (1973) *The Americans: The Democratic Experience*, New York, Random House, pp. 5–88. Chicago Plan *Proceedings*, p. 86. When Moody accepted the position of managing director with the CPC, R. W. Butler, a member of the CPC, wrote Daniel Burnham that "from this time forward the work will be pushed by the 'Chief of all Pushers' – Mr Moody." Butler to D. H. Burnham, January 20, 1911, Burnham Papers, The Art Institute of Chicago.

8 The origins, underwriting, and unveiling of the *Plan* have been copiously documented; see Ira Bach (1973) "A reconsideration of the 1909 'Plan of Chicago,'" *Chicago History*, 2, 132–41; Francoise Choay (1969) *The Modern City, Planning in the 19th Century*, London, Studio Vista; Patrick Geddes (1915) *Cities in Evolution*, London, Williams & Norgate; Werner Hegemann and Elbert Peets (1922) *The American Vitruvius: An Architect's Handbook of Civic Art*, New York, The Architectural Book Publishing Co.; Vilas Johnson (1977) *A History of the Commercial Club of Chicago including the First History of the Club by John J. Glessner*, Chicago, Commercial Club of Chicago; Lewis Mumford (1961) *The City in History, its Transformations; and its Prospects*, New York, Harcourt, Brace & World; John Reps (1965) *The Making of Urban America*, Princeton, Princeton University Press; and Lois Willie (1972) *Forever Open, Clear and Free*, Chicago, Henry Regney.

9 Helen Whitehead (1960) *The Chicago Plan Commission, A Historical Sketch, 1909–1960*, Chicago, Chicago Plan Commission, pp. 3–9.

10 Charles W. Eliot (January 1910) "A study of the New Plan of Chicago," *Century Magazine*, 79, 418; also see Perry Duis (1976) *Chicago: Creating New Traditions*, Chicago, Chicago Historical Society, p. 49.

11 On the complicated machination whereby "an alliance of businessmen, plan-ners and politicians, by persuasion, pressure and politics" set the 1909 *Plan* in motion, consult Michael P. McCarthy (1979) "Chicago business and the Burnham Plan," *Journal of the Illinois State Historical Society*, 63(3), 228–56.

12 Moody, *What of the City?*, pp. 329–32; *Chicago Tribune*, July 7, 1909, p. 3; *Chicago Record-Herald*, November 2, 1909, p. 2.

13 Moody, *What of the City?*, pp. 21–2.

14 David Noble (1958) *The Paradox of Progressive Thought*, Minneapolis, Univer-sity of Minnesota; Richard Hofstadter (ed.) (1963) *The Progressive Movement 1900–1915*, Englewood Cliffs, New Jersey, Prentice-Hall; Charles Forcey (1961) *The Crossroads of Liberalism: Croly, Weyl, Lippmann and The Progressive Era, 1900–1925*, New York, Oxford University Press, 1961.

15 Chapter II, "The new profession – city planning," *What of the City?*, pp. 18–27.

16 Robinson (1869–1917) and John Nolen (1869–1935) also contributed to the

literature of American city planning and the city planning profession. Robinson, who wrote three important books – *The Improvement of Towns and Cities*, New York and London, G. P. Putnam's Sons, 1901; *Modern Civic Art*, New York and London, G. P. Putnam's Sons, 1903; and *City Planning*, New York and London, G. P. Putnam's Sons, 1916 – was the first appointee to the first university chair of civic design (Illinois) in the United States. Nolen, a founder and later president of the American Institute of Planners, wrote *Replanning Small Cities*, New York, American City Bureau, 1912; *City Planning*, New York and London, D. Appleton & Co., 1916; and *New Ideals in the Planning of Cities, Towns and Villages*, New York, American City Bureau, 1919. On the quest for professionalism, see Burton J. Bledstein (1976) *The Culture of Professionalism: The Middle Class and the Development of Higher Education in America*, New York, W. W. Norton, pp. 80–128 and 287–332.

17 The most comprehensive assessment of the business community's involvement in the Chicago *Plan* is chronicled in Neil Harris (1979) *The Planning of The Plan*, Chicago, The Commercial Club of Chicago, and Michael McCarthy's previously cited "Chicago businessmen and the Burnham Plan," pp. 228–56.

18 W. D. Moody (1911) *Chicago's Greatest Issue: An Official Plan*, Chicago, Chicago Plan Commission; Executive Committee, CPC, *Proceedings* (June 19, 1911), p. 237. Robert Akeley (1973) "Implementing the 1909 Plan of Chicago: an historical account of planning salesmanship," University of Texas unpublished master's thesis, calculates (pp. 185–7) that there were eighty-six separate bond issues, totalling $233,985,000 falling within the recommendations of the plan.

19 *Chicago Daily News*, October 26, 1910, p. 1; on Burnham's disappointment with the inadequate promotion of the San Francisco Plan, see D. H. Burnham to Willis Polk, April 22, 1909, Burnham Papers, Art Institute of Chicago.

20 W. D. Moody (1912) *The Work of the Chicago Plan Commission During 1911*, Chicago, Address to the Commercial Club of Chicago, p. 10; *What of the City?* p. 50; "City planning and the public schools," *American City*, 6 (May 1912), 720.

21 On the visual pedagogy of the Plan's illustrations, see Robert Bruegmann (1979) "Burnham, Guerin, and the city as image," in *The Plan of Chicago, 1909–1979*, edited by John Zukowsky, Chicago, The Art Institute of Chicago, pp. 16–28.

22 Historians of American city planning have traditionally interpreted the 1909 Burnham *Plan* to have had six basic objectives: (1) improvement of the Chicago lakefront from Winnetka on the north to the Indiana state line on the south, (2) creation of a beltway/highway system on the rim of the city, (3) relocation of railway terminals and development of a complete freight and passenger traction system, (4) acquisition of an outer park system and of parkway transport circuits, (5) systematic arrangement of streets within the city to facilitate movement to and from the central business district, and (6) promotion of centers of intellectual life and civic administration so related as to provide coherence and unity for the metropolis. Carl Condit (1973) "The Chicago Plan," in his *Chicago, 1910–29; Building, Planning, and Urban Technology*, Chicago, University of Chicago Press, pp. 59–88.

23 In his highly autobiographical *What of the City?* (pp. 107–8), Moody listed his major educational achievements in advancing the plan as his work with the daily and the periodical press, his book on *Chicago's Greatest Issue*, the various lecture series he coordinated, and, of course, the *Wacker's Manual*.

24 *Wacker's Manual*, pp. 3–4. One product of Moody's teaching efforts was his

ten-volume research series (1910–11) on *Business Administration: Theory, Practice and Application*, Chicago, LaSalle Extension University.

25 On Parker's progressive pedagogy see Jack K. Campbell's well-researched life (1967) *Colonel Francis W. Parker, The Children's Crusader*, New York, Teachers College Press, and Merle Curti's assessment (1965, pp. 374–95) in his *The Social Ideas of American Educators*, Paterson, New Jersey, Littlefield Adams; for Dewey's impact in Chicago, consultant Katherine Mayhew (1966) *The Dewey School: The Laboratory School of the University of Chicago, 1896–1903*, New York, Oxford University Press.

26 Moody's inclusion of study questions (as many as sixty-seven in chapter 4), at the conclusion of each of the seventeen chapters, gave his text a highly catechetical tone reminiscent of the predetermined memorization, disciplined recitation, and rote learning that the progressive educators wished to eradicate.

27 John Dewey, *Education and Democracy*, pp. 100–2; *Wacker's Manual*, p. 10. Another example of the progressives' interest in education and city planning reform can be seen in Randolph Bourne's discussion (1916) of the curriculum unit, "The city: a healthful place to live" in *The Gary Schools*, Boston, Houghton Mifflin, pp. 117–19.

28 *Wacker's Manual*, pp. 4, 8, 97.

29 D. H. Burnham (1902) "White city and capital city," *Century Magazine*, 63, 619–620; also see Burnham's speech (1910) "A city of the future under a democratic government," *Transactions of the Town-Planning Conference, Royal Institute of British Architects*, pp. 368–78.

30 Thomas S. Hines (1973) "The paradox of progressive architecture," *American Quarterly*, 25, 427–48. For Hine's extended treatment of this facet of Burnham see his biography (1974) *Burnham of Chicago: Architect and Planner*, New York, Oxford University Press, chapters 8 and 14.

31 Richard Hofstadter (1955) *The Age of Reform, From Bryan to F.D.R.*, New York, Vintage, pp. 5–6.

32 William J. Adelman (1980) "Robber barons and social reformers," *Inland Architect*, 24(3), 12–15.

33 *Wacker's Manual*, pp. 140–5; *What of the City?* pp. 412–30; also see McCarthy, "Chicago businessmen and the Burnham Plan," p. 233.

34 Commercial Club of Chicago (1910) *The Presentation of The Plan of Chicago*, Chicago, Chicago Plan Commission, p. 29.

35 Stow Persons (1958) *American Minds, A History of Ideas*, New York, H. Holt, pp. 349–52.

36 Burnham's famous credo – "Make no little plans, they have no magic to stir men's blood and probably themselves will not be realized. Make big plans; aim high in hope and work, remembering that a noble, logical diagram once recorded will never die" – is but another example of what David Burg (1978) calls "The aesthetics of bigness in late nineteenth century American architecture" in *Popular Architecture*, edited by Marshall Fishwick and J. Meredith Neil, Bowling Green, Ohio, Bowling Green University Popular Press, pp. 108–14.

37 Consult Hofstadter, *The Age of Reform*, on the role of print in progressivism, pp. 186–97.

38 *What of the City?* pp. xi, 4; on Parsons, see Persons, *American Minds*, pp. 366–8. Other theorists of public opinion discussed in this context include A. Lawrence Lowell (1913) *Public Opinion and Popular Government*, New York, Longmans, Green & Co., Walter Lippmann (1922) *Public Opinion*, London, Allen & Unwin,

and Edward L. Bernays (1923) *Crystallizing Public Opinion*, New York, Boni & Liveright.

39 *Wacker's Manual*, p. 45. Moody was particularly taken with Howe's critical study on Düsseldorf, Germany, because in addition to insisting on constant publicity of plan purposes and educational programs, the Düsseldorf plan (like the Burnham Plan) planned for city life a half century in the future and, perhaps best of all, it was a plan originally sponsored by the city's business-men.

40 *Wacker's Manual*, p. 4.

41 Robert H. Wiebe (1967) *The Search For Order, 1877–1920*, New York, Hill and Wang; an earlier study that buttresses the Wiebe thesis is Samuel P. Hayes (1957) *The Response To Industrialism*, Chicago, University of Chicago Press.

42 *Wacker's Manual*, pp. 4, 17, 104, 8.

43 Burnham's proposed municipal building (see *Plan*, pages 115–18) was modeled, in part, after Richard Morris Hunt's administration building at the 1893 World's Fair and the building that prompted Henry Adams to muse:

> One sat down to ponder on the steps beneath Richard Hunt's dome almost as deeply as on the steps of Ara Coeli, and much to the same purpose. Here was a breach of continuity – a rupture in historical sequence! Was it real, or only apparent? One's personal universe hung on the answer, for, if the rupture was real and the new American world would take this sharp and conscious twist towards ideals, one's personal friends would come in, at last, as the winners in the great American chariot race for fame (*The Education of Henry Adams*, New York, Modern Library, 1931, pp. 340–1).

44 *Wacker's Manual*, pp. 135–7.

45 ibid., pp. 13, 66–70; *What of the City?*, pp. 38–60. Moody was also something of a historic preservationist in that he opposed the destruction of old structures having aesthetic, historic, and functional utility. He always argued for "the value of permanency in city building," especially since there were "many sites within Chicago that, within the space of seventy years, have been occupied by three, four, or five different buildings." *Wacker's Manual*, p. 69.

46 *Fifty Million Dollars For Nothing!*, Chicago, Chicago Plan Commission, 1916.

47 Samuel Haber (1964) *Efficiency and Uplift: Scientific Management in the Progressive Era, 1980–1920*, Chicago, University of Chicago Press; Samuel P. Hayes (1959) *Conservation and The Gospel of Efficiency*, Cambridge, Mass., Harvard University Press.

48 On Haussmann see Howard Saalman (1971) *Haussmann: Paris Transformed*, New York, G. Braziller.

49 Michael P. McCarthy (1970) "Businessmen and professionals in municipal reform: the Chicago experience, 1887–1920", Northwestern University: unpublished Ph.D. dissertation, p. 106; McCarthy, "Businessmen and the Burnham Plan," *Journal of Illinois State Historical Society*, p. 231.

50 John Dewey, "Waste in education," in *The School and Society*, edited by Jo Ann Boydston (1976) in *John Dewey: The Middle Works*, volume I: 1889–1924, Carbondale, Illinois, Southern Illinois University Press, pp. 39–56; Shailer Mathews (1912) *Scientific Management in the Churches*, Chicago, University of Chicago Press; Charlotte Perkins Gilman (1913) "The waste of private housekeeping," *Annals of the American Academy of Political and Social Science*, 48, 91–5.

51 On the differences between these two modes of planning see John W. Reps (1965) *The Making of Urban America: A History of City Planning in the United States*,

98   *The American Planner*

Princeton, Princeton University Press, pp. 331–9, and William H. Wilson (1964) *The City Beautiful Movement in Kansas City*, Columbia, Missouri, University of Missouri Press, pp. 40–54; Moody's argument for the Burnham Plan as primarily one of the "City Practical" can be found in *What of the City?*, pp. 15, 93.

52 *Wacker's Manual*, pp. 4, 145, 80–1.

53 Henry Blake Fuller. "The upward movement in Chicago," *Atlantic Monthly*, 80; "Chicago's higher evolution," *The Dial* (October 1, 1892), pp. 205–6; *Wacker's Manual*, pp. 80–1.

54 *Wacker's Manual*, p. 133.

55 *American Nervousness*, New York, G. P. Putnam's Sons, 1881, p. 96; also see Beard (1884), *Sexual Neurasthenia (Nervous Exhaustion): Its Hygiene, Causes, Symptoms, and Treatment, With a Chapter on Diet For The Nervous*, edited by A. D. Rockwell, New York, E. B. Treat, p. 238n.

56 Charles E. Rosenberg (1976) *No Other Gods: On Science and American Social Thought*, Baltimore, The Johns Hopkins University Press, p. 107.

57 *Wacker's Manual*, p. 97.

58 Geoffrey Blodgett (1976) "Frederick, Law Olmsted: landscape architecture of conservative reform," *Journal on American History*, 62(4), 869–89; Michael McCarthy (1972) "Politics and the parks: Chicago businessmen and the recreation movement," *Journal of the Illinois State Historical Society*, 65(2), 158–72; Peter J. Schmitt (1969) *Back To Nature: The Arcadian Myth in Urban America*, New York, Oxford University Press.

59 *Plan of Chicago*, p. 105.

60 Scott, *American City Planning since 1890*, p. 108; *Plan of Chicago*, p. 109.

61 Roy Lubove (1962) *The Progressives and The Slums: Tenement House Reform in New York City, 1980–1917*, Pittsburgh, University of Pittsburgh Press, pp. 217–56.

62 Civic League of St Louis (1907) *A City Plan for St Louis*, St Louis, Civic League.

63 Akeley, "Implementing the 1909 Plan," pp. iii, 52.

64 Scott, *American City Planning*, p. 139.

65 *What of the City?*, p. 108.

66 Scott, *American City Planning*, p. 140.

67 William T. Stead (1894) *If Christ Came to Chicago!*, Chicago, Laird & Lee, pp. 421–2. Akeley, "Implementing the 1909 Plan" (p. 31), recognizes one similarity between the two reformers in noting that both saw the Chicago citizenry as "full of a boundless elan and full of faith in the destiny of their city."

68 On Stead in Chicago, see Joseph O. Baylen (December 1964) "A Victorian's 'crusade' in Chicago, 1893–1894," *Journal of American History*, 51(3), 418–34; also "Stead in the slums," *Chicago Sunday Tribune*, November 12, 1893, p. 1.

69 *Chicago Tribune*, January 19, 1919, p. 1.

70 Stead perished aboard the *Titanic* when it sank in 1912.

71 Robert L. Wrigley, Jr (1960) "The Plan of Chicago: its fiftieth anniversary," *Journal of the American Institute of Planners*, 26, 37.

72 Lois Wille (1972) *Forever Open, Clear and Free: The Struggle for Chicago's Lakefront*, Chicago, Henry Regnery Company, p. 88.

73 Moody, *What of the City?*, p. x.

74 Chappell, "Chicago issues: the enduring power of a plan," p. 14; Scott, *American City Planning*, p. 139.

75 In Chicago, some of the most important progeny that have followed in the wake of the 1909 Burnham Plan are: *Harbor Plan of Chicago* (1927): *The Outer*

Drive Along the Lake (1929); *The Axis of Chicago* (1929); *Building New Neighborhoods: Subdivision Design and Standards* (1943); *Master Plan of Residential Land Use of Chicago* (1943); *Planning the Region of Chicago* (1956); *Development Plan For The Central Area of Chicago* (1958); the *Comprehensive Plan* (1966); *Chicago 21* (1973); and *Riveredge Plan* (1974). A summary of several of the post-1909 plans are also found in a report written by J. T. Fink (1979) entitled *Grant Park Tomorrow*. (All works listed here published by the Chicago Plan Commission.)

76 *Wacker's Manual*, p. 8.

5 From the autobiography of Edward M. Bassett

Introduction by Donald A. Krueckeberg

Introduction

A momentous occasion was when two or three of the boys and George and I mounted the roof of a temporary shed almost overhanging the sidewalk in front of our house. With a thread and bent pin we hooked the hat of a policeman and to our surprise the hat came off and was left dangling in the air. The policeman spied us on the roof and although he did nothing to us we had a first rate scare.[1]

When in the fall of 1868 Grant ran for President the candidates, I remember distinctly, were Grant and Colfax, Seymour and Blair. Great excitement among the boys! I shouted Grant and Colfax but the Irish got me down and punched me till I shouted Seymour and Blair.[2]

That was the 6-year-old boy in Brooklyn, Eddie Bassett, son of a traveling peddler, later to become a US Congressman, distinguished New York lawyer, and the father of American zoning.

Edward M. Bassett's American roots reach back to William Bassett's arrival in Plymouth, Massachusetts, from England, in 1621.[3] Edward's father, whose family had lived on farms for two hundred years, was the seventh child of a seventh child, and so, as was common of the youngest in those days, left the farm for a trade, peddling silk, later gold pens. His mother taught school as a young woman. Edward was born on February 7, 1863 in Brooklyn, New York, where he began school, with his brother George.

I started public school, going to the Gates Avenue school near the corner of Broadway. School was always a great treat to me. Words to me were spelled as they sounded, and I quickly learned to read fairly large words when I was five, possibly on the verge of six. Returning from school one day George and I got over the fence to gather some ink berries. The woman owner spied us, gave us chase and ran after us all the way home. She complained to Mother, but Mother finding us, explained to her that we were going to squeeze the ink berries and use the ink at school. It was difficult for me to see why this mellowed up the lady but it did and she was loud in praise of George and me because we were so industrious. She had thought we were stealing corn.[4]

The walk to and from school was too far and on this account Mother probably made a change. We went for a time to a private school on Herkimer Street near New York Avenue. This little school of about twenty scholars was on the north side of Herkimer Street five or six houses east of New York Avenue. Here I began geography which I thought was the most interesting study that ever was. All the studies seemed so easy that they were mere play.[5]

In 1871 the family moved two hundred miles north to Watertown, New York, where his father had decided to sell dry goods and "Yankee notions" from a wagon to surrounding villages. Edward thrived there; in high school he excelled in Greek, Latin, mathematics, and debating. At one point he thought he might like to run a dry goods store when he finished school. He recalled that "Frank W. Woolworth began a 5 and 10 cent counter in Moore and Smith's dry-goods store in Watertown. He was eight or ten years older than I but I knew him well. This was the first 5 and 10 cents store in this country."

He finally decided to be a teacher of Greek and Latin. "Mother agreed with me on my going to college but Father was not enthusiastic. None of the family had ever gone to college and Father thought that life was too serious and the need of earning some money too great to warrant spending four years with a doubtful result." But with the help of his mother and a scholarship he went off to Hamilton College in Clinton, New York.

His first year went well. What he has written makes it clear that he was an outstanding student. The summer after his freshman year he took a job as a book agent, selling the *Royal Path of Life or Aims and Aids to Success and Happiness*, to farmers and mill workers in Columbia County, New York. His first night on the road he got so homesick that he could not eat, his nose bled, and he was "completely woebegone." Later in life he would declare that "education from travel is better than education from books." He recalls the difficult customers and his skills as a salesman.

The house of Stupplebeen was said to be especially down on book agents. I learned the ropes beforehand, went to the farmhouse at the right time and entered the front gate. The father was mowing in the front yard and informed me that it would do me no good to go to the house. I went to the front door and the mother opened it a crack and told me to go. I said I was tired and could I go around on the side porch and rest a few minutes. She allowed I could and I went there knowing that the married daughter had two rooms that opened on the porch. After I sat there five or ten minutes the married daughter made her appearance and we got acquainted. I said I would gladly pay if they would let me stay to dinner. She put me up a chair and I ate with all the family, farm hands and everybody. After dinner I began a speech on the wonders of my book. I got a subscription from the old man, one from the son-in-law and one from one of the farm hands.[6]

After a year and a half at Hamilton he transferred to Amherst, where, for the first time in his life, Bassett was not leading the class. He came up against young men well-trained in schools such as Boston Latin and Phillips-Andover Preparatory. He was good in Greek and Latin, but they were better, even in debate. Bassett had been encouraged in a flamboyant style of oratory at Hamilton, but here the professors wanted "the meat, not the trimmings." He improved and by graduation in 1884 had won several prizes.

Law school came next. He enrolled in Columbia Law School in New York City, teaching school during the day and attending law classes in the afternoon and evening program. After receiving his LL.B. in 1886 he joined his brother George in Buffalo. They built a business, constructing and operating waterworks for towns in western New York State, Bassett Bros., Engineers and Contractors. George did mainly the engineering side of the work, Edward the legal work, stocks and bonds, titles, and the details of management with boards of trustees. Over a period of six years their business ran its course and closed successfully, on the eve of the Baring panic, all debts paid and a modest profit.

Edward was eager to establish a law practice. He returned to Brooklyn and engaged in an independent practice in New York City and became somewhat active in local Democratic politics. In 1902 he was elected to the US House of Representatives (D-Brooklyn) and served one term. He did not seek reelection.

His law practice involved him in many real estate cases, generating a real awareness of the need for sound planning for the physical development of the city.[7] He was a strong advocate of the construction of more bridges and tunnels crossing the East River and an altered transit fare structure to promote a city with a more "round" shape for efficiency. He pursued these causes as a gubernatorial appointee of the first Public Service Commission, which included New York City and Long Island, from 1907 to 1911.

His experience with public utilities later led to his successful handling of a legal case that was the first of its kind in the country to limit successfully the power of a state legislature in obtaining reasonable rates for public service corporations.

Bassett was a charter member (1917) of the American City Planning Institute and president of the National Conference on City Planning in 1928–29. He was said to have conceived of the term "freeway" to describe the limited access parkway.[8] The tone throughout his *Autobiography* is usually modest and often understates his accomplishments. He almost glosses over his chairmanship of the Commission on Building Districts and Restrictions which in 1916 drew up New York City's zoning ordinance, the first comprehensive zoning ordinance in the United States. He received the Medal of Honor for City Planning in 1943 from the New York and Brooklyn chapters of the American Institute of Architects, the metropolitan section of American Society of Civil Engineers, and the New York chapter of the American Society of Landscape Architects.

If one reads carefully the last few pages from these autobiographical chapters, on the "Master Plan" and "Congestion," only the slightest hint can be seen of his defense against his critics. He was a major advisor to Thomas Adams, director of the Regional Plan of New York and Environs. The plan was criticized severely by Lewis Mumford in a bitter public exchange with Adams. Bassett's conservative bent led away from policies of direct public intervention in the market, certainly not going beyond public purchase of land. He is blamed, therefore, for contributing to the plan's perceived lack of treatment of either public housing or a policy for deconcentration of the metropolis, a policy much sought after by Mumford and the Regional Planning Association of America.

Bassett's conservatism was, of course, deep rooted. He speaks fondly of his grandparents, for example:

They were not rich but they never thought of such a thing as taking money from anybody outside the family. They were just as proud of their independence as Rockefeller is today. When Mother was nine or ten there was an epidemic of smallpox in the cluster of houses near the scythe factory. Some children had it in the same house. Grandmother fed her large family on hasty pudding for several weeks and none of them caught smallpox.

I sometimes think of these conditions of American life when there was almost no wealth but at the same time there was no poverty and almost no dependence.[9]

His strategy in early zoning was to write ordinances so carefully limited as to avoid any possibility of a constitutional challenge in court. And he was successful. His second book, *The Master Plan*, took a similarly cautious tack, restricting the scope of the master plan to seven specific physical elements.[10]

The selections that follow pick up his professional career in 1905 after his Congressional term. Much of his *Autobiography* also logs his worldwide travels, usually in the company of Mrs Bassett, in the course of which he acquired quite a knowledge, and collection, of Oriental and Navajo rugs and Japanese pottery. Bassett was a dedicated layman and charter member of the Flatbush Congregational Church in Brooklyn and was chairman of its Board of Trustees for over twenty years. The father of five children, he died in Brooklyn, October 27, 1948. Today another Edward M. Bassett, his grandson, practices law in the firm of Bassett and Bassett, since 1922 at 233 Broadway, Woolworth Building, New York.

From the autobiography of Edward M. Bassett

Chapter XII: Streets and parks

After my term in Congress came to an end I gave special attention to increasing our law practice. Almost every day I was in court on trials or motions. Political conferences took a good deal of my time and I fear kept me from home evenings a great deal. I served on a large number of street and park opening commissions. The city charter was badly in need of revision on these subjects. Mayor McClellan appointed a commission of three lawyers headed by Michael Furst. Charles S. Taber and I were the other members. For several months off and on we worked on improvements to the charter provisions regarding street and park openings. These amendments were later adopted and they are still in force. Among them was a provision that eminent domain could be used for aesthetic purposes. This was a novelty in the city charter and even today is not included in many city charters. It has always seemed to me that aesthetic matters can properly be the basis for eminent domain although there is much doubt whether they ought to be the basis for police power regulations.

There was no provision in our charter or any other city charter for excess condemnation. Experience had shown that the necessity of limiting condemnation to exact street lines as mapped was often extremely expensive and in many cases produced gores and slices of land owned by private persons after the condemnation was over. Lawson Purdy, Luke D. Stapleton and I were a self-appointed committee to ascertain what could be done regarding a constitutional amendment for excess condemnation in this state. Our form was adopted in part but not so completely as we wished. A legislative enactment which we drew gave the power of excess condemnation to the City of New York. I spoke in several meetings in this city and Buffalo on excess condemnation. I also put out a pamphlet over my name. During these years I wrote a good many pamphlets on subjects that interested me. Usually I paid the whole expense of printing and distribution but sometimes the expense was paid by organizations. Copies of these pamphlets are in my attic and copies of the more recent ones are in our office. They relate to streets, parks, plats, congestion, police power regulation, rapid transit and zoning.

Chapter XIII: Public Service Commission

In 1905 the subject of traffic congestion became important. There was only one crossing of the East River – the Brooklyn Bridge. This bridge was terrifically crowded at the terminals even to the point of danger. I helped to start a movement to increase the bridges and tunnels over and under the East River, making speeches where anyone would listen to me, the gist of which was that a long city like Manhattan was the smallest area with the longest distances from the center, whereas a round city was the largest area with the shortest distances to the center. I pointed out that London, Paris, and Berlin were round cities. My thesis was that if the west end of Long Island could be brought into a five-cent fare relationship

Plate 5.1 Edward M. Bassett, 1910.
Source: Edward M. Bassett and The Harbor Press.

to Manhattan the city would assume a rounded form. It could then grow north, east, and south without great congestion.

Brooklyn felt the injury of the lack of gangplanks over the East River and it was only natural that the main turmoil should center in that borough.

The so-called Citizens' Central Committee was formed, being initiated by twenty or thirty Brooklyn citizens who perceived the importance of a solution of these problems. These men were Messrs Blum, Gunnison, Hammitt, Pounds and others including many industrialists. I went in with them and was asked to be president of the committee. Walter B. Brown was the moving spirit and for a salary gave practically all his time for a year to this organization. It reached a membership of fully 4000 men. I appointed committees covering the main fields of activity, perhaps twelve in all, and saw to it that these subcommittees had meetings and made reports.

Our committee became rather famous as the nominations for governorship approached and a number of candidates sought the endorsement of our active and growing body. We threw our favor toward Charles E. Hughes who was nominated and elected. After he was governor his first public acts were to bring about, so far as he could, a loosening of the jams between Manhattan and Brooklyn, cooperating with our large committee in many things.

This situation was the beginning of the Public Service Commission. Governor Hughes pointed out that there was no public regulation whatever of public utilities and that reasonable regulation of the transit companies would help ameliorate the congestion. He thought that the Public Service Law should embody the then existing Rapid Transit Act. I assisted in the drafting of the first Public Service Commission Law. It was the earliest law of its sort in this country.

The new Public Service Commission began its duties July 1, 1907. It superseded the Rapid Transit Commission of New York City and the Railroad Commission and the Gas Commission of the state. Its field was Greater New York and Long Island. There was another commission of five who administered the same law governing the rest of the state. This was commonly called the Upstate Commission. Governor Hughes asked me to be a member of the Downstate Commission. The salary was $15,000 a year and there is no doubt that it was the greatest honor that had come my way up to that time. I was appointed for three years but served almost four.

My duties on this commission took practically all my time although with the consent of Governor Hughes I did not withdraw from the law office. My personal work had to be done in any case and it would have taken a fraction of each day if the office had not done it. Then, too, the continuity of my law practice was preserved.

I worked on a multitude of subjects in the commission. Practically every evening was given to these duties. During the last two years of my service I was in Manhattan many evenings attending meetings of our joint committee of the Board of Estimate and the Public Service Commission working out the so-called dual subway contracts. Many of these nights I slept in Manhattan.

I will speak of only two or three topics in connection with this work.

I early became convinced that stub-end terminals of rapid transit lines, both elevated and subway, were the chief cause of transit congestion. If we could gradually adopt the pendulum method of train movement it would be a great benefit. I first became familiar with this method in Philadelphia and later in Berlin. In the latter city through letters of introduction to Mr Kemmann, chief engineer, I learned broader ideas of rapid transit distribution than we practiced in New York City. I was the first in official circles in New York to propose and work upon the pendulum movement of trains and the abolition of stub-end terminals. The pendulum movement was nothing more than a train starting in the suburbs going through the business part of the city and out again into another suburb. This would distribute the peak load at many stations and would tend to create two-way traffic instead of one way. Now the pendulum movement is so well established in this city that most people have forgotten the crowded stub-end terminals that existed at South Ferry, Brooklyn Bridge Terminal, Atlantic and Flatbush Avenues and other places.

I specialized on changes in the Rapid Transit Act in order to bring about a longer allowable period than twenty-five years for a contract by an operating company. Twenty-five years were too short for amortization. The existing law prevented any operating company from bidding on the operation of a city-owned subway. This twenty-five year period had been brought about by an uproar after the first subway was built by the city and the operation contracted to the Interborough Company. Firebrands said that the streets were paved with gold and that the gold was all given to the Interborough Company.

This talk was reflected in the legislature at Albany so that any reasonable period of contractual operation was prevented. No subways were built from the completion of the first subway up to the appointment of our Public Service Commission. The amendments to the Rapid Transit Act which I helped prepare were approved by my fellow commissioners and by Governor Hughes. Later they were embodied in the law. They brought about a more attractive prospect to the subway operator and the result was that the so-called Dual Subway Plan was adopted. This was a plan costing the city $300,000,000, part subways and part additions to elevated structures, one system operated by the Interborough which owned the Manhattan and Bronx elevated railroads and was already the contractual operator of the first subway, and the other system by the BMT which owned the Brooklyn elevated lines and desired an extension into Manhattan. Our joint committee brought about an enormous extension of rapid transit in all the boroughs except Richmond.

The shortcomings of transportation before the Dual Subways were becoming intolerable and if the problem had not been solved the natural growth of the city would have been restricted. Before I left the Public Service Commission the protocol was signed with the Interborough and the BMT and I joined in the signing. The contracts took about a year and a half to frame in detail. So I was not in office when the consummation of my rapid transit work was reached.

The importance of this work is shown from the fact that in 1907 the only way to go from Manhattan to Brooklyn was on the Brooklyn Bridge or the various ferries. Six years later three additional bridges were in use with rapid transit cars running over them. Two two-way tunnels were in use and four were contracted. The handicap of Brooklyn was the 10c fare to go to central Manhattan – 5c to go to Manhattan and 5c more to go uptown. This new work brought the 5c fare to Brooklyn, thus making Brooklyn an integral part of the round city.

While in Washington I gave considerable attention to the Interstate Commerce Act, attending the meetings of the Judiciary Committee of the House and conferring with the active members. At this time there were no teeth in the Interstate Commerce Act. The commission could direct and advise but not enforce. While I was in Congress the method of enforcement was framed, consisting of the rule of conduct of reasonable rates, adequate service and safe appliances and giving the commission power to enforce this rule. When the work on the New York State Public Service Law began I pushed the use of these words as the rule of conduct for public utility regulations. They were adopted. Public utility regulation in this state was entirely novel and I was fortunate to be in the Public Service Commission during the initial efforts on this subject.

One of my main drives while on the commission was to make new subways of a size and cost that would allow the riders to pay the expense of operation, interest, and amortization. The then existing subway built by the Rapid Transit Commission did this. There was constant pressure in my time to build on a large scale, placing part of the future burden on the taxpayers. Some of my colleagues thought I was too anxious to keep down the cost and limit the amplitude. One of them (in the best of good will) said many times that I was cheeseparing.

The Fourth Avenue (Brooklyn) subway to Coney Island was intended to be city owned and operated. It was evident that it could not be self-supporting and that the taxpayers would have to pay the excess. Mr Maltbie and I opposed it and succeeded in holding it up until the new Dual Subway Plan developed. The latter was carried out and the proposed Fourth Avenue subway to Coney Island was never built. I held that as a means of making new subways self supporting, outlying subways should be built in whole or part by assessment on the land benefited. Oliver C. Semple and I prepared a statutory method of accomplishing this. It was made part of the Rapid Transit Act and is still the law although it has never been put into actual use.

After I left the Public Service Commission his pressure to place part of the burden of subways on the taxpayers became too strong to resist.

I suppose that if I had remained on the commission my opposition would have been ineffective. The Dual Subways, built since then, have always depended on the taxpayers meeting large deficits. The Independent Subway owned and operated by the city and costing twice what the Dual Subways cost the city has been a far heavier burden for the taxpayers.

My familiarity with these new laws and their method of application caused public utility corporations to seek my assistance as a lawyer after I left the commission. Property owners' organizations in Kings and Queens Counties also retained me to advise them on securing rapid transit for their localities. All these things meant an increase of legal practice and made me very busy indeed.

Rate-making cases began to come to me. The Brooklyn Borough Gas Company case, the first of the kind in this country, was won by our office after many appeals. The Public Service Commission after an appraisal and hearing fixed the rate at 92c per 100 cubic feet of gas. The state legislature desiring the credit of doing still better for the consumers fixed a rate of 90c without any investigation whatever, disregarding the fundamentals of costs of making and distribution and regardless of a fair profit to the company. In our action in behalf of the company we claimed and established unlawful confiscation. Many later court cases involving reasonable rates for services of public utility corporations followed our methods and forms in this case.

It is likely that we could have established a large law office for public utility corporation work. In about 1915, however, I deliberately decided that I did not want my future to be public utility corporation law, not because it was in any way unpatriotic or unethical but entirely because defending public utility corporations did not seem to me to be building up laws related to progress. I probably had somewhat the same feeling as my brother George and my son Preston. They always wanted to be doing new things. I wanted to be connected with new laws that improved living conditions, especially the better distribution of residences, business, and industry.

Chapter XIV: Zoning

On my second trip to Germany in 1908 I went to the town planning exhibition at Düsseldorf. Werner Hegeman of Berlin had prepared what seemed to me a tremendous exhibition of models and illustrations showing improved streets, parks, public buildings, rapid transit, docks, and buildings for all sorts of purposes. Later I became well acquainted with Mr Hegeman in Germany and this country and he visited at our home in Flatbush. I was taken off my feet by the impressions given me by these new fields of work. I had little more than returned to New York when

Nelson P. Lewis, then Chief Engineer of the Board of Estimate, a long-time intimate friend of mine, urged me to join the National Conference on City Planning. The first meeting had lately been held in Boston and a meeting was before long to be held in Chicago. I joined. I realized that I had found the kind of work that interested me and I foresaw that the whole subject was almost unexplored in this country and that it offered a vast field of progressive legislation. I also realized that most of the objects could be secured through the police power and not necessarily by taxation.

My appointment by a Republican governor on the Public Service Commission had put me somewhat out of touch with Democratic politics. Senator McCarren, Brooklyn Democratic leader, was a good friend of mine and had helped me from time to time on legislative matters in Albany pertaining to the Public Service Commission work. He always said that Governor Hughes put me on the commission because he (McCarren) requested it and that I was the representative of the Democratic party on the commission. This view was incorrect but suited me all right because I always enrolled as a Democrat. I also voted for many Republican and Fusion candidates.

The prospect of the city planning field at once convinced me that I could make friends throughout the whole country among engineers, architects, and legislators with whom I would be more at home than in the ordinary political associations. This turned out to be true. I always enjoyed my city planning friends and meetings more than I did practical politics.

Alfred T. White and Frederic B. Pratt called at my office shortly after I left the Public Service Commission and asked me to become their paid helper in advancing the city planning of the Borough of Brooklyn. I was only too willing to accept their invitation with or without pay. We formed the Brooklyn City Plan Committee. Frederic B. Pratt was chairman, Alfred T. White and I were vice-chairmen and I was counsel. Practically all the leading businessmen and philanthropists of the borough were members of this association.

In 1911 Daniel H. Burnham of Chicago, famous as the architect of the Chicago City Plan, visited Brooklyn and pointed out in general terms how the borough might be rehabilitated, dwelling on the possibilities of Jamaica Bay. His partner, Edwin H. Bennett, was made director of the plan. Our work under Mr Bennett reached the stage of well considered drawings but as Brooklyn was only one of five boroughs the city appropriations to ratify or carry out these plans could not be wholly obtained. Mr Bennett, Mr Pratt and I inspected the locations of many problems and at meetings we talked over their solution.

Messrs Pratt and White bought land costing about $300,000 at Gerritsen Basin on Jamaica Bay and later made a gift of it to the city. It was the starting point of the great Marine Park. I represented them as legal counsel in obtaining and ceding this land to the City of New York.

We devised a plan for carrying the Fulton Street Elevated tracks across Brooklyn Bridge, continuing them under Centre Street on the Manhattan side. This plan was for a time favored by the city officials and work preparatory to carrying out this plan was done at the Manhattan end of the Brooklyn Bridge. A ramp for carrying the elevated cars from the bridge through the Centre Street subway (soon to be built) was partly constructed at an expense of about $200,000, and this ramp still exists although never used. Strangely enough, the organizations on the Hill, and especially along Fulton Street, began to oppose this connection on the ground that their neighborhood should have subway transit the same as Flatbush and nothing else would be tolerated. With Brooklyn divided against itself it was difficult to progress this very sensible plan. The result was that the Fulton Street neighborhood depended for the next twenty-five years on the Fulton Street Elevated which terminated at the Manhattan end of Brooklyn Bridge. There passengers had to change to the north and south subway lines, paying a total 10c fare to go to almost any point in Manhattan. This extra fare undoubtedly held back the development of the Hill section in Brooklyn. It began to depreciate rapidly and now many parts of it are occupied by negroes. I have always thought that this change might have been prevented if the Fulton Street Elevated cars could have been introduced into the Centre Street subway, thus giving a 5c fare to the great Hill district.

During this period and about 1912 I met from time to time with George McAneny, Otto M. Eidlitz, Lawson Purdy, and Nelson P. Lewis to discuss the possibilities of supplementing the Dual Rapid Transit Plan by regulations that would prevent the exploitation of spots rendered accessible by the new subways. The danger had already begun to appear. It was that along with distribution in the outlying parts of the city would go extreme congestion of buildings in eligible spots inside Manhattan. It was apparent that if the result of the new subways was to overbuild certain localities with enormous skyscrapers the full benefit of the subways might be impaired. They might be a means of causing congestion and concentration instead of distribution.

In New York at this time there was no regulation of skyscrapers. They could be built to any height, cover the entire lot and no space had to be left for light and air from the ground to the roof. The first skyscraper would sometimes monopolize half a block because other similar buildings were rendered impractical. George McAneny was then in the Board of Estimate. He proposed the appointment of a Heights of Building Commission to report on the possibilities of regulating height. I was on this commission and was asked by the Board of Estimate to be its chairman. I went into the work with avidity. We had a small appropriation for a working staff. I looked about for a suitable director and obtained George B. Ford who came to my office carrying his inevitable cane and said he would like the job. He was a wonder. He had been trained as an architect but had the beginning of a wide knowledge of city planning.

At the next National Conference on City Planning he and I put our heads together to find out what was going on in American cities to regulate skyscrapers. I called the roll of the delegates and Mr Ford took notes. There were about five cities, Boston and Chicago among them, that possessed a little statutory power to regulate skyscrapers. All the other cities including New York were entirely unregulated. This was the first step in the program that culminated in the New York City ordinance and was the beginning of comprehensive zoning in the United States. I should not take the space here to tell the story of the gradual upbuilding of the law of zoning and of obtaining the approval of courts for this sort of regulation. My book *Zoning* covers my connection with it.

After the zoning plan was adopted by the City of New York, a few of the workers on the plan, of whom I was one, met at my office to discuss the formation of a citizens' committee to watch the new enterprise and see that the plan was not relegated to the scrap heap. This small meeting requested me to be chairman and I consented. Then Otto Eidlitz said that we must have counsel who could give steady attention to the legal developments. I asked whether the counsel should be paid, and when they said yes I declared that I would like to be counsel instead of chairman. They readily assented to this. My compensation was fixed at $4000 per year. During the previous five years while I had given perhaps a third of my total time to the subject of zoning I received no pay whatever from any source and I was glad enough to have zoning earn me some money. We called this body the Zoning Committee of the City of New York.

In later meetings Mr Purdy and I said that inasmuch as the zoning depended on the police power, and court approval of police power regulations depended to a large extent on the general use and application of that form of regulation, we ought to spread zoning throughout the country. This spreading process became part of my work as counsel.

During the next twenty years I visited every state and all the large cities of the country. This work, however, was not gratuitous. I established a uniform charge of $100 per day for time away from the office including travel time, plus travel expenses. In going to Florida, the far west, New Orleans or the Pacific Coast our office would arrange a paid itinerary. On these trips I made talks before boards of trade, legislative bodies, both state and city, assisted in drawing zoning ordinances and state enabling acts for zoning, tried zoning cases, and argued test cases before appellate courts. From 1917 to 1927 I had about all of this work that I could do and still have some time to spare for my necessary office work.

All my zoning work connected with New York City, outside of my annual salary as counsel, has been gratuitous. This statement applies to several years of preliminary work and all the period while I was counsel whether with or without pay. Many retainers have been offered to me, some by owners of large buildings in New York City willing to pay well for my legal services. The reason why I have never taken a dollar is because during a large part of the time the Board of Estimate, Board of Appeals, Chief Engineer, Corporation Counsel, and the five building commissioners have depended somewhat on me in solving new situations. If it were known that I represented clients they would have been afraid to invite me into their councils. But it has been generally known that I have been a disinterested advisor on all New York City zoning problems. I was so keen to see zoning succeed in this city both for the benefit of the city and as an example to the rest of the country that I did not want to leave a stone unturned.

After 1927 and with the progress of the great depression this zoning work fell off, especially the distant work. Many cities developed specialists who could help as well as I. My field became nearer and nearer New York. Since the beginning of the great depression I have been advisor to many cities, towns and villages within 400 miles of this city and it has been possible to do more and more of my work at my office.

In the fall of 1936 as I was then seventy-three years old I announced to the Zoning Committee that I would like to serve as counsel without pay. The committee assented on my insistence. It was becoming more difficult for me to stand up at meetings of the Board of Estimate, the Board of Standards and Appeals, and the City Planning Commission to argue in favor of zoning matters, and it was especially difficult to stand up in the crowd in the Board of Estimate while waiting for items on the calendar to be reached. Then, too, many benevolent citizens contributed to the Zoning Committee. The system of making contributions was under my direction and most of the letters were composed by me although I did not sign them. It seemed to me to be best to be counsel without pay because as I grew older I could not cover public meetings as well as before. Certain contributors, however, desired to continue their annual contributions. These went to pay our necessary expenses, a sum for office rent and the work of Miss Wallace. Our helpfulness in this city is not so vital to zoning as formerly because the City Planning Commission has been established which has taken over the details of zoning.

When we began the zoning study in about 1912 I supposed we would work on it all my lifetime and that others might carry it on to actual completion. The subject developed so fast in its early stages that all the five boroughs of Greater New York were actually zoned on the height, area, and use maps on July 25, 1916. Not only was the city ready for it but the entire country took hold of it rapidly. Every large city in the country is zoned except Detroit. Each adopted the New York City method. At present it is not extending as fast as before because country districts, towns, and unincorporated areas do not feel the need for zoning so much as cities.

My recollection goes back to the earliest days while our District Commission was trying to get started. I prepared a pamphlet "Principles of Zoning." The principles as set forth were very nearly what zoning has become at present. I tried for two and one-half years to have the National Conference on City Planning recommend this set of principles. The Conference was not averse to studying them, and its criticisms and cooperation were one of the greatest helps in perfecting the phraseology. Lawrence Veiller was the most severe critic but on the whole he was a great help as it turned out. He was a constructive critic. The National Conference would never actually endorse the pamphlet although I changed it from time to time to meet criticisms. Notwithstanding all these things I consider that the National Conference was one of the main helpers in the beginning of zoning.

To show the small beginnings I will tell of our little office in a backroom at 113 Broadway. Mr Ford had one young man and a young woman typist. This was all his staff. I went there every day. Mr Ford made soap models of skyscrapers with setbacks and towers. I remember that he and I got the subcommittee together at his office and with the help of the soap models we reviewed the possibilities of coverage, height, and setback regulations. I little dreamed that the skyline made by these models sitting on our table would become the actual skyline of Manhattan fifteen years later.

The success of the zoning round table at the National Conferences showed how rapidly interest spread in zoning. In about 1913 I invited three different friends to sit with me at different meals. I constituted myself the leader and said we would talk of nothing but zoning and one person should speak at a time. At the next Conference I placed a notice on the bulletin board that the Zoning Roundtable would be held at certain meals at certain hours. To my surprise about fifteen members attended. It continued to grow until at the Los Angeles Conference at least two hundred attended my Zoning Roundtable. I had to be a good deal of a czar, otherwise the noise and disturbance would ruin the table. I postponed my own meal to give all my energy to the management. Proceedings began at the minute fixed. There was never a delay. I would tell the waiters to go on with their duties making as little noise as possible. I announced the rules of the Roundtable which were that each speaker should rise, that only one person should speak at a time, that persons not on their feet should keep still and not converse, and that nothing should be talked about except zoning. The method was that any person could ask questions or state his own ideas. In the early days the members hardly believed that I was in earnest when I said the doings would begin at 7.30 am. Many would come along about 8.30 and they were surprised to see that the meeting was half over. Next time they would be apt to come on the dot. More than once the room was entirely filled when I stepped to my place at the head of the table at the minute advertised.

These Roundtables were attended by governors, mayors, councilmen, city engineers, city attorneys, college professors, and land specialists of all kinds. After zoning was actually started in most cities these Round-tables were largely attended by members of zoning commissions, boards of appeals, and city planning commissions. They became rather famous throughout the country. I kept the steam at high pressure so that they would not drag. I would never wait for an answer to any question but answer it myself if no one volunteered immediately. I fear that many of my quick answers were not very good but there was no time for much deliberation or else people would begin to talk with one another. I always considered that the success of the Zoning Roundtable was due to my extremely arbitrary methods. Strangely enough no one ever got provoked for being called down. All were so much in earnest that they would forgive almost everything if the intention was to promote zoning.

During all these years devoted intensively to zoning and the master plan my constant colleagues and advisors were Frank B. Williams and Robert Whitten. The death of the latter in 1936 caused me a loss which words fail to describe. He contributed far more to the upbuilding of zoning in this country than I did.

My zoning work has been the best contribution of my life. Parallel with this I have tried to systematize the entire subject of community land planning. My work on this last subject is more comprehensive than zoning but it has not been so popular and the statutes which have accompanied this more general work have not been applied so widely. This general work might be entitled "Master Plan."

Chapter XV: Master Plan

In about 1922 the Russell Sage Foundation formed a committee called "Regional Plan of New York and Its Environs." I was invited to attend the first meeting of this committee which was held at the home of C. D. Norton, Fifth Avenue near the Metropolitan Museum. This was the starting point of an enterprise on which the Foundation spent more than $3,000,000. A little later I was asked to head the legal research and was paid a good salary for this service. Frank B. Williams was my very competent associate. I studied the possibilities of legislation for several years, talking with state and city officials in many places on my zoning trips.

Existing laws governing platting, official maps of streets and parks and the prevention of misplaced buildings, were ineffective in all the states. Many statutes in the books were not enforceable and cities did not try to enforce them. In the beginning my efforts centered on methods of producing small parks for playgrounds by platting without the use of condemnation. I attended a number of park conferences which were carried on with large attendances. My talks were printed and without intention I became a sort of by-product as a park authority. The entire subject of community land planning began to arrange itself in my mind. In 1925 I prepared a booklet on this growing subject and for brevity as well as because it is the first printed document on this sort of legislation in this country I quote the title page:

RPNY 10 – Regional Plan of New York and Its Environs – Planning of Unbuilt Areas in the New York Region – A form of State Enabling Act with Annotations – Prepared by Edward M. Bassett – Providing for the establishment of an official map or plan at the option of every municipality, the approval of plats, the protection of mapped streets, the setting aside of small parks for playgrounds, the modification of zoning in platted areas, and the control of building permits – Regional Plan of New York and Its Environs, 130 East Twenty-second Street, New York City – 1925.

This form was the basis of three laws which we prepared and which passed at Albany, one an amendment to the Town Law, one an amendment to the Village Law, and the last an amendment to the General City Law. As New York City had for several generations depended on its own charter in these matters this city has never taken advantage of these laws. They are all permissive and no municipality is compelled to adopt them but could adopt them if it so elected. These laws became the basis of similar laws throughout the country, their phraseology being copied in whole or part from the form in the above pamphlet.

In 1928 Mayor Walker appointed me an assistant corporation counsel of the City of New York in relation to new laws for better city planning. My pay was on my usual per diem basis. I prepared a pamphlet, the title page of which is as follows:

Board of Estimate and Apportionment – Statutory Set-Up of a Planning Board for Greater New York – Prepared by Edward M. Bassett – December 15, 1928 – Revised January 10, 1929 – Presented by his Honor the Mayor at the meeting held January 10, 1929.

I spoke before legislative committees at Albany in favor of the charter amendment which was part of my set-up, and the new law was reported favorably in both branches of the legislature. There was no visible opposition to it from any source. But when the time for adjournment neared and after the governor had sent a special message in favor of the amendment to the legislature Senator Kleinfeld who had introduced the bill refused to move it for adoption, absenting himself from the Senate Chamber. Other senators did not want to take his place and thus in the closing hours of the session the bill failed. It is likely that it was well understood among the legislators representing the five boroughs that this bill would take away to a certain extent the existing borough autonomy. Political leaders in Kings, Queens, and Richmond were very likely quietly opposed to the bill.

In the fall of 1936 a Charter Commission submitted a new short charter to the voters for adoption which was approved by the voters. This new charter went into effect January 1, 1938. It copied the main provisions of my set-up including the city planning commission and the master plan. The City Planning Commission has been appointed and is now functioning.

My book *Master Plan* was printed by the Russell Sage Foundation under date of 1938. I used this title as a vehicle to present my elements of the community land plan. These views had been stated by me in many talks all over the country and in pamphlets but I never before prepared and printed a complete outline of my whole system of city planning. Since the advent of the New Deal the word "planning" has been applied to almost everything. Counties, states, and the federal government have gone into the subject of planning, and I suppose that today at least 100,000 men and women are employed by states and the federal government on what is called planning. Planning has become confused with architecture, landscape architecture, municipal engineering, and all kinds of rehabilitation work whether connected with the land or not. My efforts have been to separate city planning from architecture, landscape architecture, and cognate callings. It has seemed to me that the present tendency is to broaden it so that city planning becomes meaningless and vast sums of tax money are spent in collecting data that will never be useful.

My idea has been that attention should be concentrated on the elements of community land planning and the coordination of these elements. They are streets, parks, sites for public buildings, public reservations, zoning districts, routes of public utilities, and harbor lines. This is my own list. My book *Master Plan* shows how these are all the elements that we know about today. In phrasing statutes for master plans the minds of legislators tend to center on these elements, but now and then some stray subject appeals to the legislators and is thrown in along with the true elements. These strays are getting very common and show that the mind of the legislature has no groove to travel in. The object of my book was to develop in simple language all the elements that can be shown on a Master Plan and to point out how no other subjects can be shown as elements. It was a plain statement of some very stubborn facts. Legislators, however, the last few years have been quite willing to ignore simple and stubborn facts in all fields of economics and in community planning as well.

Chapter XVI: Congestion

For thirty years my work outside of my regular law practice has been the prevention of congestion. My aim has been the distribution of light and air – openness – whether in residences, stores, offices, or industries. When I was on the Public Service Commission I urged the round city instead of the congested city. Many builders and officers of transportation companies then claimed that a city of crowded buildings is more economical than openness. They wanted subways to develop to the utmost one segment of a city before another segment was supplied with transit. They called Queens the "corn fields" although Queens is nearer the Grand Central Station than The Bronx. At that time the evils of dark buildings were not so obvious as now. New York has since then produced many blighted districts, every one of which has dark rooms due to congestion in building. In my mortgage work I have always sought to invest in the sunshine. I have preferred one-family detached houses to block houses or tenements. I have sought to have lots for each house 30 feet or more wide. Bungalows have been favorites because they make sunlight communities. Houses that will rent permanently have no dark rooms.

My interest in zoning was largely based on sunlight. The progress of this country toward sunlight houses and the lessening of the human burden on the land continued until the federal government began erecting more than a billion dollars worth of so-called slum clearance houses four stories and over in height and in all cases increasing the human burden on the land.

For more than forty years our law office has made first mortgages for clients, following these general considerations. Our mortgages have been safe. For fourteen years I have been a member of the board of directors of Thrift, a large Brooklyn corporation under the state banking department. It was founded by Charles Pratt to make twelve-year amortizing mortgages on small homes in Long Island including Brooklyn and Queens, and is connected with Pratt Institute.

Notes

1 Edward M. Bassett (1939) *Autobiography of Edward M. Bassett*, New York, The Harbor Press, p. 7.
2 ibid., p. 8.
3 "Edward Murray Bassett" (1962) *The National Cyclopedia of American Biography*, vol. 44, New York, James T. White & Co., pp. 548–9.
4 Bassett, op. cit., p. 8.

5 ibid., p. 10.
6 ibid., p. 52.
7 Stanley Buder (1974) ''Edward Murray Bassett'', *Dictionary of American Biography*, Supplement Four: *1946–1950*, New York, Charles Scribner's Sons, pp. 55–7.
8 *The National Cyclopedia of American Biography*, op. cit., p. 549.
9 Bassett, op. cit., pp. 29–30.
10 Bassett's two most important books are: (1936) *Zoning: The Laws, Administration and Court Decisions During the First Twenty Years*, New York, The Russell Sage Foundation; and (1938) *The Master Plan*, New York, The Russell Sage Foundation. For further critical discussion see Buder, op. cit., and Mel Scott (1960) *American City Planning since 1890*, Berkeley, University of California Press.

6 Bettman of Cincinnati

Laurence C. Gerckens

In a period of fiscal uncertainty and potential for renewed commitment to the optimization of scarce financial resources, it may be of value to recall that some of the most basic components of current American city planning practice were initiated and enthusiastically supported in circumstances of economic retrenchment. The story of Alfred Bettman at Cincinnati is not only the story of the emergence of the urban general plan as a basis for rational capital planning, but also the story of a personal crusade for civic rationality and participatory democracy that grew out of the Cincinnati experience.

The old Fifth Street Market was demolished in Cincinnati on February 24, 1870, clearing the site for the Tyler Davidson Fountain that would become the symbol of the city and the focal point of a future Fountain Square.[1] The refreshing murmur of falling water was still new to the hot streets of the riverboat-dominated Queen City of the Ohio River West on August 26, 1873, when the former Rebecca Bloom[2] presented her husband, Louis Bettman, a German immigrant and a clothing manufacturer, with their first son – Alfred. Raised in an environment of bold municipal creativity and individual opportunity, of mob violence and political corruption, Alfred developed both a sincere enthusiasm for his city and a deep concern for its future.

George B. Cox, a local bar-keep soon to become the Republican "boss" of Cincinnati whose political "machine" would dominate Cincinnati politics for more than a quarter of a century (1886–1912), began his nefarious career in 1880 (Vexler, p. 38). His political activity would lead the city to financial disaster and shape young Alfred's future in reform. Cincinnati in the 1880s was a city in which both beer and blood flowed freely and frequently. On March 28, 1884 a race riot filled the streets with barricades and soldiers; the Court House was burned.[3] To man's mayhem, Nature added its own that year, sending one of many periodic floods to devastate the lower central business district.

The coming of the railroads threatened Cincinnati's riverboat-based prosperity. To assure continuation of the city's role in providing stockyard, machine-shop, and agricultural products to the American inland South, the City of Cincinnati built the Cincinnati Southern Railroad, the only municipally owned railroad in the United States. In 1869 the city raised $10,000,000 through the sale of bonds to finance the Cincinnati Southern. Completed in 1880, running from Cincinnati to Chattanooga on 339 miles of city-owned right-of-way, the Cincinnati Southern, a bold expression of municipal creativity (Condit, pp. 61–71), saved the economy of the city upon the demise of the riverboat era. Another such expression was the Centennial Exposition of 1888 that celebrated the founding of the city and extolled its civic virtues just four years after the Court House Riot. The exposition featured an exhibition hall that straddled the Hamilton Canal, providing taxi service by gondola inside the building! And in sharp contrast to the civic background of currruption, riot, and debauchery, Isaac Mayer Wise, the most prominent American Jew of his time, made Cincinnati the center of a progressive reform Judaism movement in the 1890s that would shape the futures of young Alfred, Cincinnati, and America.[4]

Gilbert Bettman, one of Alfred's three brothers, was born in 1881. Both Alfred and Gilbert would follow careers in law and become deeply involved in political processes in Cincinnati, in Ohio, and in the federal government, but through divergent careers; Alfred joined Rabbi Wise in following the route of progressive reform; Gilbert followed the route of Boss Cox in machine politics.

As with most sons of successful Midwestern merchants, Alfred traveled East to complete his education following graduation from Cincinnati's old Hughes High School in 1890. He earned a B.A. degree at Harvard in 1894, and completed both a M.A. and a law degree there in 1898. When he returned to Cicinnati in 1898, the city's per capita debts were among the highest in the nation while its urban services were among the worst, thanks to the irresponsibilities and political corruption of the Boss Cox machine, earning for Cincinnati its undisputed title as "the worst governed city in America" (Bent, pp. 308–9).

Families such as the Bettmans were referred to in the Cincinnati press of the 1890s as "German Jews", a term viewed solely as descriptive and in no way anti-Semitic. There was little such prejudice in Cincinnati at that time because their German–Jewish ways did not identify them for prejudicial action in a city that was commonly more German than American (Miller, p. 129). Reform Judaism, as developed by Rabbi Wise in Cincinnati during the last two decades of the nineteenth century, became a new "urban gospel" in which service to mankind was a medium of religion intended to

change the mode of life in the immigrant sectors, transform the appearance of the city, broaden the activities of municipal and state governments, and rescue politics from the sordid abyss into which it had fallen. (Miller, p. 132)

Wise's "urban gospel" became a foundation for the Social Gospel Movement in the United States and for twentieth-century American liberalism.[5]

When the German Jews began to arrive in the wealthier suburbs of Cincinnati during the early years of this century they brought with them a new commitment to the city, to government, and to reform. They eagerly participated in, and initiated, local actions to increase the effectiveness and justice of American democracy (Miller, p. 135). When Alfred Bettman returned from Harvard in 1898 to practice law in Cincinnati, he joined this community of reform-minded Jews to participate in a movement in social and political reform that reached its early maturity (1910–15) simultaneous with his first direct involvement with city politics. Alfred's new activities in municipal reform met the community service obligations of a rising, financially successful professional who was an Eastern-educated son of a wealthy clothing manufacturer and a socially conscious Cincinnati German Jew of the turn-of-the-century.

Alfred married Lillian Wyler on June 20, 1904. They would be childless. Alfred devoted his time away from his law practice to Lillian and to his avocations, among which he would count reform of a city very much in need of reformation. Appalled by the corruption and economic waste of government under the political machine,[6] Alfred found himself drifting toward Democratic, anti-Cox, reform politics. His brother, Gilbert, who also went to Harvard, earning an A.B. in 1903, an A.M. in 1904, and his law degree *cum laude* in 1907, was admitted to the Ohio Bar in that year. He took advantage of the opportunities of the machine to begin his rise in Ohio Republican politics.

The modern urban planning movement in Cincinnati began in 1906 when a Parks Commission was appointed and $15,000 was appropriated for the development of a parks system plan (Vexler, p. 47). In 1907, George E. Kessler of Kansas City was hired to execute the parks plan, which was completed and adopted in 1908, becoming the official guide to the development of the Cincinnati parks system (Hebble and Goodwin, pp. 150–6).

Alfred entered the political arena in 1909, at the age of 36, when he began a two-year term as an assistant county prosecutor for Hamilton County (Cincinnati). He came to the attention of Henry T. Hunt, a Democrat, who sought his support in opposing the Republican machine. In an astounding political upset in November of 1911, the voters of Cincinnati rejected Louis Schwab, the machine candidate for mayor, electing Democrat Hunt as mayor (1912–13) and Alfred Bettman as city solicitor. Hunt was fiscal reform personified. He held that city spending had to be based on concepts of municipal efficiency and not on the political spoils system; he believed in government by experts, with experts in charge of each municipal department. Mayor Hunt undertook a comprehensive topographic survey of the city to serve as the basis for future capital investment decisions and authorized a national expert,

Plate 6.1 Caricature of lawyer Alfred Bettman
c. 1905.
Source: Newspaper Cartoonist Association of
Cincinnati. From *A Gallery of Pen Sketches in Black
and White of "Cincinnatians as we see 'em,"*
Cincinnati, Ohio, The Association, © Angus McNeill,
Treasurer, p. 29, "Alfred Bettman, Attorney at Law,"
by "J.A.W.".

Bion Arnold, to produce a plan for integrating the interurban railways
into a rapid transit system (Hebble and Goodwin, p. 237). He introduced
scientific budget-making. Under Hunt, each department would itemize
expenses and their purposes. These lists would then be reviewed by
citizen advisory groups and would be debated in lengthy public hearings
before final budget decisions were made. Mayor Hunt operated the City
of Cincinnati in 1913 on a budget that was a quarter of a million dollars
less than in 1912, yet covered the cost of several new projects (Miller,
pp. 214–15).

In his capacity as city solicitor, Bettman became involved with the liquidation of turnpikes, toll roads, and interurban railroads, becoming intimately aware of issues of public finance, capital construction, and the influence of land development patterns (Segoe Tape 1, p. 22). Alfred Bettman gained his first direct exposure to rational budget-making, to municipal public works planning, and to the virtues of citizen participation in policy-making through his day-to-day involvement with this revolutionary, but short-lived, Democratic reform administration. These Hunt Administration innovations became the cornerstones for a lifetime of contributions to municipal reform and to American city planning (Simpson, p. 83). During 1912–13 Bettman also served as an attorney for the Trustees of the municipally owned Cincinnati Southern Railroad.

The Republican machine regained City Hall in 1913 following a series of destructive ice plant and street railway strikes.[7] Mayor Hunt was defeated; Alfred Bettman lost his position as city solicitor; their reform efforts were aborted. But this brief exposure to machine politics, to municipal potential, and to the corruption that surfaced in virtually every investigation into the affairs of previous administrations, was sufficient to motivate Bettman to declare war on the political machine and on the fiscal mismanagement it represented. In 1913, when Alfred Bettman was 40, he returned from the fifth National Conference on City Planning, his first, as a true believer in urban planning as a vehicle for needed reform, particularly in the area of public capital investments.[8] He saw city planning as a means by which the citizen, through policy participation in what he called "the art and science of both the placing and timing of the use of land" (O'Brian, p. 2), could check the power of corrupt politicians and create rational, public-interest-founded policies on capital construction that could achieve Hunt's ends of municipal honesty and economy. Bettman's enthusiasm, intellect, and immediate political experience commended him to this young organization. He was appointed to the National General Committee of the Conference in 1914, and served on the Executive Committee the following year.

A new charter proposal for Cincinnati that included a department of city planning as an integral part of city government, headed by a citizen commission, was defeated at the polls in 1914 (Charter 1914, pp. 50–3). On January 4, 1914, Alfred Bettman assisted in the founding of a group that in 1915 would become the United City Planning Committee. This group of reform-minded businessmen included representatives of the city planning committees of various civic organizations, among which were the City Club and the Chamber of Commerce (Ford, p. 37). The United City Planning Committee, primarily anti-machine Republicans among whom Democrat Bettman was in the minority, was dedicated to the goal of starting a city planning movement in Cincinnati, and creating a

rational, public-interest-focused "master plan" for the future development of the city to stop the seemingly endless series of capital investment
disasters that had plagued the city under the pork-barrel politics of the
Republican machine[9] (NCCP 1924, pp. 35–6). The constitution of this
group specified its purposes as those of conducting an educational campaign, raising funds, and serving as an organizational contact between the
people of the city and its government relative to the proposed master plan
(ibid., p. 36).

The United City Planning Committee took its first major action when it
turned its attention to the Statehouse in Columbus. What Ohio's cities
needed, according to the committee, was a state act authorizing creation
of municipal planning commissions that gave such citizen groups the
authority to create a master plan for the city as a guide to capital construction and to enforce it over the objections of a machine-corrupted city
council. Without such authority, the committee reasoned, no plan could
be effective in channeling capital funds to their most cost-effective and
community-interest-determined use. Alfred drafted such a bill, requiring
a two-thirds vote of city council to overrule a decision of the planning
commission concerning public construction "whenever the commission
shall have made a plan of the municipality, or any portion thereof" (State
of Ohio, p. 145). The United City Planning Committee experienced its
first victory on May 27, 1915, when this bill was unanimously approved
in both houses and was enacted by the Ohio legislature to be effective
January 1, 1916 (ICRPC 1925, p. 325).[10] With passage of this act, Alfred
Bettman's capabilities in urban planning legislation came to national
attention, initiating a lifelong career as the primary author of planning
enabling legislation in the United States. In 1915 Alfred also served as
attorney and Trustee for the municipally owned Cincinnati Southern
Railroad.

For the next thirty years virtually all of the planning enabling legislation adopted by the State of Ohio would be drafted by Alfred Bettman
(Simpson, p. 51). Although enacted, this enabling legislation, being permissive and not mandatory, was not implemented in Cincinnati where
the machine politicians feared the power of the city planning commission
to override city council once a master plan was prepared. Instead, an
unofficial "advisory" commission was created that was completely
under the control of the political machine (Vitz, p. 5; Official City Plan,
1925, p. 26).

In 1917, George B. Ford, in a national survey of planning progress in the
United States, recognized Alfred Bettman as a leading figure in support of
city planning in Cincinnati (Ford, p. 38) while faulting the machine-
government for not implementing the "enabled" official city planning
commission:

Of the leading cities in America, in point of size and population, Cincinnati (410,476) is one of the few that has been tardy in giving official recognition to city planning. (ibid., p. 37)

The ninth National Conference on City Planning was held at the Muehlebach Hotel in Kansas City in May of 1917. Twenty-three persons who attended this meeting elected to create the American City Planning Institute (ACPI), the first professional organization for city planners in the United States.[11] Alfred Bettman was among the fifty-two persons invited during the course of the following months to become charter members of the new institute. The ACPI was officially organized on November 24, 1917, in New York City (Black, p. 29). Alfred became a member of the Board of Directors. Among the first actions of the new institute, upon conception in Kansas City, was an offer of its services to President Wilson. It was 1917 and the United States was at war. Active promotion of the Plan of Cincinnati was deferred, and the United City Planning Committee went inactive for the duration of the war (NCCP 1924, p. 36).

President Wilson appointed Alfred Bettman as a special assistant to A. Mitchell Palmer, Attorney General of the United States. He was assigned to the War Emergency Division of the US Department of Justice and put in charge of Espionage Act cases. Together with John Lord O'Brian, Bettman took the major responsibility for prosecuting hundreds of Americans for violation of wartime Sedition and Espionage Acts. Bettman did most of the legal drafting on the sedition cases himself, including *Schenck* v. *US* and *Debs* v. *US* that resulted in the imprisonment of Eugene Victor Debs, the Socialist Party candidate for president of the United States in 1912, for making an anti-war speech in Canton, Ohio, in the spring of 1918.

At the end of the war, upon the recommendation of both Bettman and Palmer, President Wilson granted clemency to over one hundred of the 239 persons still in prison for violations of the Espionage Act, most of whom were put there by the successful prosecutions of Bettman and O'Brian (Coben, pp. 200–1). Bettman and O'Brian recommended pardons or commutations of sentences in 109 cases involving Espionage Act convictions (Sterling, p. 151). However, in March of 1919 Bettman advised against the pardoning of Debs (Coben, p. 201). As a result of these war-related activities, Bettman had created, in less than two years, a national reputation for effective criminal prosecution. In conservative circles he became known as "the man who jailed Socialist Debs." The war being over, and the national-defense-in-wartime logic of the Espionage and Sedition Acts no longer being applicable, Bettman and O'Brian resigned their positions with the Department of Justice in May of 1919.

Responding to local public pressures, the Republican-machine-dominated city council of Cincinnati created an official city planning commission, consistent with the Bettman-drafted enabling act of 1915, that began to function on January 1, 1918 (ICRPC 1925, p. 324). This commission, headed by the machine-mayor, was in no hurry whatsoever to create that master plan that would limit the machine's political power! The commission contracted with the Technical Advisory Corporation of New York City to execute a preliminary survey of Cincinnati to highlight the city's problems and potentials (Segoe Tape 1, pp. 21–3).

On June 2, 1919, less than one month after Bettman's resignation from the Department of Justice, Attorney General Palmer's house was bombed by radicals. Shaken by the experience, Palmer, a former progressive Democrat and a liberal, turned away from liberal clemency. Following the lead of a Red-scared, arch-conservative Republican Congress, Palmer carried out what may well have been the greatest executive restriction on personal freedom in the history of the country (Coben, p. v). During the era of the Palmer Raids (1919–20), simple suspicion of unAmericanism was sufficient to warrant a jail sentence or deportation for sedition; approximately 1400 Americans were arrested under the state anti-sedition laws (Sterling, p. 95). Bettman and O'Brian were angered by this wholesale violation of civil liberties (Coben, p. 208). Bettman opposed Palmer and the new rash of peacetime sedition laws at every opportunity. And he had ample opportunity! In reaction to labor strikes and rumors of an imminent "Red Revolution," the Ohio Legislature passed the Criminal Syndicalism Act on May 7, 1919. This act, passed without a dissenting vote in both houses of the Legislature (105–0 in the house; 30–0 in the senate), penalized the mere advocacy of insurrection in any form. Bettman traveled repeatedly to Washington, D.C. after the war, at his own expense, to appear before Congressional committees in opposition to such repressive legislation (O'Brian, p. 5), and particularly to oppose peacetime anti-sedition laws (Coben, pp. 241–2). Bettman testified to the Committee on Rules of the US House of Representatives on January 23, 1920 against the Graham Bill. This proposed federal peacetime anti-sedition bill imputed criminality from mere membership in an organization, irrespective of personal guilt in an illegal act undertaken by other members. Bettman fought this "guilt-by-association," arguing that conspiracy was covered under existing laws once two or more people act illegally, and that to advocate change is not to advocate violence against the United States unless and until that violence actually occurs. Under the Graham Bill, *talk* of violence would be illegal. Bettman held that this act cut at the very foundations of Anglo-Saxon law and American democracy (Bettman 1920). His reputation as "the man who put Debs behind bars" rapidly changed to that of being the most outspoken legal advocate for free speech and association in America.

Alfred returned to Cincinnati in 1919 where, as president of a revitalized United City Planning Committee, he set out to raise $100,000 in private donations, an amount determined by the committee to be the minimum required for the preparation of a comprehensive plan for the future growth of the city that could serve as a rational guide to capital investment in community facilities (Vitz, p. 6). He also collaborated with Robert H. Whitten, planning consultant to Cleveland,[12] and with a group of Clevelanders in founding the Ohio State Conference on City Planning, now known as the Ohio Planning Conference (OPC), the first statewide citizen's organization in support of planning in the United States, which would become the model for the future American Society of Planning Officials (ASPO). Bettman became the first Ohio Conference vice-president in 1919, and its president in 1920–1 and 1922–3. From the beginning, because of his success in drafting the 1915 Ohio enabling act, he chaired the Ohio Conference Committee on Legislation (Simpson, p. 5). His new activities in support of the United City Planning Committee and the Ohio Conference did not diminish his commitment to earlier associations, however. He remained active in the National Conference on City Planning, serving on its Board of Directors for ten of the next seventeen years (1919–36). Primarily due to Bettman's leadership, the twelfth annual meeting of the Conference was held in Cincinnati, April 19–22, 1920.

All of Bettman's efforts in support of city planning through conferences, the drafting of legislation, and creating the framework for the emerging Plan of Cincinnati, as well as his work in support of civil liberties, was avocational. His vocation was corporate law; everything else was done in his spare time. In his own words, "An ordinary but continuous law practice has served to finance a non-lucrative activity in the legal, legislative and administrative phases of urban planning" (O'Brian, p. 3). His financially rewarding employment in 1921 was as a partner in the law firm of Moulinier, Bettman and Hunt, and as director general and counsel for the Title Guarantee and Trust Company of Cincinnati.

Alfred's national reputation in criminal prosecution was recognized in 1921 by appointment as an advisor to the National Conference on Law Observance and Enforcement, while his brother, Gilbert, rising in those Republican machine-politics to which Alfred was so constitutionally opposed, was elected vice-mayor of Cincinnati. On November 8, 1921, the voters of Cincinnati supported a referendum creating a city manager form of government in an effort to replace machine-politics with good government. Although supported, it would not be implemented for four years (Vexler, p. 51).

Among Alfred Bettman's greatest contributions to American law were his "mortality tables" for criminal cases, tracing the progress of each case from arrest to prosecution and conviction. First undertaken for the Cleveland Foundation Crime Survey in 1921, they indicated frequent failure of prosecution at the pre-trial stages, exposing the lax and often corrupt nature of criminal law enforcement in the United States (Bettman and Burns 1922). In recognition of his emerging reputation in criminal law reform, Bettman was appointed in 1923 to membership on the Judicial Council of Ohio where he would serve for sixteen years, recommending improvements and reform of the judicial system.

By 1922 the United City Planning Committee had succeeded in raising $105,000 from 5000 donors in support of its master plan for the city (Vitz, p. 41). The largest donation was $15,000; the smallest $1.00. The Plan of Cincinnati was included in annual Cincinnati Community Chest (United Way) fund drives for contributions "specially designated." Virtually all collections were made this way. The original idea was that the United City Planning Committee would raise $70,000 and the city would contribute $30,000. The city, in fact, contributed nothing (NCCP 1924, pp. 36–7).

With these funds committed, Bettman and a committee of four appointed by him drafted a contract with the Technical Advisory Corporation (TAC), then at work on their survey of the city for the city planning commission, authorizing the Corporation to prepare a general plan for the city (Vitz, pp. 6–7). The plan was projected to cover a period of fifty years (ICRPC 1925, p. 326). Funds raised by the United City Planning Committee were turned over to the official Cincinnati City Planning Commission, which worked with TAC to produce the plan (NCCP 1924, p. 36; ICRPC 1925, p. 324).

The Technical Advisory Corporation, the first private urban planning consulting firm in the United States, was founded by George B. Ford and Ernest P. Goodrich in 1912. Ford and Goodrich visited Cincinnati frequently during the preparation of the plan and assigned Ladislas Segoe, a 28-year-old recent arrival from Hungary, to be their fulltime onsite project supervisor. Segoe was so new to America that he had to ask an uncle to help him look in a Rand-McNally atlas to see where it was! (Segoe Tape 1, p. 24). Segoe, paid $37.50 a week by TAC to be the onsite producer of the Cincinnati Plan (Segoe Tape 1, p. 31), thus began an intimate day-to-day working relationship with the president of the United City Planning Committee, Alfred Bettman, "a very close, almost a father and son, relationship" (Segoe Tape 1, p. 51), that resulted in the mutual evolution of both the concepts and details of the Plan of Cincinnati.[13] The plan, begun in 1922, was timely, founded as it was in the imperative to realize municipal economy and rationality in the expenditure of public funds: Cincinnati was virtually bankrupt. In an effort to defuse a politically explosive situation, the Republican members of city council voted to reduce their own salaries to aid in solving the financial crisis (Vexler, p. 51). But the "last straw", in terms of both machine-politics and civic economics, was the Cincinnati subway.

Mayor John Galvin (1909–10, 1918–21), a machine Republican, inaugurated the construction of the Cincinnati Rapid Transit System in 1920. This scheme was based on Hunt's survey executed by Bion Arnold, funds from a pre-First World War bond issue, and the building of an extensive subway section under the now-derelict Hamilton Canal in the downtown area (Condit, pp. 165–73). This expensive program, originally instituted by Mayor Hunt and City Solicitor Bettman but undertaken by the political machine with out-of-date financial data and little concern for its overall effect on the postwar finances of the city, had a profound effect on Cincinnati's future. Imposed on a city already suffering from the highest public debts in America, this project severely strained both the economy and the political credibility of the city. Two years after construction began, the city stood on the brink of bankruptcy, and the economic precariousness of the still unfinished and soon-to-be-abandoned subway was publicly revealed. The subway was about half complete when studies made in support of the emerging Plan of Cincinnati determined that the system would not be cost-effective (Upson, pp. 311–13). Construction was "temporarily" halted in 1923, never to be resumed, and $6,000,000 worth of tunnels, stations, and graded rights-of-way were abandoned (Condit, p. 173).

By 1923 political and financial conditions in Cincinnati were simply intolerable. Under Republican Mayor George P. Carrel (1922–5) streets were impassable and the police and fire departments were undermanned. There was so little faith in government that essential tax levies consistently failed at the polls in spite of political-machine support (Bentley, p. 5).

Continuing his work with Ohio planning enabling legislation, Alfred Bettman drafted a bill, adopted in 1923, that gave cities with adopted master plans the right to regulate subdivisions within three miles of their boundaries. Bettman believed that without such "extra-territorial" controls, developers wishing to avoid development restrictions would simply build just outside the municipal boundaries.

While incompetence, corruption, and lack of rational public planning for municipal expenditures were leading Cincinnati to disaster, Alfred Bettman's capabilities in drafting planning-related legislation and his more recent activities in support of state and national planning organizations brought him to national attention for his contribution to city planning, complementing his national recognition for criminal prosecution and for defense of civil liberties. In 1924 he was appointed to Secretary of Commerce Hoover's Advisory Committee on Housing and Zoning for which he drafted a Standard State Zoning Enabling Act that was published by the federal government and used throughout the country, encouraging the establishment of numerous zoning commissions.

Conditions in Cincinnati were deteriorating to the point of absolute frustration. Perhaps seeing "the handwriting on the wall," the Cincinnati City Council unanimously passed the first element of the Plan of Cincinnati, the zoning ordinance, on April 1, 1924 (ICRPC 1925, p. 324) in an effort to identify municipal fiscal economy and rationality with the machine-dominated administration. Bettman could announce the following year that the "city officials are quite committed to the idea" of planning (ibid., p. 325). Nevertheless, a group of reform-minded Cincinnati businessmen under the leadership of the Cincinnatus Association and Murray Seasongood, met on June 15, 1924 to create a "Charter Party" dedicated to revision of the city charter as a means toward permanent removal of the machine from City Hall (Bentley, p. 6). Most were non-machine Republicans. Thanks to Alfred Bettman's leadership of the United City Planning Committee, which had a city plan nearing completion and which had pushed the official city planning commission to a position in support of planning, planning for municipal economy became a basic plank of Charterite politics and now had *both* machine and reformer political support. In the municipal elections of November 1924 the people of Cincinnati voted overwhelmingly in support of the new city charter (92,511 for, 41,105 against), a victory gained by the active participation of a massive number of citizen volunteers. The City Charter Committee was created at a dinner celebrating this bold political upset in order to assure continued political success (Bentley, pp. 6–7).

The Plan of Cincinnati, sponsored by the United City Planning Committee, paid for by public donations, and created between 1922 and 1924 primarily by Alfred Bettman and Ladislas Segoe, under the guidance of George B. Ford and Ernest P. Goodrich of the Technical Advisory Corporation (TAC), was presented to Mayor George P. Carrel's official Cincinnati City Planning Commission as a gift of the people of Cincinnati. The Plan was completed in the middle of 1924, primarily through the day-to-day efforts of Segoe and Bettman, with either Goodrich or Ford coming out to Cincinnati from New York one week each month to monitor the progress and to provide guidance. The final plan document, involving the synthesis of the local studies, was primarily the work of George B. Ford (Segoe Tape 1, pp. 30–1). The Plan of Cincinnati was officially adopted by the commission, with machine-mayor Carrel as its chairman, in the Spring of 1925 (ICRPC 1925, p. 324), becoming the first such long-range master plan for community development to be officially adopted by the planning commission of a major American city. Segoe observed, "How Alfred managed to engineer that I do not know, . . . He wasn't even on the commission" (Segoe Tape 1, pp. 24–5). Having completed the plan in mid-1924, Segoe returned to Hungary, where he was seeking a place to open an office when he received a telegram from TAC offering him a junior partnership in the firm if he would return to America to do an industrial survey for Cincinnati and a master plan for Dayton. He returned to Ohio (ibid., pp. 31–2).

It should be noted that the Plan of Cincinnati, in its two parts, the zoning element (1924) and the capital improvements component (1925), was adopted by the City of Cincinnati *before* the political revolution that brought reform government to Cincinnati, and that both a strong planning commission, operating under Bettman's 1915 guidelines, and the Plan of Cincinnati were in place prior to the election of 1925.

The revised charter, authorized in the election of 1924 and completed in 1925, declared comprehensive planning to be a necessary and permanent part of Cincinnati city government (Bentley, p. 5; Upson, pp. 399–401). In the 1925 elections, the first under the new charter, the Charterites under the leadership of the Cincinnatus Association and Murray Seasongood elected six council members, four non-machine Republicans and two Democrats, against three for the Republican machine (Bentley, p. 7). The machine was defeated! On December 30, 1925 the new Charterite-dominated city council elected Murray Seasongood mayor and appointed Colonel Clarence O. Sherrill as Cincinnati's first city manager, charging Sherrill with bringing businesslike objectivity and economy to the operation of municipal affairs (Vexler, p. 51). It also reaffirmed the powers of the official city planning commission and its commission-adopted plan. The Cincinnati City Planning Commission, the first in the nation to be specifically empowered to establish and officially adopt a comprehensive plan (Kent, p. 200), was now assured political support for the implementation of the Plan of Cincinnati.

Although the Republican machine suffered a fatal setback in Cincinnati, Gilbert Bettman continued his career in party politics when the Ohio Republican organization appointed him chairman of the Republican State Convention in 1924, permitting him to rise in Republican state politics where prospects for future success were much brighter.

Murray Seasongood, the first Charterite mayor of Cincinnati (1926–9), became chairman of the city planning commission in 1926, assuring political implementation and enthusiastic promotion of the Plan. In May of 1926, Alfred Bettman was appointed to the city planning commission that his efforts had created.

Insofar as the primary purpose of the Plan of Cincinnati was that of acting as a guide to rational public investment in capital projects, Bettman suggested shortly after taking his seat on the commission that a capital budget be prepared based on the plan. This concept, developed jointly by Bettman, Segoe, and John B. Blanford, Jr of the Bureau of Government Research (Segoe Tape 1, pp. 56–7), was rapidly adopted in various forms throughout the United States, usually under the title of a Capital Improvement Program

(CIP). But, for many years this was simply referred to as "The Cincinnati Plan," a plan for municipal financial efficiency through long-range capital investment planning based on a comprehensive plan (Scott, pp. 253–4). That is what the comprehensive plan, and the city planning revolution in Cincinnati, was all about.

By 1926 Cincinnati had an operating official city planning commission with strong local support and implementation powers, a master-plan-based capital improvements planning system, and a commission-adopted master plan that was to become the foundation for the evolution of the comprehensive plan idea in America. In two short years, from 1924 to 1926, but based on a decade of preparation, Cincinnati was changed from "the worst governed city in America" to "the best governed city," thanks to Alfred Bettman's concepts of city planning as reform and municipal economy, his implementation of Hunt's concepts of participatory democracy and capital planning, and the Charterite political revolution.

In the 1920s American city planning commissions were generally volunteer committees of laymen that were almost totally lacking in in-house expertise. They were virtually always either grossly underfunded by public sources, or totally dependent on charitable contributions for the continuation of their work. In 1926, when Bettman took his seat on the Cincinnati City Planning Commission, he immediately addressed these two issues; he initiated actions to assure the continuing financial support of the planning function in Cincinnati with public funds (Vitz, p. 9), and arranged for Ladislas Segoe to be employed by the city as a "planning engineer." Segoe thus became a full-time municipally employed professional planner charged with continuing studies and with formulating the implementation actions needed to fulfill the promise of the adopted master plan.

Segoe, who was employed at that time by the TAC, was at Dayton, Ohio, where he was working on a Dayton version of the Cincinnati Plan. He left Goodrich and Ford to accept Cincinnati's offer of $6000 per year and the directorship of a city planning department that consisted of himself, a draftsman, a secretary, and a total annual budget of about $14,000 (Segoe Tape 1, pp. 32–3). This made Segoe the head of one of the best funded municipal planning agencies in the United States.

On January 27, 1926 oral arguments were conducted before eight members of the United States Supreme Court in the case of *Village of Euclid et al.* v. *Ambler Realty Company*, the first such constitutional test of comprehensive zoning. Bettman viewed land use zoning as the most direct tool for guiding private development toward fulfilling the objectives of the comprehensive planning program. Two years earlier, as an appointed member of Secretary of Commerce Herbert Hoover's Advisory Committee on Housing and Zoning, he had drafted a Standard

State Zoning Enabling Act that was published by the federal government and was used throughout the country. By this means, Bettman became the primary author of those state enabling acts that supported the zoning actions that were now being contested as unconstitutional. He not only viewed the zoning power as critical to the success of the comprehensive planning idea, he also viewed zoning and the comprehensive plan as an integral unit. He told the attendees of the 1924 meeting of the Ohio State Planning Conference, "Cincinnati . . . started from the beginning upon the principles of a comprehensive city plan, the zoning ordinance being conceived simply as a part of this plan" (Simpson, p. 12). Through *Euclid*, a primary component of his comprehensive plan idea, a component for which he had been the primary legal author, was under attack as unconstitutional.

The Village of Euclid, Ohio, adopted a zoning ordinance on November 13, 1922. This ordinance, for all intents and purposes, was the New York City Zoning Code of 1916, the first comprehensive zoning code to be adopted by an American city, with the names and locations changed to fit this tiny village located a short distance to the east of Cleveland (Toll, p. 231). The Ambler Realty Company had 68 acres in Euclid that were not zoned to its liking. It instituted legal action. The ordinance being upheld in the Ohio courts, Ambler claimed violation of the "due process" clause of the US Constitution and entered the federal courts. James F. Metzenbaum, noted Cleveland attorney and advocate of planning control actions, the attorney who had amended the New York City Zoning Code to fit Euclid (Toll, p. 229), represented the Village. Newton D. Baker, former reform mayor of Cleveland, and President Wilson's Secretary of War, represented Ambler. Judge Westenhaver of the US District Court for the Northern District of Ohio found for Ambler. Metzenbaum took the case directly to the US Supreme Court (Metzenbaum, 1:57).

Chief Justice William Howard Taft, a Cincinnatian and personal friend of Alfred Bettman, presided over the oral arguments in *Euclid* v. *Ambler*. At the end of the day, Metzenbaum realized that he had failed to convince the court and filed a request for permission to file a reply brief. Chief Justice Taft concurred, taking this opportunity to correct a critical oversight. Alfred Bettman had been promised the opportunity to file a brief in support of the zoning power which, due to the forgetfulness of a court clerk, had not been requested and thus had not been heard (Scott, pp. 238–9). Reopening the case permitted Taft to fulfill the obligation to Bettman. While the case was being reopened to argument, Judge Sutherland, the one Justice absent during the earlier oral arguments, began to draft the majority opinion of the court in support of Ambler, holding that comprehensive zoning is unconstitutional!

Taft's friendship with Bettman and, one may suppose, his long-term support of planning[14] led him to schedule reargument of the case, permitting Metzenbaum to sharpen his arguments and Bettman to present his promised brief in support of the zoning power. It has also been reported that Justice Sutherland's convictions became clouded while he was developing the majority opinion against zoning, contributing to Chief Justice Taft's decision to rehear the case (McCormack, p. 712). Such reargument was a Supreme Court rarity. Bettman's *amici curiae* brief changed the course of American urban history.[15] Bettman's brief, a brilliant defense of the zoning power, is credited with swaying the court toward support of Euclid's position. On November 26, 1926, the Supreme Court issued its opinion: a 6:3 vote for Euclid, with Mr Justice Sutherland writing the majority opinion *in support* of the zoning power! (Metzenbaum, 3:1904). *Euclid* is the constitutional foundation for all current American zoning. Before *Euclid*, although eleven states had upheld the zoning power in state courts, more states had decided against zoning than had decided for it. Bettman, through his *Euclid* brief, reversed the tide, thus saving the day for both zoning and comprehensive planning in America.

In mid-1928 Ladislas Segoe left the employ of the City of Cincinnati in favor of a locally based private consulting practice (Segoe Tape 1, p. 36). Myron D. Downs replaced Segoe as the director of planning for Cincinnati.

Bettman's views on the integration of zoning and comprehensive planning, "The Building Zone Ordinance printed herein . . . is an integral part of the City Plan" (*Official City Plan*, 1925, foreword), were to be forcefully expressed again when *A Standard City Planning Enabling Act* was published by Secretary Hoover's Department of Commerce in 1928. The result of a three-year effort by a nine-person committee, this proposed state enabling act was primarily based on Alfred Bettman's legal draftsmanship. The Standard Act accepted zoning, the immediate control of private property rights, as a part of the comprehensive plan. It permitted piece-at-a-time adoption of components of the comprehensive plan, and it stated that zoning, to be legal and to be effective, had to be based on and intended to fulfill the purposes and objectives of a comprehensive plan. As Kent observes (p. 33), this uncharacteristically confused work, although totally supported by all of Bettman's earlier work at Cincinnati, where these conditions had been fulfilled with positive results, created a plethora of state enabling acts that in fact permitted, and fostered, the adoption of zoning ordinances that were not based on comprehensive planning at all. Under the terms of this Standard Act, any zoning, once adopted, could be claimed to be "part one" of a comprehensive plan and therefore always based *on* a comprehensive plan (itself!), even when executed totally out of context of a comprehensive planning process. Instead of creating the legal foundations for a system assuring that local land use control is predicated on long-range comprehensive community development objectives and capital investment implications, as was clearly intended, this "model," widely adopted in the United States, had the reverse effect. It discouraged comprehensive planning and confused public understanding of it by making the act of zoning, by definition, synonymous with comprehensive planning. This legal confusion still characterizes planning and zoning in vast areas of the United States today, a half century after this strange lapse in Bettman's usually clear thought and normal careful channeling of legal efforts to assure the desired results. Bettman later realized the error of including zoning in the comprehensive plan. When the next Plan of Cincinnati was being prepared under his direction, in the 1940s, a careful distinction was made between long-range land use planning in the comprehensive plan and immediate land use control through zoning (Segoe Tape 1, p. 60).

Alfred Bettman's national reputation for effective criminal prosecution kept pace in the late 1920s with his growing national impact on American urban planning. In 1929 Alfred began a four-year term as a member of President Herbert Hoover's Commission on Criminal Prosecution Procedure, the "Wickersham Commission." In that same year his brother, Gilbert, still rising in Ohio Republican machine-politics, began a two-term, four-year, period in office as Attorney General of the State of Ohio, sworn to uphold all of Ohio's laws, including those anti-sedition laws to which his brother, Alfred, was so strongly opposed.

The Ohio Criminal Syndicalism Act of 1919, an anti-sedition act that had seen many arrests but no convictions in its ten-year history, was applied on July 12, 1929 when two members of the Communist Party were arrested for the crime of distributing leaflets outside a steel plant in Martins Ferry. In reaction, on "International Red Day," August 1, 1929, three members of the party from Cleveland came to Martins Ferry to pass out handbills that threatened "revolutionary mass action" and predicted "the overthrow of capitalism." They were arrested, found guilty, and sentenced to five years in prison, although they had not distributed a single leaflet, having been arrested before the meeting began. The International Labor Defense (ILD), a clear adjunct of the American Communist Party, established an appeal. Being underfunded, the ILD asked the American Civil Liberties Union for help. The ACLU, in turn, asked one of the leading American spokesman for civil liberties, Alfred Bettman, to defend the Communists. The case, *Johnson et al.* v. *State of Ohio* (Gilbert Bettman, Attorney General) was heard under appeal in the 7th District Court of Appeals for Belmont County, St Clairsville, Ohio (Sterling, pp. 94–7).

Plate 6.2 Alfred Bettman *c.* 1930.
Source: Cincinnati Historical Society.

The Communist Party wanted to use the trial as a propaganda device, preferring to *lose* the case after maximum publicity in order to create class martyrs and to stimulate increased labor agitation. Alfred Bettman refused the Communist Party the help of the ACLU unless the case was fought solely on legal and constitutional ground, and was fought to win. Being without funds, the party had no choice but to agree. The case was heard against the background of the financial "Crash" of October, 1929.

Bettman prepared a careful brief, focusing on the fact that, since none of the handbills had been distributed prior to the arrest, the State of Ohio was using this act to prevent an opinion from being heard. He argued that this was a clear violation of the US Constitution's guarantee of free speech. On May 24, 1930 the court upheld Bettman's views, adding that even if the handbills had been distributed they did not incite an unlawful act. The Communist Party lost both its propaganda and its martyrs (Sterling, p. 150). Seven months later, Bettman won a similar case at Cadiz, Ohio.[16] In both cases he donated his services in defense of civil liberties against his brother's sworn duty to uphold the laws of Ohio.

Murray Seasongood, the first Charterite mayor of Cincinnati, resigned the chairmanship of the Cincinnati City Planning Commission in 1930. Alfred Bettman was appointed to replace him. He would serve as chairman of the Commission until his death in 1945. As chairman, Bettman kept the City Planning Commission together during the darkest days of the Great Depression, from 1930 to 1933, when planning commissions throughout the country lost their meager funding and their staff positions to municipal economy drives generated by the deepening economic crisis (Simpson, p. 29). The major capital construction projects projected in the 1925 Plan of Cincinnati, such as the Western Hills Viaduct (1930–2) and the immense Cincinnati Union Terminal passenger railroad complex (1929–33), became the vehicles for Depression-era unemployment relief. The Union Terminal complex, consisting of twenty-four buildings, was financed by a city-backed $42 million bond issue that was floated just one month before the Crash of 1929, giving the city cash-in-hand for unemployment relief construction at the very beginning of the economic catastrophe. It also permitted construction with pre-Depression dollars at Depression wages and prices, resulting in an even more grand facility than originally contemplated (see Condit, pp. 215–73 for a superb account of these projects). In 1931, as the Depression deepened, Alfred Bettman again answered Herbert Hoover's call, this time to serve as a member of the City Planning Committee of President Hoover's Conference on Home Building and Home Ownership. This conference revealed the true extent of the national economic problem and the total collapse of the American home-building industry.

In 1932, in the depths of the Depression, Alfred Bettman, the chairman of the Cincinnati City Planning Commission, served once again as the president of the Ohio State Conference on Planning (now known as the Ohio Planning Conference), and championed concepts being propounded by his friend Ernest J. Bohn, a member of the Cleveland City Council (1930–40) and future chairman of the Cleveland City Planning Commission, that called for the public construction of low cost housing and a 50 per cent federal subsidy for such housing (Simpson, pp. 36–7). These concepts, formulated and propounded in the more liberal environment of Cleveland and Cincinnati, were decidedly unpopular with the dominant conservative Republicans at the Statehouse in Columbus, and with the Hoover Administration in Washington. But the Columbus Republicans were out of step with emerging public values. In the election of November 1932,

Gilbert Bettman, running as a Republican candidate for the US Senate from Ohio, was swept aside, his national political aspirations crushed, by the anti-Republican, anti-conservative, and anti-Hoover Democratic landslide that brought Franklin Delano Roosevelt and the New Deal to Washington.

Alfred Bettman's long-term high national repute in such areas as planning and zoning, criminal prosecution, and the defense of civil liberties, combined with the fact that in 1932 he was serving as president of both the Ohio Planning Conference and the National Conference on City Planning, being the visible head of the planning movement in both Ohio and the nation as a whole, brought him to the attention of the New Deal. Thanks to Alfred Bettman's maintenance of the City Planning Commission during the "dark days" of the early 1930s, Cincinnati was among the few American cities that were adequately staffed with planners and ready to take advantage of New Deal programs when they began to flow in 1933 (Simpson, p. 29). Cincinnati became a New Deal showcase for federal new town construction (Greenhills)[17] and for the implementation of Ernie Bohn's public housing concepts.

Bettman, a Democrat, a legal expert, and an experienced public planner, was particularly valuable to the Roosevelt Administration. In 1933 he was appointed legal consultant to a federal commission charged with the development of the Tennessee River. His work led directly to the creation of the Tennessee Valley Authority ("Chairman," *New York Times*, 1/23/45). From 1933 to 1941, he promoted state planning. This concept was eagerly supported by the Secretary of the Interior, Harold Ickes, and was implemented throughout the country at that time, creating the foundation for most current state planning activity in America. But not in Bettman's own Ohio where Statehouse Republicans consistently defeated every attempt to create a state planning board. In 1934 Bettman accepted the chairmanship of the Fourth Region of the new National Planning Board, consisting of the states of Ohio, West Virginia, Tennessee, and Indiana, and served the newly created American Society of Planning Officials, now the American Planning Association, as its first president (1934–8).

The last half of the 1930s were fruitful years for the indefatigable corporate lawyer chairman of the Cincinnati City Planning Commission. In 1935, in *US* v. *Certain Lands in Louisville*, Bettman produced legal arguments in support of Ernie Bohn's housing concepts that were then being implemented by the Roosevelt Administration through the Public Works Administration. These arguments, published at the time in an article entitled "Is housing a public use?" would later be accepted by the US Supreme Court, creating the legal foundations for all future public housing programs in America. Bettman also began to write a section of the

ASPO Newsletter in 1935 called "Planning law and legislation," that came to be a separate publication called *Zoning Digest* (Vitz, p. 40), and the only book ever written by Alfred Bettman, *Model Laws for Planning Cities, Counties and States*, co-authored with Edward Murray Bassett, Robert Whitten, and Frank B. Williams, was published by Harvard University. From 1935 to 1938 he served one of many three-year terms as a member of the Board of Directors of the American City Planning Institute. In 1936 he became the chairman of the Ohio Valley Regional Planning Commission. His national visibility in leadership roles in planning associations, his clear support for public housing, and his legal contributions to the public housing issue in *US* v. *Certain Lands in Louisville* led, in 1936, to his chairmanship of the ASPO committee on the federal Wagner Housing Bill. This bill became the US Housing Act of 1937, the first major federal legislative commitment to public housing in America. The 1937 act implemented Ernie Bohn's concepts on a national scale. Bettman's committee became ASPO's permanent Committee on Planning Legislation, which he would chair until 1942 (Vitz, p. 43).

Alfred Bettman's planning-related activities in the 1930s were not limited to the United States. In 1937 he represented the United States on the Executive Committee of the International Congress for Housing and Town Planning. A member of the British Town Planning Institute, he spent many summers in attendance at town planning courses in the United Kingdom. But war clouds were gathering in Europe and Asia. As America walked to the brink of the Second World War, Alfred Bettman served as a member of the Board of Governors of ASPO (1938–40) and saw the American City Planning Institute, that he helped to found in 1917 and which he served as a member of the Board of Governors from 1935 to 1938, become the American Institute of Planners in 1939.[18]

In 1941 Bettman was serving as a consultant to the National Resources Planning Board, drafting the planning statutes for Puerto Rico. These statutes are commonly recognized as the most advanced planning enabling legislation ever enacted in America. 1941 also saw his brother, Gilbert, still involved in Ohio Republican politics, elected as a Justice of the Ohio Supreme Court, the position he held when stricken, at the age of 60, by a fatal heart attack on July 17 of the following year.

As with the early Depression years, the early years of the Second World War devastated local planning departments: staff positions were abolished and budgets were cut to support programs more directly related to the war efforts and to reflect grossly diminished available manpower. Most American cities did little during the war years with regard to long-range urban planning, permitting their planning processes, staff, and local support to atrophy and exhibiting little concern for the future postwar era. But at Cincinnati things were different. Again, as in the

Plate 6.3 Alfred Bettman *c.* 1944.
Source: Courtesy of Professor Jay Chatterjee, Director,
School of Planning, The University of Cincinnati.

Depression, Alfred Bettman held the planning commission together during trying times and made positive progress toward planning for the future. While other planning agencies slowed their non-war-related activities to a crawl, the Cincinnati City Planning Commission continued its technical studies. Realizing the need for a total reevaluation and expansion of the comprehensive plan for the city that had been originally adopted more than fifteen years earlier, Bettman used the war years to execute new long-range planning studies of the Cincinnati region toward the end of the adoption of a new master plan for the city as soon as possible following the end of the war. An appropriation to the City Planning Commission to prepare the revised master plan was provided by an ordinance passed by City Council on February 16, 1944 (*Official City Plan*, 1948, foreword). But preliminary studies had been begun much earlier. In the course of these studies, Bettman concluded that control of perimeter development, the key issue in planning during the 1920s, would have to be complemented in the new plan with new devices for the reconstruction of the older deteriorating core areas of the central city. 1941 to 1943 "were the formative years for his pioneering work in urban redevelopment enabling legislation" (Vitz, p. 41), when he served as chairman of the ASPO Urban Redevelopment Committee (Bettman, 1943). Bettman built the legislative bases for the area redevelopment program, now commonly referred to as the "urban renewal" clearance program, to fulfill the postwar need for rebuilding the deteriorated areas of the city of Cincinnati and to fulfill the promise of the new comprehensive plan that was taking shape under his leadership and that of Myron Downs and Sherwood Reeder, director of Master Plan Studies for the City of Cincinnati. As chairman of the Legislative Committee of the American Institute of Planners, he drafted model state legislation to support such central city redevelopment, including an Ohio Urban Redevelopment Act, in which reconstruction was to be primarily undertaken by private enterprise with local project control. But he argued that the financing of such large-scale undertakings was beyond the capacities of a local municipal government and had to be carried by either state or federal government. "He was utterly devoted to the cause of urban redevelopment" (Hansen, p. 38).

Alfred Bettman's wartime vision resulted in Cincinnati's being virtually the only American city that was ready to meet the challenge and promise of the postwar era. Thanks to his efforts, the new Cincinnati Master Plan, adopted on November 22, 1948, a decade in advance of most other American cities and the first to be adopted by a major American city following the end of the war, coordinated postwar construction and reconstruction activities in Cincinnati in an unprecedented manner, permitting the careful targeting of capital projects and redevelopment activities in the context of a coherent overall program of public policies. This master plan was primarily the work of Bettman, Myron Downs, Sherwood Reeder, Malcomb Dill, and consultants Ladislas Segoe and Tracy Augur. The plan's adoption was dedicated to the memory of Alfred Bettman (Official City Plan, 1948, introduction) who did not live to see this fruit of his efforts.

Robert A. Taft, US Senator from Ohio, known throughout the nation during the mid-to-late 1940s as "Mr Republican," was a friend of Alfred Bettman, a fellow Cincinnatian, and son of Chief Justice William Howard Taft who manipulated the outcome of the *Euclid* decision. Robert A. Taft, while a member of the Ohio Legislature, had introduced rural zoning bills for Alfred Bettman although he was politically lukewarm to these ideas being by nature a staunch conservative (Simpson, p. 38). Alfred solicited Taft's support for federally funded urban redevelopment legislation that he drafted to permit America's postwar cities to undertake the large-scale urban reconstruction that his ongoing studies toward a new comprehensive plan for Cincinnati indicated as essential. He also solicited his support for "test case" legislation to be introduced in Congress establishing such a redevelopment program for the District of Columbia as a model for the rest of the country. Most significantly, Bettman, the Democrat, convinced "Mr Republican" Taft of the need for a new postwar federal public housing program to replace the now-financially-depleted US Housing Act of 1937 that had resulted from the Wagner Housing Bill. He further convinced Taft that this new US Housing Act should be a vehicle for fulfilling public housing and area redevelopment purposes, and to encourage overall comprehensive planning. Conservative Republican Taft, convinced that such a program was essential by Bettman's wartime studies of the postwar needs of his own home town, Cincinnati, was no longer a lukewarm friend to such planning ideas, and introduced this legislation in Congress with the support of Senator Allen J. Ellender and liberal Democrat Robert F. Wagner of New York. This legislation, debated during the end-of-the-war years, became the US Housing Act of 1949, the foundation for American postwar central city reconstruction and public housing activities, and for the future "701" comprehensive planning assistance provision of the US Housing Act of 1954. Taft's support of these programs, embodied in a bill co-sponsored with arch-liberal Wagner, probably cost him his presidential aspirations as such "Rooseveltian" approaches were anathema to most conservative Republicans.

Because of Alfred Bettman's wartime activities, Cincinnati was ready in 1949, upon passage of the new US Housing Act including both area redevelopment and public housing programs, to utilize immediately these programs in the context of the new master plan Cincinnati had adopted the year before, fulfilling those specific and local needs in Cincinnati *that they were created to address.*

During the first week of January, 1945, while the US Supreme Court, in *Cleveland* v. *US*, supported the constitutionality of public housing programs based on the legal logic that had been developed by Bettman in *US* v. *Certain Lands in Louisville* ten years earlier, Alfred Bettman traveled to Washington with his wife, Lillian, to testify to Senator Taft's Subcommittee on Housing and Urban Redevelopment of the Senate Special Committee on Postwar Economic Policy and Planning (Bassett, Jan. 1945). He testified as chairman of the American Bar Association Committee on Planning Law and Legislation, and as a representative of the American Institute of Planners,[19] specifically as chairman of the Institute's Committee on Federal Activities (Scott, p. 418). He spoke in support of postwar redevelopment legislation, urging the federal government to adopt a program, such as that which he had drafted for Ohio, permitting cities to demolish deteriorated central city areas and to lease or sell these areas to private enterprise for proper guided reconstruction ("Alfred Bettman," *Cincinnati Enquirer*, 1/22/45; Hansen, p. 38). He argued the need for federal finance of such projects (Evans, p. 4). Following his testimony on behalf of the American Institute of Planners, he appeared again as legal counsel to the National Capital Park and Planning Commission to promote these concepts further (O'Brian, p. 3). While in Washington he attended a meeting of the Board of Directors of the American Planning and Civic Association (Bassett, Jan. 1945), and then proceeded to New York City, where he attended a meeting of the American Institute of Planners.

> Alfred Bettman passed away yesterday en route home from New York.
> *(Telegram from Sherwood Reeder to Ernest Bohn, January 22, 1945)*

In the early morning hours of January 21, 1945, while returning to Cincinnati with Lillian, Alfred Bettman suffered a fatal heart attack aboard a Pennsylvania Railroad train as it passed through Altoona, Pennsylvania. He was seventy-one. His remains were returned to his beloved Cincinnati, where they were buried in United Jewish Cemetery.[20]

In all probability, no single person contributed more to the development of American city and regional planning between 1920 and 1945 than Alfred Bettman of Cincinnati. He published about eighty-five works on planning and housing during his lifetime (Bettman, 1946, p. 41). "In fact, a full list of his planning activities would parallel the historical evolution of the American movement for municipal, state, and national planning in all of its aspects" (ibid., p. xvi). Cincinnati, the State of Ohio, and the federal government became his laboratories for experimental statutes, ordinances, bills, and planning methods intended to "make planning not merely to fit into, but actually preserve and strengthen democracy" in America (Vitz, p. 46). He did all of this as an avocation, as a hobby, as a self-fulfilling uncompensated service adjunct to his vocation of corporate law. When asked how he could afford to donate so much of his time and effort to his planning interests,[21] Bettman said, "Well, when I come to the end, I would like to feel that I have been a part of the life of my time" (O'Brian, p. 6). Alfred Bettman was not only "a part of the life" of his time, but also a primary shaper of modern American urban planning practices and, through them, a primary shaper of the modern American city . . . and he did it all in his spare time.[22]

Notes

Portions of this paper were presented at a session of the Annual Conference of the Association of Collegiate Schools of Planning held at Howard University, Washington, D.C., on Friday, October 23, 1981.

1 The Tyler Davidson Fountain, a gift to the people of Cincinnati from Henry Probasco in honor of his late brother-in-law, Tyler Davidson, was dedicated

on October 6, 1871. Designed by August von Kreling, the 43-foot high fountain is topped by a figure of the "genius of waters," "beckoning" to the City of Cincinnati.

2 Alfred's mother, Rebecca, was born in Cincinnati of immigrant parents from Alsace.

3 The 1884 riot resulted from protest over the results of a trial in which two men, one white and one a mulatto, were convicted of murdering their employer. The white man received a lighter sentence than the mulatto, precipitating a violent outburst of mob action (Vexler, p. 41).

4 Isaac Mayer Wise founded Hebrew Union University in Cincinnati in 1875. He died March 26, 1900.

5 Among the more prominent Christian proponents of the Social Gospel was Washington Gladden (Solomon Washington Gladden) who directed the First Congregational Church in Colombus, Ohio, from 1882 to 1914. He preached that religious principles must be applied to current social problems. Among his more influential works were *Social Salvation* (1902) and *Where Does the Sky Begin?* (1904). He died July 2, 1918.

6 In 1906 George B. Cox and others were brought to trial for taking money from the city treasury. The court ruled that taking the money, under the circumstances, was not a criminal act! Cox was tried again in 1914 for the misapplication of state funds. The case was dismissed (Vexler, pp. 47, 50).

7 Street railway strikers broke into violence on May 19, 1913. The city seized six strike-closed ice plants on the advice of the Board of Health, ice being essential then for the safe preservation of food.

8 The first National Conference on City Planning was held four years earlier, in Washington, D.C., in 1909.

9 The entry in the *Dicionary of American Biography*, Supplement Issue: *1941–1945*, would appear to be in error when it reports relative to Bettman that "in 1917 [sic] he joined the United City Planning Committee."

10 The entry in the *Dictionary of American Biography* (see n. 9, above) would also appear to be in error in stating that in "that year (1917) the committee successfully lobbied for an enabling act, drafted by Bettman, which allowed cities in Ohio to create planning boards."

11 The American City Planning Institute was created under the initiative of Flavel Shurtleff, an attorney from Boston, and Frederick Law Olmsted, Jr, landscape architect, from Cambridge. They developed the idea of a professional institute for planners at an earlier Boston meeting and during the train ride to Kansas City (Scott, p. 163).

12 Robert H. Whitten had previously been secretary to the New York City Commission on Building Districts and Restrictions, receiving national recognition when the report of this group became the New York Zoning Code of 1916, the first comprehensive zoning code to be enacted in the United States.

13 "We spent some weekends picnicing together, we went to the conferences, traveled together, we spent summer vacations on Georgian Bay fishing, feeding worms [sic], and gathering berries together, and canoeing together and we were together much of the time we were talking about planning" (Segoe Tape 1, pp. 51–2).

14 William Howard Taft, former dean of the University of Cincinnati Law School, received Daniel Burnham's Plan of Manila when he was Secretary of War, called the first National Conference on City Planning in 1909, and signed into law, as President, the federal act creating the National Commission of Fine Arts that acted to implement the McMillan Plan for Washington, D.C.

15 The Ohio State Planning Conference provided Bettman with the sum of $382 in support of his *amicus* brief in the *Euclid* case and his travel to Washington, D.C. (Simpson, p. 14).
16 *Gannet and Yoki* v. *State of Ohio*.
17 The federally built new town of Greenhills was located at Cincinnati because of the city's history of good planning during the previous decade (Scott, p. 337).
18 The American Institute of Planners (AIP) is now known as the American Institute of Certified Planners (AICP).
19 Alfred Bettman served as a member of the Board of Governors of the American Institute of Planners from 1941 to 1944.
20 Lillian passed away three years later, on July 19, 1948.
21 The donation of so much of his time to public service projects resulted, for a corporate lawyer, in a rather frugal and modest life style.
22 The author wishes to recognize the contributions of Luis Roberto Martinez, graduate student in the City and Regional Planning Department at The Ohio State University, who assisted in the basic research upon which this paper is based. The cooperation of The Ohio Historical Society, in locating historic views of Cincinnati that helped the author to comprehend the physical realities of the city over time, is also most sincerely appreciated.

References

"Alfred Bettman dies suddenly when returning aboard train from business trip to East," *The Cincinnati Enquirer*, January 22, 1945, pp. 1, 6.

American Planning Association (1980) *The Ladislas Segoe Tapes*, transcript of an interview with Ladislas Segoe conducted May 22–24, 1978 in Cincinnati, Ohio by Sydney H. Williams, AICP, Washington, D.C. and Chicago, The American Planning Association.

Bassett, Edward M. (1945) "In Memoriam, Alfred Bettman 1873–1945," *Planning and Civic Comment*, 11, 65.

Bassett, Edward M., Williams, Frank B., Bettman, Alfred, and Whitten, Robert (1935) *Model Laws for Planning Cities, Counties and States*, Cambridge, Mass., Harvard University Press.

Bent, Silas (1926) "Liberating a city," *The Century Magazine*, pp. 304–11.

Bentley, Henry, chairman, Committee on Citizen's Charter Organization (1934) *The Cincinnati Plan of Citizen Organization for Political Activity*, New York, National Municipal League, September.

Bettman, Alfred (1920) *Do We Need More Sedition Laws?* Testimony before the Committee on Rules of the House of Representatives, National Popular Government League Pamphlet no. 20, New York, Graphic Press.

——— (October 1928) "The Paris International Housing and Town Planning Congress," *City Planning*, 4, 261–8.

——— (1935) "Is housing a public use?" *Proceedings of the Joint Conference on City, Regional, State and National Planning*, Chicago, National Association of Housing Officials, pp. 63–8.

——— (1943) "Federal and state urban redevelopment bills," *American Planning and Civic Annual*, pp. 166–71.

——— (1946) *City and Regional Planning Papers*, in Comey, Arthur C. (ed.) Cambridge, Mass., Harvard University Press.

Bettman, Alfred, and Burns, Howard (1922) *Prosecution: Criminal Justice in Ohio, Part II*, Cleveland, The Cleveland Foundation.

Black, Russell VanNest (1967) *Planning and the Planning Profession: The Past 50 Years, 1917–1967*, Washington, D.C., American Institute of Planners.

"Chairman of Cincinnati Planning Board dies on train," *The New York Times*, January 23, 1945, obituaries, p. 19.

Charter Commission of the City of Cincinnati (1914) *The Charter of the City of Cincinnati*, Cincinnati.

The Cincinnati Metropolitan Master Plan and the Official City Plan of the City of Cincinnati (1948) Cincinnati, City Planning Commission.

Coben, Stanley (1963) *A. Mitchell Palmer: Politician*, New York, Columbia University Press.

Condit, Carl W. (1967) *The Railroad and the City: A Technological and Urbanistic History of Cincinnati*, Columbus, Ohio, The Ohio State University Press.

Dictionary of American Biography, Supplement Issue: *1941–1945*, s.v. "Bettman, Alfred."

Evans, Lee "Boon to cities envisioned in plan to reclaim slums," *Cincinnati Enquirer*, January 22, 1945, p. 4.

Ford, George B. (ed.) (1917) *City Planning Progress in the United States, 1917*, Washington, D.C., The Journal of the American Institute of Architects.

Hansen, Alvin H. (1945) "Institute affairs: Alfred Bettman," *Journal of the American Institute of Planners*, 11, 38–9.

Hebble, Charles R., and Goodwin, Frank P. (eds) (1916) *The Citizens Book*, Cincinnati, Stewart & Kidd, Co.

International City and Regional Planning Conference (1925) *Planning Problems of Town, City and Region, Papers and Discussions at the International City and Regional Planning Conference* held at New York City, April 20–25, Baltimore, Norman, Remington Co.

Kent, T. J., Jr (1964) *The Urban General Plan*, San Francisco, Chandler Publishing Company.

McCormack, Alfred (1946) "A law clerk's recollections," *Columbia Law Review*, 45, 710–12.

Metzenbaum, James F. (1955) *The Law of Zoning*, 2nd ed., 3 vols., New York, Baker Voorhis & Co.

Miller, Zane L. (1968) *Boss Cox's Cincinnati*, New York, Oxford University Press.

National Conference on City Planning (1924) *Planning Problems of Town, City and Region, Papers and Discussions at the Sixteenth National Conference on City Planning* held at Los Angeles, California, April 7–10, Baltimore, Norman, Remington Co.

O'Brian, John Lord (1945) "Alfred Bettman, 1873–1945," *Journal of the American Institute of Planners*, 11, 1–6.

The Official City Plan of Cincinnati, Ohio (1925) Cincinnati, City Planning Commission.

Scott, Mel (1969) *American City Planning since 1890*, Berkeley and Los Angeles, University of California Press.

Simpson, Michael (1969) *People and Planning: History of the Ohio Planning Conference*, Bay Village, Ohio, The Ohio Planning Conference.

"State of Ohio: An Act to Provide for a City Planning Commission in Municipalities" (1916) *Proceedings of the Eighth National Conference on City Planning*, Boston, University Press, Appendix III, pp. 144–6.

Sterling, David L. (1969) "The 'naive liberal', the 'devious Communist' and the Johnson Case," *Ohio History*, 78, 94–103.

Toll, Seymour I. (1969) *Zoned American*, New York, Grossman Publishers.

Upson, Lent D. (ed.) (1924) *The Government of Cincinnati and Hamilton County*, Cincinnati, City Survey Committee.

Vexler, Robert I. (1975) *Cincinnati: A Chronological and Documentary History 1676–1970*, Dobbs Ferry, New York, Oceana Publications, Inc.

Vitz, Martin H. (1964) "The contribution of Alfred Bettman to city and regional planning," Master's thesis, The Ohio State University (typewritten).

Other sources

"Alfred Bettman 1873–1945" (1945) *American Society of Planning Officials Newsletter*, p. 14.

Bettman, Alfred (1931a) "Master plans and official maps," *Planning Problems of Town, City and Region, Papers and Discussions at the Twenty-Third National Conference on City Planning* held at Rochester, New York, June 22–24, Philadelphia, Wm. F. Fell Co.

—— (1931b) *Report on Prosecution. National Commission on Law Observance and Enforcement*, Washington, D.C., United States Government Printing Office.

"Bettman's work draws praise; Mayor Lauds fame as planner," *Cincinnati Enquirer*, January 22, 1945, p. 6.

Cincinnati Facts and Figures (1918) Cincinnati, Times-Star Co.

"An expression of our appreciation," a tribute to Frederic A. Delano and Alfred Bettman (1943) *American Society of Planning Officials Newsletter*, p. 74.

"Gilbert Bettman, Ohio jurist, dead," *The New York Times*, July 18, 1942, obituaries, p. 13.

Goss, Charles F. (1912) *Cincinnati: The Queen City 1788–1912*, 4 vols., Chicago, Clarke Publishing Co.

"Mrs A. Bettman, 71, clubwoman in Ohio." *The New York Times*, July 20, 1948, obituaries, p. 23.

National Municipal League (1934) *The Cincinnati Plan of Citizen Organization for Political Activity*, New York.

Nolen, John (ed.) (1929) *City Planning*, New York, D. Appleton & Co.

"Planning Metropolitan Cincinnati" (1947) *Planning 1947: Proceedings of the Annual Meeting of the American Society of Planning Officials held at Cincinnati, Ohio, May 5–9, 1947*, Chicago, ASPO.

US Congress, Senate (1945) Special Committee on Postwar Economic Policy and Planning, *Hearings before the Sub-Committee on Housing and Urban Redevelopment* on S.B. 102, pt 9. 79th Cong., 1st sess.

Walker, Robert A. (1941) *The Planning Function in Urban Government*, Chicago, University of Chicago Press.

Who Was Who in America, 1943–1950, vol. 2, 1950 edn, s.v. "Alfred Bettman."

7 Woman-made America: the case of early public housing policy

Eugenie Ladner Birch

The 1937 Wagner–Steagall Act provided for the first permanent public housing program subsidized by the federal government. Although immediate economic conditions caused by the Depression provided the direct impetus for its passage, a painstakingly constructed intellectual background and grass-roots political support created the climate for its acceptance. This atmosphere was the product of the work of many housing reformers. However, two women, Edith Elmer Wood and Catherine Bauer, stand out as leaders having the most significant impact on the formulation of the new policy. As women, they contributed two major facets to it: the recognition of the need for government construction of dwellings when the private sector did not build; the demand that publicly constructed homes be positively supportive of family life.

The August 19, 1937, headline announced: "Housing Bill voted by House as gag blocks opponents . . . measure is pushed through heated night session."[1] The last obstacle to the Wagner–Steagall Act fell away. As public housing became a reality, its supporters breathed with relief. For the first time, the federal government took tentative steps toward accepting permanent responsibility for the construction of decent, low-cost homes and for the elimination of hazardous, unhealthy slums. Like most social decisions in pluralistic America, neither the president nor Congress had generated this policy directly. Instead strong interest groups had captured the support of New York Senator Robert F. Wagner, and he promoted the Housing Act which responded to their ideas. In this way, housing became a legitimate national concern, to be broadened later by more ambitious legislation passed between 1949 and 1968.

The federal presence in housing matters was a major change from former practice. Until the New Deal, localities, under their police powers, were perceived as responsible for maintenance of adequate dwellings. Cities limited the scope of their work by intent and practice to regulation in the form of tenement and house codes. Traditionally, private enterprise provided all residential construction and rebuilt declining urban areas when economically feasible. However, with increasing frequency in the twentieth century, this sector had been unable or unwilling to perform these functions completely, leaving a vacuum to be filled by public endeavor.

Plate 7.1 Catherine Bauer.

The new federal role was the product of the efforts of the American housing movement. Consisting of an amorphous, sometimes divided, coalition of social workers, economists, labor leaders, lawyers and municipal officials, the housers waged their battle between 1914 and 1937.

Although this coalition and its approach were similar to many other alliances of the period, it differed in one significant way.[2] It was led predominantly by women. Springing from traditional female interests in social housekeeping on local levels, it grew to national importance as

Plate 7.2 Edith Elmer Wood.
Source: Avery Library, Columbia University.

women united to promote their ideas. Along the way, women supplied the intellectual basis, political leadership, and executive expertise as well as the rank and file support which gave early housing policy a distinct character. This article will focus on the development of female leadership.

Two features of early housing policy can be clearly attributed to female influence. The first was the insistence that government was to build homes for the low-income slum dweller because the private sector would not do so. Earlier reformers, primarily men such as Lawrence Veiller and E. R. L. Gould, had supported publicly financed slum clearance but not governmental construction of new units. The second was the demand

Plate 7.3 Mary Kingsbury Simkhovitch.

that the publicly constructed homes be positively supportive of family life, not merely provision of minimal shelter. Public housing architecture would reflect domestic needs as long as women participated in the implementation of the program.

Key women of the early housing movement

In the evolution of these ideas, two women played key roles. They were

Edith Elmer Wood (1870–1945) and Catherine Bauer (1905–64). Daughter of and wife of naval officers, Wood spent a good part of her life at military stations throughout the world. When she was a child, her father tutored her in languages and math. An honors graduate from Smith College at the age of eighteen, she and her mother were suffragists. An accomplished novelist, Wood became interested in housing through personal experience with unhealthy servants and the death of one of her four sons from contagion. A theorist, she approached reform by first taking a Columbia doctorate in political economy and later applying these principles to housing analysis.

Catherine Krouse Bauer, a generation younger, grew up in New Jersey where her father was the state's chief highway engineer. Her mother, too, was a suffragist. A graduate of Vassar, she had dropped out temporarily to study architecture at Cornell. A self-styled bohemian, she held a variety of jobs before meeting Lewis Mumford who stimulated her interest in housing and encouraged her to write on aesthetics and architecture.

Wood and Bauer had many common characteristics. Their parents encouraged self-expression and learning. They had similar educational backgrounds at women's colleges. They had literary ambitions which they turned toward achieving social good. They had pragmatic personalities which led them to temper reform theories with political reality. They differed in one major way. Wood's approach to housing reform came from the social sciences while Bauer's stemmed from architecture and planning.

Since the late nineteenth century, many other women intimately involved in housing were: Indianapolis reformer Albion Fellows Bacon; Washingtonians Mrs Ernest P. Bicknell, Mrs Archibold Hopkins, and the first Mrs Woodrow Wilson; and New Yorkers Mary Kingsbury Simkhovitch, Helen Alfred, and Loula Lasker. Nonetheless, Wood and Bauer had the most significant impact on the formulation of the new policy. Wood was the pioneer who redefined the housing problem and formulated the new goals. Bauer joined her to create legislative solutions and bring political support and interest to the cause. Together, they were responsible for the passage of the Housing Act of 1937.

Redefining the housing problem

In the 1930s, the new federal housing policy evolved from a revised perception of the problem. The laboring class became the focus. The argument held: not only had the Depression caused many workers to be unemployed, but more importantly, even in the best of times, those who did have jobs were not able to purchase or rent adequate homes at reasonable prices. As a result, the majority of low-income families were forced to live in slums or substandard units – a situation unacceptable to

American society. The Wagner–Steagall Act, responding to this dilemma, would aid the worker in two ways: providing decent shelter and creating employment. Its succinct preamble stated the issue in this context. It defined the housing problems as the need:

to provide financial assistance to the States and political subdivisions thereof for the elimination of unsafe, unsanitary housing conditions, for the eradication of slums, for the provision of decent, safe and sanitary dwellings for families of low income and for the reduction of unemployment and the stimulation of business activity.[3]

Although shelter has always been a basic need, governmental concern, stemming from the conditions caused by nineteenth-century urbanization and industrialization, is relatively new. American housing reform was born in New York, scene of some of the worst examples of residential crowding, poor sanitation, and disease. Public interest was first aroused in the 1890s when *Tribune* reporter, Jacob Riis, whose vivid photographs and poignant accounts of "how the other half lived" caused progressive Governor Theodore Roosevelt to appoint a state Tenement House Commission at the turn of the century to study New York City dwellings. Headed by veteran settlement house worker, Lawrence Veiller, the commission's recommendations were embodied in the 1901 Tenement House Law, a prototype after which all of the nation's housing codes would be modeled.[4] The law established minimum standards of windows, toilets, and fire escapes in the city's multiple-unit dwellings.[5] The effect was regulatory, local, and limited. It was based on Veiller's view that poor housing, caused by the unscrupulous landlord and careless tenant, was a threat to the general health, safety, and public welfare and therefore must be controlled. Writing in the early 1900s, Veiller stated:

The housing problem is the problem of enabling the great mass of people who want to live in decent surroundings and bring up their children under proper conditions to have such opportunities. It is also to a very large extent, the problem of preventing other people who do not care for decent conditions or are unable to achieve them from maintaining conditions, which are a menace to their neighbors, to the community and to civilization.[6]

For twenty years, the Veiller ideas swept the nation as reformers from Indianapolis to Philadelphia sought to introduce housing codes into their communities. Basically, these civic groups, heavily dominated by women, wished to exert social control over the slum dwellers. They never questioned the rationale nor results of their campaigns.[7] Typical of their attitudes was the declaration of a Washington, D.C. activist, Mrs Ernest P. Bicknell, who referred to the 1914 effort to use the rules to close alley dwellings, slums peculiar to the Capital. "Our greatest desire [is] that these people might some day be forced to live where they would be subjected to the supervision and restraint of the public street."[8]

Wood challenges Veiller

One volunteer worker in the Washington effort raised her voice in doubt, challenging the existing dogma. In 1913, Edith Elmer Wood undertook a survey of hundreds of alley dwellers questioning them about their conditions. She found that people lived in slums because they had no alternative. She roundly condemned "any remedial measure which simply forces them out of the alleys and makes no provision for their future as a very great hardship upon . . . people who in the majority of cases are deserving of every consideration."[9]

For the next five years, she broadened her studies by surveying major US cities. In her first book, published in 1919, *The Housing of the Unskilled Wage Earner*, she concluded that poor housing was not the result of the malfeasance of a few landlords and tenants but of the malfunctioning of the modern industrial system and therefore must be treated differently from the traditional regulatory approach used by Veiller. In her analysis, she did not view slums as a moral problem, but as an economic issue which demanded governmental attention. To her mind, adequate shelter had to be provided through public welfare procedures. She argued,

If our modern civilization requires workers to congregate in cities and the great value of land there puts the control of their housing outside of the hands of the workers and good housing out of their reach, then it would seem logical that housing should be accepted as a community problem – as a public service even as water, light, transit or education – to be controlled and regulated and where necessary owned and managed by the community.[10]

In addition, Wood emphasized that the minimum standards established by Veiller were outdated and too limited for universal application. Drawing from the 1912 housing statement of the National Conference of Charities, she pointed out that the concept of adequate housing was not limited to insuring the basic health and safety of the inhabitants but also mandated decent surroundings. She established standards of density: no more than one person per room. She outlined an economic stricture: maximum rents of 20 per cent of family income. She included locational demands: accessibility to places of employment.[11]

Wood desired to raise housing minimums because she realized that, although in New York City they had eliminated the worst conditions, the codes had not accomplished enough. She granted that after several years of the law's application, "There were no accumulations of filth . . . no dilapidation or extreme disrepair . . . no privy vaults . . . [and] there was running water in almost every apartment." Nonetheless, she charged: "only in a comparative sense can even the new law tenements be said to represent a satisfactory . . . standard." For there were still conditions of crowding, unpleasant and poorly designed high-density development, and relatively high rents which could be improved only by radical change.[12]

Housing needs analysis on a national basis

Using her new standards, Wood reviewed the housing problem in a wider context, embracing the nation. At this time, Wood made the first estimates of national housing conditions. Determining the number of sub-standard dwellings in the country was a difficult task before the US Bureau of the Census collected housing and income distribution figures. As early as 1919, Wood used primitive government statistics for average wages, number of wage earners, and costs of housing to report the dramatic finding:

Roughly one third of the people of the United States are living under subnormal housing conditions which fall below the minimum standard and about one tenth are living under conditions which are an acute menace to health, morals and family life.[13]

Wood continued to be the sole monitor of housing conditions during the following years. Although some writers such as Lewis Mumford and Louis Pink covered the issue, they did not deal with the statistics. The residential market fluctuated wildly in the 1920s: severe shortages and high costs in the immediate postwar period were followed by glut and inflation in the latter part of the decade.[14] Wood distinguished parameters of the problem. Writing in 1931 she observed,

By 1926, the end of the shortage was in sight. By 1928, it had been reached. In a nationwide numerical sense, there was no longer a housing shortage. We were back where we were before the War with qualitative rather than quantitative needs. So far as net progress was concerned, ten years had been lost.[15]

Finally, when the Department of Commerce published the 1934 Real Property Inventory, Wood found figures that "block out . . . in vivid colors the extent of the slum clearance task that lies before us. [And it] contains facts on which to base a rational division of the field between private enterprise and public."[16] Her newsmaking analysis of the data, *Slums and Blighted Areas in the United States*, published in 1935 by the Public Works Administration, substantiated the earlier conclusion that one-third of the nation was ill-housed. By 1937, even Roosevelt would cite this figure in his second inaugural address. The absolute numbers of her findings of 11 million substandard units made national headlines as the *New York Times* and other newspapers gave coverage to the new conception of the housing problem.[17]

Most professionals in the field accepted Wood's analysis immediately. For example, when she published her tentative estimates in 1919,

Plate 7.4 Conditions in New York surveyed by Wood and
Bauer.
Source: Avery Library, Columbia University.

architect-houser Carol Aronovici in the *American Journal of Sociology*
hailed her writing as the first "scientific discussion of the whole
problem." By 1931, executive secretary of the Public Administration
Clearing House Charles Ascher reported that public administrators
regarded her work, *Recent Trends in American Housing*, as the "bible of
housing." And in 1935, New Deal officials Jacob Crane and Leon Keyserling relied upon her *Slums and Blighted Areas* as "a solid factual book."[18]

Resistance to her definition of the housing problem came from two
areas: older housing reformers led by Lawrence Veiller and the real estate
industry. Veiller refused to acknowledge her work because he was

Plate 7.5 Exhibit in San Francisco attempted to focus public attention on the need for adequate housing.
Source: Avery Library, Columbia University.

vehemently opposed to government construction of housing. The real estate industry shared Veiller's objections. It cried that the public sector should not compete with the private, that the state was not a good landlord, and that the workingman would become too dependent upon society if he lived in a publicly sponsored dwelling.[19]

Formulation of new goals

Simultaneously with redefining the housing problem, Wood articulated new goals for social policy for its solution. Linking substandard units with their location in center city slums, she called for a program of clearance, building, loans, and code enforcement. Beginning with her 1919 book, she recommended elimination of all slums, direct public construction of new dwellings for the lowest economic third of the population, and financial assistance for the second economic third to purchase houses. These goals would be explicitly stated in the 1949 and 1968 housing acts. The Housing Act of 1949 declared that the nation was responsible for the provision of "a decent home and suitable living environment for every American family." The Housing and Urban Development Act of 1968 would reaffirm this objective and create legislation to build 26 million new residences through public and private efforts in ten years.

Wood generated these goals to be consistent with her public welfare analysis. She argued that if all citizens had a right to adequate shelter, the government must take proper action to guarantee that right. She pointed to traditional constitutional interpretations to justify this point of view. She quoted the eminent jurist Ernst Freund to demonstrate that the police power "should not only restrain and command but also render aid and service . . . to serve public welfare."[20] By 1949, the preamble to the housing act would clearly state this principle: "The Congress hereby declares that the general welfare and security of the Nation and the health and living standards of its people require housing production and . . . clearance of slums."[21]

Public support and interest for the cause: women and labor

While Wood designed her comprehensive program, she also addressed the strategic problem of how to promote its acceptance by the American public and its passage by Congress. She understood that the effort would require the demonstration of widespread political support and strong vocal alliances as well as painstaking lobbying. As early as 1914, she correctly identified two groups as having natural sympathies to her brand of housing reform. They were women and labor.

Being a suffragist, she believed women of all classes had common interests. She thought they would respond to the need to create a decent living environment for the nation's children. She, like other college-educated women, was convinced that the graduates had a special responsibility to lead the movement.

I want to see the university women of the nation become acutely – even painfully – conscious of the hardships under which more than half the mothers of our land now labor in trying to bring up children and make a real home in the cramped depressing tenements of obsolete rundown houses which are all the family income can command. . . . It is not impossible to bring this about but it is far from easy. It will not be done until the women of the nation organize to do it.[22]

In 1914, Wood convinced the Washington branch of the American Association of University Women (AAUW) to form a housing committee. By 1916, this local group proved to the central leadership that its work should be incorporated into its national program by arguing,

The Association . . . is better fitted than any other group to determine the right direction . . . [for solving] the problem of securing wholesome homes for wage earners . . . because its members have trained minds and the habit of critical analysis, because its members are mothers who realize with special vividness the influence of environment on child life, because among its members are to be found architects, physicians, social workers and social economists – representatives of all the professions covering the approaches to the housing problem, and finally because as an organization, it has always been distinguished for a deep sense of responsibility to the community.[23]

Wood, as head of the national housing committee during its fifteen-year existence, directed its program in two ways. The first was to develop a nationwide network of city based supporters. By 1921, there were fifty-two local groups of university women. Each one supported the reform policy and was engaged in various parochial endeavors. The Boston project participated in a housing code campaign, the New York effort lobbied on the state level for public assistance for low-cost housing construction, and the Chicago activists promoted a zoning plan which was under consideration.

Under Wood, the national committee's second function was to articulate goals and programs and use the American Association of University Women as a political base to promote them. Although the 1920s were a decade in which public sympathy for housing matters was limited, the committee did have some achievements. Among its projects were lobbying for a building and housing division in the US Department of Commerce established in 1922 and pressuring the Census Bureau to measure overcrowding in its 1930 tabulations.[24]

In 1929, the association's governing board, citing its interests in other areas, abolished the national housing committee. This was a great disappointment to Wood. However, this action convinced her of the need for an organization dedicated solely to housing reform. She could see from the results of the AAUW work that such a group could successfully function on grass-roots and national levels.

Wood's early efforts to generate labor support were more narrowly focused. Nonetheless, in 1914, she convinced the Central Labor Union of the District of Columbia "to instruct their delegate to the national convention of the American Federation of Labor at Philadelphia to present a resolution favoring government loans for workingmen's houses and municipal lodging."[25] Subsequently, the union adopted the motion which later became an important part of its policy.

Role of the Regional Planning Association of America

Wood's work with the American Association of University Women brought her into contact with Frederick Ackerman and Clarence Stein, members of a small circle of architects and writers centered around Charles Harris Whittaker, editor of the *Journal of the American Institute of Architects*. These men became interested in the design of low-cost dwellings during the First World War when they served as advisers for US government sponsored defense housing projects. Among their number were Lewis Mumford, Benton MacKaye, Henry Wright, and Robert Kohn.

In 1923, they formed the Regional Planning Association of America (RPAA) and invited others to join, including Edith Elmer Wood and Catherine Bauer. Through their meetings they exchanged information, encouraged each others' publications, and collaborated on experiments such as Radburn, New Jersey, a garden city. In 1933, the group divided on the issue of slum clearance. But while the RPAA lasted, it had a profound influence upon housing thought because it served as a meeting ground for leading reformers. Clarence Stein writing to Catherine Bauer recollected,

It brought together some of those who were in search of a saner planned develop-ment on a regional basis here in the USA. Being together, talking together and working together clarified their own objectives and helped mold their own activities.[26]

Organizing lobbying groups

From the RPAA discussions Wood and Bauer gained ideas which they used in developing two major housing lobby groups. The first was the National Public Housing Conference (NPHC) founded in 1931. An out-growth of New York socialist Norman Thomas' Committee on Civic Affairs, it quickly became independent and established, as its primary goal, the promotion of "good housing through governmental loans and public construction to those people who cannot be adequately housed at rents they can afford to pay." Women predominated in the leadership of the National Public Housing Conference. Mary Kingsbury Simkhovitch served as president. Edith Elmer Wood, Edith Abbot, Mary Harriman Rumsey, and Cornelia Bryce Pinchot were among the vice-presidents. Grace Abbot, Elizabeth Coit, Loula Lasker, and Lillian Wald were some of the women who acted as the advisory committee. Helen Alfred was the executive director.[27]

The second was the Labor Housing Conference (LHC) sponsored by the Pennsylvania Federation of Labor in 1934. Its purpose was to "organize and promote a powerful and intelligent demand for workers' housing and to assist workers' groups in the formulation of their requirement." The Labor Housing Conference was the creation of architect Oscar Stonorov and union leader John Edelman of the United Hosiery Workers of Phila-delphia. They were stimulated to act by the fact that in the early years of the Depression about one quarter of the union had lost homes through foreclosure. Searching for an executive secretary, they chose Catherine Bauer, author of the recently published *Modern Housing*, a book whose thesis was that America could have government sponsored housing only if workers organized to demand it.[28]

A third lobby group, the National Association of Housing Officials (NAHO), began in 1933. Wood also was among its founding members.

Its purpose was to "be a clearinghouse to collect and disseminate information and to act as a service bureau for public housing officials." Coleman Woodbury, its first permanent executive director, emphasized that its primary role was to promote better public administration.[29]

All these organizations were to be highly instrumental in the passage of New Deal housing legislation. The National Public Housing Conference initiated efforts as early as 1932. The Labor Housing Conference and the National Association of Housing Officials, founded after the first programs were in effect, became important in the fight for a permanent program.

Federal housing legislation

The new breed of reformers, led by Wood and Bauer, was centered primarily in the East. Consequently, New York continued to be a fore-runner in housing as these activists cast about for ways to incorporate their ideas in governmental programs. In 1926, the New York State legis-lature passed a landmark housing law allowing tax exemptions for limited dividend companies building low-cost dwellings. Although its supporters had hoped to ease credit through a state housing bank, the legislators deferred to real estate industry complaints and deleted the provision. Wood, who viewed the program as "what is left of an effort to put my out-line of a state housing policy into effect for New York," became an advisor to the state housing board, the administrator of the new law. The program would later serve as a model for the federal government.[30]

Three years after the passage of the New York law, the Depression devastated the construction industry. Urban building, which had peaked in 1925, halved by 1936. National housing starts reflected the slump — the 1925 high of almost a million fell to 93,000 by 1933. Of 13 million workers unemployed in that year, one-third were in the building trades.[31]

Responding to the panic, President Herbert Hoover called a National Housing Conference in December 1931. True to the Republican Adminis-tration's leanings, the proceedings were premised on Secretary of Interior Roy L. Wilbur's warning, 'Unless businessmen . . . accept the challenge of providing an adequate supply of housing at moderate prices, housing by public authority is inevitable.'[32]

Even though the conference's climate was unsympathetic to her ideas, Wood joined more than 3700 delegates who attended this first federally sponsored housing effort. Organized around twenty-five issues ranging from financing to minimum standards, the final recommendations were predictably conservative. The sole legislative result was the 1932 Federal Home Loan Bank Act, designed to aid beleaguered homeowners unable to meet mortgage payments. Nonetheless, in a few committees there was some debate on an expanded government role for inexpensive housing and slum clearance.

Relief and Construction Act: some provision for housing loans

At this time National Public Housing Conference leaders began to monitor the Washington scene carefully. They were in close communication with New York Sen. Robert F. Wagner through their president,

Plate 7.6 The Pleasance at Roehampton, distinctive public housing built by the London County Council.
Source: Avery Library, Columbia University.

Plate 7.7 Los Angeles interpretation of the European model, adapting the aspects of low density, large scale, and ample open space.
Source: Avery Library, Columbia University.

Mary K. Simkhovitch. Simkhovitch had worked with Wagner on many local issues connected with her New York City settlement, Greenwich House. They respected each other and had a long-standing friendship. (In addition, Simkhovitch was on close terms with Eleanor Roosevelt and Secretary of Labor Frances Perkins. She used these connections to promote the cause.) Later, Wagner, with his labor sympathies, would be receptive to Bauer's overtures on behalf of the Labor Housing Conference.

As the Depression worsened, Wagner and others pressed for federal action. The National Public Housing Conference lobbyists were on the spot suggesting housing construction as an aid to recovery. The first piece of legislation they influenced was the 1932 Relief and Construction Act setting up the Reconstruction Finance Corporation to prevent industrial bankruptcies. Wagner slipped in the NPHC provision for federal loans to limited dividend companies producing low-cost homes.[33]

Although only two projects received loans, the inclusion of this provision boosted the housing movement by bringing new sources of support. Chicago observer Charles Ascher reported to Wood,

There is no doubt that the ineptly worded clause in the Relief Act has given great impetus to thinking about the problem: housing has become respectable to big business. As one of the editorial writers for the Chicago *Tribune* . . . said to me, ''We are opposed in principle to the government's going into the banking business but as long as it's there, we want to see Chicago gets its fair share.'' But also some of our civic leaders – big bankers and industrialists – have suddenly begun to see housing on an enormous scale as the thing to break the back of the depression: being big businessmen, they talk in terms of $100,000,000 in a fashion to take away the breath of us little folk who know that there is no plan in existence by which such work could be undertaken.[34]

National Industrial Recovery Act and formation of the housing division

Such talk died down with an economic rally in the summer of 1932. However, shortly after the November election of Franklin D. Roosevelt, the system faltered again and the country experienced some of the most difficult months of the Depression. The first hundred days of the presidency, featuring the creation of the early New Deal package, were to be extremely important for housing reform as activists took this opportunity to inject their ideas into federal legislation. When the National Industrial Recovery Act, a comprehensive proposal containing many items, reached Congress in May, the housers had contributed the sections creating a housing division to construct or aid in the construction of low-cost dwellings and slum clearance projects. It could make loans at 4 per cent interest to limited dividend companies or grants to public authorities of up to 30 per cent of costs, or directly condemn land and rebuild. Senator Wagner, with the persuasion of the National Public Housing Conference had placed these provisions in the act.[35]

Shortly before its passage, Helen Alfred, the conference's executive director, wrote jubilantly to Wood,

What do you think of the Public Works Bill? Pretty interesting – eh? Immediately upon reading detailed news of it, we communicated with the President and a number of key people in Washington in regard to paragraph D under section 202 of Title II. We definitely requested that this paragraph read: *"Construction by public bodies* or under public regulation and control of low cost housing and slum clearance projects."[36]

Even while Congressional debate on the bill took place, housing reformers began to define the ways to implement it. In Philadelphia, the United Hosiery Workers drew up plans for what would be the first PWA housing project, the Carl Mackley homes. In New York, members of the Regional Planning Association of America outlined policy directives.

The first objectives of national emergency housing policy

The housing faction of the association – Wood, Stein, and Kohn – worked feverishly on a position paper entitled "A housing policy for the United States Government." They knew they were faced with a unique opportunity. Kohn wrote to Wood, "It seems likely I can make this statement the declared policy of the new Public Works Administration under the Recovery Act."[37] He was right. On June 16, Roosevelt signed the act and made Harold Ickes head of the Public Works Administration. One week later, Ickes named Kohn chief of the PWA Housing Division. When the program officially started in early July, the division had a staff of about ten and an equal number of consultants including Wood and Simkhovitch of the National Public Housing Conference.

The Regional Planning Association of America document, which was published widely, illustrated the first principles of federal housing policy. Primarily concerned with physical and social aspects of low-cost housing, it had two distinct considerations. First, the location of the projects was to be determined by regional planning and economic criteria. Second, "the complete neighborhood community [was to] be taken as the basic unit of housing." Not only should programs be dedicated to producing dwelling units, but also they should be concerned with their arrangement in large-scale developments in which provision would be made to minimize street traffic, maximize open space and parks, insure sun and air, and provide buildings for community activities.[38] Wood had emphasized these ideas in her 1923 book, *Housing Policy in Western Europe.* Bauer would repeat them in 1934 in *Modern Housing.*

The emergency housing program had a slow start. Hampered by the reticence of Congress to appropriate money, an interagency feud between Controller General John R. McCarl and Administrator Ickes, and the confusion of starting a completely new agency, the housing division had processed only seven applications by the end of 1933. The program suffered further setbacks in the next years. The 1934 National Housing Act, setting up the Federal Housing Administration (FHA) to guarantee home mortgages, pitted Ickes against FHA administrator James Moffet who jockeyed for leadership in the field.[39] Later in the year, Roosevelt impounded $110 million of PWA housing funds; and in January 1935, a Kentucky court struck down federal use of eminent domain for slum clearance.[40]

The need for a permanent housing policy

These events convinced housers that the emergency programs were impractical. Between the spring of 1935 and the summer of 1937 they hammered out the actual details of a permanent housing policy. Through Wagner and others, the Labor Housing Conference and the National Public Housing Conference brought legislation before three sessions of Congress. The 1935 versions never moved past the hearing stage. The 1936 bill passed the Senate but never got out of the house committee. With these failures, it became evident that there would be no act unless Roosevelt was behind it.

Finally, the lobbyists, through Senator Wagner, secured a campaign commitment from the president. Speaking in October, Roosevelt promised a New York City audience of 300,000,

We have too long neglected the housing problem for our lower income groups. . . . We have not yet begun adequately to spend money in order to help the families in the overcrowded sections of our cities live as American citizens have a right to live. You and I will not be content until city, state and federal government have joined with private capital in helping every American live that way. . . . I am confident that the next Congress will start us on our way with a sound housing policy.[41]

Following Roosevelt's election, Wagner's legislative assistant, Leon Keyserling, along with National Association of Housing Officials director Coleman Woodbury and government economist Warren J. Vinton, refashioned the previous year's bill for presentation to Roosevelt and the 1937 Congress. In the process, they frequently consulted Bauer, Wood, and Simkhovitch.

Legislative campaign: LHC and NPHC leaders work non-stop

While this group prepared the bill, Catherine Bauer cultivated grass-roots support.[42] The National Public Housing Conference and the National

Plate 7.8 Women housers promoted all aspects of domestic life, including model kitchens in Memphis.
Source: Avery Library, Columbia University.

Association of Housing Officials supplemented her efforts. Bauer worked from the Housing Legislation Information Office (HLIO) which she and Ernest Bohn, a Cleveland politician, long enthusiastic about federal funding for municipal problems, had started in 1936. From these headquarters, two windowless rooms located behind the stairwell of the Hays Adams Hotel, she orchestrated a masterful plan to put pressure on Roosevelt, Wagner, Rep. Henry Steagall of Alabama, head of the House Banking and Currency Committee, and other congressmen.

In the two previous years, Bauer had systematically built labor support. Personally visiting state and local labor unions from Minneapolis to Birmingham, she convinced them to pressure the American Federation of Labor to take a strong stand on public housing. She based her strategy on the work Wood had started in 1914. By 1935 her efforts paid off. The national organization passed a resolution stating that it was in favor of "a long term permanent program to guarantee a minimum standard of decency in housing for all families." In addition, it called for the formation of local housing committees to "take the lead in developing an active demand for housing, to initiate suitable projects and to represent, protect and promote the interests of labor and consumers in the location, design, construction and management of public housing projects."[43]

This was the mandate Bauer needed. From that point on she begged, bullied, and convinced the locals to create their housing committees. She wrote innumerable pamphlets, sponsored regional labor housing meetings with leading housers as speakers, sent out periodic bulletins, gave dramatic press releases, pushed for an American Federation of Labor Housing Advisory Council of prominent leaders, and maintained constant letter and telegraph communications with key AFL supporters.

Bauer used her considerable personal talents to bring local officials into line. John Edelman, one of the Labor Housing Conference founders, never ceased to be amazed by Bauer, recording,

The prompt and easy way in which Catherine established her relationship with the fairly hardboiled labor skates . . . was something no other woman . . . [had] accomplished. . . . She got herself some respectable clothes . . . and snuggled up to the building trades boys. And those old goats, always to a man opposed to public housing and to women's rights, to a man they fell in love with her . . . and introduced her around.[44]

At one critical point, she wired state federations of labor in Delaware, Maine, and Nevada saying that each state was the only one in the nation failing to give public endorsement to housing and innocently asked, "Does this mean you don't need housing or construction?" Their positive, supportive replies were prompt.[45]

Thus, she gathered labor support, instructing locals to barrage their representatives and the president with resolutions (based on a sample written by herself), letters, and telegrams of endorsement. In addition, she worked with Helen Alfred of the Public Housing Conference to round up others – civic groups, women's clubs, and government officials.

The National Public Housing Conference centered its activities in arousing grass-roots support among tenement dwellers, particularly the women who struggled to raise families in the slums. As early as the 1935 hearings on the first bill, the conference bussed a thirty-seven-member delegation of New Yorkers who presented the Senate committee with a 25,000-signature petition and heart-rending testimony of their hopeless plight in the miserable homes for which they paid exorbitant rents. The mothers' descriptions of the infant mortality, debilitating disease, and criminal activities which characterized life in the slum brought increased public awareness as the *New York Times* and other newspapers gave dramatic coverage to this event. Wood's 1914 strategy: college women organizing support for housing among women and labor was coming to fruition.[46]

Roosevelt backs the bill

In the spring of 1937, Wagner met with Roosevelt to discuss the bill. At that time, the senator reminded the president of the reformers' work. They had endorsements from 525 local unions, 40 state federations of labor, 250 social and civic groups, 47 city councils, 34 mayors, 17 state governments, 45 religious organizations, 22 housing authorities, and 79 prominent individuals.[47]

Finally, Wagner convinced Roosevelt, who had been under considerable pressure from Secretary of Treasury Henry Morgenthau to oppose it, to make good on his campaign promise and promote the bill. The president sent word to House Banking and Currency chairman Henry Steagall to move it along. Party loyalty transformed the Alabama congressman's initial opposition to support. When Bauer, Bohn, and Keyserling went to him to talk strategy he retorted, "I'm against it, it's socialism, it's Bolshevist, it will bankrupt the country but the leader wants it."[48] Hearing this concession, the lobbyists realized that they had conquered the worst obstacle. Although there would be more skirmishes in the congressional floor debates, the act passed the Senate, 64 to 16, and the House, 274 to 68, by the end of August.

Implementation of the Wagner–Steagall Act

The Wagner–Steagall Act called for the provision of "decent, safe and sanitary" housing. It established the United States Housing Authority to interpret this directive. Although women had played a critical role in the composition and promotion of the legislation, they did not gain leading positions in the newly formed agency. Nonetheless, they continued to have a significant impact on policy because they were important repositories of the technical knowledge which the authority's administrator, Nathan Straus, and his two deputies, Jacob Crane and Leon Keyserling, did not have. Bauer as director of information and research and Wood as a consultant on constant retainer were vitally involved in all the authority's initial activities.[49]

These women were particularly important because the new program differed considerably from the PWA one. In the new situation, local authorities would build units whose legislated cost could be no more than $4000, not the $6200 average of former years. New financial arrangements would permit lower-income tenants, and the 1938 budget allocation of $500 million provided for a more massive program than the $36 million total of the PWA.

In these circumstances, the neophyte officials relied upon the wide European expertise of Wood and Bauer. Wood was particularly concerned with the issues of defining minimum standards for the units, establishing tenant selection practices, and developing financial arrangements to yield a maximum number of dwellings. Bauer helped incorporate these ideas into designs promoting community and family life.

The results reflected many of Wood's and Bauer's values. Between 1937 and 1941, the USHA sponsored 130,000 new units in 300 projects scattered throughout the nation. They were large-scale developments containing one- to three-story dwellings. They averaged 25 per cent lot coverage. They featured such community facilities as meeting rooms and playgrounds. Only 4 per cent of the total units were in six-story buildings and less than one per cent in ten stories. Tenants paid no more than 20–25 per cent of their incomes in rent. They lived in the city, near their work. Wood's standards of density, rent–income ratios, and physical location were met in these projects. Also, the requirement for slum clearance led to the elmination of 79,000 substandard units.[50]

War ends early housing program — postwar projects are different

The Second World War brought an end to this phase of the public housing program. Under the wartime Lanham Act the government channeled funds into hastily constructed temporary dwellings for defense workers. Late in 1949 Congress passed the second major act providing for public construction and slum clearance. By this time the guiding lights of the earlier movement were gone. Wood had died in 1945 and Bauer had retired to California to a career of teaching and consulting. Leadership of the National Public Housing Conference passed to others, and the Labor Housing Conference was inactive. A few women such as Elizabeth Wood continued to take part in the housing program but not on national policy-making levels. In addition, architectural ideas of Le Corbusier were becoming popular among designers. In this later program some of Wood's and Bauer's ideas survived but many atrophied. High density development, new tenant selection policies, and shifting American settlement patterns changed the character of public housing. Bauer, writing in 1957, bitterly criticized the new thrust of the postwar efforts. She harshly denounced them as being unfaithful to earlier plans stating, "Life in the usual public housing project just is not the way most American families want to live. Nor does it reflect our accepted values as the way people should live."[51]

Effects of women's participation

Like women's activities in the settlement house movement, consumer's leagues, and child welfare programs, female participation in housing

Plate 7.9 After passage of the 1949 Housing Act,
many original conceptions of public housing
architecture were put aside as government projects
turned to high-rise units.

172   *The American Planner*

reform had social acceptability because the reformers operated within the traditional sphere of women's interests which they merely expanded from their own homes to the city, and later, the nation. Once involved, however, women challenged contemporary definitions of the housing problem and supplied new standards and solutions. They succeeded in transferring the emphasis of housing efforts from regulation to construction. They moved motivation from social control to social justice. They allied class and sex interests to promote the cause. They influenced the shape and form of public housing architecture, making sure it safeguarded family life. Finally, they created a new profession, that of houser, as they moved from well-meaning volunteers to executive directorships of housing lobbying groups to some positions in government.

Even though women were successful in exercising this leadership in the early years of the modern housing movement, they did not sustain it. In one important sense, they failed. For when the stakes became high, in terms of large government expenditures, they lost dominance. As later housing policy demonstrates, they had not convinced their followers of the necessity of their design concepts, nor even of the efficacy of a widespread national housing program. So as they lost position, their clearly stated goals and ideas vanished also.

Author's Note

A different version of this article was presented to the Columbia University Seminar on the History of the City, June, 1977. The assistance and counsel of George Collins, Deborah Gardner, Kenneth Jackson, Robert Kolodny, and Chester Rapkin in encouraging the research for the preparation of this article is gratefully acknowledged.

Notes

1 "Housing Bill voted by House," *New York Times*, August 19, 1937, p. 1.
2 John Buenker (1973) *Urban Liberalism and Progressive Reform*, New York, Charles Scribner's & Sons.
3 Francesco Cordasco (ed.) (1967) *Jacob Riis Revisited: Poverty and the Slum in Another Era*, Garden City, Doubleday & Co.
4 Roy Lubove (1962) *The Progressives and the Slums: Tenement House Reform in New York City, 1890–1917*, Pittsburgh, University of Pittsburgh Press.
5 Lawrence Veiller (1910) *A Model Tenement House Law*, New York, Russell Sage Foundation.
6 Edith Elmer Wood (1919) *The Housing of the Unskilled Wage Earner*, New York, Macmillan, p. 18.
7 Albion Fellows Bacon (1913) *Beauty for Ashes*, New York, Dodd, Mead & Co.
8 Mrs Ernest P. Bicknell (1914) "The homemaker of the White House," *The Survey*, October 13, p. 19.
9 Edith Elmer Wood (1914) "Four Washington alleys," *The Survey*, December 6,

pp. 251–2; statement of Mrs Albert N. Wood (1914) "Hearings before the Subcommittee of the Senate Committee on the District of Columbia, Inhabited Alleys of the District of Columbia and of Unskilled Workingman," 63rd Congress, 2nd sess., pp. 23–4.

10 Wood, *Housing the Unskilled*, p. 249.

11 ibid., p. 249.

12 ibid., p. 10.

13 ibid., pp. 43–6, 72, 76.

14 US Bureau of the Census (1961) *Historical Statistics of the United States*, Washington, D.C., US Government Printing Office, Series N106–15, A242–4.

15 Edith Elmer Wood (1931) *Recent Trends in American Housing*, New York, The Macmillan Co., p. 83.

16 Edith Elmer Wood to Loula Lasker, November 24, 1934, Edith Elmer Wood Collection, Avery Library, Columbia University, Box 90-M (hereafter referred to as the EEW Collection).

17 Edith Elmer Wood (1935) *Slums and Blighted Areas in the United States*, Washington, D.C., US Government Printing Office; "11,000,000 homes put in slum class," *New York Times*, June 13, 1935, p. 7; "The Inaugural Address," *New York Times*, January 21, 1937, p. 1.

18 Carol Aronovici (1919) "Review of *The Housing of the Unskilled Wage Earner*," *American Journal of Sociology*, pp. 507–8; Charles Ascher, interview, New York City, October 21, 1975; Henry Churchill (1935) "Slums and blighted areas," *Bulletin of Federation of Architects, Engineers, Chemists and Technicians*, December 17, p. 1.

19 Lubove, *Progressives*, p. 180.

20 Wood, *Housing*, p. 244.

21 Daniel R. Mandelker (1972) *Housing in America*, New York, Bobbs Merrill, p. 273.

22 Edith Elmer Wood to Maxine Creviston, October 17, 1932, EEW Collection, Box 52-A.

23 Association of Collegiate Alumnae, 1919, "Report of the Committee on Housing." (The Association of Collegiate Alumnae later changed its name to the American Association of University Women.)

24 In 1929 the US Bureau of the Census agreed to undertake a pilot study of overcrowding in four cities but at the last moment backed out. EEW Collection, Box 25-A.

25 Edith Elmer Wood (1919) "Reminiscences of a housing reformer," *Smith Quarterly*, p. 30.

26 Clarence Stein to Catherine Bauer, September 27, 1961, Clarence Stein Papers, Cornell University.

27 "Letterhead," National Public Housing Conference, 1931, EEW Collection, Box 39-B. Stein and Mumford later dropped out over a disagreement of emphasis. They did not favor slum clearance linked with public housing.

28 "The Reminiscences of John W. Edelman," Oral History Collection, Columbia University, 1960, pp. 91–2; Welfare Council for New York City, Housing Section (1934) "Labor organizes for housing," *Housing Information Bureau Monthly Letter*, vol. 2, June 1.

29 Coleman Woodbury, interview, Madison, Wisconsin, June 2, 1975. In 1934, NAHO held its first national conference. Bauer and Wood were among its eighty attendants. At that meeting the membership passed "A housing program for the United States," a memorandum criticizing current policy and suggesting new directions for the future. Although some scholars, such as

Mel Scott in *American City Planning since 1890*, view this document as the first comprehensive outline for what would become the 1937 Wagner–Steagall Act, Wood had presented the ideas much earlier in her widely read *Housing of the Unskilled Wage Earner* (1919).

30 Edith Elmer Wood to John Millar, December 16, 1932, EEW Collection, Box 32-E.

31 US Department of Labor, *Building Operations in Principal Cities*, #424, 440, 500, 524, 545; Bureau of Census, *Historical Statistics*, Series N106–15, N189, D654–68; William E. Leuchtenburg (1963) *Franklin D. Roosevelt and the New Deal*, New York, Harper & Row, pp. 13–15.

32 Mel Scott (1969) *American City Planning since 1890*, Berkeley, University of California Press, p. 285.

33 Joseph Huttmacher (1958) *Senator Robert Wagner and the Rise of Urban Liberalism*, New York, Atheneum, p. 206.

34 Charles Ascher to Edith Elmer Wood, August 16, 1932, EEW Collection, Box 52-A.

35 Timothy McConnell (1957) *The Wagner Housing Act*, Chicago, Loyola University Press, pp. 29–30.

36 Helen Alfred to Edith Elmer Wood, May 22, 1933, EEW Collection, Box 39-B.

37 Robert Kohn to Edith Elmer Wood, June 9, 1933, EEW Collection, Box 6-B.

38 Regional Planning Association of America (June 1933) "A housing policy for the United States Government," *The Octagon*, pp. 28–30.

39 Harold L. Ickes (1953) *The Secret Diary of Harold L. Ickes: The First Thousand Days, 1933–36*, New York, Simon & Schuster, pp. 230–43.

40 *United States* v. *Certain Lands in City of Louisville*, 9F. Supp. 137.

41 Russell B. Porter (1936) "City throngs cheer Roosevelt and Landon as they open final battle for the East," *New York Times*, October 29, p. 1.

42 The most thorough account of Catherine Bauer's work in these years is: M. S. Cole (1975) "Catherine Bauer and the public housing movement: 1926–1937," unpublished Ph.D. dissertation, George Washington University; Ernest Bohn, interview, June 3, 1975, Cleveland, Ohio.

43 Warren J. Vinton, "Resolution on a public housing program," Warren T. Vinton papers, City Planning Collection, Cornell University.

44 John Edelman to Douglas Haskell, January 25, 1967, John Edelman papers, The Archives of Labor History and Urban Affairs, Wayne State University, Detroit.

45 Cole, "Catherine Bauer," p. 545.

46 "Slum dwellers plead to Senators," *New York Times*, June 5, 1935, p. 2.

47 Telegram to President Roosevelt, March 11, 1937, State Historical Society of Wisconsin, American Federation of Labor, Files of the Executive Secretary of the Labor Housing Conference.

48 Cole, "Catherine Bauer," p. 621.

49 Wood was the only houser to remain as a federal consultant from the beginning of federal involvement in 1933. Coleman Woodbury observed: "Mrs Wood anticipated a large proportion of the issues of the thirties. When some newly born expert . . . would come in, he'd be busting out with [some idea]. Mrs. Wood in a quiet way, would pick it up and analyze it. She had thought about it well before and knew what ought to be done." Interview, June 2, 1975.

50 US Department of the Interior (1939) *Annual Report of the United States Housing Authority, 1938*, Washington, D.C., US Government Printing Office, pp. 70–96.

51 Catherine Bauer (1957) "The dreary deadlock of public housing," *The Architectural Forum*, May 1, pp. 140–1.

References

Bacon, Albion Fellows (1913) *Beauty for Ashes*, New York, Dodd, Mead.

Bauer, Catherine (1957) "The dreary deadlock of public housing," *Architectural Forum*, 48, p. 140.

Bicknell, Mrs Ernest P. (1914) "The homemaker of the White House," *The Survey*, 43, p. 19.

Buenker, John (1973) *Urban Liberalism and Progressive Reform*, New York, Charles Scribner's & Sons.

Cole, M. S. (1975) "Catherine Bauer and the public housing movement: 1926–1937," Ph.D. dissertation, George Washington University

Cordasco, Francesco (ed.) (1968) *Jacob Riis Revisited: Poverty and the Slum in Another Era*, Garden City, Doubleday.

Huttmacher, Joseph (1959) *Senator Robert Wagner and the Rise of Urban Liberalism*, New York, Atheneum.

Ickes, Harold L. (1953) *The Secret Diary of Harold L. Ickes: the First Thousand Days, 1933–36*, New York, Simon & Schuster.

Leuchtenburg, William E. (1963) *Franklin D. Roosevelt and the New Deal*, New York, Harper & Row.

Lubove, Roy (1962) *The Progressives and the Slums: Tenement House Reform in New York City, 1890–1917*, Pittsburgh, University of Pittsburgh Press.

Mandelker, Daniel R. (1972) *Housing in America*, New York, Bobbs Merrill.

McConnell, Timothy (1957) *The Wagner Housing Act*, Chicago, Loyola University Press.

Scott, Mel (1969) *American City Planning since 1890*, Berkeley, University of California Press.

US Department of Commerce, Bureau of the Census (1961) *Historical Statistics of the United States*, Washington, D.C., US Government Printing Office.

US Department of the Interior (1939) *Annual Report of the United States Housing Authority*, Washington, D.C., US Government Printing Office.

Veiller, Lawrence (1910) *A Model Tenement House Law*, New York, Russell Sage Foundation.

Wood, Edith Elmer (1914) "Four Washington alleys," *The Survey*, 43, 251.

_____ 1919a *The Housing of the Unskilled Wage Earner*, New York, Macmillan.

_____ 1919b "Reminiscences of a housing reformer," *Smith Quarterly*, p. 30.

_____ 1931 *Recent Trends in American Housing*, New York, Macmillan.

_____ 1935 *Slums and Blighted Areas in the United States*, Washington, D.C., US Government Printing Office.

Part 2   The regionalists

---

8 Charles Dyer Norton and the origins of the Regional Plan of New York

Harvey A. Kantor

The passage of the nation's first comprehensive zoning law in 1916 brought a great deal of attention to the urban planners of New York City. The "promising start" that zoning represented vaulted New York to the forefront of the national planning movement.[1] The next step to be taken would be important in setting a trend for the planning profession in general.

The New York planners did not abdicate their leadership role. The route chosen after 1916 was a broadened concern for regional, rather than mere city planning. The scientific techniques of surveying and data gathering employed during the zoning campaign would now be applied to the entire metropolitan area. The result of these expanded efforts – *The Regional Plan and Survey of New York and Its Environs* – would again be a model of comprehensive achievement.[2]

The man who singlehandedly inspired the New York Regional Plan was Charles Dyer Norton. Through influential connections in the community and a personal dynamism, Norton was successful in overcoming the timidity of his contemporaries and in converting his vision into concrete proposals. The New York Regional Plan was the boldest effort at mastering a metropolitan area yet attempted by urban planners of the day.

Norton's background

Charles Norton was not a planner himself, but he had a reputation for interest in urban planning activities. Born a clergyman's son in Oshkosh, Wisconsin, in 1871, Norton worked hard to save enough money to attend Amherst College. After graduation, he returned to the Midwest to work for the Northwestern Mutual Life Insurance in Chicago.[3] In 1897, tall, handsome Norton married Katherine McKim Garrison, niece of Charles Follen McKim, the architect. It was this contact with McKim which stirred his interest in planning.[4]

While working in Chicago, Norton was active in the Commercial Club and helped to obtain Daniel Burnham as head of the Chicago Plan project. Indeed, the inauguration of this plan, so influential in the planning

Plate 8.1 Charles Dyer Norton.

movement, may be credited largely to Norton.[5] He became imbued with Burnham's enthusiasm and vision, and for the remainder of his life followed Burnham's dictum – ''make no little plans.''

Norton left Chicago in 1909, the year in which the Chicago Plan was published and turned over to city officers. He went to Washington as an assistant secretary in charge of the fiscal bureau in the Treasury Department. There he caught the eye of the President, and from 1910 to 1911 he served in the White House as personal secretary to William H. Taft. In his capacity, Norton worked on planning in another sense. He was a guiding figure in the efficiency drive in the government, and Taft credited him with designing the new system of budgeting ultimately adopted by the federal government. He also promoted establishment of a bureau of research as a permanent center for efficiency studies.

Norton's work in the White House points up the close connection between the joint interests of city planning and budget management. In many ways, the impulses toward greater efficiency and management are the same in both of these areas, and they tend to complement each other. Locally, for instance, New York City established a Bureau of Municipal Research in 1906 and soon after began working on zoning as a means of efficient land use control.[6] Thus, Norton's experience as a presidential secretary was valuable for his interest in planning; and he earned the complete respect of the President as well. Taft later wrote of Norton, "his interest was catholic, his mind constructive, his energy intense, and his vision broad and confident."[7]

Norton left Washington to become vice-president of the First National Bank of New York. Once in the city, he immediately became engaged in a number of financial, social, and civic activities.[8] George McAneny, the Manhattan Borough president who was interested in planning, quickly realized the value of someone like Norton; and when he attempted to bolster public support for his new City Planning Committee in 1914, he asked Norton to head the Advisory Commission.

Norton accepted McAneny's offer because he had become completely fascinated by the planning possibilities in New York. He found the streets, squares, and towers of the city magnificent and took long walks around New York to acquaint himself with the charms of its neighborhoods.[9] His experience as head of the City Planning Advisory Commission was unproductive, however, as that group which McAneny had worked so hard to create never really got off the ground. As Norton stated, "our Advisory Committee met in a beautiful room in the City Hall once or twice and wisely resolved to give our advice only when asked for, which was never."[10]

A vision too big to be believed

The experience was valuable in one respect, though. It led Norton to think about having a private group support the kind of planning he wished to promote for New York. On November 27, 1915, he drew up a memorandum that became the basis for extended discussions on future planning in the city. In the memorandum, Norton maintained that before a plan would succeed in New York, it had to encompass all the areas in which New Yorkers earned their living and made their home. Thus, "from City Hall a circle must be swung which will include the Atlantic Highlands and Princeton; the lovely Jersey hills back of Morristown and Tuxedo; the incomparable Hudson as far as Newburg; the Westchester

182   *The American Planner*

lakes and ridges of Bridgeport and beyond, and all of Long Island.''[11] Clearly, Norton was indulging a Burnhamesque vision in calling for a community plan that would take in all of New York City and its environs. But he believed firmly in the concept and wanted to test his ideas on his New York contemporaries.

After meeting several times with friends, Norton found their reaction sympathetic, but non-committal. McAneny was too concerned with current zoning problems, and Frederic Pratt was too involved in his own Brooklyn planning projects. John Pine, a lawyer friend who had been a member of the city's Municipal Art Commission, probably expressed the sentiment of all when he wrote to Norton: "It does not seem to me wise to include so wide an area in your City plan. I do not myself see the connection between Princeton, Tuxedo, and Stamford, and our immediate problems, and I think that the issue will be greatly confused if so much is attempted.''[12] Norton's vision seemed too advanced for his associates in 1915.

The skepticism of his contemporaries, as well as the demands of his own work, caused Norton to shelve his idea of a regional plan for the moment. President Wilson had appointed him to the Red Cross War Council, and this demanded a great deal of his attention. But in 1918, Norton was named to the Board of Trustees of the Russell Sage Foundation, and he saw renewed hope there for advancing his ideas.

The Russel Sage Foundation backs the plan

The Russell Sage Foundation had already shown its interest in urban planning by sponsoring the Forest Hills Gardens project in 1911. Since that time, the Foundation had not engaged in further planning endeavors, but its personnel had changed little. Robert W. DeForest, active in a broad range of civic enterprises, was still influential as president of the Foundation's Board of Trustees; and John M. Glenn was the organization's secretary. Glenn had experience in public charity work, primarily in Baltimore, and he was an able fiscal administrator.[13] Also serving on the Board of Trustees was Alfred T. White, a Brooklyn philanthropist who had sponsored model tenement projects in Brooklyn in the 1880s and 1890s and who was closely associated with the Brooklyn planning movement.[14]

When Norton assumed his new position as trustee, DeForest asked him to give thought to projects the foundation might undertake, and Norton proposed his scheme for a regional plan. He discussed the project with DeForest, Glenn, and White several times late in 1919, but again met the response that the idea was too grandiose.[15]

Gradually, Alfred White was converted to Norton's way of thinking and in December 1920, he supported him at a meeting with Glenn, DeForest, and Nelson Lewis, who had recently retired from his position as chief engineer of the City of New York. DeForest was still appalled at the enormous amount of territory Norton wanted to survey but ultimately agreed to employ Lewis for a preliminary investigation of the area.[16]

Alfred White's death a setback

Norton finally had a foot in the door. He suffered a setback, however, when his main supporter, Alfred White, drowned on January 29, 1921, just before the two were to present their plan formally to the entire Board of Trustees of the Foundation.[17] Norton carried on, nonetheless, working with Lewis and McAneny on a draft of the proposal, which he presented at the Trustees' meeting on February 7, 1921.[18] Happily, the Russell Sage Foundation now viewed his ideas with sympathy. They established a committee to prepare a new city plan for the New York region and authorized $25,000 for the services of specialists to work on it. Several months later, the Foundation made a larger commitment in the form of an additional $25,000 for immediate use as well as an authorization to spend up to $300,000 over the next several years.[19]

Once he had received formal permission, Norton began to organize the work. On February 11, 1921, he called a confidential meeting in his apartment at 4 East 66th Street for some of the city's and the nation's leading figures in urban planning. Present at that historic first working session of the Regional Plan group were Norton, Glenn, and DeForest of the Russell Sage Foundation; Frederick Law Olmsted, Jr, a leading American planner; George McAneny, Lawrence Veiller, and Edward Bassett, leaders in the New York housing and planning movements; Frederic B. Pratt of the Brooklyn planning movement; Lawson Purdy, the former vice-chairman of the Zoning Commission; E. P. Goodrich, a civil engineer who had been on the technical staff of the Zoning Commission; and Shelby Harrison, a social worker and member of the Sage Foundation staff.[20]

At this meeting, Norton read aloud his draft of a proposal of a new plan for New York. Citing the Sage Foundation's sponsorship of Forest Hills Gardens as precedent for involvement in planning, Norton tried to stir the imagination of his listeners with a call for boldness and vision in planning endeavors. He then carefully laid out his tentative scheme for the preliminary survey of a regional plan.

This outline called for Nelson Lewis to visit personally every municipality in the plan area and to map and record local conditions. Shelby Harrison would study and report on the social aspects of the area; E. P. Goodrich would study transportation facilities; Edward Bassett would relate problems of zoning to general planning considerations; Veiller would study housing, Purdy the tax structure, Olmsted, Jr the parks; and Frank Williams would be called upon for legal counsel, other advisors would be asked to consult their respective professions and to submit recommendations to the general group. These advisors would include Herbert Hoover for engineers, Bert Fenner for architects, James Greenleaf for landscape architects, Daniel French for sculptors, Francis Jones for painters, Arnold Brunner for the Fine Arts Federation, and Eugenius H. Outerbridge for business interests.[21]

Norton had devised one of the most comprehensive ventures in the history of American city planning. The area he sought to encompass in planning was the largest yet attempted for this purpose and contained more people than any area of similar size in the United States. In addition, the personnel he proposed were the finest and most experienced in the nation. Norton was truly a giant among promoters of greater planning for the New York area.

After the February 11 meeting, Norton continued working behind the scenes to modify and refine his suggestions. He felt it was necessary to avoid publicity until a definite proposal could be announced to the general public.[22] And he worked closely with all members of the group that he had called together in order to get a wide range of opinion.[23]

Norton's association with Frederic A. Delano

During this period before the Regional Plan was announced publicly, the individual upon whom Norton relied most was his very close friend Frederic A. Delano. Delano had worked with Norton in Chicago as vice-chairman of the Chicago Plan and had since moved to New York. Norton was eager to get Delano involved in his new project and had proposed his election as a Trustee of the Sage Foundation at the meeting of the Board on Februry 7, 1921.[24] Once this was accomplished, the two Chicago friends renewed their close relationship and talked almost daily on matters concerning the new planning endeavor.[25] From their activities sprung the statement that ''the leadership in New York planning has been borrowed from Chicago.''[26]

Delano, a Harvard-trained engineer, had worked his way up the ranks of railroading, beginning as an apprentice machinist. Eventually he became president of the Gould railroads, the Wabash–Pittsburgh Terminal and the Wheeling and Lake Erie, which were in financial difficulty. In 1904, Delano proposed the consolidation of all but one of Chicago's railway terminals into one central spot. This idea spurred his interest in more general planning, and his railroad scheme was later incorporated into the Chicago Plan. After he left Chicago, Delano was appointed by President Wilson to the Federal Reserve Board on which he served until the War, during which he was Major of Engineers for the American Expeditionary Force. When he returned to the United States, he resumed directorship of several railroads; and it was then that Norton sought him out to work on the Russell Sage designs for a New York Regional Plan.[27] Norton intended that Delano initially be in charge of collecting data on harbor and railroad terminal problems for the area.[28]

Delano was extremely enthusiastic about the possibilities New York offered to planners to test some of their methods, and he wrote to Norton about his ideas for double-decking arteries of traffic in order to accommodate greater volume.[29] But Delano insisted that any new suggestions for planning in New York be approached with caution and urged Norton to make a careful study of each suggestion and to build public opinion step by step to gain maximum support for an overall scheme.[30]

Thomas Adams inspects the working model

Throughout 1921, Norton continued to seek advice from the men he had originally called together, and on November 3 he prepared a memorandum for the Sage Foundation's planning committee which reflected these deliberations. The report reiterated Norton's beliefs that a man of Burnham's stature should lead the project and also that a series of preliminary inquiries should be made before the actual plan was developed. Unlike his February 11 announcement, the memorandum of November 3 grouped the subjects to be treated under four major headings – headings which would eventually form the framework for the actual survey of the regional plans. These broad categories were: (1) physical, which included railway and water transportation, highways, parks, buildings, and density and distribution of population; (2) economic; (3) legal, inquiring into various statutes on zoning, excess condemnation, and stabilization of official city maps; and (4) social and living conditions.[31]

Norton was almost ready now to make his plans public and to begin the project. Characteristically, however, he decided to seek one more opinion on his working model, that of Thomas Adams of the Town Planning Commission of London. Adams, a Scot, had had extensive experience in city planning in England. He was a founder and secretary of the Garden City Association, which in 1900 established Letchworth, the first garden city in England, inspired by the writings of Ebenezer Howard. He was also an early mover and first president of the Town Planning Institute of Great Britain in 1904. From 1913 to 1921, as advisor on town planning to the Canadian government, he received much praise for his work on connecting urban centers with agricultural districts, as well as for his advice on controlling the use of natural resources. While in Canada, Adams also took part in early planning conferences in the United States; he had even testified before the 1916 New York City Zoning Commission. In 1921, however, he returned to England to set up his own firm and made plans for several towns in Great Britain. The following year he came to America as a visiting lecturer on town planning at MIT.[32]

The views Adams held regarding regional planning are perhaps best expressed in his address to the National Conference on City Planning in 1919. Here he contended that "the real controlling factors" determining industrial growth are "physical and natural to a greater extent than they are administrative and artificial." He saw the regional survey as "the investigation and mapping of the existing physical, industrial and residential features of a region that has interests and problems in common, which need comprehensive and coordinated treatment without regard to arbitrary administrative boundaries." A regional plan, he said, involved the general planning of the area included in a regional survey. "It is a skeleton and tentative plan of a region within which there is comprised a series of municipal units in juxtaposition to one another and having overlapping and interrelated problems."[33]

Clearly, Adams had anticipated the kind of surveying techniques that Norton was proposing. He was frank with Norton and made constructive comments on every point in his outline. In the first place, he disagreed that the project should be led by a strong figure in the tradition of L'Enfant, Haussman, or Burnham. Adams felt this approach invited charges of "singlehandedness" and that "it would create dissatisfaction among the staff, who were bound to feel that they were doing the work and only one person was getting the credit." He thought that a group of specialists was far preferable to a single planner with a famous reputation.[34] Adams endorsed the suggestion for a series of preliminary investigations and suggested that the men who were ultimately to carry out the plan also should be involved in the early studies. He further cautioned against expending too much energy and too many resources on the preliminary efforts, lest everything be dissipated before the actual planning took place.[35]

Adams approved the four categories of subject matter that Norton had set up for the survey, but he made valuable suggestions under each. His most important suggestions dealt with the economic study. Here he stressed that all aspects of the value, method of development, and uses of land had to be carefully analyzed. He also pointed out that in the occupational surveys distinctions should be made between those pursuits that created populated districts and those that followed population. This difference between manufacturing and retail concerns was vital in understanding the relationship of business to population; and Adams felt that it would not show up if all businesses were studied the same way.[36]

Public approval of plan

Adams' comments in hand, Norton was at last convinced that he had done enough homework on his plan and that it was time to begin the actual surveys. On the evening of May 10, 1922, Norton's dream of a regional plan for New York and its environs was announced to the public. A special meeting was held in the auditorium of the Engineering Societies Building. Present were about six hundred prominent citizens from the New York metropolitan region. Robert W. DeForest, president of the Board of Trustees of the Russell Sage Foundation, opened the meeting and introduced Norton. Norton explained the project and set out the four fields of inquiry – physical, economic, legal, and social – that the Regional Plan Committee would tackle. He took obvious pleasure in outlining the project and chided the commissioners of 1811 for fearing that the amount of territory they had chosen to plot might be so large that it would become "a subject of merriment."[37] For now, just a little over a century since the first New York plan, Norton was proposing surveys of an area embracing three states, three hundred municipalities, and nearly ten million people.[38]

Speaking immediately after Norton, Herbert Hoover, then Secretary of Commerce as well as a noted engineer, praised the Sage Foundation for its foresight in sponsoring the plan and asserted that the lack of planning not only was wasteful but prevented cities from making the contribution they should to the national life:

The enormous losses in human happiness and in money which have resulted from lack of city plans which take into account the conditions of modern life, need little proof. The lack of adequate open spaces, of playgrounds and parks, the congestion of streets, and misery of tenement life and its repercussions upon each new generation, are an untold charge against our American life. Our cities do not produce the full contribution to the sinews of American life and national character. The moral and social issues can only be solved by a new conception of city building.[39]

Other speakers were Lillian Wald, John J. Carty, Elihu Root, Charles Dana Gibson, and Mrs August Belmont; and each lauded the vision of the men working toward the Regional Plan.

The press reacted enthusiastically to the proposal for a regional plan.[40] *The New York Times* gave ample news coverage to the speeches of all the participants. It also published an editorial entitled "City conservation," which interpreted planning of the metropolitan area as "the application of those principles which have long been approved in regard to forests and mines."[41] The planning movement had always drawn on the methods used by the conservation movement, but never before had this relationship been made explicit for the citizens of New York.[42] Now, *The Times* believed, an end to wasted natural resources could come about, not only by traditional conservation means but also by regional planning, which could develop New York into "an economically ordered, a healthful and a beautiful metropolis."[43]

Endorsement by the press was followed by that of the New York Architectural League, the New York Section of the Society of Civil Engineers, and the National Conference on City Planning.[44] Such application was heartening to the men working on the plan, and they needed all the encouragement they could get. For before their project was finished, seven years of hard work would pass.

The sheer size of the territory their plan was to encompass and the comprehensive manner in which they proposed to treat the subject were the primary reasons the task was to take so long to complete. The region contained 5528 square miles, roughly the commuting radius of New York City, and represented the greatest aggregation of population and industry in any comparable area in the world. The 1920 Census recorded the area's population at 8,979,055 and projected continued growth. The number of manufacturing plants had increased from 19,416 to 57,753 between 1900 and 1920, and the number of employees from 655,170 to 1,209,447. The Port of New York, which was primarily responsible for this tremendous industrial expansion, comprised 125 miles of waterfront, accommodating 868 piers. Thirteen railroads served the region, with annual freight tonnage of 88,000,000 tons. It was estimated that more than 2,800,000 commuters and visitors entered and left Manhattan below 59th Street every day. A total of 858,000 cars were registered in the area.[45]

In attempting to deal with a problem of this magnitude, the Regional Plan Committee formulated a body of doctrine containing the principles upon which their work would be based. Their central purpose was to promote better living conditions for all people in the New York region. A second major premise was the desirability of a more balanced pattern of growth for the region. For example, standards for open spaces had to be maintained, business areas needed to be more concentrated for efficient functioning, and better transportation links were necessary to promote growth of satellite and neighborhood communities, thereby relieving core-city congestion. The third goal, closely related to the second, was the maintenance of certain major activities in central areas, particularly the financial center in Lower Manhattan and the trade activity of the port. A fourth assumption was that all transit and transportation facilities had to be expanded; new highway construction was crucial. Fifth, all public expenditures had to be confined to essential social needs – such as government, public health, education and recreation. And sixth, the highest standards of architectural design were to be applied to all projects undertaken within the jurisdiction of the master plan.[46]

Thus, at the outset, the Regional Plan Committee viewed its task as one of blending the logic of the lawyer, the technique of the artist and engineer, and the idealism of the prophet. This sensitive balance was needed in planning and preserving land and water areas for the best functioning of the region and for determining what areas were best suited for business, industry, residence, and recreation.[47]

Work begins with expertise and controversy

With public enthusiasm attending their initial announcement and their task clearly outlined before them, the Regional Plan Committee vigorously embarked upon its activities in 1922. Serving on the committee at this time were Charles Dyer Norton, chairman; Robert W. DeForest, John M. Glenn, and Frederic A. Delano; Dwight W. Morrow, a Trustee of the Sage Foundation and a partner of J. P. Morgan and Company; and Frank L. Polk, lawyer and former acting Secretary of State under Woodrow Wilson. Added to this group at various times during the 1920s were John H. Finley, an associate editor of *The New York Times* and former editor of *Harper's Weekly*, as well as professor of politics at Princeton; Frederick B. Pratt, president of the Pratt Institute; Lawson Purdy, then active in the Charity Organization Society; George McAneny, then executive editor of *The Times* and also chairman of the New York State Transit Commission; and Harry James, lawyer and Trustee of both the Rockefeller Institute for Medical Research and the Carnegie Corporation. These men comprised the overall Regional Plan Committee.[48]

Norton naturally carried out most of the early organizational work. He asked Nelson Lewis to continue his studies of the region's physical outline and called in as economic consultants Columbia University professors Robert M. Haig and Roswell C. McCrea. Shelby Harrison, who had edited the important *Pittsburgh Survey*, agreed to head the social division, and Edward Bassett the legal division. Frederick P. Keppel, secretary of the International Chamber of Commerce, was persuaded to leave Paris to become executive secretary of the group. These individuals and their assistants formed the working staff of the Regional Plan at its inception.

Norton, in his restless search to recruit the best talent and advice available, turned to Raymond Unwin, chief architect for the British Government on Housing and Town Planning. The internationally known planner agreed to come to New York to advise Norton.[49] After studying Norton's scheme, Unwin expressed his belief – expertly stated in his famous essay ''Nothing gained by overcrowding'' – that decentralization ought to be the regional planners' guiding hypothesis. He warned against reliance on increased transportation facilities as a means of curing congestion, reminding his host that, in fact, the opposite might result. He argued against the promotion of travel by private automobile and stressed the need for dispersal of industry away from the city's central core. He also encouraged the development of new suburbs or garden cities.[50]

Unwin's admonitions were not endorsed wholeheartedly by the staff of the Regional Plan Committee. Haig and McCrea, who were working on the economic survey, felt transportation was essential to the region's continued economic growth. Their response to Unwin's criticism of multiplying traffic facilities was that transportation must be developed in any way "suited to the topography and suited to the type of economic activity for which the Region is best adapted."[51] This disagreement over the relation of traffic facilities to decentralization of population, while only a minor argument in the early stages of the Regional Plan, exploded into the major controversy when the plan was finally completed.

Because he was genuinely seeking advice and not just looking for support, Norton continued his search for objective opinions from outside experts. In 1923, he requested that a group of architects suggest aesthetic improvements for the area's physical appearance, particularly Manhattan. Cooperating with Norton on his project were famous New York architects Cass Gilbert, D. Everett Waid, William A. Delano, Harvey Corbett, Thomas Hastings, John Russell Pope, and Hugh Ferriss. Before their deaths, Arnold Brunner and Burt L. Fenner also worked briefly on the Regional Plan.[52]

Besides the architects, Norton solicited a group of city planners to aid the preliminary studies. Meeting for the first time on February 22, 1923, at the committee's headquarters at 130 East 22nd Street were five leaders of the urban planning profession – Thomas Adams, Harland Bartholomew, Edward H. Bennett, George B. Ford, John Nolen, and Frederick Law Olmstead, Jr.[53] Each planner agreed to take an area of the region and to survey its needs by mid-September.[54]

The plan loses Norton

Norton had assembled a spectacular group of individuals to work on the initial stages of the Regional Plan. By the middle of 1923, he had not only a competent professional staff working full-time but the benefit of expert opinion from those working on an advisory basis. Everything was moving along smoothly; then tragedy struck.

Norton had been ill on several occasions during 1922. Late in the year, he came down with a "tremendous cold" which put him to bed for most of December.[55] His cold worsened, and complications set in. For two months he survived, but then on March 6, 1923, he died at the age of fifty-three.[56] The man who single-handedly had launched the great project of the Regional Plan was sorely missed. William Howard Taft, his former boss and now Chief Justice of the United States Supreme Court, glowingly

praised him in a long letter to *The New York Times.*[57] The paper itself
extolled Norton's virtues and praised him for "dreaming Burnham's
dream for New York."[58] The work of the Regional Plan continued, and
throughout the process there seemed almost a hallowed reverence for the
memory of Charles Dyer Norton. When the project was finally completed, it was dedicated to him.

One year later, Nelson Lewis passed away also; and the Regional Plan
lost a second major figure. Lewis had been a pioneer in all the work that
had been done in modern city planning in New York. He had taken part
in virtually every effort for greater planning. In 1920, with Lewis's completion of a twenty-one-year tenure as the city's chief engineer, Mayor
John Hylan justly claimed that he could "rightly take unto himself much
credit for the advancement which the city has made to its present stage of
municipal pre-eminence."[59]

But even though he had ended a career that would have filled most
men's life, Lewis had been receptive to Norton's overtures for working on
the huge Regional Plan. Although somewhat tired (he confessed to
George McAneny in 1923 that "after a month or more spent in some of
the unspoiled places I am more and more convinced of the foolishness of
living in the city unless one has to"), he endeavored to survey all of the
New York region, and his studies were the basis for all the planning done
by the group.[60] Upon his death in March 1924, Herbert Hoover, speaking
as one engineer about another, said that Nelson Lewis had rendered "a
public service of a most enduring type."[61]

With the death of Norton and Lewis, and the loss of Keppel to the presidency of the Carnegie Corporation, major restructuring of the Region Plan
Committee had to take place. Robert DeForest was anxious that replace-
ments be named as soon as possible and that he not be one of them. DeForest
himself was getting old; and although he had gone along with Norton's
original plans, his heart did not seem to be in the Regional Plan project. For
one thing, DeForest never really seemed to grasp the significance of what
was being done. In January of 1922, he made the unbelievable statement
that the Regional Plan was starting at a particularly fitting time because
"the factors which might have changed radically a City Plan are no longer
liquid, or uncertain. The Erie Canal is located. There will probably be no
more trunk railroad lines terminating in New York."[62] DeForest's lack of
recognition of what the automobile might have in store for the New York
region was revealing, even for a statement made in 1922. Besides his failure
to grasp the significance of the Regional Plan for New York, DeForest was
anxious not to spend too much of the Russell Sage money. He was constantly pressing for the group to finish its work, present it to the public, and
then let some other civic-minded body be formed to promote its implementation.[63] Clearly, DeForest was not the man to take Norton's place.

The man selected by the Regional Plan Committee was Frederic A. Delano, an excellent choice. Probably Norton's closest associate, Delano knew more than anyone else the possibilities the Regional Plan had for the future. While Delano assumed the leadership of the committee on the Regional Plan, Thomas Adams was named director of the general staff in 1923. Adams, too, was a fine selection, and together Frederic Delano and Thomas Adams saw the work through and completed the project initiated by Norton.

The significance of the plan

Eight volumes of survey material were published at various times during the 1920s, and the two volumes of the completed Regional Plan were presented in 1929 and 1931.[64] Containing 470 proposals for the 5528 square miles, 10 million people, and 421 communities in the region, the final product was a monument to the organization and foresight of its staff. The Regional Plan represented the most extensive survey and plan of a metropolitan area yet attempted in the United States. But apart from the sheer size of the project, its significance for urban planning history can be seen in several other important ways. First, by accepting the prospect of continued growth for the New York area, the Regional Plan identified itself as the helpmate of further urban congestion. The project in effect planned *for* growth, rather than attempting to *direct* it in any way. By adopting this strategy, the Regional Plan lost a golden opportunity to become an instrument for the "balanced growth" it advocated and won the everlasting antipathy of such critics as Lewis Mumford.[65] Second, by placing primary emphasis upon the private automobile as the major means of transportation for the area, mass transit was relegated to a secondary role. Highway plans were always foremost in the minds of the men working on the project, and the precedent they set in this regard had enormous consequences for the development of the New York area. Third, by concentrating on such a large geographical area, the plan was an early promoter of the concept of regionalism, and its impact was felt nationwide. Upon receiving his copy of the published document, President Franklin Roosevelt said, "now we are really getting somewhere, and all of the fine work which your Association did is bearing fruit. I hope, of course, that all new projects will be studied in light of regional planning."[66] Roosevelt, a man the planners felt could be "counted upon as a lifelong friend," did not forget the Regional Plan.[67] He appointed its head, Frederic Delano (also his uncle), to his newly created National Planning Board to try to apply the New York planning techniques on the federal level.[68] Finally, the plan spurred the organization of a private group, the Regional Plan Association, to work for implementation of the projects.[69] This important group still exists as one of the most active promoters of urban research and design.

On balance then, the Regional Plan of New York has a mixed record. Although it aided the further agglomeration of people in the metropolitan area and increased dependency upon the automobile, it nonetheless heightened an awareness for the larger urban region and created a commitment in the private sector to the ongoing examination of that region. It is this commitment which is the legacy of the promotional skill and imagination of Charles Dyer Norton.

Notes

1 George McAneny to Flavel Shurtleff, September 26, 1916, George McAneny Papers, Princeton University. For a convenient summary of the status of American city planning immediately after the passage of the 1916 Ordinance, see George B. Ford (ed.) (1917) *City Planning Progress in the United States, 1917*, Washington, D.C., American Institute of Architects.

2 Brief accounts of the Regional Plan appear in Mel Scott (1969) *American City Planning since 1890*, Berkeley and Los Angeles, University of California Press, pp. 199–204; Roy Lubove (1963) *Community Planning in the 1920's: The Contribution of the Regional Planning Association of America*, Pittsburgh, University of Pittsburgh Press, pp. 115–27.

3 "Biographical sketch of Charles Dyer Norton," Russell Sage Foundation Papers, Russell Sage Foundation, New York City, and *National Cyclopaedia of American Biography*, VI, 489–90.

4 Christopher Tunnard (1968) *The Modern American City*, Princeton, Van Nostrand, p. 77.

5 Charles Moore (1921) *Daniel H. Burnham, Architect, Planner of Cities*, Boston and New York, Houghton Mifflin, pp. ii, 11, 14, and 45.

6 See Jane S. Dahlberg (1966) *The New York Bureau of Municipal Research*, New York, New York University Press, esp. pp. 81–92.

7 *The New York Times*, March 10, 1923.

8 "Biographical sketch of Charles Dyer Norton," Russell Sage Foundation Papers.

9 The major source of information on Norton's interest in planning and his activities in setting up the Regional Plan Committee of New York is an extended letter he wrote to Frederic A. Delano on November 24, 1921. The letter was updated and privately published in 1923 under the title, *The Plan of New York with References to the Chicago Plan*, New York. The original letter is in the files of the Regional Plan Association in New York City. Future references will be from the original, "Norton Letter of 1921."

10 ibid., p. 4.

11 ibid., p. 7.

12 ibid., p. 9.

13 "Biographical sketch of John M. Glenn," Russell Sage Foundation Papers, Russell Sage Foundation, New York City.

14 Robert H. Bremner (1967) *From the Depths: The Discovery of Poverty in the United States*, New York, New York University Press, p. 207.

15 "Norton Letter of 1921," p. 14.

16 ibid., p. 16.
17 ibid., p. 17.
18 "Norton Memorandum," January 31, 1921, George McAneny Papers, Princeton University.
19 "Norton Letter of 1921," p. 18.
20 ibid.
21 ibid., pp. 20–2.
22 Charles Norton to George McAneny, May 10, 1921, George McAneny Papers, Princeton University.
23 Charles Norton to George McAneny, February 5, 1921, George McAneny Papers, Princeton University.
24 "Norton Letter of 1921," p. 17.
25 Charles Norton to Frederic A. Delano, November 8, 1922, Regional Plan Association Papers, Regional Plan Association, New York City.
26 Thomas Adams (1929) "Regional planning in the United States," *American Civic Association Pamphlet*, 4, 3.
27 David C. Coyle (1946) "Frederic A. Delano: Catalyst," *Survey Graphic*, 45, July: 250–69; and *National Cyclopaedia of American Biography*, Supplement, A, pp. 410–11.
28 "Norton Letter of 1921," p. 20.
29 Frederic A. Delano to Charles D. Norton, April 27, 1921, Regional Plan Association Papers, Cornell University.
30 Frederic A. Delano to Charles D. Norton, April 4, 1921, Regional Plan Association Papers, Cornell University.
31 Charles D. Norton, "Memorandum for City Plan Committee," November 3, 1921, Regional Plan Association Papers, Cornell University.
32 John M. Glenn, Lillian Brandt, and F. Emerson Andrews (1947) *Russell Sage Foundation 1907–1946*, New York, Russell Sage Foundation, II, 442–3.
33 Thomas Adams (1919) "Regional and town planning," *Eleventh National Conference on City Planning, Proceedings*, pp. 77–88.
34 Thomas Adams to Charles D. Norton, April 14, 1922, Regional Plan Association Papers, Cornell University.
35 ibid.
36 ibid.
37 "Program of meeting of May 10, 1922," Regional Plan Association Papers, Regional Plan Association, New York City.
38 "Planning for an urban population of thirty-seven million" (1922) *American City*, 26, 533.
39 "Program of meeting of May 10, 1922," p. 11.
40 *The New York Tribune*, May 14, 1922.
41 *The New York Times*, May 11, 1922.
42 Roy Lubove (1967) *The Urban Community: Housing and Planning in the Progressive Era*, Englewood Cliffs, N.J., Prentice-Hall, pp. 2–6.
43 *The New York Times*, May 11, 1922.
44 *The New York Times*, May 13 and 18, 1922; *Fourteenth National Conference on City Planning, Proceedings*, 1922, 198.
45 Thomas Adams (1927) *Planning the New York Region*, New York, Committee of the Regional Plan of New York and Its Environs, pp. 17–22.
46 ibid., pp. 23–30.
47 Regional Plan Committee (1923) *Report of Progress*, New York.
48 Forbes Hays (1965) *Community Leadership*, New York, pp. 15–16.
49 *The New York Times*, October 15, 1922.

50 Raymond Unwin, "New York and Its Environs as a regional planning problem from a European point of view," summarized in Adams, *Planning the New York Region*, pp. 42–3. A good recent account of Unwin's general planning views may be found in Walter Creese (1967) *The Legacy of Raymond Unwin*, Cambridge, Mass., The MIT Press.

51 Adams, *Planning the New York Region*, p. 44.

52 ibid., p. 10.

53 *The New York Times*, February 23, 1923.

54 ibid., February 25, 1923.

55 Charles D. Norton to Eleanor Robson Belmont, December 2, 1922, Eleanor Belmont Papers, Columbia University.

56 *The New York Times*, March 7, 1923.

57 ibid., March 10, 1923.

58 ibid., March 11, 1923.

59 John Hylan to Josiah Fitch, December 7, 1920, Nelson P. Lewis Papers, Cornell University.

60 Nelson Lewis to George McAneny, September 8, 1923, George McAneny Papers, Princeton University.

61 Herbert Hoover to Mrs Nelson P. Lewis, April 1, 1924, Nelson P. Lewis Papers, Cornell University.

62 Conference on Fundamental Considerations in City Planning, "Report," January 4, 1922, Regional Plan Association Papers, Regional Plan Association, New York City.

63 Robert DeForest to Frederic A. Delano, January 22, 1926, and Delano to DeForest, February 5, 1926, Russell Sage Foundation Papers, Russell Sage Foundation, New York City.

64 Committee on the Regional Plan of New York and Its Environs (1929) *The Graphic Regional Plan*, vol. I, New York; Thomas Adams, assisted by Harold M. Lewis and Lawrence M. Orton (1931) *The Building of the City*, vol. II, New York. An explanatory volume published under the auspices of the Regional Plan Committee is R. L. Duffus (1930) *Mastering a Metropolis*, New York, and a condensed version of the entire plan may be found in a brief descriptive brochure also published by the Regional Plan group (1929) *A Close-Up of the Regional Plan of New York and Its Environs*, New York.

65 The Mumford attack may be found in Lewis Mumford (1932) "The Plan of New York," *New Republic*, 71, 121–6 and "The Plan of New York, II," *New Republic*, 71, 146–53. A rebuttal appears in Thomas Adams (1932) "In defense of the Regional Plan," *New Republic*, 71, 267–70.

66 Franklin D. Roosevelt to George McAneny, August 7, 1933, George McAneny Papers, Princeton University.

67 Frederic Delano to Lawrence Orton, December 7, 1931, Regional Plan Association Papers, Cornell University.

68 Scott, *American City Planning*, pp. 300–11. Also see John L. Hancock (1967) "Planners in the changing American city, 1900–1940," *Journal of the American Institute of Planners*, 33, 299–300.

69 Regional Plan Association (1931) *Annual Report, 1930*, New York, pp. 1–10.

9 Benton MacKaye: the Appalachian Trail

John R. Ross

In 1921 Benton MacKaye, a lover of wilderness, a conservationist, and a regional planner, proposed the Appalachian Trail. He projected a wilderness footpath as the backbone of an Appalachian domain consisting of camp, recreational and industrial communities. The Appalachian Trail developed solely as a footpath, but MacKaye viewed it as a primeval barrier to the spread of metropolitanism. The Appalachian Trail became a psychological resource for the hiker and an essential part of what MacKaye called the indigenous environment: the rural, and the primeval.

Introduction

In 1921 Benton MacKaye proposed the Appalachian Trail as a project in community planning. The Committee on Community Planning of the American Institute of Architects sponsored the proposal because it epitomized the regional planning ideas advocated by the Committee. The Appalachian Trail was to be the beginning of an Appalachian domain, a counterpoise to the unplanned spread of the metropolitan environment. MacKaye projected a wilderness footpath as a base line for community development. The primary goals were recreation, a respite from a worldly commercial life, and the creation of communities based on cooperation rather than competition. As such, the communities would be the antithesis of the profit motive and the speculation in natural resources characteristic of American society. MacKaye was not advocating an escape from industrial society. Instead he envisioned the use of industry as an aid to real "living" and as a tool to lighten the burden of toil. Contact with nature would enable the worker to place industrialism in proper perspective. Consequently, MacKaye's proposal presupposed the rational use of natural resources, the conscious planning of industry and commerce, and the subordination of the profit motive to social needs.

MacKaye was born in Stamford, Connecticut, in 1879, educated at Harvard, receiving an A.B. and an M.A., and joined the Forest Service in 1905, the year it was organized under Chief Forester Gifford Pinchot. Much of his work with the Forest Service involved advising farmers and landowners on wood lot management, but he came to realize that forestry

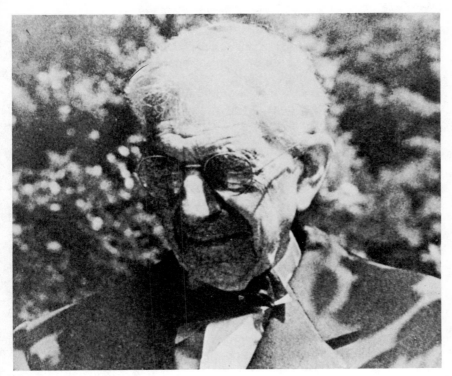

Plate 9.1 Benton MacKaye.

involved more than silviculture, that the manner and method of resource use had social consequences.[1] Forestry schools taught the scientific management of forests, but, MacKaye noted, they taught nothing about the human problems of the lumberjack.[2] In 1915 he began studying the relationship between resources and employment, and thus began his career in planning.

He continued his studies for the Forest Service until 1918 when he transferred to the Department of Labor. Secretary of Labor William B. Wilson was developing a policy to create employment opportunities through the utilization of natural resources. Not content to seek "manless jobs" for "jobless men," Wilson sought to develop a positive labor policy. Wilson's assistant, Louis F. Post, was responsible for MacKaye's transfer to the Labor Department and assisted MacKaye in his work. Post was a single-taxer, an economist, and owner of *The Public, A Journal of Democracy*. Like Wilson, Post wanted to remedy some of the defects of the old homestead policy, prevent speculation in land, and create opportunities for employment.[3]

MacKaye's Report on employment and natural resources

MacKaye's report, prepared for the Labor Department, presented the most advanced thinking of the conservation movement: public protection of natural resources, the elimination of speculation in land, and constructive action by public authorities to aid in land colonization. He outlined farm, forest, and mining communities based on cooperation in economic affairs and arranged as community units rather than as isolated farms. The land and resources in the communities would be publicly owned with title to farm lands based solely upon beneficial use. The public mineral lands in the West and in Alaska would be leased by the government rather than sold. Water power on the public domain and on navigable streams would be developed and controlled by the government to assist in development of the communities.

The objective of MacKaye's plan was to assure the settler a livelihood and the semblance of civilized life. The first step was to connect the communities with city markets. His plan had the government preparing the farms by plowing and clearing land, erecting buildings, and providing machinery and livestock, so that the farmer would begin his venture with the same chance to succeed that an industrial worker had.[4] MacKaye had seen farmers lose their homesteads because they were unable to earn a living wage and pay the mortgage while developing their land.

To remedy the labor problems in the lumber industry, MacKaye proposed logging communities made possible by the sustained-yield management of the public forests. Forests would be cut in units so the lumberjack could return home at the end of each day. Although the logging communities might have to be moved from time to time, timber culture would lead to more permanent communities than timber mining. MacKaye was also concerned about working conditions for miners. He expected government supervision of mining communities to establish standards for safe working conditions. The mining communities could be developed in conjunction with farming communities. These communities were expected to reduce the cost of living by moving laborers from congested industrial pursuits and placing them on idle land to produce agricultural products.[5]

Plan fails

MacKaye's plan was submitted to Congress as a bill in 1919 when demobilization was turning a labor shortage into a labor surplus. A pilot bill introduced in 1916 was drafted to appeal to all homesteaders; the bill of 1919 was designed mainly to attract returning soldiers, sailors, and marines. Neither bill drew support, even though the latter bill was designed to stimulate immediate employment through public works and eventual employment through colonization. The bill embodying Mac-Kaye's plan never cleared the House Committee on Labor because the Department of the Interior and the Department of Agriculture, agencies which were to assist the Labor Department in administering the bill, did not support it.[6] Assistant Secretary of Labor Post blamed Secretary of the Interior Franklin K. Lane for the failure of the bill. Lane was sponsoring a bill of his own for soldier colonization similar to Labor's bill, except for the leasing provisions. Post thought that Lane's bill would permit speculation in land, the feature that MacKaye and others blamed for the failure of the homestead policy and the exploitation of natural resources. Lane's bill encountered the opposition of established farmers, farm organizations, and state and federal agricultural agencies. Both bills ran counter to the general view that the answer to agricultural and labor problems was intensive agriculture and steady industrial employment rather than more farmers.[7]

However, President Woodrow Wilson was interested in the colonization idea and during the war was making funds available for the establishment of a colony in New England. A soldier's colony was to be established, by the Fuel Administration, the Forest Service, and the Labor Department, in the White Mountains at Wild River Valley near the Maine boundary. One hundred thousand dollars had been granted to the project from funds that Congress had given the president to spend as he saw fit. The war ended before they had a chance to set up the colony.[8]

In 1920 bread riots in New York City renewed MacKaye's interest in the high cost of living brought on by wartime inflation. MacKaye made his views known in a series of articles written at the request of Frederick M. Kerby, manager of the New York Bureau of Newspaper Enterprise Association. Kerby felt that MacKaye was able to present complex economic problems in a way that made them comprehensible to the layman. His work was not popular, but Kerby considered his article the clearest analysis of complex problems. MacKaye recommended the public ownership of the major facilities in the meatpacking industry, the public development of oil, coal, and water power, and a colonization plan similar to his proposal for the Labor Department.[9]

MacKaye's marketing system

Although most of his articles did not attract widespread support, a marketing system which he outlined for Washington, D.C. received favorable comment in the newspapers, according to MacKaye.[10] Under this plan, the postal roads system would be utilized to collect produce from the farmers and transport it directly to the city consumer. MacKaye estimated that such a system would substantially reduce the cost of living. Direct connection between the farmer and the citizens of Washington would save them one million dollars annually on each of three products: potatoes, eggs, and butter. MacKaye drafted the system on the instructions of Fourth Assistant Postmaster General James Blakeslee. The Post Office Department was operating a marketing system between Gettysburg, Pennsylvania and Washington, D.C., and Blakeslee wanted to expand it.[11] MacKaye intended only to establish general principles, not the details. However, he outlined a route between a proposed farm colony in Fairfax County and Washington. A marketing system between the two points could be established as a postal marketing system, as a farm colony, or as a garden city. Like many of his proposals, his marketing plan was not implemented. Even MacKaye considered his scheme utopian, but workable. However, his plan was commended to the American Society of Landscape Architects who were establishing a committee to draft a regional plan for the Baltimore and Washington, D.C. areas.[12]

The Northwest Plan

MacKaye was becoming a regional planner. His studies reflected his interest in using resources for employment opportunities, for eliminating waste through conservation, and for reducing the cost of resources by eliminating artificial barriers between the producer and the consumer. He also wanted to locate manufacturing and urban areas close to the source of resources.

A study he helped conduct in 1920, the Northwest Plan, indicated his grasp of regional planning. MacKaye, Stuart Chase, an economist with the US Food Administration, and Charles Harris Whitaker, editor of the *Journal of the American Institute of Architects*, conducted a preliminary economic study of the seven northwest states of Wisconsin, Minnesota, North and South Dakota, Montana, Idaho, and Washington designed to reduce the cost of living. They proposed the establishment of producing and consuming units located at strategic intervals and connected by postal roads for the exchange of goods between farm and city. Manufacturing centers would be located near raw materials and power sources, modeled after the "new town" concept of Letchworth, England. These new towns or garden cities would combine industrial plants in the central area and dwelling and farming lands in the surrounding belt. The Northwest Plan was a model for a more detailed and extensive plan should the opportunity arise. Consequently, it was intended only for private consumption and was never published.[13] It did, however, indicate the scope of MacKaye's thinking about resource use and the economic and social consequences of the use.

Appalachian Trail proposal

It was as a regional planner that MacKaye drafted his proposal for an
Appalachian Trail in 1921. The proposal was precipitated by a conversation with Charles Harris Whitaker at Whitaker's home in the highlands of
New Jersey. MacKaye and Whitaker had worked together on the Northwest Plan, and the latter was receptive to using the *Journal of the American
Institute of Architects* to advance regional planning. Whitaker was a single-
taxer and an advocate of English garden city communities.[14] Whitaker
introduced MacKaye to Clarence Stein at the Hudson Guild Farm in
Netcong, New Jersey, and Whitaker and Stein suggested that MacKaye
write up his trail idea for publication in the *JAIA*. Stein was chairman of
the Commission on Community Planning of the American Institute of
Architects (CCP-AIA) and agreed to sponsor the Appalachian Trail.

Stein's interest in the trail grew out of his conception of the role of the
architect. He also was an advocate of the garden city idea and wanted to
see community planning move beyond the limited goals of housing,
zoning and street construction. Community planning to Stein meant
regional planning, and the trail idea was to him the boldest contemporary
scheme for regional planning. Stein wanted to control the growth of cities
and preserve the outlying land for agricultural or recreational use. He
would plan for work, habitation, and recreation and wanted the architect
to take the lead in relating the physical city to the human needs of its
inhabitants. Stein, like MacKaye, would curb speculative profits and unproductive methods of operation.[15]

In a short article MacKaye proposed a footpath over the crest of the
Appalachians through or near primeval areas. The trail would be built by
volunteer groups and supplied with shelters separated by the distance of
a day's hike. Adjacent to the most populous eastern cities, the trail would
be accessible to workers who wanted to escape a worldly commercial life
for a period of recreation, for the recuperation of health or the regaining
of sanity. MacKaye hoped that the worker who hiked the trail would con-
template his life and work and come to use industrialism "as a means in
life and not as an end in itself."[16]

Shelter camps

The footpath was hopefully to become the base line for an Appalachian
domain. MacKaye saw the possibility of shelter camps growing into community camps developed by a non-profit group where workers could
spend their vacations growing their own food and developing a community spirit. New camps would be established when the need arose to
avoid overcrowding. The camps would be owned by the community,

possibly purchased by a wealthy individual and held to avoid speculation. There would be no place for the "yegg-man" and the profiteer.[17]
MacKaye did not want communities to develop near the trail and now
regrets having included community planning with the proposal for the
trail.

Food and farm communities

Secondly, MacKaye envisioned food and farm communities developing
along with the camping communities. Food and timber for the camp communities could be provided by food and farm communities which
included forest areas. The latter communities would create an opportunity for the city worker who wanted to escape the city for a rural vocation; in this case the communities would reverse the flow of migration to
the cities that was draining the countryside of population.[18]

Industrial communities

The third development in the trail idea would be the growth of industrial
communities which would grow out of the recreational communities.[19]
The development and transmission of electric power made it possible to
locate factories near the source of raw materials. MacKaye expected the
hiker and the outdoorsman to support the idea of recreational communities; labor, radical, and advanced liberal groups would endorse the
idea when they realized its possibilities for employment as well as recreation. He expected the ultra-conservatives to be hostile and to label the
idea "visionary" or "bolshevistic." Big business would be strongly
opposed.[20] MacKaye presented no concrete plan for implementing the
community aspect of his proposal, leaving the financial problems up to
the labor and recreation groups. He thought the whole scheme should be
above politics since regional planning was primarily concerned with
ordering the physical aspects of man's environment.

MacKaye's goal in presenting the Appalachian Trail proposal was to
unravel the complexity of industrial civilization. He wanted to introduce
the worker to a little of what he considered real living and freedom, and
to inspire the worker to demand leisure as well as employment.[21] He
hoped that a firsthand acquaintance with nature would "provide an
understanding of the forces of nature and their power to emancipate man
and make him a higher being."[22] In MacKaye's opinion, only a few
experts knew how to utilize resources; the user of the trail could become
more familiar with natural resources. Then workers could begin to
demand the use of resources to create a more livable environment.

Formation of the RPAA

The assumption of MacKaye's thought was that industrialism was sweeping man's physical and psychological environment before it. MacKaye and the CCP-AIA believed that industrialism and the spread of urbanization were becoming a monolith on the landscape. In 1923 MacKaye and a group of his associates began to call attention to the spread of metropolitanism. Brought together by Clarence Stein, the group called themselves the Regional Planning Association of America (RPAA) and met informally to discuss regional development, geotechnics, and new communities.[23] Stein was hopeful that the RPAA would help control the haphazard growth of cities. As a counterpoise, the association advocated the deliberate planning of entire regions and the creation of new population centers where natural resources would be preserved for the community, where industry would be conducted efficiently, and where houses, gardens, and recreation grounds would ensure a healthy and stimulating environment. The Appalachian Trail project embodied the goals of the RPAA. However, MacKaye and the CCP-AIA were focusing on the recreational features of the trail project as the most feasible way to gain popular understanding and support for regional planning.[24]

Association with the RPAA proved to be a stimulating contact for MacKaye. The significance of the trail project shifted from community development per se to regional development. After 1921 MacKaye focused on the wilderness nature of the trail. He came to envision it as a primeval barrier to the spread of the metropolitan environment. The influence of the members of the RPAA was apparent in MacKaye's conception of the trail.

The RPAA members

Each member of the RPAA contributed to the thought and focus of the group. MacKaye understood why cities grew and became congested. He charted the flow of raw materials and population into the city and the consequent spread or sprawl of the city. Stein understood why the city broke down physically. He was aware that city planning, residential and industrial, was effective only in the context of planning beyond the city limits. Stuart Chase portrayed the inefficiency of hauling coal and other raw materials from their source to feed the remote and sprawling city. Robert Bruere realized that giant power, an integrated and decentralized power grid, made the creation of new towns possible. Giant power could revitalize the countryside through regional planning and could also be used to pile mechanical energy upon mechanical energy in congested metropolitan areas.[25] It was Lewis Mumford who brought these concepts together under regionalism.

Lewis Mumford

Mumford was a writer by vocation, a historian by avocation, and an architectural and social critic by inclination. Both Mumford and MacKaye proposed a new conservation: the conservation of natural resources for social goals. Mumford would approach the problem of urban congestion and rural isolation by achieving a balance between the two. He would bring the urban and rural together in garden cities built for habitation and industry. These garden cities would be limited in growth but large enough to provide the cultural and social amenities requisite for an urbane society. In extolling the garden city, Mumford was not presenting a cut-and-dry plan. He was advocating a concept of city building. Regional planning would depend upon the soil, the climate, the vegetation, the culture, and the industry of a region. His thinking presupposed designing for living rather than solely for profit; it meant seeking a pattern of industrial growth which would keep the city and countryside desirable places to live. It was a conscious attempt to alter the uncontrolled spread of the metropolitan environment.[26]

Appalachian Trail: indigenous environment

For MacKaye, the Appalachian Trail, as a wilderness footpath, became a key to preserving a balanced and habitable environment. In *The New Exploration*, first published in 1928, MacKaye presented the indigenous environment as the goal of regional planning. The indigenous environment was composed of the primeval, the rural, and the urban as distinct environments. The flow of metropolitanism, as MacKaye labeled urban sprawl, was sweeping over the village and the countryside. To preserve the indigenous environment, he suggested the erection of levees and dams in the form of open space between urban areas. The Appalachian Trail was such an openway and a barrier to the heedless flow of metropolitanism.[27]

MacKaye's indigenous environment provided a variety of environments; the business and culture of the city, the personal contact of the village, and the influence of nature in the primeval area. It would also involve the ordering of commerce and industry by region and the use of technology for social ends. MacKaye's philosophy of regional planning entailed the rational use of natural resources; it also posited a new resource, the psychological resource of environment. The Appalachian Trail as a wilderness footpath was conducive to the realization of the psychological environment. This environment was created in the mind of the individual on the trail. MacKaye quoted Thoreau to explain the effect of wilderness on one's outlook: "It is the highest of arts to effect the very medium of the day." Appreciation of the wilderness would lead to the preservation of the trail.[28]

The Appalachian Trail developed as a hiking trail; the community planning aspects of the trail were forgotten. MacKaye expected the trail to develop as a recreation project before the process of community building began. After 1921 he never referred to the community planning aspects of the trail. In helping to organize the trail he emphasized camping and hiking and the benefits of escaping industrialism in the wilderness. He was apparently aware that community building was too "visionary" for Americans.

Conclusion

However, the Appalachian Trail was a primary tenet in MacKaye's philosophy of regional planning which was based on the indigenous environment: the urban, the rural, and the primeval. MacKaye's career was devoted to creating a more habitable environment. The Appalachian Trail, the Wilderness Society, and the townless highway or modern turnpike are ideas that MacKaye publicly advocated to improve habitability. In 1966 the Department of the Interior awarded MacKaye the Conservation Service Award for proposing the Appalachian Trail and for co-founding the Wilderness Society. His work for the Tennessee Valley Authority and the Rural Electrification Administration pointed toward the planned use of resources for social and economic needs. Many of MacKaye's ideas are as relevant today as when he proposed them, including those that have been implemented.

MacKaye is optimistic about his regional planning ideas; more optimistic now at the age of ninety-five than he was during the 1920s. He thinks planning has a better chance now than it had forty-five years ago because the situation has grown worse. "People didn't realize forty-five years ago what a hell of a mess was developing." Now they are more aware and more interested. The Appalachian Trail developed because people were interested in it for its recreational value. Regional planning could be accepted in the same way. In originating the Appalachian Trail, MacKaye was prescient in recognizing the transformation that industrialism was working on the physical and psychological environments of Americans. The trail was a response to the psychological needs of Americans; regional planning and community planning are practical responses to economic and social needs. They are a way to preserve a healthy environment which MacKaye thinks is both possible and practical.

Notes

1 "Benton MacKaye, Biographical Sketch," January 8, 1946, Wilderness Society Records, Washington, D.C.

2 Benton MacKaye (1918) "Some social aspects of forest management," *Journal of Forestry*, p. 210, Benton MacKaye Papers, Harvard University.

3 Louis F. Post, "Living a long life over again," manuscript in Louis F. Post, Library of Congress; Statement by Department of Labor, September 21, 1919, MacKaye Papers; Memorandum for the Secretary, June 3, 1918, RG #174, Department of Labor, Chief Clerk's File, National Archives.

4 Benton MacKaye (1919) *Employment and Natural Resources*, Washington, D.C., Government Printing Office, pp. 13–14, MacKaye (1918) "The soldier, the worker, and the land's resources," *Monthly Review*, p. 1.

5 MacKaye, *Employment and Natural Resources*, pp. 11 and 13; "The soldier, the worker, and the land's resources," pp. 3–6; Statement issued by the Department of Labor, September 21, 1919; MacKaye (1919) "Making new opportunities for employment," *Monthly Labor Review*, p. 126, MacKaye Papers.

6 Memorandum for the Secretary, June 3, 1918; Elwood Mead to Louis F. Post, April 23, 1918, RF #174, Department of Labor.

7 "Lane & Mondell-Real Estate" (1919) *The Public, A Journal of Democracy*, p. 821; Post, "Living a long life over," p. 329; See Bill G. Reid (1967) "Agrarian opposition to Franklin K. Lane's proposal for soldier settlement, 1918–1921," *Agricultural History*, 41, 167–77 for an account of the opposition to Lane's bill; an article in the *Pittsburgh Dispatch* September 23, 1919, MacKaye Papers, also explains opposition to the bills.

8 Interview with Benton MacKaye, June 18, 1973, Shirley Center, Massachusetts.

9 Benton MacKaye, "A plan for handling the living problem," F. M. Kerby to Benton MacKaye, August 18, 1919, MacKaye Papers.

10 Interview with Benton MacKaye, June 18, 1973.

11 Benton MacKaye (1920) "A plan for cooperation between farmers and consumer," *Monthly Labor Review*, 11, 1–2, 13 and 19–20.

12 Stephen Child to the Board of Trustees, American Society of Landscape Architects, January 4, to 1922, Mackaye Papers.

13 The Northwest Program; Harry Chase, Benton MacKaye, Stuart Chase to Herbert Brougham, June 14, 1920, MacKaye Papers.

14 Roy Lubove (1963) *Community Planning in the 1920's*, Pittsburgh, University of Pittsburgh Press, p. 39.

15 "Report of Committee on Community Planning, March 30, 1922," *Proceedings of the Fifty-fifth Annual Convention of the American Institute of Architects, held at the Chicago Beach Hotel, Chicago, Illinois, June 7, 8, and 9, 1922*, pp. 101–2.

16 Benton MacKaye (1921) "An Appalachian Trail, a project in regional planning," reprinted from the *Journal of the American Institute of Architects*, pp. 1–5, MacKaye Papers.

17 ibid., p. 6.

18 ibid., 6–7.

19 MacKaye, "An outdoor recreation system," pp. 5 and 7, MacKaye Papers.

20 MacKaye, "Memorandum, regional planning and social readjustment," pp. 27–34, MacKaye Papers.

21 MacKaye, "Project for an Appalachian Trail, a new approach to industrial problems," p. 2.

22 MacKaye, "Appalachian Trail, a project in regional planning" (synopsis), p. 2, MacKaye Papers.

23 Clarence Stein (1951) *Toward New Towns for America*, Liverpool, The University Press of Liverpool, p. 21.

24 "Report of the Committee on Community Planning," *Proceedings of the*

Fifth-sixth Annual Convention of the American Institute of Architects, Washington, D.C., May 16, 17, and 18, 1923, p. 106.

25 MacKaye, "The new exploration," pp. 153–7; Clarence Stein, "Dinosaur cities," pp. 134–8; Stuart Chase, "Coals to Newcastle," pp. 143–6; Robert Bruere, "Giant power–region builder," pp. 161–4, *The Survey*, 54, May 1925. This issue of *The Survey* was devoted to the regional planning views of the RPAA.

26 Lewis Mumford, "Regions–to live in," *The Survey*, 54, 151–2; Lubove, *Community Planning*, pp. 87–8.

27 Benton MacKaye (1962) *The New Exploration*, Urbana, University of Illinois Press, pp. 135 and 200.

28 ibid., pp. 201–14.

10 Henry Wright: 1878–1936

Henry Churchill

One of city planning's truly great men is remembered by his
colleague and friend – himself one of that small but indomitable
group that made the 1920s and the 1930s a golden age of creative
thought and accomplishment. It is both humbling and exciting for
those of us who are their unknowing heirs to review their work. It
ranged from state-wide regional planning, to plans for new cities, to
designs for housing and residential districts; it included some of the
most sophisticated commentary on the city and city life that has yet
been written. They left answers to many of our current questions
imbedded there, waiting to be rediscovered. And without doubt, the
richest vein in that too-often-forgotten mine was a capacity for
creative thought, a driving enthusiasm, and a dedication to
improving man's lot. Wright, with his biographer, was among the
best of them.

He was a nice man to know. He knew what he knew, but he would take
great pains to tell it to you. If, as sometimes happened, you knew something too, he would listen; and if, as sometimes happened, what he
learned from you upset something he had thought before he learned it, he
did not get mad. He would revise what he had thought he knew to what
he now knew.

It was this spirit of inquiry, this lack of dogma, that gave Henry Wright
his place of importance among the pioneer "planners." There was no
arrogance about him, but he could be obstinate. His continual search for
something better, his refusal to compromise, made it difficult for him to
work with clients. He worked best in a group, and he was fortunate in
that the group into which he was drawn was composed of similar talents,
eager for the catalyzing properties of the minds of others.

Wright came from St Louis. He was by training and practice a landscape
architect, which meant that he planned subdivisions and did the grading,
drainage, and road design as well as specified "plant materials." He later
became an architect and a Fellow of the American Institute of Architects,
although he did not "build" or practice in the accepted use of the term. I
do not know when he got his degree, but Frederick Bigger, to whom Pittsburgh is so much indebted, thinks that he and Wright were at Penn at
about the same time.

Frederick Bigger also recalls that Wright for a time was Chairman of the
AIA Committee on Community Planning. This committee was very

active in stimulating the architects to an interest in community planning instead of brooding about the City Beautiful and great, big but no-little-plan Uncle Dan. Bigger followed Wright as chairman; Stein had also been chairman some time before. During the First World War he worked on war housing, and it was Robert D. Kohn of New York, who was in charge of the program, who induced him to come East and who introduced him to Clarence Stein.

Stein was the main driving force of a group of men of diverse technical training and interests, whose common focal point of interest was the use of land. They called themselves the Regional Planning Association of America. It had nothing to do with the Regional Plan Association of New York, a rich outfit that was (and still is) doing a splendid job of an entirely different kind. Several of the members of the RPAA were deeply immersed in the nascent Housing Movement; all stimulated and influenced each other's ideas. There was for instance, Frederick L. Ackerman, who was associated as architect with Stein and Wright on Radburn and other jobs. He was a Technocrat and a disciple of Veblen, who was then teaching at the old New School for Social Research. Later he was a powerful force in shaping the policies of the New York City Housing Authority. There was Lewis Mumford, and there were others, economists and administrators. There was Benton MacKaye, who almost single-handed created the Appalachian Trail, and who was a great assistance to Stein and Wright when they were developing the really remarkable first "comprehensive" study for a region – New York State – for the New York State Commission for Housing and Regional Planning under Governor Smith in 1926.[1] Stein was chairman.

This was the first study in the United States that took into account all the resources of a region: the agricultural land of varying kinds, the forests and wild areas, the watersheds and the grand drainage basins, the minerals and the power potentials, industry and the transportation and trade routes, the cities and the eventual distribution of people in the light of the rising new technical developments – electricity and the automobile. It is broad, it is beautifully presented as analysis, clear and simple as synthesis. This simplicity and clarity is perhaps its greatest virtue, the distillation of essentials from what must have been, as always, a vast amount of data. It is very short, only 82 pages octavo, but it says all that needs to be said to comprehend the basic resources and potentials of the state. The maps, which were Wright's particular contribution, tell the whole story: there are no tables, for none are needed. The succinct summation of what it is all about, with brilliant suggestions for the future, takes eleven pages of text and seven pages of maps. It is too bad that New York State never did anything constructive about it.

Stein and Wright were the perfect team, and they worked together so

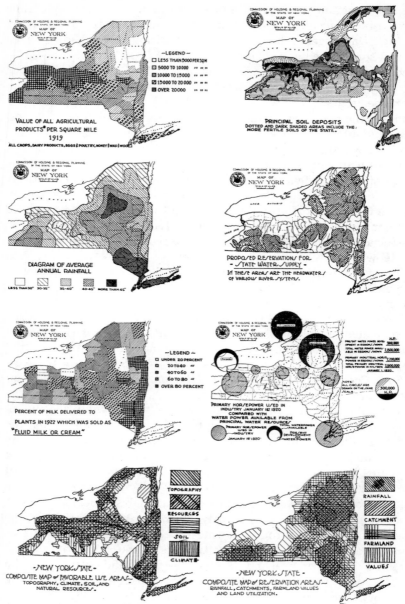

(A) The most valuable agricultural section of the state has now been found in practice to be the area bounding the southern shores of lakes Ontario and Erie.
(B) Restoration of forests throughout the headwaters of the rivers would cause a less rapid flow off of rain and melting of snows, and thus a greater regularity in the volume of stream flow.

Epoch I: Rapid development of natural resources; small towns economically independent; industry served by local water wheels and canal system; all widely distributed over state. Toward end of period drift to new rail lines had set in. *Epoch II:* Development of central rail routes, change of industry to steam power, and competition in agriculture of fertile west combine to concentrate growth in central valley belt and undermine the industrial prosperity of towns off main-line transportation. *Epoch III:* Comparable in importance with the railroad and the steam engine in determining the character of development in the second industrial epoch are the modern factors of the automobile, good road, and electric transmission line. These modern forces do not portend a return to the widely distributed development of the first epoch. Rather they will lend themselves to a more effective utilization of all the economic resources of the state and to the most favorable development of areas especially adapted to industry, agriculture, recreation, water supply, and forest reserve.

Figure 10.2 These three maps with the accompanying captions concluded the *Report of the Commission of Housing and Regional Planning to Governor Alfred E. Smith.* Chairman of the Commission was Clarence S. Stein. Maps were drawn by Henry Wright.

well that in the design aspects of their collaboration it is not possible to separate their work. Besides the State Regional Plan, Sunnyside, Radburn, and Chatham Village are their joint efforts. They would not have come into existence without Stein and his organizing ability, but development of the concepts and their physical form was due to collaboration. There were, of course, many others who shared in the work. It is all set down in meticulous detail and with due credit in Stein's *Towards New Towns for America.*[2]

What, then, was Wright's particular contribution to planning? There were several. Perhaps the most important was demonstrating that site-planning, town-planning, is a socio-economic function which, in spite of – or because of – its multiple effects on what is now called the "structure" of a community, could not be considered as a mere mechanical process of laying out lots. That this idea had a long history in the Garden City and in Patrick Geddes and informed the teaching of Mumford is obvious; it goes back to Robert Owen and the Fourierists. But

---

(C) Surplus milk produced near New York City is sold as fluid milk; the surplus produced far from New York City is made into cheese.
(D Left) This map shows a composite of areas that are generally favorable for more intensive agricultural development.
(D Right) This map shows a composite of areas more suited for reforestation.
Figure 10.1 A portfolio of maps by Henry Wright, selected from the *Report of the Commission of Housing and Regional Planning to Governor Alfred E. Smith,* May 7, 1926.

as practical and applied planning it was ignored in this country, and any reference to its sources was considered not even "socialism" – which would have been to take it seriously – but as just plain crackpot. What Henry did was to evolve a qualitative as well as quantitative analysis of land-planning and house-planning, considered as an unitary and indivisible process. He developed economic analysis to match, and to justify, social reform. Thus, by a process of indirection, he gave respectable status to "social values." All costs were included in his method: pavement, sidewalks, curbs, drains, watermains, sewers, laterals, grading, party vs non-party walls, the cost of corners, of maintenance and of operation. Previously all costs had been gross, cubic foot costs, and a breakdown of site costs was unknown. Money was lent solely on cubic content: the greater the cube the greater the loan – larger cubage meant more materials. Maintenance costs, except for heating, were not even considered.

He demonstrated not only that proper site layout combined with the proper type of house (or apartment) design could squeeze the waste out of the speculator's routine plats, but that at the same time the saved land could increase the value of the investment by increasing amenities – common open space, more pleasant gardens, safer and more accessible play space. This combination was consequently not only saving immediate dollars, but also was an insurance against obsolescence.

This has now become so commonplace that it is taken for granted; indeed the statistical analysis is often so overdone by unimaginative bureaucrats as to be obstructive to new proposals. Yet there was a time when the only acceptable method of subdividing was to cut up the surveyor's standard block into standard lots for standard free-standing houses eight feet apart. That, said the developers, was what people wanted. (There were exceptions – there always are – but most of the exceptions were for high-priced dwellings in "restricted" subdivisions.) It was official doctrine, too, which then as now is automatically against innovation. Stein notes that at Sunnyside they had to fit the housing to the blocks because it was officially "impossible" to close a mapped street, even if it dead-ended against a railroad. And it was only because Sunnyside was zoned "industrial" that it was possible to build it at all.

Wright helped the spread of the superblock idea by pointing out the economic absurdities of conventional zoning which prevented rational development of large-scale integrally designed projects by the insistence on platting "lots." (This absurdity still persists as a legal requirement for "for-sale" projects.) Tied up with superblock design were two other ideas which he considered essential: the row-house as the most desirable as well as the most economic type of dwelling; and the facing of living rooms to the garden side of the block, with the service on the street. This latter

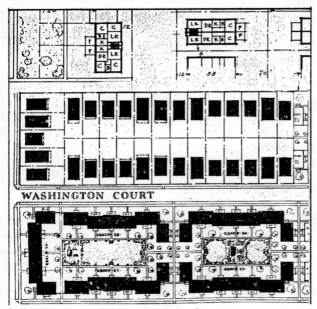

Figure 10.3 Contrasting Sunnyside with normal block plan.

Below: Sunnyside plan utilizing shallow, attached, two-room-deep dwellings in both houses and flats. *Above:* same building space as is usually wastefully arranged in free-standing, individual buildings. Typical building plans for each type also shown at top. The center park play space is about equal to the narrow side yards in upper plan.

twist too was stubbornly resisted, it was "not acceptable" to the consumer accordingly to real estate wisdom. This fight still goes on, even though it is now known how pleasant and private it is to live on the garden side, even though it saves money by eliminating the alley, even though the car is an added argument in favor of it.

These ideas were tried out over a period of years. Sunnyside was the first on any large scale. It was a row-house rental development on city land within the city pattern. Apartments followed, located in the same general area of the city, and other investors and architects – notably the Metropolitan Life Insurance Company – took up the basic formula also, thus gradually forcing acceptance by the official city departments and initiating changes in the zoning resolution.

Radburn followed. The story of The Town for the Motor Age has been well told too often to bear repeating. I want only to point out that Stein and Wright continually revisited what they had designed, and from management and occupants learned what mistakes they had made and profited by what they learned.

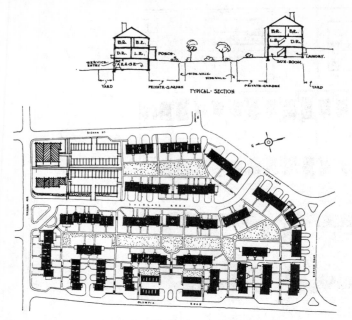

Figure 10.4 Final Chatham Village plan; and cross section
through hillside block at Chatham Village.

Below: shows the general plan of unit of Chatham Village
completed. Note interior park and walk system and streets
with parking bays. Hatched portion shows late additions.
Above: shows how on upper side of streets, houses appear
three-stories high with basement garages, while on opposite
side, houses apparently two-stories high have basement sun
rooms on rear, or garden, side.

Chatham Village, just outside of Pittsburgh, on a very difficult site, is
perhaps the most distinguished of all Wright's designs. It still repays careful study for the way in which the adjustments of levels are handled, the
parking and garaging provided for, the treatment of the open spaces, and
the architectural embellishments. Ingham and Boyd, the architects, were
sensitive and appreciative collaborators, not only in the landscape
features but in the handling of roof-lines and entrances.

During the Depression, Wright, Albert Mayer, and I were the team in
charge of Greenbrook, the "Suburban Resettlement" town which was to
have been built near New Brunswick, New Jersey. For various political
reasons it was dropped from the program, just as plans were completed.
What was interesting about it was that Wright did not repeat the Radburn
plan. He used superblocks and carefully separated main traffic streets
from secondaries, but there were fewer cul-de-sacs, and the large interior
block parks and particularly the walkways which, he felt, invaded

privacy at Radburn were more carefully located. The over-and-under passes were omitted too; schools and neighborhood shopping were accessible without crossing major streets. Yet the town was not "conventional," there was great care to develop pedestrian courts, variety of grouping, arrangements of charm, and changes of pace.

Wright and Stein took infinite pains with the design of their sites. Henry had the most delicate feeling for contours; he could walk over a fifty-acre tract and go home and sketch its contours with uncanny accuracy. His objective was always to fit the houses and the roads to the land, to save trees, to achieve beauty and variety by the arrangement of buildings, by walls, steps, adjustments of the man-made elements to the land. He really loved it. He was fortunate in having Ralph Eberlin[3] as civil engineer

Figure 10.5 Greenbrook, "ultimate" plan.
First unit (750 dwellings) shaded.

Figure 10.6 Greenbrook, first unit.
Site planner: Henry Wright. Architects: Henry S. Churchill and
Albert Mayer.

for much of his (and Stein's) work. He was that rare anomaly, an engineer
with a sensitive regard for land, trees, meadows, and even human beings.

In Wright's time "town planning" was recovering from the oppro-
brium of "the City Beautiful," but had not yet swung into the stultifi-
cation of the City Statistical. It was a rather simple time, and the statistical
approach used by Wright and others for proving something was also
simple, limited to the direct use of verifiable data. *City* planning, as it is
known today, was just starting to roll. There were not many planning
commissions, and almost all of them were moribund. The Housing Movement had not yet become a Planning Movement, in fact "planning" was
still a word of reproach. The speculative possibilities of zoning and
eminent domain for the creation of unearned increment were not then
understood by real estate manipulators. They were all too inclined to take
such things at the face value virtuous planners innocently ascribed to
them, and to scream "socialism." Nor had the fantastic profits to be
derived from borrowing-out − a practice in bad odor since the collapse of

such institutions as S. W. Straus & Company during the Depression – which were latent in the FHA, been more than tentatively explored. The heat for guaranteed, effortless profits was not yet on, and the analytical theories of Henry Wright, and their resultant application to good sub-division design, were built into the manuals of FHA in its early days by such men as Miles Colean and E. Henry Klaber. No matter how low FHA has sunk since then, those basic principles left ineradicable traces.

As has been implied, Henry was a good teacher. For some years he had an informal summer school at his home in Mount Olive, New Jersey. This, unlike the school of the Greater Wright, was not exploitative. It was explorative, learnful, and his methods and ideas were spread by men and women who absorbed a method and later, almost unwittingly, applied it as their own. His "Town-planning Studio" at Columbia was a first step towards formal teaching of the subject, perhaps the first in a major university.

Another of his activities during the Depression was as a director, guide, and mentor of the Housing Study Guild. This had been started, almost informally, in the first days of unemployment, with the aid of private funds, by Albert Mayer, Mumford, Ackerman, and others. It was set up to do research in the field of housing. As the Depression deepened, it was taken over by the WPA, and a considerable staff was assembled. Henry, as usual, provided not only guidance but inspiration.

When Henry died he was only 58, which is not old, but I always thought he was younger. The bibliography which accompanies these comments ·was put together for the Resettlement Administration by Benjamin Gruzen. His library, pamphlets, and notes were given to Avery Memorial Architectural Library of Columbia University.

Wright's book, *Re-Housing Urban America*,[4] has fallen into unbecoming disuse, for it is one of the few primary textbooks we have on site and town design along with Stein's *Toward New Towns for America*, Frederick Gibberd's *Town Design*,[5] and Klaber's *Housing Design*.[6] They are all by architects. The Wright and the Stein books must be taken together, the Then and the Now, for now, as then, the two men are necessary to each other.

Perhaps this may serve as a summary of Henry Wright's contribution to planning, and its importance:

> His contribution was pervasive and
> consequently cannot be measured; its
> importance is that of a quiet stream that
> makes a land rich.

A chronological list of references written by, in collaboration with, or about Henry Wright, compiled by Benjamin M. Gruzen

This list of references was prepared in the Library of the Division of Suburban Resettlement, U.S. Resettlement Administration, December 31, 1936.

1913

"Co-operative group planning; suburban development work of Henry Wright, architect and landscape architect," by David E. Tarn. (In the *Architectural Record*, NYC, vol. XXXIV, no. 5, November, pp. 467–75, photographs, plans, plats.) "It is with the hope of suggesting some basic principles that a most interesting study has been made by Henry Wright of St Louis in his treatment of a new residential subdivision known as Brentmoor Park, St Louis, Mo."

1915

"The economic side of city planning," by Henry Wright, landscape architect. Read before the Engineer's Club of St Louis, January 6. (In the *Journal of the Association of Engineering Societies*, vol. 54, February, pp. 79–93, maps of St Louis.)

1920

"Allotment and community planning," by Henry Wright, St Louis. (In the *National Real Estate Journal*, Chicago, Illinois, vol. XXI, no. 2, January 19, pp. 15–20, photographs, plans, elevations.)

"Platting city areas for small homes," by Henry Wright, advisor in allotment and community planning, member Committee on community planning, AIA, Assistant town planner in the housing developments of the Emergency Fleet Corporation during 1918–19. Foreword by John Irwin Bright, chairman of the Committee on Community Planning. (In the Supplement to the *Journal of the American Institute of Architects*, August, 16 pp., floor and site plans.)

1921

"Architect's ideal home," by Henry Wright. (In *Good Housekeeping*, New York, vol. 72, June, pp. 64–5.)

"Shall we community plan?" by Henry Wright. (In the *Journal of the American Institute of Architects*, vol. IX, no. 10, October, pp. 320–24, site plans and elevations.)

1923

"Site planning practice," a review by Henry Wright of the book by F. Longstreth Thompson. (In the *Journal of the American Institute of Architects*, vol. XI, no. 10, October, pp. 405–7, illustrations from Thompson's book.)

"Preliminary study of a proposed garden community in the New York City region," by Alexander M. Bing, Henry Wright, and Clarence S. Stein, NY, n.p., 38 pp., typewritten, plans, charts.

1924

"Testimony of Mr Henry Wright." (In New York Commission of housing and regional planning. Tax exemption hearing; minutes. Wednesday, February 20, pp. 137–48, typewritten.)

"Town planning in England," a review by Henry Wright of *Town Planning and Town Development* by S. D. Adshead. (In the *Journal of the American Institute of Architects,* May, pp. 222–4, illus.)

1925

"The road to good houses," by Henry Wright. (In the *Survey Graphic,* vol. 54, May, pp. 165–8 and 189.)

"Testimony of Mr Henry Wright." (In the NY State department of architecture, Commission of housing and regional planning. Emergency rent law hearings; minutes. Friday, November 13), vol. two, pp. 605–17, mimeographed.

1926

"Vicious 'own-your-home' propaganda," an abstract of the report of the Committee on community planning, by Henry Wright, chairman of the Committee. (In the *Journal of the American Institute of Architects,* vol. XIV, no. 1, January, pp. 35–6.) Acceptance of this report by the AIA Board of Directors is printed on page 134 of the March 1926 issue of the *Journal.*

"Home ideal versus reality," by Henry Wright. (In the *American Federationist,* vol. 33, January, pp. 65–9.)

"Lo! the poor one-family house," by Henry Wright. (In the *Journal of the American Institute of Architects,* vol. XIV, no. 3, March, pp. 118–21, diagrams.) This is found in a section called "Community planning," which also contains two short articles, signed: Henry Wright, chairman.

"Housing: how much for how much?" by Henry Wright. (In the *Survey Midmonthly,* vol. 55, March 15, pp. 673–7.)

"The six-cylinder house with streamline body," by Henry Wright. (In the *Journal of the American Institute of Architects,* vol. XIV, no. 4, April, pp. 175–8, floor plans.)

"Studies of forces which have shaped the economic history of New York State." (In the New York Commission of housing and regional planning; Clarence S. Stein, chairman. *Report to Governor Alfred E. Smith,* May 7, Albany, J. B. Lyon Co., 82 pp. charts and diagrams.) Henry Wright, active Planning Adviser.

"Regional planning in East Kent," a review by Henry Wright of the *East Kent Regional Planning Scheme* by Patrick Abercrombie and John Archibald. (In the *Journal of the American Institute of Architects,* vol. XIV, no. 5, May, pp. 224–6, 2 maps.)

"Cottage and tenement in the USA; some determining factors," by Henry Wright. (In the *International Housing and Town Planning Congress,* Vienna, 1926, Part One, pp. 261–73.

"Report on the 1926 conference of the International federation for town and country planning and garden cities, Vienna," by Henry Wright, chairman of the AIA Committee on community planning. (In the *Journal of the American Institute of Architects,* vol. XIV, no. 11, November, pp. 499–500.)

"Report of the Committee on community planning," by Henry Wright, chairman. (In the *Journal of the American Institute of Architects,* vol. XIV, no. 12, December, p. 550.)

1927

"Primer of housing," by Arthur C. Holden in collaboration with Henry Wright and Clarence S. Stein . . . with a preface by William J. Tracy, NY, Workers Education Bureau Press, 48 pp., illus., charts. (Workers Education Bureau of America, Workers' Education Pamphlet series no. 11.)

"Exploiting the land," by Henry Wright, chairman of the Institute's Committee on community planning. (In the *Journal of the American Institute of Architects*, vol. XV, no. 10, October, pp. 305–6.) This article tells a little of what was before the Committee as a result of the resolution passed at the 60th Convention of the AIA and recorded on page 227 of the June 1927 (vol. XV, no. 6) issue of the *Journal*. The resolution ends as follows: "Resolved that the Institute, through its Committee on Community Planning, make special study of the problems of land development and regulation, and report its findings to the next convention."

1928

"For block playgrounds," by Henry Wright. (In *Playground*, vol. 21, January, p. 540.)

"Is the low cost house a myth?" by Henry Wright. (In the *National Conference of Social Work, Proceedings*, 1928, pp. 161–5.)

"Costs of utilities; basis of estimates for land studies at the Garden Suburb." 1928 data, 1 sheet, typewritten.

"Cul-de-sac streets effect marked economies," by Henry Wright.

1929

"The modern apartment house," by Henry Wright. (In the *Architectural Record*, March, pp. 213–45, illus.) Important article extending from page 212 to 288.

"Planning a town for wholesale living," by Henry Wright. (In *Playground*, vol. 22, March, pp. 682–4).

"Inner block playgrounds," by Henry Wright. (In *Playground*, vol. 23, July, pp. 257–9.)

"How to plan and build group housing," by Henry Wright. (In the *Building Developer*, vol. IV, no. 5, August, pp. 28–31, 58–62, plans, diagrams, charts.) Note: the text was delivered in the form of an address before the Subdividers' Division of the recent convention of National Association of Real Estate Boards in Boston.

"Application of apartment house data to an actual layout," by Henry Wright. (In the *Architectural Record*, vol. 66, August, pp. 187–9, plans.)

"How to reduce the cost of land development," by Henry Wright. (In the *National Real Estate Journal*, Chicago, Illinois, vol. XXX, no. 18, September 2, pp. 17–22.) Second article appears in the Sept. 30 issue.

"The Radburn plan; illustrating the public and private advantages of group building and planning," by Henry Wright, consulting architect, New York. (In the *National Real Estate Journal*, vol. XXX, no. 20, September 30, pp. 74–6, illus. by a plan of Radburn, a cul-de-sac plan and 2 house drawings.) Editor's Note: This is the second article to appear in the *Journal* based upon Mr Wright's address before the Homebuilders' and Subdividers' Division of the National Association of Real Estate Boards at the Boston Convention. Mr Wright was associated with C. S. Stein as a town planner for Radburn, NJ. (The first article appeared in the Sept. 2 issue.)

"Wastefulness of gridiron street plan," by Henry Wright. (In the *National Real Estate Journal*, vol. XXX, no. 21, October 14, p. 24.) "Before" and "after" street plan and a paragraph of explanation.

"Some principles relating to the economics of land subdivision," a paper delivered at the November 1, 1929, meeting of the American City Planning Institute, by Henry Wright (*American City Planning Institute, Paper*, New York, 1930, Series 1930, number 1, pp. 1–20, plans.)

1930

"Picturesque architecture," by Henry Wright. (In the *Architectural Record*, vol. 67, no. 2, February, pp. 172–3.) Contains a photograph of Ruislip, England, housing.

"Place of the apartment in the modern community," by Henry Wright. (In the *Architectural Record*, vol. 67, March, pp. 207–38, illus.)

"Wanted: a substitute for the Gridiron street system," by Henry Wright. (In the *American City*, vol. XLII, no. 3, March, pp. 87–9, street layouts, tables.) (Also May 1930, p. 100.)

"Autobiography of another idea," by Henry Wright. (Reprint from the *Western Architect*, September, 7 pp.)

"Can the architect promote more business?" by Henry Wright. (In the *Architectural Record*, vol. 68, October, pp. 288–90.)

1931

"The architect, the plan and the city," by Henry Wright. (Reprint from the *Architectural Forum*, February, pp. 217–23.)

"The apartment house – a review and a forecast," by Henry Wright. (In the *Architectural Record*, vol. 69, March, pp. 187–95.)

"Machine-made house," by Henry Wright. (In the *New Republic*, vol. 68, Sept. 2, p. 76.)

"Summary and further development of 'A housing research' for the consideration of the Temporary housing commission of Illinois," by Henry Wright. No place of publication given, December 11, variously paged, typewritten.

"What does the architect know about small house costs?" by Henry Wright. (In the *Architectural Record*, vol. 70, December, pp. 431–4, tables, illus.)

1932

"Large-scale operations," by the Committee on Large-Scale Operations; Henry Wright, research secretary. (In the *President's Conference on Home Building and Home Ownership*, vol. III, Slums, large-scale housing and decentralization, pp. 66–142, illus.)

"Costs of housing," by Henry Wright. (In the *Architectural Forum*, March, pp. 299–305, tables.)

"How can apartment facilities be provided for the lower income groups?" by Henry Wright. (In the *Architectural Record*, vol. 71, March, pp. 147–56.) Portrait (supplement 38).

"Comparative cost studies of new group dwellings," by Henry Wright. (In the *Architectural Record*, vol. 71, March, pp. 213–16 and 44.)

"Re-search versus research," by Henry Wright. (In *Shelter*, May, p. 50.)

"Was weiss der Architekt von den Kosten des Kleinwohnhaus?" von Henry

Wright. (In *Moderne Bauformen*, June, pp. 309–12.) This article was taken from the *Architectural Record* of December 1931, "What does the architect know about small house costs," by Henry Wright. The American currency costs were changed into marks, and the measurements into the metric system.

"The in-betweens of community planning," by Henry Wright. Mimeographed statement used for university students, 1932.

"Economics of site-planning and housing," prepared by the AIA Committee on Economics of Site-Planning and Housing; Frederick Bigger, chairman; F. L. Ackerman, G. F. Cordner, G. H. Gray, P. J. Horner, E. H. Klaber, C. W. Stedman, C. S. Stein, and Henry Wright. (In the *Architectural Record*, June, pp. 369–75.)

"A self-starter for the building industry; a search for a national housing type which will meet the average income and replace blighted areas . . . A search for the simplest way to start profitable, non-competitive building activity," by Henry Wright. First article. (In *Building Investment*, vol. VII, no. 12, August, pp. 12–16, plans, photos.)

"To plan or not to plan," by Henry Wright. (In the *Survey Graphic*, vol. 68, October 1, pp. 468–9.)

"Hillside group housing," by Henry Wright and his Summer School students. (In the *Architectural Record*, October, pp. 221–2.)

"City planning in relation to the housing problem," by Henry Wright, architect and city planner, NYC. (In the *National Conference on City Planning. Planning Problems of Town, City and Region*, 24th conference, Pittsburgh, Pa., November 14–16, 1932.) Pp. 17–22.

"The architect and small house costs," by Henry Wright. (In the *Architectural Record*, vol. 72, December, pp. 389–94, illus.)

"To plan or not to plan," by Henry Wright. (In *Die Neue Stadt*, Frankfurt-am-Main, Germany, December, pp. 194–5.) Reprinted in German from the *Survey Graphic* of Oct. 1, 1932, with an English summary.

1933

"Servicing apartments for lower rentals," by Henry Wright. (In the *Architectural Record*, vol. 73, March, pp. 223–9, illus, plates.)

"The sad story of American housing," by Henry Wright. (Reprinted from *Architecture*, March, pp. 123–30, illus.)

"Are we ready for an American housing advance?" by Henry Wright. (Reprint from *Architecture*, June, pp. 309–16, illus.)

"A national housing and rehabilitation policy." Preliminary report of the Committee on economics of site-planning and housing, AIA. (In the *Octagon*, vol. 5, no. 7, July, pp. 8–10.) Committee signed as follows: F. L. Ackerman, G. F. Cordner, Detroit; G. H. Gray, New Haven; P. J. Hoener, St Louis; R. D. Kohn, NY; E. F. Lawrence, Portland, Ore.; W. S. Parker, Boston; C. W. Stedman, Cleveland; C. S. Stein, NY; Henry Wright, New York; E. H. Klaber, chairman, Chicago.

"Remarks by Mr Henry Wright." (In the National Conference on Slum Clearance, *Proceedings*; Cleveland, Ohio, July 6 and 7.) Pp. 105–7.

"Housing – Where, when, and how?" by Henry Wright. Part I. (In *Architecture*, July, pp. 1–32, illus.)

"Housing – Why, when and how?" by Henry Wright. Part II. (In *Architecture*, August, pp. 79–110, illus.)

"Sinking slums," by Henry Wright. (In the *Survey Graphic*, vol. 22, August, pp. 417–19.)

"Planning and financing of low cost housing," by Henry Wright. (In the

National Conference on Low Cost Housing, Proceedings of October 25, 26, 27.) Pp. 3–7.

"Cost analyses of Cleveland and Indianapolis plans," by Henry Wright and his Housing Laboratory group. New York City, n. pub., 1933. Unpaged, manuscript report, blueprints, and schedules.

1934

"New homes for a new deal." "I. Slum clearance – but how?" by Albert Mayer. "II. Abolishing slums forever," by Henry Wright. "III. The shortage of dwellings and direction," by Lewis Mumford. "IV. A concrete program," by Albert Mayer, Henry Wright, and Lewis Mumford. (Reprinted from the *New Republic*, vol. 78, February 14, Feb. 21, Feb. 28, and March 7.)

"A study of a regional area comprising 488 acres in Astoria–Queens, New York City," by Carol Aronovici, Henry S. Churchill, William E. Lescaze, Albert Mayer, Henry Wright, associates. Drawings by Charles K. Agle. March–April 1934. 27 pp. plates. The plates and a short article were also printed in the *Architectural Forum*, July, pp. 49–55, under the title of "Realistic replanning."

"The New Housing problem in the large city," by Henry Wright. (In *America Can't Have Housing*, Carol Aronovici, editor. New York, published for the Committee on the housing exhibition by the Museum of Modern Art, c.1934.) Pp. 63–5.

"Housing conditions in relation to scientific machine production," by Henry Wright. (Reprint from the *Journal of the Franklin Institute*, October, pp. 485–98.)

"A housing problem for the United States," a report prepared for the National Association of Housing Officials by Sir Raymond Unwin, Mr Ernst Kahn, Miss Alice M. Samuel, Mr Henry Wright, Mr Ernest J. Bohn and Mr Coleman Woodbury. Chicago, Public Administration Service, 1935. 42 pp. (Public Administration Service publication no. 48.) The "Summary of a housing program for the United States" – herein printed as an appendix – was also printed earlier (November 1934) as a 22 pp. pamphlet.

1935

"Housing and education," by Henry Wright. (In the *Housing Study Bulletin No. 6*, March, pp. 1–2.)

"Housing and the FHA," by Henry Wright. (In the *Housing Study Bulletin No. 7*, May, pp. 4–6.)

"Preliminary report on Hamilton Heights," by the Town planning studio, School of Architecture, Columbia University. Henry Wright in charge. Henry S. Churchill, Assistant. New York City, the *Studio*, May, 24 pp., charts, tables, maps, plans.

Rehousing Urban America, by Henry Wright, New York, Columbia University Press, 3p.l. (xi)–xxii, 173 pp., 1 l. front., illus. (including plans). 2 representative reviews of the above book follow: "No mere facial uplift can cure the wrinkles of our cities," by Henry S. Churchill. (In the *American City*, June, pp. 55–6.) "Rehousing urban America," by Albert Mayer. (In *Architecture*, July, pp. 29–32.)

1936

"Henry Wright," by Coleman Woodbury. (In *National Association of Housing*

Officials Bulletin No. 93; 850 East 58th Street, Chicago, Illinois. July 17, 2 pp. mimeographed.)

"The passing of Henry Wright," an editorial. (In *The Nation*, 20 Vesey Street, New York City, vol. 143, July 18, p. 59).

"An editorial on the death of Henry Wright." (In the *New Republic*, 40 East 49th Street, New York City, vol. 87, July 22, pp. 308–9.)

"Henry Wright," by Lewis Mumford. (In the *New Republic*, vol. 87, July 29, pp. 348–50.)

"Necrology – Henry Wright." (In the *American Society of Planning Officials News Letter*, vol. 2, no. 7, July, p. 51.)

"Deaths . . . Henry Wright." (In the *Architectural Forum*, August, pp. 56, and 58 [adv.] photograph). A challenge to the younger men in the planning profession, by Flavel Shurtleff. (In the *American City*, August, p. 64.) "The roll [of those who have died] is too long for the comparatively short span of the planning movement, and the death of these leaders has placed a heavy responsibility on the profession at a critical time when there is a great need for counsel."

"Henry Wright, town-planner, dies suddenly." (In the *Architectural Record*, vol. 80, August, p. 83, photograph.)

"Obituary." (In the *American Magazine of Art*, vol. 29, August, p. 540.)

"Henry Wright . . . 1878–1936," by Clarence S. Stein. (In the *American Architect and Architecture*, August, pp. 23–4, photograph.)

"Site planning and sunlight as developed by Henry Wright." (In the *American Architect and Architecture*, August, pp. 19–22, illus.) Sunlight control on a scientific basis now affects both site planning and architectural form according to studies carried on in the late Henry Wright's Town Planning Studio at Columbia University. This article is illustrated with the work of two of Mr Wright's students. Photographs by Henry Niccolls Wright.

"Henry Wright, site planner of Village, is taken by death; outstanding career as pioneer in housing and town planning left rich heritage." (In the *Chatham Village News*, Pittsburgh, Pa., vol. V, no. 3, August 29, p. 2.)

"Henry Wright: creative planner," by Albert Mayer. (In the *Survey Graphic*, vol. 25, September, p. 530, portrait.)

Notes

1 *Report of the Commission of Housing and Regional Planning to Governor Alfred E. Smith.* Albany, J. B. Lyon Company, 1926). "The Committee on the Plan of New York and Its Environs" was established by the Russell Sage Foundation in 1922 with Frederick A. Delano as chairman. The "environs" were a fifty-mile radius from New York City. "The Niagara Frontier Planning Board," covering some 1550 square miles, turned in a report in 1925.

2 New York, Reinhold Pub. Corp., 1957.

3 Ralph Eberlin once said in a conference, to another engineer who purportedly was saving money by redesigning something: "If you'd designed it right in the first place there wouldn't be anything to save." As Colonel Eberlin he had a very large part in the building of the Burma Road. This note is just to point out a characteristic of this group of collaborators – they were *really* tough, but they were not ashamed to be sensitive, and they strove for perfection.

4 New York, Columbia University Press, 1935.

5 London, Architectural Press, 1953.

6 New York, Reinhold Publishing Corporation, 1954.

11 Rexford Guy Tugwell: initiator of America's Greenbelt New Towns, 1935—6

David Myhra

Between 1935 and 1936, the United States Department of Agriculture (USDA) initiated a public housing program that resulted in the construction of planned new communities called Greenbelt Towns. The prime mover behind this effort was Rexford Tugwell. The significance of this idea was his advanced concept of resettling the rural poor in planned towns at the edge of urban areas. Tugwell recognized, earlier perhaps than many of his colleagues, the "push-pull" tendencies emerging in American society in the 1930s. Arguing that urban growth was inevitable, Tugwell's Greenbelt concept was to demonstrate how housing could be surrounded with a more pleasing environment in order to accommodate the expanding rural to urban migration. In less than two years Tugwell's Resettlement Administration planned and constructed three new communities and litigated a fourth. By all standards, these accomplishments demonstrate an unprecedented speed record for action by a bureaucracy.

Background of the idea

Urban planning literature becomes cloudy when describing the ideological origins of America's Greenbelt New Towns of the 1930s, the first completely planned communities to be built in this country. Available material is full of references to Ebenezer Howard and his English Garden City movement.[1] However, a closer examination indicates that these towns originated largely through the effort and persistence of one man in Franklin D. Roosevelt's Administration, Rexford Guy Tugwell. The Greenbelt New Town program was Tugwell's idea;[2] it was an extension of his land use programs which he envisioned as correctives to the problems of rural poverty facing millions of farm families during the "Great Depression" in the 1930s.[3]

Tugwell was not an urban planner, but an agricultural economist, on the faculty of Columbia University. He was invited to become an economic advisor to Roosevelt during his presidential campaign of 1932, becoming one of the original members of FDR's "brain trust" and later, Undersecretary of Agriculture. One of Tugwell's prime functions was as

Roosevelt's "idea man." Referring to the problems of the nation, Tugwell noted in his diary

Whatever the situation we were in, I tried to think of ways out. I took literally dozens of these [ideas] to the President, sometimes after consultation with others, sometimes after going to the length of drafting a memorandum, and sometimes just as a suggestion to catch his mind as it worked on a problem.

One such idea that Tugwell presented to Roosevelt was his Resettlement concept. This hoped to establish a comprehensive program of action to alleviate the socioeconomic problems then confronting the American farm population.

The very heart of the Resettlement conception was the simultaneous attack on the wastage of people and the inefficient use of resources. Resettlement undertook to remedy all this. It meant to assist the families in the worst situations to find new and more economic farms or to locate elsewhere in other occupations with a prospect of work and income. (Tugwell, 1959, p. 160)

The plight of American farmers

In the 1930s, American farmers were in trouble. Soil erosion, labor displaced by mechanization, overproduction in the early 1920s, and changing

Plate 11.1 Rexford Guy Tugwell.
Source: *Center* magazine.

food consumption patterns were causing widely ranging difficulties for most farmers and farm families.[4] Millions were on direct relief and thousands were flocking into urban areas in search of jobs and housing. The cities were not able to accommodate them because of their own lack of housing.

Something had to be done in order to ameliorate these problems. What resulted grew not only out of an altruistic attitude, but also from the belief that rural America was on the verge of a revolution (Lowi, p. 290). Steps had to be taken, and Tugwell believed that these steps had to occur in the city (Mann, 1952). The city became for Tugwell the corrective for the amelioration of rural poverty problems (Tugwell, 1959, p. 160).

Tugwell the economist

Tugwell entered governmental service with extensive experience in college teaching and holding a Ph.D. in economics from the University of Pennsylvania. His economic theories may be described as Institutional, a concept which prevailed at the beginning of the twentieth century. Through such men as Thorstein Veblen and Simon N. Patten, economic thinking underwent its great reformation. The economic heterodoxy that permeated American thinking was in sharp contrast to that which had prevailed before the turn of the century. There came into being a greater empiricism, a more rational outlook, and a more practical application. When closing the gap between economic theory and practical application, heterodox economists such as Tugwell provided a significant challenge to what had been known as economic orthodoxy (Mann, 1952).

Veblem, Simon and, later, Tugwell found their strength in the fact that their theorizing was relevant to the problems facing the American economy. By adopting a pragmatic outlook and relying upon cultural sciences for support, institutional economists presented a body of doctrine which had the welfare of the public as its goal, to be accomplished through social reform and an experimental approach.

In the strictest sense, the Resettlement Administration is not in the housing field at all. It is building houses, true, but its considerations go beyond the fact, important as that fact is, that millions of Americans need new homes if a minimum standard of decency is to be attained. What the Resettlement Administration is trying to do is to put houses and land and people together in such a way that props under our economic and social structure will be permanently strengthened. (Tugwell, 1936, p. 28)

Tugwell's interpretation of economic development involved a consideration of what he described as cultural equilibrium. The economic process was one in which there was movement (push-pull) from one cultural equilibrium to another. He found that American institutions such as farming were reaching a new equilibrium. Consequently, maladjustments were witnessed, which had to be harnessed in order to obtain the maximum welfare. Tugwell believed, as did many of the "institutionalists," that man had to shape institutions rather than men so that both undesirable or antisocial impulses and economic activities would be corrected. This attitude stemmed from the belief that basic human drives were too strong to be channeled by police methods. Thus the desire to change institutions rather than men was accompanied by a belief in democracy and planning (Sternsher, p. 15).

Tugwell as an "institutionalist" believed that man had to respond to changing social and economic conditions through planning. There was no choice. He believed that men could assure progress by designing social mechanisms to meet specific needs, emphasizing experimentation as the technique of planning. But at the same time he rejected the dogmas of Marx and classical liberalism. Tugwell maintained that effective social policies had to be dictated by contemporary resources, techniques, and circumstances; that they had to be tuned to the times rather than to an imaginary environment in some Utopia (ibid., p. 15).

As an economist, Tugwell reached the crest of importance in 1932, when he was called by Franklin Roosevelt into the services of the New Deal. Tugwell had many novel ideas about economics and its application to the difficulties confronting rural America at that time. In fact, many of his economic theories are still in opposition to current "growth pole" economic thoughts regarding regional and rural development. In this context, regional development or rural development, broadly defined, is a nationwide effort to develop the resources of rural areas in order to improve economic, educational and cultural conditions for those who wish to live there.

However, if people remain on scattered settlements of thinly populated cities and towns, requirements for economic and social investments are created that tend to be uneconomical. Tugwell's belief is that those who argued in 1935, as well as those who argue now in 1974, that rural development is a viable corrective to rural poverty are failing to be pragmatic. In other words, they are failing to accept rural decline as inevitable in the face of increasing technology. Small communities and towns, even if grouped together under the "growth pole" concept, require centralized sewerage and water systems, education, police and fire protection, roads and highways, and so on. Tugwell's response says in essence, "Wouldn't it be better to capitalize on our already existing social and economic investments in the larger cities, and construct examples of how housing might be surrounded by a more pleasing environment?" Tugwell's ideas were manifested in the Greenbelt New Town program.

The Greenbelt New Town program

America's Greenbelt New Town program officially began on April 30, 1935, when President Franklin D. Roosevelt signed Executive Order No. 7027, creating the Resettlement Administration, with Dr Rexford Guy Tugwell as its director (Rosenman, 1950). This agency came under the auspices of the Department of Agriculture where Tugwell had served as Undersecretary since 1933. Funding was provided through the Emergency Relief Appropriations Act of 1935 (Emergency Relief Appropriations Act of 1935, US Statutes at Large). However, the entire construction was halted a mere eighteen months later on May 18, 1936, when this Act was declared unconstitutional (*Franklin Township* v. *Tugwell*). After 1936, the federal government maintained what had been completed, finally selling its interest in 1955 to private developers. However, during its brief eighteen-month existence, Tugwell's staff of architects, city planners, and engineers, many of them America's foremost authorities, managed to plan and construct three new towns and litigate a fourth, setting an excellent speed record for action by a government bureaucracy.

Problem of displaced farm workers

Rexford Tugwell had initially joined Franklin Roosevelt's campaign staff as an agricultural economist in 1932, later becoming Undersecretary of Agriculture. In his position as Undersecretary, Tugwell was pushing the United States Department of Agriculture into land reform and soil conservation programs in an effort to improve economic conditions on American farms.

He recognized, perhaps earlier than his colleagues, that farming as an institution was changing because technology was increasing the yield. This resulted in a displacement of surplus farm workers. These displaced rural people had few options open to them except migration into the cities, seeking work. The farmer, in particular, had been affected by the "Great Depression" of the 1930s, with more than five million families living in quiet desperation, dependent at one time or another on local, state, or federal relief (Tugwell, 1959). A large number of farm families were living on land so poorly adapted to farming that they could no longer subsist from it. Other families whose land was more productive had been severely handicapped by excessive financial burdens through overproduction, when strong European markets for grains disappeared after the First World War. Uneconomical methods of farm management and inadequate farming equipment were also contributing factors, together with soil erosion. When grouped together, these facts made the American farmer suffer more during the Depression than perhaps any other socioeconomic group, except for the Negroes.

None of these conditions were new. They had been developing over a period of decades, becoming intensified in the late 1920s and early 1930s. As early as 1900, people were becoming concerned over the way the land had been mistreated in the rush for increased yield. Reckless deforestation practices by "lumber barons," for example, prompted Theodore Roosevelt and Gifford Pinchot to establish a National Conservation and Forest Service to save what then remained of our once boundless timberlands. But the immense demands of many European countries for foodstuffs during the First World War checked the young policy of conservation and, in fact, reversed it. "We were told that wheat would win the war"; as a result, the prairies were ploughed up far beyond the limits of economic productivity in order to take advantage of abnormally high wheat prices abroad (Tugwell, 1935, p. 3).

After the War, attempts were made to check the results of overpricing, overfarming, deforestation, and soil exhaustion, although very little was achieved. All through the 1920s, as most European countries became agriculturally self-sufficient, American farmers were suffering from overproduction and low prices. In addition, a new dimension to the growing farm problems was becoming evident when, as early as 1931 and 1932, dust storms began to blow away the top soil in western Kansas and eastern Colorado. Year by year the area affected by these storms increased until the great drought of 1934 threatened to make a large section of inland America into desert land. Nebraska, Kansas, Wyoming, New Mexico, Colorado, Texas, Oklahoma, and even the Dakotas, Iowa, and Minnesota were affected by this drought. Feed crops withered, water sources dried up, starving cattle slowly died, and farm families departed by the thousands for the cities, seeking housing and employment. To Tugwell, this was not a temporary trend, but a fundamental socio-economic change that could be expected to continue. Tugwell felt that a radical reorganization of agriculture along industrial lines was in process. Even the demand for products was changing. The American diet, for example, was evolving from starch to protein, the development of synthetic fibers was lessening the demand for cotton, and farms were being mechanized. All these factors led to the same conclusion: the release of large numbers of farmers and farm laborers from their jobs, homes, and means of livelihood (Tugwell, 1936b, p. 38).

Two major problems confronted the New Deal administration. One had to do with the need for an extensive land reclamation program. The other had to do with the displaced farm family. The first problem was by far the more easily corrected. Farm lands damaged by ignorant, short-sighted, or wasteful methods of farming could be improved by better methods or techniques. Exhausted soil could be checked by the use of chemical fertilizers, rotation of crops, and other methods of scientific agriculture. But the task of resettling farm refugees was another matter. Most of the displaced farmers were seeking employment and housing in the larger cities. Tugwell felt conditions there were no better because a lack of imaginative city planning was creating problems equally as grave as those found in rural areas (Conkin, p. 153).

Tugwell opposes Roosevelt's "back to the land" concept

However, there was a considerable difference of opinion as to the best methods for relieving this situation. Roosevelt felt that rural poverty was correctable at the source, through better farm management and rural sub-sistence homes. He believed vast areas of American cities should be razed (slum clearance, he called it), and the people released to rural home-steads, a "back to the land" movement.[5] Tugwell, on the contrary, felt that this would not correct the problems inherent in the farm situation. Although he was concerned about existing urban problems such as the lack of housing, his priority lay with the rural people whom he felt had been neglected for too long. Poor land makes for poor people, Tugwell believed, so it was necessary either to find these poor people better land and teach them to work it profitably, or to relocate those who could not continue to farm close to employment opportunities in the cities.

Tugwell's correctives to rural poverty were just the opposite of what FDR envisioned. Roosevelt would not or could not recognize the forces that were pushing the population off the farms and into the cities.

Plate 11.2 Greenhill, Ohio.

Tugwell did; consequently he felt that urban areas had to be prepared to absorb very large numbers of people from the farms, and he believed very strongly that rural poverty could only be corrected in the city (Tugwell, 1935). These correctives would be industrial employment and the growing opportunities in the service industries. Industrialization in rural areas as an alternative was unacceptable because it was too slow and uncertain as a definite process, as well as inefficient and uneconomical for business itself. Besides, Tugwell felt that industry could not be encouraged to locate in rural areas. Rural industrialization simply was not a viable alternative.

The correct approach toward the elimination of rural poverty, Tugwell believed, lay in the creation of new urban resettlement projects (new towns) that would house the displaced farm family while the father, or head of the household, could obtain employment in nearby industry.

In this regard Tugwell differed from Ebenezer Howard. Although both men believed that the city was basically unfit for human habitation, each proposed different solutions. Tugwell saw uncontrolled urban growth and a lack of planning as part of the problem (Conkin, 1959). This situation could easily be corrected, he believed, through demonstration projects in suburban settings, physically illustrating how urban growth could be developed if a conscientious effort was made to surround housing with a more pleasing environment. Howard, on the other hand, believed urban form could be made more livable only if city dwellers were removed entirely and located in rural, self-sufficient garden cities. Tugwell did not agree with so drastic a measure. He believed in the city and was confident of its continued growth and development. However, the laissez-faire attitudes in handling urban growth would continue to create distress because of the impact of advancing technology on farming and farm workers.

Franklin Roosevelt, however, remained an ardent admirer of the pastoral life. He was absorbed with land, forests, and waters, in his continued search for a better design for national living. "Utopia," Schlesinger wrote, "still presented itself to him in the cherished image of Hyde Park . . . tranquility in the midst of rich meadows and farmlands, deep forests, and a splendid flowing river" (Schlesinger, p. 319). In the 1920s FDR had discussed the possibility of keeping people on the land by combining farming with part-time local industry. As Governor of New York, he had talked of redressing the population balance between city and countryside, "taking industry from crowded urban centers to airy villages, and giving scrawny kids from the slums opportunity for sun and growth in the country" (ibid., p. 319). "I want to destroy all this," he once said of cities, "this is no way for people to live. I want to get them out on the ground with clean sunshine and air around them, and a garden to dig

Highlights of the program

In capsule form, these are the highlights of the Greenbelt New Town program:

February 1935	Tugwell suggested his concept of Greenbelt New Towns to President Roosevelt.
March 1935	FDR gave Tugwell permission to begin staffing and formulating plans.
April 1935	FDR signed Executive Order #7027, creating the Resettlement Administration within the United States Department of Agriculture, with Tugwell as director, to build the Greenbelt New Towns.
May 1935	Tugwell's initial staff began studying 100 cities in the United States as potential sites for new planned communities.
July 1935	Tugwell pared the list to twenty-five possible sites.
September 1935	FDR approved eight cities for Greenbelt New Towns and allocated $68 million for their construction. Tugwell actually received only $31 million and the number of New Towns was further reduced to five. They included sites at St Louis, Cincinnati, Milwaukee, Washington, D.C. and New Brunswick, N.J. Plans for the proposed Greenbelt New Town in St Louis were dropped after disagreement with the St Louis Plans Commission.
October 1935	Construction began on three of the four Greenbelt sites: Washington, D.C., Milwaukee, and Cincinnati. The New Jersey site experienced delays due to opposition.
December 1935	Franklin Township (New Brunswick, N.J.) prepared for a legal battle in its efforts to stop the Greenbelt New Town project, asking the Federal District Court in Newark to issue an injunction restraining the Resettlement Administration from proceeding with construction. The court refused to do so.
January 1936	Franklin Township hired Dean Acheson as counsel and reinitiated their suit in the Supreme Court of the District of Columbia against Rexford Tugwell. Franklin Township's objections were again over-ruled.
February 1936	Dean Acheson appealed the decision.
May 1936	The United States District Court of Appeals for the District of Columbia handed down a decision prohibiting the construction of the fourth Greenbelt New Town in New Jersey. The other three New Towns were unaffected. In addition, however, the Court of Appeals ruled that the Greenbelt program's funding source, the Emergency Relief Appropriations Act of 1935, represented unconstitutional delegation of legislative power to the President; therefore the entire Act was unconstitutional. All monies for the Greenbelt New Towns program ran out.
June 1936	Plans to appeal the decision to the Supreme Court of the United States were abandoned. Plans for Greenbrook, New Jersey, were also abandoned, and the other three Greenbelt New Towns were finished as far as possible with monies already appropriated. Tugwell became increasingly harassed by Congressional leaders who wanted his resignation.
December 1936	Tugwell resigned, hoping then that Congress would leave the Resettlement Administration alone to finish its work. However, the entire organization was dismantled, being absorbed by other federal agencies. The United States Government retained ownership and managed all three existing New Towns.
January 1955	The Federal Government sold its Greenbelt New Town interest to private developers, ending Tugwell's initial effort to surround urban housing with a more pleasing environment.

in. Spread out the cities, space the factories out, give people a chance to live" (ibid., p. 364).

To FDR, the Great Depression and the Presidency provided new opportunities to move toward a balanced civilization. Against the backdrop of drought and dust, Roosevelt hoped to awaken in the American people a sense of urgency about their ultimate basis in nature.

Tugwell could not accept this concept. He felt that the meaning of wilderness had been confused by a strange sort of romanticism which had its roots in the writings of Rousseau, Chateaubriand, and other French writers just before the outbreak of the French Revolution – men who were fascinated by the idea of "back to nature." In the 1920s and 1930s tales and verses abounded, setting forth the triumphs of man in rural areas. The writings of Jack London, the tales of Stewart E. White, and the verse of Robert W. Service all spoke of situations in which the rural life cured men of their weaknesses. On a more sophisticated level and with greater literary skill, Rudyard Kipling romanticized the prophylactic qualities of nature. As a result, FDR and other "back to the land" advocates revived the theory that American pioneers and existing farmers drew strength from the land (Roosevelt, 1970).

Tugwell questioned this concept of the spiritual influence of the land. It may have been true that the westward trek was epic and that the men, and particularly the women, who crossed much of the continent on foot were a tough breed. But they won not because the land and nature had given them spiritual strength, but because they had overcome the wilderness. Their physical endurance was fortified by the vast amount of labor they had to perform in order to survive and not because of imaginary forces supposedly spawned by rural living. Instead of inspiring them, the wilderness actually embittered them. They were at the mercy of the seasons and of the weather, they endured thirst and hunger, and many of the weak died (Roosevelt, 1970).

Tugwell strongly believed that rural life was bleak and irrational. For the more competent farmers with equity in substantial acreages and with able-bodied sons, the farm was a beneficial institution (Baldwin, 1968, p. 87). But for the chronically insecure small farmers, it often became a trap. To Tugwell there was no romance in agriculture and rural life and, in 1930, he painted the following picture:

A farm is an area of vicious, ill-tempered soil with not a very good house, inadequate barns, makeshift machinery, happenstance stock, tired, overworked men and women . . . and all the pests and bucolic plagues that nature has evolved . . . a place where ugly, brooding monotony that haunts by day and night, unseats the mind. (Tugwell et al., 1930, p. 85).

In particular, he fundamentally disapproved of the whole rural homestead approach. The family farm seemed to him to be as much a monument of the primitive past as was the small business; both were structured defects in an economy committed to large-scale units. Tugwell felt that this "back to the land" ideology went against technology, and to do that was to go against history. If the family farm or the rural homestead had a role, it was at best peripheral, exacting a far higher economic cost than social value justified (Schlesinger, 1958, p. 369). "I am inclined to believe," he wrote in 1933, "that such settlements will function merely as small eddies of retreat for exceptional persons and that the greater part of our population will prefer to live and work in the more active and vigorous mainstream of a highly complex civilization" (ibid., p. 369).

The city as corrective

The correct approach to mitigate rural poverty, he felt, was in the cities. The cities themselves could also benefit, for here was a rare opportunity for almost limitless experimentation in land use planning, community planning, massive rural conservation programs, and a better life for exhausted people. But the opportunity for the concurrent correction of rural poverty and urban problems was not being taken advantage of. In addition, Tugwell in his position as Undersecretary of Agriculture was becoming disappointed. His private hopes for awakening the conservative USDA to the needs of the marginal farmer were not materializing (Baldwin, 1968, p. 88).

Steps toward creation of resettlement administration

By 1935, business was showing signs of improvement, and the older members of Congress were beginning to question many of the recovery methods used by Roosevelt to stimulate the depressed American economy. Many felt that some of FDR's programs were too socialistic and radical. Tugwell realized that if socio-economic improvement was to occur, it was necessary to take action immediately. But a close inspection of the USDA revealed that agencies dealing with land and poverty programs were working independently of, and often competing with, one another. Tugwell felt that a program consolidation under one agency was necessary to implement improvement of rural poverty conditions, thus permitting a better use of the land. FDR knew this also, for both had discussed a centralization of these programs, but, due to administration difficulties and interagency rivalries, reorganization had not been accomplished. In early 1935, Tugwell decided that there was little he could accomplish without this reorganization, and began to consider leaving the USDA (Baldwin, 1968, p. 88).

On February 18, 1935, Tugwell suggested in conversation with FDR that he wanted to resign his position. FDR refused to consider such a move; in fact, Tugwell wrote in his diary, "He regarded me as a distinct political asset . . . he had no intention of letting me go at all." During the days that followed, he and FDR discussed several courses to follow. FDR's intention was the implementation of "new" policies outlined in his State of the Union message of January 4, 1935. These included three types of security: livelihood, hazards of life, and housing. The type of housing reform FDR advocated was a form of slum clearance. Tugwell, however, was not in agreement because, in his opinion, FDR's plan would not go far enough in correcting the problems of the rural poor.[6] Still dissatisfied, Tugwell again discussed possible resignation with FDR, who then suggested that he consider other approaches regarding the slum clearance issue and work out possible solutions. On March 3, he again talked with Roosevelt:

FDR let me off slum clearance, though he laughed at me for not wanting to do it. I talked to him about satellite cities as an alternative and it interested him greatly. My idea is to go just outside centers of population, pick up cheap land, build a whole community and entice people into it. Then go gack into cities and tear down slums and make parks of them. I could do this with good heart and he now wants me to. (Diary, March 3, 1935.)

Four days after Tugwell had spoken with Roosevelt about his "satellite cities" plan, he reported, "I submitted my charts and plans to FDR and he approved completely, giving me permission to get the things organized" (Diary, March 7, 1935). His attitude was reminiscent of a piece he had written twenty years earlier for the Intercollegiate Magazine while a sophomore at the University of Pennsylvania – a piece which would provide a great deal of pleasure for his critics in the years to come.

> I am strong
> I am well made
> I am muscled and lean and nervous
> I am frank and sure and incisive.
>
> I bend the forces untameable;
> I harness the power irresistible–
> All this I do; but I shall do more.
>
> I am sick of a nation's stenches,
> I am sick of propertied czars . . .
> I have dreamed my great dream of their passing,
> I have gathered my tools and my charts;
> My plans are fashioned and practical;
> I shall roll up my sleeves . . . make America over.
>
> (Bolles, 1936, p. 77)

Plate 11.3 Greendale, Wisconsin

The automobile and Greenbelt

Literature is replete with statements that the men who designed and laid out the Greenbelt towns drew on a rich international heritage of town planning theory and practice (Arnold, p. 3). Particular reference has been made to Ebenezer Howard and his Garden City movement. However, there is little evidence to suggest that Tugwell was influenced by Howard to any great extent. According to John Lansill, Tugwell's director of the Suburban Resettlement Administration, both men were highly influenced by other American planned communities during this period, communities associated with the introduction of the automobile in the 1920s (Lansill, 1972).[7] As Mel Scott notes, after 1920 people began to buy automobiles by the millions, 2.3 million in 1922 and more than 3.0 million annually from 1923 through 1926. In 1927 sales went to 3.8 million and reached 4.5 million in the climactic year of 1929 (Scott, p. 186). The sheer number of automobiles contributed enormously to environmental and financial stress. Many problems were created, among them a demand for better streets and roads, and for better paving and wider streets on the part of the merchants, who complained that the existing streets were choked with traffic. An additional strain was placed on municipal treasures which had to purchase expensive traffic and road maintenance equipment. The boom in automobiles had a very grim aspect also; by 1925, traffic accidents were claiming approximately twenty-four thousand lives annually.

According to Scott, the incidence of fatalities and injuries caused by the automobile was the factor which prompted some of the most constructive endeavors of the times and did much to stimulate interest in city and town planning (Scott, p. 188). In the 1920s, developer William Harmon stated that all his future housing plans would include their own recreational sites because automobile traffic had made streets literally death traps for children and pedestrians. Clarence Perry was designing residential areas that would be free from noise, fumes, and the hazards of automobiles. Radburn, a typical example of what Perry had in mind, was described as "a city for the motor age." It had superblocks of thirty to fifty acres in which there were interior parks where children could play without fear of falling beneath the wheels of cars. A host of other housing developments throughout America in the 1920s and 1930s were designed to restrict the use of the automobile and make the environment safer. Among these were Shaker Heights in Cleveland, designed by the Van Sweringen brothers; Torrance, California, designed by J. S. Torrance; and the Country Club District of Kansas City, designed by Jesse Nichols. The Van Sweringens employed many of the features of suburban residential development later to be used in planning the typical Greenbelt New Town: abandonment of the traditional gridiron and substitution of curving and semi-elliptical roads leading from main automobile boulevards, the preservation of natural park areas throughout, and strict architectural requirements (Glaab and Brown, p. 283).

For these reasons, Lansill maintained that the Greenbelt New Town program initiated by Rexford Tugwell owed few direct intellectual debts to Howard, instead drawing heavily on the newly created American school of thought concerning urban development. Walt Creese notes that

an exercise can be prepared to show that the United States, with its rapid growth in the nineteenth century and its receptivity to novel schemes, contributed substantially to the impetus of the garden city movement. It would require only a little chauvinism to persuade us that most of the basic premises of the garden city movement in England originated here in the United States. (Creese, p. 1).

Early Greenbelt designs

For Beltsville, Maryland, Tugwell originally envisioned a group of skyscrapers fifty or sixty stories high, cruciform in plan and very widely spaced, containing housing, administrative, and commercial space. These designs were greatly influenced by Le Corbusier's Ville Contemporaine, the city designed for three million inhabitants which was displayed at the Paris Exhibition of 1922. Le Corbusier's city was surrounded by a "green belt" several miles wide, permanently isolating and protecting it; industrial districts were situated to the east, with farms and a sports arena to the northwest. The optimum population of three million was not to be exceeded; additional new cities would be built to accommodate the excess. With the possible exception of Tony Garnier's Plan for an Ideal City of thirty-five thousand (1901–4), Le Corbusier's Ville Contemporaine was the first really contemporary vision for a new metropolis: an imaginative exercise in ideal city planning, bringing into play all the then known and anticipated technological advances and building forms (Anthony, p. 281).

However, John Lansill, Tugwell's friend since their days as students at the University of Pennsylvania, was appalled by Le Corbusier's design. Lansill, upon graduation from the Wharton School of Finance, had entered a Wall Street brokerage house and had lived and worked among the concrete canyons of Manhattan. It was an architectural form he never enjoyed, and he thought the idea of purposefully designing a city from the beginning and constructing it in this manner was insane. Lansill was able to convince Tugwell to abandon Le Corbusier's Ville Contemporaine idea in favor of single- and multi-family housing units.

The first fruits of the Greenbelt New Town program were not altogether encouraging. "One of the major problems in getting the program started was the difficulty of getting together a staff capable of handling a huge building problem" (Lansill, 1972). To its distress, the Resettlement Administration was handicapped by the nationwide ignorance about housing. In addition, it appeared that Tugwell had a bias against architects and town planners (Lansill, 1972). Part of the reason stemmed from the experiences of the Public Works Administration (PWA) in its attempts to construct low-cost housing in urban areas, in conjunction with minor slum clearance programs. PWA had found that most American architects and town planners had conceptual difficulties in attempting to design reasonable low-income housing within the constraints established by budgets and land use requirements.[8] Tugwell also believed that architects and town planners were too utopian and idealistic. Consequently, the Resettlement Administration did not immediately turn to city planners or designers for advice, but rather to its own engineering staff which had considerable experience in designing many rural low-income subsistence homestead projects (Arnold, p. 47).

The first design for Greenbelt, Maryland, represented a typical subdivision of the period, calling for a grid land use plan with over sixty miles of streets. This might have been the model for all the succeeding Greenbelt New Towns if it had not been for Warren Vinton. Vinton was the chief economist of the Resettlement Administration and he had mentioned the Greenbelt design to a group of friends, several of whom were architects. Sketching out the plans as he remembered them, Vinton was persuaded that the engineers had produced an undistinguished, unimaginative design for a housing project of Greenbelt's magnitude (Baldwin, 1972). John Lansill was later approached about the inadequacies of the design and with Tracy Augur, Tennessee Valley Authority's chief town planner, they agreed to approach Tugwell with the recommendation that all the engineers be replaced with professional town planners. Tugwell, though reluctant, allowed the change to take place. The engineering staff was dispersed, and a separate planning and architectural team was designed for each of the four Greenbelt towns (Lansill, 1972). (See Table 11.1.)

Planning the four towns

The planning of the four towns intentionally reflects four different approaches to the problem. Setting up four parallel, vertical organizations may seem, on superficial view, extravagant in its duplication and cumbersome in procedure. However, John Lansill felt that as the head of a new type of venture and as a layman dependent on the technicians to carry out the program, he could not afford to rely on any one theory of design procedure. Moreover, the projects were in four widely differing localities; local laws, prejudices, habits, and wants would all have to be considered. After an abortive start with the in-house architectural engineers, Lansill felt that the time for standardization was not yet here. Because the whole venture was in the nature of an experiment, the more talent that could be enrolled, the better the chances for success.

According to Arnold, this type of thinking was quite remarkable (p. 83). The Resettlement Administration could have stayed with the dull, unimaginative designs put forth by the initial engineering group. It could have met its primary responsibility by merely constructing a large number of simple dwellings. But the receptivity of Tugwell and Lansill to design criticism was unusual; as a result the enthusiasms of the planners and architects in the Resettlement Administration became widespread. They were inspired, said Lansill, by the standard set by Tugwell to create a demonstrable example and set it before the American people (Lansill, 1972). As the project evolved they became increasingly convinced that they were involved in one of the most significant American experiments in city building the nation had ever seen. Will Alexander says, "The young architects felt sure that this Resettlement Administration was going to revolutionize the concept of urban built form" (Arnold, p. 50). Marquis Childs recalled the enthusiasms of the planners who kept the lights burning far into the night, and said, "They thought they were planning a new world" (ibid., p. 50).

No one within the Resettlement Administration posed his own ideas on the planning staff. Therefore, each separate team worked independently of the other town planning staffs. This was necessary because each town site was different in topography, population, economy, and legal structure.

Table 11.1 Greenbelt New Town organizational structure

Henry C. Wallace *Secretary, Department of Agriculture*
Rexford Guy Tugwell *Director, Resettlement Administration*
John Scott Lansill *Director, Suburban Resettlement*
Henry Wright *General Consultant*
Clarence S. Stein *Architectural Consultant*
Tracy Augur *Regional Consultant*
Earle Draper *Policy Formation*
Catherine Bauer *Special Consultant*
Russell Bloch *Special Consultant*
Tilford Dudley *Land Acquisition*
Reid W. Diggs *Budget & Finance*
Warren S. Vinton *Social & Economic Research*
Frederick Bigger *Chief of Planning*

Section	Greenbelt	Greenhills	Greendale	Greenbrook
Architects	Reginald S. Wadsworth	Roland A. Wank	Harry A. Bentley	Albert Mayer
	Douglas D. Ellington	G. Frank Condner	Walter G. Thomas	Henry S. Churchill
Planners	Hale Walker	Justin Hartzog	Elbert Peets	Henry Wright
		William A. Strong	Jacob Crane	Allen Kanstra
Engineers	Harold B. Bursley	William T. Powell	Walter E. Kroening	Ralph Eberlin
			Charles D. Putnam	
Regional Coordinator	William Richards	Albert Miller	Fred L. Naumer	Isaac McBride

Each planning staff had three departments: town planning, architecture, and engineering. Subsections were established to plan electrical, heating, utilities, and landscaping. The planning staff was headed by one or two men designated as chief town planner, chief architect, or chief engineer, but the group was collectively responsible for the whole project.

The Greenbelt town plan included a sweeping crescent-shaped town along a beautifully wooded ridge with the open end of the crescent facing prevailing summer breezes. Greenhills was built along the crest of a number of small ridges cut by ravines and resulted in a somewhat irregular town pattern. Greendale is laid out on very gently rolling land, and the tract is cut in by a small creek running through its very center. Greenbrook would have been built on nearly flat terrain.

Low residential density was considered desired for all the towns. In the residential area of Greendale there were approximately 5 families per acre. At Greenhills, there were 8.5 families per acre and at Greenbelt, 4 families per acre.

At Greenbrook and Greenbelt the curvilinear streets were designed to form superblocks which were intended to form a physical basis for the development of neighborhoods, as had been done at Radburn and several other new towns. The Greendale planners rejected the superblock as well as curvilinear streets. Elbert Peets, the town planner, was attracted to traditional architectural styles, particularly that of colonial Williamsburg. Peets later said, "It was not quite an accident that in its skeleton organization the plan of Greendale is much like the plan of Williamsburg" (Arnold, p. 94).

The exterior design of the buildings for all three of the Greenbelt towns is generally considered disappointing. Henry Churchill, an advisor, called the exteriors "competent and undistinguished." There was no conscious effort to follow any set precedent in the design of the buildings, and if one had to label the style, it could be called "functional" or "contemporary" (Arnold, p. 102). Basically, Greenbelt's architecture is an example of what the designers of the 1930s regarded as the "New Tradition" (now called the International Style in architecture), a reaction against the ornamentation and sentimental traditionalism of Victorian styles which held their own in the United States up to and including the 1920s. Greendale, from the aesthetic point of view, is considered to be the most interesting. Peets, the head architect, patterned his houses on the American colonial pattern, close to the street with small fenced yards on the side and rear. Nevertheless, each group of planners for the Greenbelt towns showed remarkable imagination and thoroughness in the face of great pressures during the depression days of the mid-1930s and with a back-breaking schedule to achieve these accomplishments in a period of one and one-half years.

Greenbelt opposition and the courts

It was no secret that the Greenbelt New Town program was pioneering a new pattern of rural–urban industrial life. However, not everyone appreciated the pioneer spirit of Tugwell and the Greenbelt town planners. When the plans for the fourth new town, Greenbrook, were announced, this lack of appreciation appeared in the form of a legal challenge.

Greenbrook was to have been the largest of the Greenbelt projects, containing over twenty thousand people. Its location was between New Brunswick and Princeton, New Jersey. By a three-to-one decision in the United States Court of Appeals in the District of Columbia on May 18, 1936, the Resettlement Administration was enjoined from proceeding with its construction. In arguing the case before the court, Dean Acheson, counsel for the township, pleaded that this new town would cause something of a revolution in the character of the township, changing it from rural to urban in nature almost overnight and adding to the cost of local government without supplying a compensating source of revenue. Another factor was that Greenbrook was designed to accommodate twenty thousand people, and many residents within the township feared that existing property values would drop if a United States government-subsidized new town were constructed. The township had other than monetary interests in the Greenbrook case; by forcing an unwanted development upon it by the federal government, it was argued, the township would be in danger of losing its home rule (*The United States Law Week*, 1936, p. 6).

In a lengthy opinion, the court also held that the provision of the Emergency Relief Appropriations Act of 1935, pursuant to which the Resettlement Administration was created, constituted an invalid delegation to the President of the Congressional power to legislate because (Minutes of the United States Court of Appeals for the District of Columbia, 1936):

1 There was no adequate definition of the subject;
2 There was nothing in the Act directly prescribing the powers and duties of the President with respect to housing; and
3 The declaration of purpose was too vague.

Ordinarily Congress may lay down policies and establish standards, leaving it to the appropriate government agencies to make subordinate rules within prescribed limits to fill in details, and to determine the facts to which the policies declared by the legislature apply. Under this Act, the Court declared that no policies or standards were laid down, and the President was improperly free to decide when, where, and how housing projects could be established (Robbins, p. 5).

This objection could have been cured by amendment to the original Act or by new legislation. However, the court went further and held that the federal government had no power to engage directly in housing activities for two reasons:

1 That such activities are not within the scope of the powers granted to Congress, because housing projects "have no connections with the general welfare"; and
2 That such activities are reserved for action by the states alone. Therefore, legislation by Congress for that purpose is forbidden (Minutes, 1936).

Although the Circuit Court's decision seemed to doom the entire Resettlement program, the United States Attorney General announced that the decision would be limited to the New Jersey project, Greenbrook. An appeal to the Supreme Court was dropped, and the other projects which remained unchallenged were pushed toward completion with the funds already allocated to them. However, new projects could not be initiated because the Emergency Relief Appropriations Act which provided the funds to build the new towns had also been declared unconstitutional (Minutes, 1936). For all practical purposes, the Circuit Court's decision brought to a halt America's first large-scale attempt to integrate all the factors that go into making a balanced community – towns planned from the beginning according to a definite conception of purpose and overall balance.

Opposition to resettlement

As Lash noted, both Eleanor and Franklin Roosevelt supported the

Resettlement Greenbelt project. But even this support was not enough. By 1936, the mood of the country, and especially that of Congress, was growing hostile to the whole idea of publicly planned communities. The political environment had become unfriendly to such social experimentation and to such reformers as Tugwell who wanted to "make America over" (p. 413).

Eleanor Roosevelt, a strong supporter of the rural subsistence homesteads, felt saddened about the opposition to the Resettlement project:

If experiments like Resettlement are not justified, [she said] "we must go along the beaten path and be contented with the same type of living which has driven people out of rural districts in the past and into the cities where they have become equally unhappy under present industrial conditions. (Lash, p. 417)

However, the lessons of the Greenbelt New Towns went unappreciated. Instead of a planned approach to the related problems of the flight from the farms, urban congestion, and industrial decentralization, the outcome was left to the unchecked operation of social and economic forces that had produced the crisis of the cities in the first place (ibid., p. 417).

Tugwell had hoped to construct a good many projects; at a press conference he once remarked that we need three thousand new towns instead of the three being planned. But the entire Administration came under such fierce attack that the program was limited to three, which were never completed, and were later disposed of by the government to speculators. Tugwell thought the attack stemmed from the belief that the Resettlement Administration was doing something for those who had done nothing to deserve it: an administration of extravagant do-gooders (Tugwell, 1959, p. 163).

Planning

Another source of conflict between Congress and the Resettlement Administration was the stress placed on planning, especially the idea of land use control, and the retiring of land no longer suitable for agricultural use. Congress met this idea with "complete scorn." They let us know that this was a fancy idea devised by intellectuals, therefore, it was wholly impractical; and they refused to have anything to do with it," Tugwell wrote (1959, p. 161).

Critics may have disagreed about Tugwell's ideological commitments but on one point there was agreement, that he was basically an iconoclast (Baldwin, p. 88). Hostile to the traditional laissez-faire attitude with its tendency toward anarchy, Tugwell saw national salvation lying not simply in productive efficiency, technological innovation, and improving the market mechanism, but also in growth guided by public planning and control.

Although he did not expect ideality to be just around the corner, Tugwell knew that planning implied a revolution, with new attitudes, new disciplines, revised legal structures, unaccustomed limitations on freedom, and an end to privatism (Conkin, p. 151). He felt that people were generally opposed to planning; that there were strong emotional and physical investments in the status quo; that the effectuation of planning required change in institutions, a realignment of vested interests, and the displacement of people; and that planning involved conclusions and commitments with respect to an indefinite future (Tugwell, 1947). He had realized that it was perhaps more difficult to plan than not to plan, seemingly easier to wait until the situation was self-evident and decisions were forced upon him. He felt that these were limitations to be overcome rather than reasons not to proceed. When Tugwell looked around him, he saw trends in society which suggested that there were no alternatives to increased planning, the growing technological and organizational complexity of business and government, population growth and migration patterns, the continued specialization of labor, and the foreseeable exhaustion of many of the natural energy sources on which the nation relied.

To Tugwell his Greenbelt towns represented a pioneer effort. Through them he hoped to weave a new pattern of rural–industrial life, a method of land use in which the old, wasteful practices never had a chance to get started:

I really would like to conserve all those things which I grew up to respect or love and not see them destroyed. I grew up in an American small town and I've never forgotten it. No one was very rich there, but no one was very poor either. I can't make this Park Avenue country club life seem right, along with slums and breadlines, ballyhoo, speculation; I can't make this fit into my picture of American institutions.

I'm for decentralization, for simplicity of life, along with a recognition of the complexity of industrial and scientific civilization. It seems to me that electricity, vacuum tubes, Diesel engines and all those other things ought to make it possible for us to approximate that "no riches–no poverty" kind of life in which I grew up. (Lord, p. 360)

Congress kills Resettlement Administration

But young intellectuals such as Tugwell who influenced the President and who disregarded traditional political methods were bound to arouse a mounting resentment and rebellion on the part of Congress. Their lack of a definite mandate and their lack of political experience proved to be a decided weakness.

Tugwell wrote, "We were a Presidential protégé; and we were among the first to suffer from the inevitable upsurge of antipresidential emotions following his great second term victory" (1959, p. 163). He felt that Congress as an institution could not tolerate its being outshone by the President.

Plate 11.4 Greenbelt, Maryland.

When the 1936 election was over, Congress was in a mood to assert its prerogatives, and the Resettlement Administration was one of the first programs to be eliminated.

On December 31, 1936, Tugwell resigned his position as the head of the Resettlement Administration. His organization was under attack from several sides and he felt that if he left then, the legislators might be content with his resignation and leave the Administration alone to do its work. But he was mistaken. In fact, it was completely dissolved. Twenty-three years later he had this to say to younger successors in governmental service:

> If you feel impelled to organize a constructive attack on social ills, be sure that you are riding a drift of support likely to register at the source of funds. In other words, the Congress must have a bad conscience too.
>
> Be sure that those who will be benefited will be able to, and will, register their support whenever the struggles for your continuance occur.
>
> My final advice to those who are thus moved by injustices and human needs, and who think they perceive better possibilities through social organization, is to go ahead. Fail as gloriously as some of your predecessors have. If you do not succeed in bringing about any permanent change, you may at least have stirred some slow consciences so that in time they will give support to action. And you will have the satisfaction, which is not to be discounted, of having annoyed a good many miscreants who had it coming to them. (Tugwell, 1959, p. 164)

Conclusion

The three completed Greenbelt New Towns represent the Federal Government's initial efforts in building new towns in America. They were not the garden cities of Ebenezer Howard, economically complete, but satellite suburbs, made possible for the first time because of the universal and economical availability of the automobile. Howard's garden cities may be thought of as being escapist, reflecting a desire to leave London entirely. Tugwell, on the other hand, believed existing cities could be made more livable but he was dismayed by their deficiences, which were due to lack of order, management, and control. In addition, with technology displacing farm workers and releasing them to industrial employment in the cities, Tugwell believed that urban growth and development had to be controlled, not stopped or abandoned, but guided and regulated through planning. The Greenbelt New Towns would demonstrate this belief. However, Tugwell's demonstration of more orderly growth, his efforts to surround housing with a more pleasing environment went unappreciated and ultimately were rejected. It was simply a road not taken. In the late 1940s or early 1950s, Tugwell wrote:

I am, after all these years, still bitter about the disappearance of the Resettlement Administration and still harbor, in spite of myself, a good deal of stubborn resentment. No one paid any penalty for killing Resettlement. But I still believe that something like it must be done for the sake of the people and the land. I hope in its next incarnation it will meet with greater success. (Diary, section 7, p. 34)

Acknowledgements

The author would like to express his appreciation to the JAIP reviewers and to Dr Virginia Yans-McLaughlin of the City College of The City University of New York for their helpful comments and suggestions in the preparation of this manuscript.

Notes

1 See, for example, Glaab and Brown, p. 303, and also Stein, pp. 120 and 130.
2 Tugwell writes: "The idea for this agency was my own, and I was made its administrator. President Roosevelt was, however, immediately interested because it touched matters he cared about a great deal" (Tugwell, 1959, p. 159).
3 Tugwell notes: "The conception of suburban resettlement came less from the garden city of England than from some studies of our own population movements which showed steady growth in the periphery of the cities . . . in other words [Greenbelt] accepted a trend instead of trying to reverse it" (Tugwell, 1937, p. 43), and Lash writes: "Tugwell's emphasis as resettlement administrator was on land reform. His program sought to 'take poor people off poor land and resettle them where good land, good organization and good advice might rehabilitate them.' In addition, he promoted the brilliant concept of the Greenbelt towns, garden communities built in wooded areas adjacent to industrial areas" (Lash, p. 413).

4 For one of the best descriptions of the plight of the American farmer during the Depression, see John Steinbeck's *The Grapes of Wrath*.
5 See Roosevelt's article about the benefits of rural life as opposed to urban living (Roosevelt, 1931), and also Slicker's descriptions of Roosevelt's "back to the land" concepts (1959).
6 Tugwell did not embrace slum clearance as did FDR. Tugwell felt that garden cities offered a better environment "for living and working" than did seeking to rebuild existing cities. "Slum clearance has to fight a good many entrenched interests; and its land costs are too high ever to protect the rights of children or ever to provide recreation for adults. Cities will not develop such projects as these; they will probably oppose them" (Tugwell, 1937, p. 43).
   Albert M. Miller's view was similar: "When an effort is made to rebuild bad areas in a city, with new housing, we are confronted with a confused background of extravagant municipal procedure, and often with mythical land values, transportation companies in receivership, defaulting of municipal debt interest and all the rest of the confusion which businessmen of the communities have allowed to grow up around them" (Speech, 1936, p. 15).
7 According to Peets: "The program, the skeleton of ideas and facts, on which Greenbelt is being planned is something like this: Automotive transportation makes it possible for men to live a considerable distance from their work; pure air, rural surroundings, and contact with the ground, are physically and psychically good; life is better in a small town where social cooperation is possible; by eliminating inflated land values, by appropriate planning, by large-scale construction, and by taking advantage of every reasonable means for reducing living costs" (p. 409).
8 For examples of these difficulties, see Hackett, pp. 1 and 4; Stein, p. 120; and Arnold, p. 88.

References

Anthony, Harry A. (1967) "LeCorbusier: His Ideas for Cities," *American Institute of Architectural Journal*, September.
Arnold, Joseph (1971) *New Deal In The Suburbs*, Columbus, Ohio, Ohio State University.
Baldwin, C. B. (1972) Interview, August.
Baldwin, Sidney (1968) *Poverty and Politics*, Chapel Hill, N.C., University of North Carolina Press.
Bolles, Blair (1936) "The Sweetheart of the Regimenters," *American Mercury*, September.
Conkin, Paul (1959) *Tomorrow A New World*, Ithaca, New York, Cornell University Press.
Creese, Walter L. (1966) *The Search For Environment: The Garden City: Before and After*, New Haven, Yale University Press.
Emergency Relief Appropriations Act of 1935, US Statutes at Large, vol. 49, p. 115.
Franklin Township v. *Tugwell*, 85F (App., D.C.) 208 (1936).
Glabb, Charles N. and A. Theodore Brown (1967) *A History of Urban America*, London, Macmillan.
Hackett, Horatio B. (1935) "Problems and policies of the Housing Division of PWA," *Housing Officials Yearbook*, Washington, D.C., National Association of Housing.
Lansill, John S. (1972) Interview, June.

Lash, Joseph P. (1972) *Eleanor and Franklin*, New York, W. W. Norton.

Lord, Russell (1947) *The Wallaces of Iowa*, Boston, Houghton Mifflin.

Lowi, Theodore J. (1969) *The End of Liberalism*, New York, W. W. Norton.

Mann, Maurice (1952) "Rexford Guy Tugwell, Institutional Economist," master's thesis, Department of Economics, Boston University.

Miller, Albert L. (1936) "Resettlement Administration," Speech before the Citizen's Committee on Slum Clearance and Low Rent Housing, Cincinnati, June 24.

Minutes of United States Court of Appeals For The District of Columbia #6619, "The Township of Franklin v. *Rexford Tugwell,"* May 18, 1936.

Peets, Elbert (1937) "Greendale," in *City Planning-Housing*, edited by Werner Hegemann, New York, Architectural Book Publishing.

Robbins, Ira (1936) "Resettlement Administration only partially unsettled," *American City*, June.

Roosevelt, Franklin D. (1931) "Back to the land," *The Review of Reviews*, October.

Roosevelt, Nicholas (1970) *Conservation: Now or Never*, New York, Dodd, Mead.

Rosenman, Samuel I. (1950) *The Public Papers and Addresses of Franklin D. Roosevelt*, 13 vols, New York, Random House.

Schlesinger, Jr, Arthur M. (1958) *The Coming of the New Deal*, Boston, Houghton Mifflin.

Scott, Mel (1971) *American City Planning*, Berkeley, University of California Press.

Slichter, Gertrude A. (1959) "Franklin D. Roosevelt's farm policy as Governor of New York State, 1928–1932," *Agricultural History*, October.

Stein, Clarence S. (1957) *Toward New Towns For America*, New York, Reinhold.

Steinbeck, John (1939) *The Grapes of Wrath*, New York, The Viking Press.

Sternsher, Bernard (1964) *Rexford Tugwell and the New Deal*, New Brunswick, Rutgers University Press.

Tugwell, Rexford Guy et al. (1930) *American Economic Life and The Means of Its Improvement*, New York, Harcourt, Brace.

Tugwell, Rexford Guy, "Diary Notes," manuscript, FDR Library, Hyde Park, New York.

___ (1935) "No more frontiers," *Today*, June 22.

___ (1936a) "Housing activities and plans of the Resettlement Administration," *Housing Officials Yearbook*, March, Washington, D.C., National Association of Housing.

___ (1936b) "Down to earth," *Current History*, July.

___ (1937) "The meaning of the Greenbelt Towns," *The New Republic*, February 17.

___ (1947) *The Stricken Land*, New York, Doubleday.

___ (1959) "The Resettlement idea," *Agricultural History*, October.

The United States Law Week (1936) "Resettlement Administration – Constitutionally Injunction," May 19.

12 Seeing things whole: a consideration of Lewis Mumford

Park Dixon Goist[1]

> Mumford is a revolutionary thinker . . . in the sense of one who
> burrows down to neglected fundamentals – the plainest human
> biological needs, the most obvious aspirations of ordinary men and
> women – and works out what modern science, skill and creative
> energy could do to satisfy these if to satisfy them were the conscious
> aim of society. (Frederic J. Osborn)

Lewis Mumford is one of America's most challenging writers. His intellectual lineage includes Ralph Waldo Emerson and Herman Melville. Like these predecessors, he is, as his friend Frederick Osborn suggests, a revolutionary thinker – one who challenges our basic assumptions about human existence. He distrusts specialization and conventional wisdom as means of achieving an understanding of life's fullness. In coming to Mumford's thought, it is necessary then to realize that his approach is basically at odds with most of our dominant perspectives. These he finds overly specialized and too narrowly scientific. Starting from a holistic view alien to specialists, he has challenged many of the assumptions we usually accept without question. Mumford maintains that our failure to cope with basic human needs is due not to inadequate technology but to our growing unwillingness to exert humane control over science and *technics*. This observation has led him to offer a radical reinterpretation of the role of science and technology in human history. In this work he has been an activist, a maker of events – not as a wielder of political power, but in the sense that by deliberate, organized thought he has actually given new meaning to the facts of human experience. In his studies of urban development and his essays on contemporary planning, Mumford has also challenged planners for frequently aggravating rather than alleviating the crisis of man's environment. His alternative is a regional approach, patterned largely after the work of Patrick Geddes, the Scottish regionalist. Mumford sees this regionalism as a first step in the fundamental, but gradual, reorientation of values which he insists must take place if our civilization is to survive and grow. Thus in calling us back to fundamentals, Mumford has emphasized the role human values must play in our plans for the future.

The hallmark of Mumford's life and work is balance and wholeness.

In asserting the need for balance in the region, the community, and the individual, he has emphasized the close interaction of these levels of human organization. Mumford defines balance as a means of providing for individual and social growth by holding in dynamic equilibrium the polarities of existence – stability and change, security and adventure, necessity and freedom. For the person, balance means experiencing both physical and mental exercise, group involvement and contemplative withdrawal, family nurture and individual experimentation. It also means an effort to avoid the unbalancing effects of specialization, for "specialism is hostile to life." Balance can also provide the individual and society with the flexibility to make the fullest response to novel situations and unexpected opportunities or demands. In community and region, balance begins by subsuming mechanical and scientific means to human ends (homes, living space, sociability, meaningful work). It involves efforts to maintain an equilibrium between urban cultural advantages and rural contact with nature, between industry and agriculture, and between work and play. Community balance also implies an economy suited to basic human wants, not to the unlimited, artificially stimulated "needs" of conspicuous consumption.

One model Mumford offers of this wholeness in life is the ecological balance sought by living organisms and the organic complexes (ecosystems) which embody such efforts. The reason nineteenth-century biology plays so vital a role in Mumford's thought is the emphasis ecologists give to the balanced interplay of organisms, functions, and environment. Such an ecological or holistic approach is exemplified for him in the works and in the very lives of such figures as Charles Darwin and Patrick Geddes. It is this model of human fullness and balance which Mumford feels must help guide our plans for the future.

His instinct for wholeness led Mumford to decide early in life, based on Geddes' example, to forgo the career, though not the experience, of a specialist. Mumford's definition of a "generalist" is an apt description of himself: one who is "more interested in putting the fragments together in an ordered and significant pattern than in minutely investigating the separate parts" (1922–62b, p. 6).[2] In pursuing the means of "putting the fragments together," he has for over half a century been America's leading advocate of a regional planning marked by individual, social, and environmental balance. Furthermore, in the face of the ecological suicide being committed by man's irrational misuse of modern technology, he has vigorously asserted the primacy of fundamental human values. Thus in Mumford's work, *wholeness, balance, organicism, ecology, integrated personality, renewal,* and *planning* are the key terms that embody his strategy for dealing with our urbanized and mechanized world. They will also be the terms which guide the following discussion of his life and writings.

Plate 12.1 Lewis Mumford

Mumford's urban origins

Lewis Mumford is an urbanite. America's largest metropolis helped shape his personality, ambitions, and interests. Descended from German fore-bearers, he was born in Flushing, N.Y. He grew up in a mixed middle-class section of Manhattan's Upper West Side. As a youngster, he visited with his grandfather many other areas of the city, and from his old nurse he came to know something of the Irish Catholic working class of the West Side. From the enclosed, even provincial, world of the West Nineties, he ventured into the wider city as a student at Stuyvesant High School. He rubbed shoulders with the sons of Russian and Polish Jews from the Lower East Side, learned of Socialism, and knew "at least at second hand" about the belly dancers who performed at the Dewey Theatre, near Sharkey's saloon. On his way to school, he recognized not only the prostitutes around Fifteenth Street and Third Avenue but also on occasional five-mile walks home watched the building of the Public Library and Grand Central Terminal. He visited job printers on John Street, practiced tennis with his team on Staten Island, went to high school games in the Bronx, and worked on a city newspaper for a short while. Before he ever became a conscious student of urban development, the city was the very stuff of his life: "in short, long before I began to think about the city, I had absorbed much of it through my pores" (1955–65, p. 147).

Young Mumford was an amateur radio operator. With the help of a friendly instrument-maker, he built a radio set at the age of twelve and wrote up his experiments for a popular technical and electrical magazine, *Modern Electrics*. These youthful scientific interests, plus the reputation of Stuyvesant's basketball team, led him to choose the technical high school. Along with his scientific courses, he gained familiarity with tools and mechanical processes, received training in cabinetmaking, smithing, wood and metal turning, and foundry work. Thus he came to appreciate the ability and integrity of the craftsman, as well as gaining a high regard for machine technology. Enamored by current technological progress, Mumford planned to become an electrical engineer.

His enthusiasm for a technical career cooled in time. From such encounters as his study of Leonardo da Vinci (the hero of an early one-act comedy by Mumford) and his discovery of Patrick Geddes, he came to value the fullness of man's existence, not only his technical ability. By the time he graduated from high school in 1912, his ambitions had changed and he took a job as copy boy with the *Evening Telegram*, with some notion of becoming a newspaper reporter. After a two months' trial, he turned his back on that career. From 1912 on, until he entered the Navy in 1918, Mumford attended courses at a number of colleges in the city, particularly City College of New York. He wrote short stories, essays, and plays during this period; and although little of it was published, he was preparing for his eventual career as a writer.

The years prior to 1920 were exciting ones for a young urbanite bent on making his way in the world of literature and ideas. Mumford had already read Cooper and much of Poe, Twain, Longfellow, Whittier, Irving, Hawthorne, Whitman, and Emerson among the native authors. Now he also heard the newer poets and philosophers in Greenwich Village, at the Liberal Club on Macdougal Street, and at lectures given by the Intercollegiate Socialist Society. The New York in which he was serving his apprenticeship shared in a new spirit of national cultural invigoration heralded by such writers as Amy Lowell, Robert Frost, Paul Rosenfeld, Walter Lippman, Randolph Bourne, Van Wyck Brooks, and Waldo Frank. Young poets and political writers, Mumford's friends and contemporaries, were finding their voices and expressing their views in a number of new journals and reviews, among them the *Little Review*, *Seven Arts*, *The New Republic*, *The Masses*, and the fortnightly *Dial*. This was the hopeful time when H. G. Wells — whom Mumford greatly admired in his adolescence — was telling his eager young American readers that, "We are going to write of wasted opportunities and latent beauties, until a thousand new ways of living open to men and women" (May, p. 238). Waldo Frank declared in 1919, as Herbert Croly had ten years before, that for the younger generation America was a promise and a dream to be realized by "a fierce passion of renewal." Years later, four of Mumford's important works constituted what he called *The Renewal of Life* series.

This American rejuvenation was part of a broader cultural revolution. A growing number of thinkers during these years were deeply affected by the shattering of once accepted scientific certainties. The close mechanical world view of Newton was being challenged from numerous perspectives. Albert Einstein's work suggested to non-scientists that time, traditionally considered a basic necessity for human thought, was itself relative. The French mathematician Henri Poincaré said that the presumed "laws" of science and mathematics really reflected only a particular way of thinking, useful but not revealing the only truth. Henri Bergson, the French philosopher who had a large following among pre-war American intellectuals, in writing about evolution emphasized the creative role of the organism rather than the merely repetitive pattern described by science.[3] The meaning of all this ferment seemed to be, as Henry May points out, that life is too diverse and many-sided to be fully encompassed by the narrow, mechanistic universe posited by the scientific method (1959, pp. 219f.). It was within the context of this international "liberation," this opening up of possibilities, that American writers and artists like Lewis Mumford sought the renewal of national life. Mumford expressed something of the imprint this vital period left on him when he noted:

Though the first World War would blacken and blight the more tender buds, those whose minds were formed in the hopeful days before chaos dawned would, for the rest of their lives, still carry order – a human cosmos – in their hearts. (1926b–57, p. ix).

During these exhilarating and formative years, Mumford encountered more directly some of the men and ideas that helped to broaden his intellectual horizons and focus his abundant energies. When one is dealing with the extraordinary range and grasp of a synthetic mind such as Mumford's, it is impossible to do justice to all the sources that played a role in his development. A few can at least be mentioned. Among those whom Mumford has singled out as particularly important for the general broadening of his interests are Herbert Spencer, "that prince of generalists," and J. Salwyn Schapiro (a disciple of the historian James Harvey Robinson) from whom he took a course in politics. Also during the period before 1917, he became familiar with the work of Thorstein Veblen. After the war, in 1919, Mumford took a course with the author of *The Theory of the Leisure Class* (1899) at the New School for Social Research. In the same year, they met when both were connected with the fortnightly *Dial*. Though Mumford never shared Veblen's hopes for the dominant role of engineers in a technocratic society, he saw the strength of his observation that capitalism viewed production primarily in terms of pecuniary profits, while ignoring human needs. Veblen's interpretation of the adverse effects capitalism has on machine technology was an analysis congenial to one more concerned with the quality of life than with the mere commitment to an "expanding economy." Not least, Mumford saw in Veblen a superb satirist whose strength was a synthetic mind which ranged easily through various areas of human effort (1931b).

The discovery of Patrick Geddes

Even more important for the future direction of Mumford's writing, particularly in regard to technology and the city, was his discovery of Patrick Geddes. Young Mumford first came across Geddes in 1914 while studying biology, and a few years later started corresponding with the Scottish botanist and social philosopher. Among Geddes' varied interests was his concern for city and regional development. In 1904, his plan for improving the park system in the city of Dunfermline, entitled *City Development*, had appeared. In the year after his young American admirer discovered him, his more widely known *Cities in Evolution* was published. It was under the impetus of Geddes that Mumford became a conscious student of the city, first New York and its surrounding region, and then other eastern seaboard cities and villages. He began systematically to walk city streets – camera, sketchbook, and notebook in hand – photographing buildings and noting urban ways of life which before he had rather taken for granted. Essentially what the young New Yorker learned from Geddes was how to see a city in its regional and worldwide context, from the perspective of its origins and in regard to its importance for human life. Geddes perhaps also awakened Mumford to the realization that he might take a hand in helping to form the city. Years later, in describing the significance of *Cities in Evolution*, Mumford noted the dearth of material on the city prior to 1920, and then continued:

It taught the reader, in simple terms, how to look at cities and how to evaluate their development. See for yourself; understand for yourself; act on your own initiative on behalf of the community of which you are a part. That summarized Geddes' message. From the moment I gathered the import of Geddes' words, I began walking through the streets of New York and planning excursions into its hinterland with a new purpose: looking into its past, understanding its present, replanning its future became indissoluble parts of a single process, a task for all citizens, not merely for professionals. (1955–65, p. 106).

In 1919, Geddes suggested to his young American student that they collaborate in writing a book on contemporary politics – a project that never came to fruition. Then in 1920, Mumford was invited to London to serve as acting editor of the *Sociological Review*, organ of the Sociological

Society founded by Geddes in 1903. Geddes himself was in Palestine at the time as a consultant to the Zionist organization planning the new Jerusalem. The Scotsman then accepted a post as Professor of Civics and Sociology at the University of Bombay and asked Mumford to join him in India as his assistant. The younger man reluctantly refused the offer and returned to America (1966, p. 11).

During his sojourn in London, Mumford spent much time walking about the city with Victor Branford, Geddes' friend and colleague. Years later, he attested that those walks had greatly influenced his thinking about cities (1961, p. 585). In this respect, Mumford believes he owes almost as large a debt to Branford as to Geddes. In his published survey of Westminster (1919), Branford conveyed what must have impressed his American visitor: a knack for "reading history backwards," of illustrating how present city forms and activities are the modern survivals of historic uses and practices. He explained this ability as a reversed historical perspective which begins with an observation of a common object and then leads to a tracing of this contemporary form backward in time to its origins. In Branford's historical perspective, in his poignant social criticism, and in his life-long acquaintance with a great city, Mumford recognized a kindred spirit (1930, pp. 43–4; 1933a, p. 585; 1948, pp. 677–95).

This insistence upon the interaction of past, present, and future, which both Geddes and Branford illustrated, was also strongly felt by another of Mumford's friends, Van Wyck Brooks. Upon his return from England, Mumford became friends with Brooks, then an editor of a new weekly, *The Freeman*. A common interest in discovering a "usable past" as part of the cultural rejuvenation of America marked their friendship. Brooks' series of books entitled *Makers and Finders: A History of the Writer in America, 1800–1915*, was not motivated by the same concern with the origins of modern man's dilemma as Mumford's *Renewal of Life* volumes. But both men were searching out the meaning of modern culture, convinced that this demanded a knowledge of the past and how it is linked to the present, as a basis for shaping the future. A publishing effort which had this goal as one of its aims was the *American Caravan* (1927, 1928, 1929, 1931, 1936), a yearbook of American literature which featured such new authors as Robert Penn Warren, William Faulkner, Morley Callaghan, Mike Gold, Hart Crane, Richard Wright, and E. E. Cummings. Mumford joined Alfred Kreymborg and Paul Rosenfield in this venture.

One immediate reason for Mumford's return to New York in 1920 was the presence there of a young editorial assistant at the *Dial*, Sophia Wittenberg, whom Mumford married in 1921.[4] They remained for a few years in Greenwich Village and then Brooklyn Heights, before moving to the planned complex at Sunnyside Gardens on Long Island where they lived for eleven years. Participating actively in the intellectual life of the city, Mumford was one of the thirty writers Harold Stearns brought together in 1921 to write a critical evaluation of civilization in the United States. Among those involved in this project was Joel Spingarn, the literary critic. Spingarn invited Mumford for a weekend of conversation with himself, Brooks, and Ernest Boyd, at Troutbeck, his country place in upstate New York (Brooks, 1957, pp. 13, 141–2, 153, 172). The Mumfords were soon spending their summers in the region, and in 1936 moved to a farmhouse in the hamlet of Amenia. Some critics were later to find irony in the fact that a writer on cities lived in a Dutchess County village (Cowley, 1938). But Mumford spent the first forty-one years of his life in New York, and since has lived half of each year (except for a half dozen years in the 1940s and early 1950s) in a city (Hughes, p. 451).

The Story of Utopias and the uses of Utopian thought

Mumford brought together his interest in city and regional development, his concern for American culture, his historical perspective, and his search for wholeness as he began to publish widely in the 1920s. In 1919, he published his first article on urban history, applying Geddes' concept of a "valley section" to explain city development in the United States. In 1921, he contributed his essay "The city" to Stearns' *Civilization in the United States*. His reviews and articles were now appearing in numerous periodicals, including the *Freeman*, *The New Republic*, *American Mercury*, the *Dial* and the *Journal of the American Institute of Architects*. Between 1922 and 1931, he published five books, all of which are still in print. Mumford's first book, *The Story of Utopias*, written when he was twenty-six, celebrates its fiftieth anniversary this year. It indicates the direction of much that was to follow and expresses an outlook and approach characteristic of all his work.

   The Story of Utopias is an audacious book. It was conceived, researched, and written in five or six months in 1922.[5] Amidst the aftermath of the First World War, when so many intellectuals felt betrayed and disillusioned, Mumford called upon his readers "to talk about fundamentals – consider Utopia!" (p. 13). In a letter to Brooks, Mumford explained:

I undertook this utopian inquiry because it seemed to me necessary to throw a rainbow into the sky at just this moment, if our generation, and the one that is on our heels, were not to become sodden in spirit as a result of the storm through which we've passed. (Spiller, p. 19)

The book posed a most basic question: What is the first step out of the present disorder? Is there a method to help us put together the pieces of our shattered world, a basis upon which we can build livable communities? There was such a basis for renewal, and Mumford recognized one expression of it in what he called the *utopian method of thought*. This method is marked by an effort to see society whole, to understand the interaction of people, place, and work, and to see the relationship between social functions, institutions, and human purposes. It is akin to Geddes' ecological or synoptic view of life, which emphasizes the interplay among occupations, social organization, and physical environment in shaping the person and his community. Mumford found that such a view marked the heroic efforts of Emerson, Thoreau, and Whitman to challenge the accepted assumptions of their day. In *The Golden Day* (1926), he argued that these writers were among those who in the mid-nineteenth century were rethinking and reevaluating their social inheritance as a basis for reordering the disparate details of experience in order to "make possible a creative renovation" (1926b–57, p. 49). In his study of Herman Melville (1929), Mumford characterized this method as an "imaginative synthesis," a "double vision which sees with both eyes – the scientific eye of actuality, and the illumined eye of imagination and dream," a view of experience emerging from an integrated life and coherent consciousness (1929–62, p. 132). In writing *Moby Dick*, Melville was not employing a single method of knowledge. Rather, every aspect of human experience was poured into constructing the reality of the whale.

In praising a *utopian method of thought*, Mumford was not then arguing for a particular utopia or attempting to formulate his own. He was pointing out the weaknesses of all utopias. For "utopia" meant not only the imaginative projections of a Plato or H. G. Wells, but also the social myths and half-truths by which we live. These included the partial utopias of radicals as well as such accepted abstractions as the national state. All of these Mumford found "dull as mud" because they were removed from the complexity and diversity of the environments in which men actually lived. They failed to connect science and the arts to the common life of men. In utopias, as in the societies from which they emerge, the arts and sciences become the possession of specialists and are divorced from one another and from the vital day-to-day life of the community.

Thus the irony of *The Story of Utopias* is that Mumford finds utopias wanting because they are out of contact with the everyday world of real men and women. The challenge is to bring our utopian inner world of ideas back into contact with the actual world. How? Essentially by bringing both arts and sciences to bear on the problems and conditions in particular communities and definite regions. The best vehicle through which this objective can be realized is, Mumford argues, the Regional Survey developed by Patrick Geddes. Through this combination of imagination and detailed, localized knowledge gained by a survey which confronts the complicated totality of a particular region, we can challenge dominant social myths and begin to build viable communities. Thus concluded Lewis Mumford fifty years ago.

The Regional Planning Association of America

The regionalism Mumford has advocated for so long was an important ingredient in drawing together, during the 1920s, a group of architects and planners concerned with housing and community planning. Prior to the war, Mumford's growing interest in the physical city led him to the pages of the *Journal of the American Institute of Architects*. Under the editorship of Charles Harris Whitaker from 1913 and 1928, the journal became a focal point for men like Frederick Ackerman and Clarence Stein, whose special interests were housing and community planning. Ackerman, as chief of Housing and Town Planning for the Shipping Board, had been in charge of several housing projects during the First World War. Stein, an architect-turned planner, had a part in designing both the San Diego Exposition (1915) and Tyrone, New Mexico, planned for copper workers in 1917. Whitaker introduced Mumford to Stein, and in 1923, together with a dozen or so others, they formed a small, loosely structured organization, the Regional Planning Association of America. Other members included Ackerman, the economist Stuart Chase, Catherine Bauer, who became a housing expert, Clarence Perry, originator of the Neighborhood Unit Idea in planning, and Benton MacKaye, the conservationist who designed the famous Appalachian Trail. They met on weekends at Stein's Hudson Guild Farm in New Jersey, and one of their first guests in 1923 was Patrick Geddes. The RPAA advocated a non-metropolitan centered conception of regionalism and devised an alternative to unlimited urban expansion. In their books, reports, plans, and articles and in the communities they designed or helped plan, this group expressed a conception of the community at variance with dominant trends in city building and planning (Lubove, 1963).

Mumford and his RPAA colleagues argued that unrestricted real estate speculation resulted in a haphazard overcrowding of houses, people, and physical apparatus (streets, sewers, etc.) in increasingly unlivable cities. They criticized planning which merely encouraged monotonous suburban subdivisions, elaborate subway and highway proposals, costly street widenings, and arbitrary zoning restrictions – or permissions. These schemes facilitated congestion when the thrust of planning should be to check it. Mumford was also critical of grandiose "city of the future" projects, such as those of Hugh Ferriss and Le Corbusier. Writing in the 1920s, he conceded that such plans, marked by soaring glass and concrete skyscrapers, showed a certain boldness in the face of the "half-baked environment" of small-town America. But the metropolitan dream too often reflected "a sort of elephantiasis of the imagination," in which "the naive fantasies of the businessman came back to him with the prestige of city planning 'authority.'" He was particularly critical of what he felt to be the foolishness and inhumanity of plans aimed at "clearing away the cluttered quarters of an ordinary city block, and putting the inhabitants in a single tall building, surrounded by a garden" (1925b, pp. 454–6; 1926a, pp. 270–5; 1930b, pp. 332–3). Mumford asserts that such building, whether the Unité de'Habitation in Marseilles or Stuyvesant Town on Manhattan, is marked by a mechanized image of the city and a failure to distinguish between tidy looking open space and the actual social uses for which people need space.

One facet of the RPAA regionalist approach was the garden city concept as formulated by Ebenezer Howard at the turn of the century (1898, 1902). Mumford had read *Garden Cities of Tomorrow* shortly after becoming a conscious student of the city, and as early as 1917 wrote an article (which was never published) on garden civilizations (Hughes, pp. 166, 202, 208–9). The City Housing Corporation, a limited-dividend company, was formed by Alexander Bing, a successful real estate operator, to carry out the building of a community along garden city guidelines. After gaining experience in urban housing for lower incomes in Queens, New York (where Mumford lived from 1925 to 1936), the City Housing Corporation projected a town for the motor age in Radburn, New Jersey – an effort brought to an end by the Depression, after one neighborhood unit was built. These and a number of other experiments are fully described in Clarence Stein's *New Towns for America* (1951).

Mumford emerged as the RPAA's leading spokesman for regionalism. In 1925, he edited a special issue of *Survey Graphic* – a magazine of social concern edited by Paul Kellogg – devoted to exploring various aspects of regional planning. Along with Ackerman, Stein, Wright, and MacKaye, contributors to the discussion included New York Governor Alfred E. Smith, C. B. Purdom, English garden city advocate, and Alexander Bing, key financial backer of the City Housing Corporation. In his introduction to the Regional Plan Number, Mumford expressed the hopes and approach of these regionalists:

Regional planning asks not how wide an area can be brought under the aegis of the metropolis, but how the population and civic facilities can be distributed so as to promote and stimulate a vivid, creative life throughout a whole region – a region being any geographic area that possesses a certain unity of climate, soil, vegetation, industry and culture. The regionalist attempts to plan such an area so that all its sites and resources, from forest to city, from highland to water level, may be soundly developed, and so that the population will be distributed so as to utilize, rather than nullify or destroy its natural advantages. It sees people, industry and the land as a single unit. (1925a, p. 151)

Nearly forty years later, Mumford reaffirmed his position by explaining that regionalism consists "not of a *metropolitan* region dominated by a single center and continuous in structure with it, but of a regional framework capable of embracing cities of many sizes, including the central metropolitan center and giving each urban unit the advantage of the whole" (1962, p. 108). Thus the regionalism which Mumford and his colleagues were working out in the 1920s has remained at the center of his planning approach ever since.

Basic to Mumford's advocacy of regionalism is the belief that we cannot deal adequately with "the urban crisis" by accepting and encouraging those very trends which have brought on that crisis. This is what he was arguing in the 1920s, and in 1967. Testifying before the Ribicoff Committee on governmental expenditures, he asked, "Is there any reason to suppose that a massive new attempt of the federal government to wipe out the existing slums . . . will succeed any better than our earlier efforts *unless we change our methods and objectives?*" (1968, p. 215, my emphasis). Mumford doesn't think so any more now than he did in the 1920s. Why? In order to answer this fully we must turn to another important facet of Mumford's thought, his interpretation of *technics*.

The *Renewal of Life* series

Of Mumford's first five books, four deal with aspects of American culture, particularly architecture and literature. He had followed his study of utopian thought with a pioneer survey of American architecture, *Sticks and Stones* (1924). In 1931, he published a more thorough examination of art and architecture at the end of the nineteenth century in *The Brown Decades*. These two works, along with the two literary studies already mentioned, reveal Mumford's ability, regardless of the specific topic – a building or bridge, a novel or poem, a city plan or painting, even an individual life – to see the connections among, and give a pattern of meaning to, apparently disparate phenomena. The special genius revealed in these early books was a gift for relating the particular object with the broader culture, "the immediate and local with the remote and universal." But these works were really preparatory notes for the comprehensive studies which followed. Van Wyck Brooks, in reading *The Brown Decades*, sensed "that all these sketches and ideas are probably fragments of the great book that has to be written" (Spiller, p. 70). As it turned out the "great book" emerged as the four *Renewal of Life* volumes. In the course of writing the first, *Technics and Civilization* (1934), Mumford projected the series as three books: one dealing primarily with technology, the second with cities (*The Culture of Cities*, 1938), and the final one with personality. The latter grew to two books: *The Condition of Man* (1944) and *The Conduct of Life* (1951). Conceived as a unity, these works reveal the wholeness of Mumford's mind in pursuing the theme of renewal. They also reflect the fruits of his holistic method.

Technics and Civilization

The first book in the renewal series argues that *technics* (the particular means of mechanical power and the habits of mind which encourage and sustain their use) is an integral part of human culture, affected by and in turn modifying the decisions and choices of men.

Technics, then, is essentially a cultural phenomenon, and the forms it takes are: (1) an expression of the values and goals of the society in which it functions, and (2) an element in helping shape the habits, ideas, and organization of that society. Technics originates in man's ability through rational conceptualization to give regularity and order to his experience. It reflects a dimension of man's personality essentially different from the more clearly imaginative aspect of his nature.

Mumford takes pains to illustrate how men became mechanized in many phases of life before ever inventing modern machinery. The routine of the Benedictine monastery, the emerging urban bourgeoisie and its infatuation with profits neatly recorded in ledger books, the abstract world of matter and motion posited by the mechanical world view of natural philosophy and experimental science, the modern army – all of these expressed an intensified will-to-order. They were part of the cultural preparation for the growing dominance of machine technology after the middle of the eighteenth century.

The direct agents of modern technics pinpointed by Mumford are mining, capitalism, warfare, and pecuniary standards of consumption. It is the historic association of machine technology with these phenomena that is responsible for the apparent maliciousness of the machine in modern affairs.

Following Geddes' lead, Mumford traces the evolution of technics through three overlapping cultural–technological stages of development. The *eotechnic* era, which dominates western Europe from the tenth to the eighteenth centuries, is based on wind, water, and wood power and is marked by improvements in navigation, glass-making, and textile industries. The *paleotechnic* era, which begins in the eighteenth century and becomes dominant between 1850 and 1890, is based on coal and iron and is marked by the steam engine, railroad, and steamship. The *neotechnic* era, which began to emerge in the 1880s, is based on electricity, lighter metals (like aluminium), and rare metals (like tungsten) and is marked by the dynamo and water-turbine.

During the course of this development, the machine is conditioned by a capitalist and expansionist milieu characterized by warfare and

pecuniary standards of consumption. The confluence of machine technology with these cultural agents fosters not only a contempt for the
natural environment but a growing disregard for life itself. It produces a
withered imagination which, while sensing something is wrong, can only
respond by advocating the production of more machines and devices to
fill the void of an empty existence.

For Mumford, the implications of these tendencies are visible in landscapes scarred by strip-mining techniques, urban slums, the trench
warfare of the First World War, and more recently, by the use of
extermination bombs against city populations in the Second World War
and the use of bombs and biocides against villages in Vietnam. Thus a
civilization given over to machine worship, which increasingly degrades
the imagination and disregards life is symbolized by the bombed-out city,
the devastated region, and the extermination camp.

What the situation calls for, Mumford argues, is first a recognition of
the value of the machine: as a controllable means of order in the world, as
a source of aesthetic experience (in photography and moving pictures for
example), as a basis of precision and economy (in standardized consumer
goods), as a way of easing individual burdens and simplifying the routine
of life, and as a source for a more objective human personality. These
features of the machine and modern technics must be assimilated by and
subsumed more fully to man's will. This can take place, he argued in the
1930s, by an orientation which emphasizes ecological balance and
conservation rather than mechanical expansion, and which works for a
synthesis of biological and social sciences as a basis for industrial, regional,
and community planning. Among the guidelines Mumford offered for
achieving this goal were socialization of raw materials and agricultural
land, and the use of regions as a basis for rational industrial and agricultural
planning in order to achieve balanced production and distribution. He also
advocated economic planning for limited human needs, not artificially
increased wants, and the establishment of a fixed equality of income with
regard to basic commodities. By reducing the hours of work, he would seek
to provide a basis for the balance between an individual's specialized job
and his pleasurable work. Mumford also envisioned the organization both
of industry to ensure unions and workers a role in establishing production
schedules and collective consumer organizations to have a say in the kind,
quality, and distribution of products. Finally he looked to state regulation
or control of industrial natural resources, capital, credit, and machines.

The Culture of Cities

In turning his attention to city development in *The Culture of Cities*, Mumford reemphasized how urban environments were connected to the

sequence of cultural–technological stages since the middle ages. He pushed his investigations even further into the past with *The City in History* (1961), which appeared twenty-five years later. Taken together these two volumes present Mumford's mature thought on the meaning, origins, and future of the city.

In tracing present urban forms back to their prehistoric origins, Mumford found that people came together temporarily for protection and religious ceremonies before cities existed. The city first emerged as the result of an "urban implosion" which drew together these preurban forms. The result was a union between settled neolithic groups and the more warlike paleolithic hunter culture. Thus at its inception the city reflected both settlement and aggression. The implosion causing this drawing together was accomplished by a sudden increase of power embodied in the institution of kingship, which fused sacred and secular authority. For Mumford the significant factor in the original structure of the city was that it heightened power in both its destructive *and* socially beneficent dimensions. But the city also gives rise to opportunities and purposes (both positive and negative) which were not anticipated in its origins. For example, though the city began largely as a center for containing and controlling a large population for the benefit of a dominant elite, there arose simultaneously a greater capacity for cooperation as well as a widened area for rational and emotional communication.

Granted the ambivalence of power at the very origins of this "bifurcated urban heritage," what does Mumford conceive to be the true purposes and meaning of the city? The human function of the city is to convert mechanical power and human energy into social and physical arrangements and into meaningful cultural forms. Thus, the regulation of power, the nurture of life, and the provision for participation in both local groups and the broader cultural existence are the main purposes of the city.

In his interpretation of city development, Mumford finds no one urban form which consistently expresses these positive urban functions. He does insist, however, that there is a relative human scale for cities, "an organic limit to city growth." In such forms as the agora and theatre of the Greek polis; the cathedral, market square and religious pageant of medieval cities like Siena and Lübeck; the neighborhood units of Venice; the commons and meeting-house of New England towns; modern Amsterdam; various contemporary "new towns" – in these he has seen evidence of the balance, "rooted dignity," human scale, and civic participation which are at the heart of his conception of urban. Far from perfect, such communities reflect a better balance than has characterized most city growth in the past three hundred years.

The most notable feature of society in general and urban development in particular since the seventeenth century, according to Mumford, has been the abandonment of limitations. Between the fifteenth and eighteenth centuries, the most significant urban transformation since the Bronze Age implosion took place under the impetus of a sense of limitlessness. Such an ethos made possible overseas exploration and exploitation as well as the great intellectual adventure of rendering the movement of heavenly bodies and the events of nature to mechanical formulas. This expansionist mind-set first took urban form in the war capitals Rome to Berlin and Paris and in grandiose planning which sacrificed homes and neighborhoods to the mathematical designs of straight, military avenues and broad vistas.

As urban expansion came under the control of capitalists in the nineteenth century, and when it became clear that profit was to be made from intensive land use, overcrowding, and speculation in urban property, the city itself was treated as just another commodity. Community services and such fundamental amenities as access to sunlight, fresh air, and open space were neglected in the scramble for private wealth. In the soot-covered slums of Manchester and Pittsburgh, "the century of progress" produced the most dehumanized environment in history – a "paleotechnic inferno." "In an age of technical progress the city, as a social and political unit, lay outside the circle of invention" (1961, p. 449). In a detailed study of the interaction between American "privatism" and urban growth in Philadelphia, Sam Bass Warner, Jr has confirmed Mumford's observation on this point (1968).

Finally in our own time, Mumford argues, megalopolis continues to deny spontaneity and self-direction by its dependence on monopolistic organization and bureaucratic centralization. Megalopolitan culture is characterized by automation and the increasing control of every aspect of life; it will provide an ideal setting for the regulated life of Roderick Seidenberg's "post-historic man" (1950). This is one possibility for the future. Another possibility, the one Mumford advocates, is that a growing sense of limitations in modern life will be coupled with the recognition of the need for regional planning based on the premise that organic limits to city growth exist and must be enforced. By planning for limited growth within a regional framework he believes that future development can avoid further urban decay.

Mumford's planning reports

During the 1930s and early 1940s, Mumford gained an international reputation primarily for his interest in cities and planning. He was invited to prepare two planning reports, a pamphlet on postwar building and a critique of *The County of London Plan* (1943). Later, in 1947, he acted as a planning consultant to Stanford University and in 1951 to the United Nations. Some of his reports and critiques were collected together with two earlier essays and published as *City Development* (the title of Geddes' 1904 Dunfermline report) in 1945. Two other books were also published during the 1940s: *The South in Architecture* (1941), based on lectures given at Alabama College, and *The Condition of Man* (1944), the third volume in the *Renewal of Life* series. Also during this period, Mumford began corresponding with Frederick J. Osborn, the planner who played such a vital role in Britain's adoption of a New Towns policy following the Second World War (Hughes 1972).

The two planning reports Mumford prepared in 1938 illustrate the practical application of his regional approach to specific areas. One was done for the City and County Park Board of Honolulu and the other, on the Pacific Northwest, for a planning group in Spokane, Washington. The report on Honolulu moves from a discussion of the unique physical and social characteristics of the city and its assets to the weaknesses in its plan. The latter included erratic and unplanned growth which resulted in neglecting to utilize fully certain natural advantages (like the sea). Also, overcrowding had blurred the distinction between natural zones and led to a low standard of housing and open space.

The answer, Mumford concluded, was not to follow the typical pattern of suburban subdivision and plans aimed at providing for increased population. It would be better to adopt a more open plan, which combined slum clearance and extensive low-cost housing, and to establish a standard of density of occupation, neighborhood planning, and a fairer distribution of open space. Mumford suggested various kinds of open space: miniblock parks, larger neighborhood playgrounds, open greens, and shaded promenades, "primeval" parks, formal gardens, and local greenbelts to help give coherence to the different zones of the city. The park system was to be closely orchestrated with drainage canals, new arterial parkways, neighborhood planning, and a public housing program. As Mumford envisaged it, "The park system is thus the very spearhead of comprehensive urban planning" (1945, p. 130).

To carry out this coordinated park and city planning program, Mumford advocated revision of the Honolulu city charter to provide for an effective city planning authority within the structure of the municipal government. He would replace the typical City Planning Commission by a three-pronged planning process. A representative City Planning Council would act as an advisory body and as a liaison between the public and a newly appointed plan director. The director with his own staff would carry out a city survey, develop a comprehensive urban renewal policy, propose a flexible master plan, and proceed with its implementation. There would also be a Board of Public Works, consisting of various city department heads, which would collaborate with the plan director in formulating planning procedure.

Mumford's other 1938 report concerned an entire region rather than a particular city. Entitled "Regional Planning in the Pacific Northwest" (1939), it was compared to the 1926 *Final Report* of the New York State Commission of Housing and Regional Planning, prepared largely by Henry Wright of the RPAA, as only a brief reconnaissance. That earlier report traced the settlement pattern of New York state, showing how a relatively well-balanced distribution of population and economic activity was unbalanced by the growth of industry and haphazard concentration of population in cities. Wright saw hope for the future of the state's crowded cities in the decentralizing potential of electricity and in regional planning which emphasized a more efficient industrial and agricultural utilization of land. The conditions Mumford found in the Pacific Northwest were different from New York State, but the tendencies toward overconcentration were the same. While the smaller capitals of Washington and Oregon (Olympia and Salem) reflected coherent development, "neither Portland nor Seattle show . . . more than metropolitan ambitions that have overreached themselves" (p. 2). The whole area cried out for increased population, but only if provided for on a rational, regional basis. The Bonneville Dam promised to provide the electrical grid which would form the basis for such regional distribution. Mumford suggested an urban interregion on either side of Portland, consisting of greenbelt towns with low-cost housing. He proposed a regional authority to treat the Columbia River Gorge as a whole, thus eliminating rivalry between Oregon and Washington. In *Culture of Cities* he had praised the Tennessee Valley Authority as the kind of regional administrative unit he had in mind, offering it as a model for such areas as the Columbia Valley (p. 362). By prohibiting the industrial exploitation of the Bonneville region and checking the metropolitan expansion of Portland, a Columbia River Planning authority could aid in achieving a better balance of people, agriculture, and industry.

Mumford's planning reports are specific examples of his larger effort to present a minority report on the modern condition. Regionalism incorporates aspects of the "organic world picture" which he offers as an antidote to the dominant mechanical world view. In the quarter century following the Second World War, he has continued to rework these themes of technics and organic balance. In four works which appeared in the 1950s – *The Conduct of Life* (1951), *Art and Technics* (1951), *In The Name of Sanity* (1954), and *The Transformations of Man* (1956) – and in his recent two-volume study of *The Myth of the Machine* (1967, 1970), Mumford has evolved an interpretation of the role of science and technology in human development strikingly at odds with conventional understanding.

In these writings, as in his planning reports, he has again challenged what he believes to be the basic assumptions of our naïve belief in technical and scientific progress.

Mumford maintains that the contemporary "overcommitment" to science and technology is based on a fundamental misunderstanding of human development. What is needed to lay the foundation for future balance in human affairs is a historical reassessment of man's interaction with technics. From Mumford's widened perspective, man's uniqueness is not his technical ability but his imaginative capacity to shape a human personality. Man is able to give purpose and self-direction to his existence not because he is primarily a tool-maker (an ability shared with other animals) but because he has been able to transfer an abundance of unused animal energy to creating the expressions of human culture. In his understanding of human development, Mumford insists that man's hands are subordinate to his brain. With the growth of a highly organized nervous system and the emergence of a human mind, man slowly became aware of his own existence. Mumford asserts that "man's cumulative capacity to give symbolic form to experience," to modify his existence by linguistic symbols, aesthetic designs, and socially transmitted knowledge, answered a more imperative need than the urge for control over external environment. Man's first concern was to gain control over himself, and the means of achieving this were his first instruments: rituals, symbols, words, images, standardized gestures and modes of behavior. "Man's most important tools at the beginning were those he extracted from his own body: formalized sounds and images and movements. And his efforts to share these goods promoted social solidarity" (1967, p. 64).

Mumford emphasizes the significance of language for man's capacity to symbolize and thereby give meaning to reality. But he points out that speech did not initially appear as a means of rational communication. Rather, it was preceded by and emerged from the human propensity for playfulness and make-believe, the ritualistic "habit of lingering over a satisfactory response in memory and working it into a meaningful pattern" (1965b–62, p. 13). Man emerging transformed himself from his animal origins through dreams, ritual, dance, totem, taboo, religion, magic, and finally language, before he ever learned to improve tools. The struggle to achieve a complex language structure took time and demanded unflagging effort. It was the central achievement of primitive man. The dream and the word are for Mumford the origin of those symbols and images by which men attempt to order and reshape the external world. Long before using stone tools, man was using his own body to explore and transform nature. But *technics* did become important to human development, by enlarging the capacities for human expression. Mumford's point is thus not to deny the significance of tools and machines but to assign them to what he understands as their proper role in human history.

In developing this interpretation, he argues that we have failed to realize this interaction of human imagination and technics. The consequence has been to view scientific and technical advances as ends in themselves, somehow beyond our ability to control. This is the "myth of the machine." How did it come about? Though there had been previous cultural preparation, it was from the sixteenth- and seventeenth-century "scientific revolution" that there emerged a world view which has since been realized in western society. Modern science has concentrated on those aspects of reality which can be weighted, measured, and controlled. It neutralizes the human observer, limiting his scope in order to ensure the greatest amount of accurate, factual knowledge. But by fixing attention on the "primary qualities" the sciences are not dealing with reality in its entirety. They have posited an abstract world of matter and motion devoid of life and individuality. It is an increasingly mechanized world already anticipated in the monastery and counting house, and realized in our own day under the aegis of what Mumford calls the American "pentagon of power." Indeed, it has even more ancient and ominous ancestors. For as Mumford presents the pentagon of power, with all its splendid gadgetry – missiles, computers, nuclear warheads – it is a modern version of the human Egyptian "megamachine" that built pyramids for the Pharaohs. Our scientific establishment is the new priesthood, and, as Mumford sees it, our exploration of the lifeless moon, by means of the completely artificial environment of space-ship, is a reenactment of the ancient worship of the dead.

Mumford asserts that our denial of human imagination reaps its own dehumanized rewards. The unconscious is an integral facet of human personality and will seek expression even when thwarted. What happens under the increasing regimentation of man's human impulses is that "spontaneity too often takes the form of criminal acts, and creativeness finds its main outlet in destruction" (1952, pp. 11–12). (This observation is strikingly similar to the statement made by Stanley Kubrick in his movie, *Clockwork Orange*.) Thus the cult of violence and meaninglessness in contemporary art and politics. Mumford has consistently denounced American acceptance, first during the Second World War and then in Vietnam, of "the indiscriminate extermination of human life, by atomic and bacterial means, as the conceivable act of a sane government engaged in War" (1954, p. 5). In the glamorization of *technics* and neglect of the organic, he believes we have brought ourselves to a point where the elimination of life is a distinct possibility – either by swift nuclear suicide, by somewhat slower pollution of water, soil, and air, or by complete social and individual regimentation. His answer to such a future has been to emphasize the need to develop integrated, rather than fragmented, personalities, on the basis of family life, neighborhood and group participation, variation of work experience, planned communities, and economically and ecologically balanced regions. Long before the current interest in ecology, Mumford was asking the cost of expensive accessories (including superhighways, rockets, and precision weaponry) in terms of healthy living conditions – houses, fresh air, recreational open space. His ecological concerns have recently been recognized by young people involved in the first national environmental teach-in (DeBell, 1970; Hughes, p. 470). But years earlier, in 1955, he was named co-chairman of the Wenner-Gren Conference on Man's Role in Changing the Face of the Earth, which warned against continued ecological imbalance.

Mumford in contemporary times

The 1950s also witnessed the appearance of two collections of Mumford's work, and two more appeared in the next decade. *The Human Prospect* (1955) is a collection of previously published essays, a few poems, and a fragment from an unpublished novel, all aimed at revealing the "singleness of vision" which has marked Mumford's work. The second collection, *From the Ground Up* (1956) is a selection of his articles from *The New Yorker*. Since 1932, Mumford had been the architectural critic for that magazine, publishing his contributions under a general heading, "The Sky Line." This volume, coupled with two other groups of essays which appeared in the 1960s – *The Highway and the City* (1963) and *The Urban Prospect* (1968) – provides a record of his criticisms of American and European city building and planning in the decades since the Second World War. A number of these articles were written at the time Mumford was working on *The City in History*, and they offer specific observations on the contemporary city which are largely missing from that essentially historical study.

The question motivating these evaluations of contemporary urban forms is the same one which guides all his other cultural criticism: What human purpose does this or that particular thing serve? Is any really human end served by a public housing project which piles fourteen thousand people into high-rise buildings on thirty-four acres of land, but fails to provide a single church or synagogue or movie house or public market in the whole area? Were basic social concerns the motivating factor behind traffic planning which increased and widened expressways into and through central Manhattan, and provided more and more precious living space for parking automobiles?

As in the 1920s, so again in the 1950s planners seemed to believe the cure for congestion was facilities for more congestion.

It would take a great mind indeed [Mumford wrote in 1955] to decide which set of planners is more irrational – the people who are piling up high structures in the overcrowded business districts of our cities, or the people who are creating cross-country expressways that dump more traffic into them. (1956a, p. 207)

In essence, Mumford's case against much of modern architecture, the architecture of Le Corbusier, Philip Johnson, Mies van der Rohe, is that it merely gives steel and glass expression to a one-dimensional emphasis on mechanical progress and aesthetic abstractions, with no concern for past forms and little regard for the amenities and sociability which enrich one's working day.

In the past twelve years (1960–72), between the ages of sixty-five and seventy-seven, Mumford has published what he considers to be three of his best books: *The City in History*, which won the National Book award for non-fiction in 1961, and the last two volumes of *The Myth of the Machine: Technics and Human Development* (1967) and *The Pentagon of Power* (1970). In the early 1970s, two volumes of correspondence were published: *The Van Wyck Brooks–Lewis Mumford Letters* (1970) and *The Letters of Lewis Mumford and Frederic J. Osborn* (1972). Also in 1971, Elmer Newman compiled *Lewis Mumford: A Bibliography, 1914–1970*, a book which runs to over 120 pages.

The distance between *The Story of Utopias* and his two most recent volumes is essentially a matter of greater maturity, breadth of learning, and depth of knowledge in reworking basic themes. But much of his work deals with the past. Why? Because Mumford is a historicist, one whose understanding of wholeness includes the *possible* and the *real*, one who sees that "the past is still present in the future, and the future as potentiality, is already present in the past" (1963, p. 164). As we have seen, he finds the one-dimensional, purely causal explanation of positive science wanting. He posits instead an organic system which "seeks to understand processes in terms of goals, the part by its relation to the whole, the past with reference to the future, and the actual as revealed in the potential" (1951, p. 241). According to this view, each generation finds itself faced with the challenge of assimilating the heritage of the past and molding the future. By reworking the materials of its social heritage, a generation escapes being victimized by whatever fashions and forces are dominant for the moment. In man's responsibility for nurturing and improving upon his cultural heritage, the present is the vital link between past and future. "The future of our civilization," Mumford noted in *Sticks and Stones* (1924), "depends upon our ability to select and control our heritage from the past, to alter our present attitudes and habits, and to project fresh forms into which our energies may be freely poured" (p. 195). Thus what Mumford finds in history is much the same quality he discovered in biology – a source of potentiality for the renewal of life. The ultimate basis of this renewal is the unfathomable possibilities of life itself, as exemplified by certain achievements and personalities of the past.

Mumford's work is truly a "thought of youth worked out in maturity." It is guided by a "singleness of vision" apparent from the very beginning of his writing career. This *vision*, the link that connects all of his work is, as suggested at the outset of this chapter, his sense of the wholeness and balance of life. For Mumford this emerges from an intuition concerning the primacy of man. For fifty years, he has given voice to the implications of a scientific method and technology which, pursued as ends in themselves, deny the ecological wholeness of man's existence.

No one questions the immense benefits already conferred in many departments by science as efficient methodology, [he notes in *The Pentagon of Power*] but what one must challenge is the value of a system so detached from other human needs and purposes that the process itself goes on automatically without any visible good except that of keeping the corporate apparatus itself in a state of power-making, profit-yielding productivity.

It is not, then, a question of rejecting science or technology but of offering the challenge of balance, that balance which will be the basis for renewal in the future. In the ecosystems of nature, in certain forms and personalities in the past and some which are emerging in our own time, and in the regional approach to community planning, Mumford has located examples and sources of this balance. His earliest efforts to recover and convey an awarness of America's historic resources (its "usable past") in buildings, bridges, art, literature, thought, planning, and conservation, were aimed at laying the foundation for renewal. His broader studies of the city in history and the interaction between technics and western culture are also directed at this end, of providing a running start in history for our plunge into a more humanly balanced future.

Mumford believes modern nations are misguided in their seemingly uncontrollable pursuit of power and wealth. But years ago he observed, "It is better to face chaos courageously than to cherish the dream of returning to an outworn synthesis." The answer to a meaningless existence is neither pragmatic or existential acquiescence in the madness of the present, nor the irrational use of violence against institutions, whereby one submits to the very forces he is opposing. "The true answer to a meaningless existence is to conceive a pattern of life that possesses meaning and purpose." He is convinced that if men do not work toward a world in which the realization of human potential is at least a possibility, they will continue by unconscious choices to bring about an environment divested of life. As Van Wyck Brooks pointed out, *renewal* is the key word in Mumford's thought, renewal as embodied in a "loving awareness of one's environment" in all its fullness and complexity (1953, pp. 136, 143). Thus it is his holistic or historicist method of understanding our total cultural and physical environment that gives his work its vitality. In fact, Lewis Mumford's capacity for "seeing things whole" is an excellent example of the wholeness and balance which he advocates.

Notes

1 I would like to thank three people for their encouragement in regard to this article. My friend John Hancock first urged me to undertake the project. Richard Bolan, editor of the *JAIP*, has been a sympathetic and understanding reader. The greatest debt I owe to my wife Doris, whose tough-minded criticism has always benefited my work.
2 In 1967, Mumford noted, "The generalist's competence lies not in unearthing new evidence but in putting together authentic fragments that are accidently, or sometimes arbitrarily, separated, because specialists tend to abide too vigorously by a gentlemen's agreement not to invade each other's territory" (p. 17).
3 In a letter to Van Wyck Brooks written in 1935, Mumford remarked of Bergson, "My own philosophy could be treated as a modification of his, for whereas he draws a distinction between intuition, which is vital, and reason, which is mechanical, and lets it go at that, I go on to point out that the mechanical itself is a creation of life and only when it is perversely divorced from all our experience, including our feeling and intuition, does it become dangerous, that is, anti-vital" (Spiller, pp. 117–8).
4 Brooks wrote of the Mumfords, "I thought of Lewis and Sophy Mumford as a new Adam and Eve, with whom the human race might well have started, for one could scarcely have imagined a handsomer pair. I always felt as if they had just stepped out of Utopia and were looking for some of their countrymen, astray on this planet, who were also waiting to get back home again" (1957, p. 67).
5 Mumford's early works are all marked by a certain breathless intensity. He cast some light on this quality by noting in 1931, "Partly as a result of my adolescent illness and disability, my whole life has been arranged, more than half consciously, on the assumption that I would die before forty: so that every work was conceived and finished on a limited scale, with a short breath, as it were, as though it were to be my last" (Spiller, p. 74).

References

Branford, V. (1919) "Westminster: a city survey for disoriented citizens," in Victor Branford and Patrick Geddes, *Our Social Inheritance*, London, Williams & Norgate.

Brooks, V. W. (1936–52) *Makers and Finders: A History of the Writer in America, 1800–1915*, 5 vols, New York, E. P. Dutton.

_____ (1953) "A prophet of our day," pp. 134–55 in *The Writer in America*, New York, E. P. Dutton.

_____ (1957) *Days of the Phoenix: The Nineteen-Twenties I Remember*, New York, E. P. Dutton.

274   *The American Planner*

Cowley, M. (1938) "Heavenly city," *The New Republic*, 95, 337–8.

De Bell, G. (1970) *The Environmental Handbook: Prepared for the First National Environmental Teach-In*, New York, Ballantine Books.

Geddes, P. (1904) *City Development: A Study of Parks, Gardens, and Culture-Institutes*, Edinburgh, Geddes & Co.

_____ (1915) *Cities in Evolution*, London, Williams & Norgate.

Howard, E. (1902) *Garden Cities of Tomorrow*, London, Swan Sonnenschein & Co.; Cambridge, Mass., The MIT Press, 1965.

Hughes, M. (1972) *The Letters of Lewis Mumford and Frederic J. Osborn: A Transatlantic Dialogue, 1938–1970*, New York, Praeger.

Lubove, R. (1963) *Community Planning in the 1920's: The Contribution of the Regional Planning Association of America*, Pittsburgh, University of Pittsburgh Press.

May, H. (1959) *The End of American Innocence: A Study of the First Years of Our Own Time, 1912–1917*, New York, Alfred A. Knopf.

Mumford, L. (1919) "The heritage of the cities movement in America: an historical survey," *Journal of the American Institute of Architects*, 7, 349–54.

_____ (1922–62a) *The Story of Utopias*, New York: Boni & Liveright, 1922; New York, Compas Book, Viking Press, 1962.

_____ (1922) "The city," pp. 3–20, in Harold Stearns (ed.) *Civilization in the United States: An Inquiry by Thirty Americans*, New York, Harcourt, Brace & Co.

_____ (1924–55) *Sticks and Stones; Architecture and Civilization*, New York, Boni & Liveright, 1924; New York, Dover Publications, 1955.

_____ (1925a) "Regions – to live in," *Survey Graphic*, 54, 151–2.

_____ (1925b) "Climax," *Journal of the American Institute of Architects*, 13, 454–6.

_____ (1926a) "The sacred city," *The New Republic*, 45, 270–1.

_____ (1926b–57) *The Golden Day; A Study in American Experience and Culture*, New York, Boni & Liveright, 1926; New York, Beacon Paperback, Beacon Press, 1957.

_____ (1929–62) *Herman Melville*, New York, Harcourt, Brace & Co., 1929; *Herman Melville, A Study of His Life and Vision*, New York, Harbinger Book, Harcourt, Brace & World, 1962.

_____ (1930a) "Victor Branford," *The New Republic*, 64, 43–4.

_____ (1930b) "The city of tomorrow," *The New Republic*, 61, 332–3.

_____ (1931a–55) *The Brown Decades; A Study of the Arts in America, 1865–1895*, New York, Harcourt, Brace & Co., 1931; New York, Dover Publications, 1955.

_____ (1931b) "Thorstein Veblen," *The New Republic*, 67, 314–16.

_____ (1934–63) *Technics and Civilization*, New York, Harcourt, Brace & Co., 1934; New York, Harbinger Book, Harcourt, Brace & World, 1963.

_____ (1938a–70) *The Culture of Cities*, New York, Harcourt, Brace & Co., 1938; New York, Harvest Book, Harcourt, Brace, Jovanovich, 1970.

_____ (1938b–45b) *Whither Honolulu? A Memorandum Report on Park and City Planning*, Honolulu, T. H., the author); reprinted as "Report on Honolulu," pp. 84–153 in *City Development*.

_____ (1939) *Regional Planning in the Pacific Northwest: a Memorandum*, Portland, Ore., Northwest Regional Council.

_____ (1941) *The South in Architecture*, New York, Harcourt, Brace & Co.; New York, Da Capo Press, 1967.

_____ (1944) *The Condition of Man*, New York, Harcourt, Brace & Co.

_____ (1945a) *The Plan of London County*, London, Faber & Faber; reprinted as "The Plan of London," pp. 198–240 in *City Development*.

_____ (1945b) *City Development; Studies in Disintegration and Renewal*, New York, Harcourt, Brace & Co.

—— (1948) "Patrick Geddes, Victor Branford and applied sociology in England: the social survey, regionalism and urban-planning," pp. 677–95 in H. E. Barnes (ed.) *An Introduction to the History of Sociology*, Chicago, University of Chicago Press.

—— (1951) *The Conduct of Life*, New York, Harcourt, Brace & Co.

—— (1952) *Art and Technics*, New York, Columbia University Press; Columbia Paperback, 1960.

—— (1954) *In The Name of Sanity*, New York, Harcourt, Brace & Co.

—— (1955–65) *The Human Prospect*, ed. H. T. Moore and K. W. Deutsch, Boston, Beacon Press, Beacon Paperback, 1955; Carbondale, Ill., Southern Illinois University Press; Arcturus Press, 1965.

—— (1956a) *From the Ground Up; Observations on Contemporary Architecture, Housing, Highway Building, and Civic Design*, New York, Harvest Books, Harcourt, Brace & Co.

—— (1956b–62) *The Transformations of Man*, New York, Harper & Bros.; New York, Collier Books, 1962.

—— (1961) *The City in History: Its Origins, Its Transformations, and Its Prospects*, New York, Harcourt, Brace & Co.

—— (1962) "Megalopolis as anti-city," *Architectural Record*, 132, 101–8.

—— (1963) *The Highway and the City*, New York, Harvest Books, Harcourt, Brace & World; New York, Mentor Book, New American Library, 1964.

—— (1966) "The disciple's rebellion; a memoir of Patrick Geddes," *Encounter*, 27, 11–21.

—— (1967) *The Myth of the Machine: I. Technics and Human Development*, New York, Harcourt, Brace & World.

—— (1968) *The Urban Prospect*, New York, Harcourt, Brace & World.

—— (1970) *The Myth of the Machine: II. The Pentagon of Power*, New York, Harcourt, Brace, Jovanovich.

—— (1972) "The scholar as activist," *New York Review of Books*, 18, 13–16.

Newman, E. (1971) *Lewis Mumford: A Bibliography, 1914–1970*, New York, Harcourt, Brace, Jovanovich.

Seidenberg, R. (1950) *Posthistoric Man*, Chapel Hill, N. C., University of North Carolina Press.

Spiller, R. (1970) *The Van Wyck Books – Lewis Mumford Letters: The Record of a Literary Friendship, 1921–1963*, New York, E. P. Dutton.

Stein, C. (1957) *Toward New Towns for America*, New York, The Town Planning Review; Cambridge, Mass., The MIT Press, 1966.

Warner, S. B. (1968) *The Private City: Philadelphia in Three Periods of Its Growth*, Philadelphia, University of Pennsylvania Press.

Wright, H. (1926) *Report of the New York State Commission of Housing and Regional Planning to Governor Alfred E. Smith*, Albany, N. Y., J. B. Lyon Co.

Part 3 The professionals

13 Harland Bartholomew:
precedent for the profession

Norman J. Johnston

When Harland Bartholomew began his career as a planner early in this century's second decade, the profession and its techniques were only beginning to emerge. By his example, the spread of his work across the nation, and his influence on others moving into planning, he was to occupy in a remarkably short time a seminal position in the profession. The nature of his approach with its structure, clarity, and thoroughness – his "science of planning" – helps us understand this impact. He initiated investigations and brought focus to key concepts with which planners continue to work.

When several years ago it came time for the American Institute of Planners to seek an appropriate chairman for its approaching fiftieth anniversary celebration it turned felicitously to Harland Bartholomew, and he in turn, in spite of the pleasures of semi-retirement, characteristically added this important responsibility to the long record of his services to the profession. It was ground, in fact, that he had already personally been over: his own fiftieth anniversary as a planning professional had been passed in 1962.[1] Now, five years later, it was appropriate that he would be chairing for the Institute the occasion of its first half century of service to planning.

Bartholomew's origins are Yankee: born near Boston in 1889, raised on a New Hampshire farm, late teens and early twenties in Massachusetts and New York, he graduated from a Brooklyn high school with the expectation of accepting the offer of work as a bank clerk. But other events intervened. At the urging of one of his high school teachers, he made inquiries at Rutgers. Some scholarship help and part time work gave him the necessary boost, and he began his studies for a civil engineering degree.

Those studies were not to continue beyond the sophomore level. Economics, work load, and academic regulations discouraged him beyond that point, and so he chose to serve engineering by a more direct route, accepting a job with E. P. Goodrich, a New York City civil engineer. (Nevertheless he was to receive degrees from Rutgers: an honorary civil engineering degree in 1921 and in 1952 their Doctor of Science for leadership in his profession.)

Again there were to be outside influences at work. In 1912, Goodrich together with George B. Ford, a New York architect, signed a contract with the City of Newark, New Jersey, for preparation of what was then a quite unorthodox document – a city comprehensive plan – and Bartholomew was chosen to be the firm's representative. Thus his anticipations of working with bridges, dams, and harbor works (the sorts of commissions for which Goodrich had a considerable reputation) were suddenly and unceremoniously channeled into the legwork of a planning contract. Nevertheless, in spite of his initial disappointments, the switch proved unexpectedly permanent.

City Beautiful/City Efficient

By 1912, the planning profession had passed through its earliest formative years, loosely grouped into an era known as City Beautiful. The leaders of the City Beautiful were likely to have been from the design professions or men allied with them: architects like Daniel Burnham and Arnold W. Brunner, landscape architects Frederick Law Olmsted, Jr and John Nolen, and journalist-turned-planner Charles Mulford Robinson. Indeed, of a listing of forty-two comprehensive plans issued prior to 1912, only eleven had not been the product of one or the other of these men. (Nolen, pp. 21–5). They dominated planning practices of the day.

Yet the visual civic art biases of that period, propagandized so effectively by the environmental imperialism of the 1893 Columbian Exposition in Chicago, had in the decade or so that followed come to be found wanting. Not that goals of urban monumentality and beautification were being dismissed out of hand, but there was a discernible shift away from their elusive promise toward what were seen as harder, more practical, and measurable objectives. Here was a different set of values whose focus was functional and social, comprising a program designed to create the City Efficient.

For these newcomers, the primacy of the visual city was displaced by a different set of priorities. Theirs too was a program for building, but its center of gravity had shifted away from civic centers, parks, and boulevards and over to sanitation, housing, transportation, and municipal efficiency. The shift was of course paralleled by shifts in the predispositions of its leaders. Political reformers, lawyers, housing officials, social workers, and engineers were more likely to be the protagonists of the new faith: Lawrence Veiller, Robert de Forest, Benjamin C. Marsh, Virgil Bogue, as well as John Nolen (who was successfully able to make the transposition). This was the context that included engineer Goodrich who in turn enlisted architect George B. Ford. And this is the partnership with its recently awarded planning contract for Newark that, in its

Plate 13.1 Harland Bartholomew.

assembling of resources in March 1912, assigned engineering aspirant Harland Bartholomew to the task.

The circumstances out of which the partnership was formed and Bartholomew's sudden involvement in its contract were characteristic of the professional informality of the day. These were formative years for planning in which somewhat spontaneous arrangements and methods arose in the absence of more structured and established procedures and precedents. Planning as a profession was still undefined, and in the relatively uncharted field the expert came with no set pattern of credentials. Professional training was non-existent. Harvard had begun some instruction in city planning in 1910 in its School of Landscape Design, but it was still alone in the field in 1912. Nor were its ambitions at that stage to educate planners but rather to enrich the breadth of its landscape program.

A similar kind of spontaneity marked the nature of the planning process. Though there might be efforts among some to clarify its functions and give structure to its service, wide variety marked the tone and detail of what the client bought from his planning expert. What data were needed? What measurements used? What values applied? What objectives sought? How to compose the parts into some structured and convincing whole? To answer such questions and others like them, one plan report could be almost entirely preoccupied with beauty, parks, and streets (Brunner and Olmsted's *Rochester Plan*), another contrastingly biased toward arterial highways, harbor improvements, and transportation (Bogue's *Seattle Plan*), and both be products of the year 1911. What was this process of planning? There were those who by 1912 might be seeking the rationale and the format, but the returns were still not yet in.

Professional beginning

When Bartholomew arrived in Newark to take up his assignment it had been the result of what was, for then, rather unique civic initiative. By 1912, there were only some thirteen cities in the United States with official planning commissions; Newark had joined their number in 1911 in response to an act the New Jersey legislature had passed in the spring of that year authorizing appointment of a nine-man city planning commission "to prepare a plan for the systematic and future development of said city" (Newark City Plan Commission, p. 3). The authorization also granted commissions power to employ "experts," and Messrs Goodrich and Ford were their choice. It was the partners' first such contract, individually or as a team; as Bartholomew has written, "Neither Mr Ford nor Mr Goodrich had prepared a comprehensive city plan, it was new to everyone, and we were groping."[2]

Groping or not, the work progressed, and by the end of 1913 the commission had before it the partners' summary report, *City Planning for Newark*, comprising two principal steps: data collecting and, after their initial analysis, a roughing out of immediate proposals. But the third and most uncharted of the steps, the development of a comprehensive plan for Newark's future, remained only a sketch as to how it was to be transposed into specific rationale and planning practice.

Bartholomew's responsibilities in subsequent work expanded abruptly when the partners' contract was not renewed, Bartholomew instead being appointed in March 1914 as the commission's "engineer" and its secretary on a salaried basis. He thus became one of the nation's first full-time professional employees of a planning commission. The earlier tentative framework of the plan was now Bartholomew's charge to complete. He had arrived at his own independent course, and though he did not realize it at the time, he was to spend the rest of his professional life giving substance to step three.

By 1916, he had moved on to St Louis as that city's planning engineer, where he followed a general planning process begun in Newark. This was the beginning of an association with St Louis that would continue to the present day: its planning engineer until 1950, the home office of the private consulting firm that carries his name,[3] and still his place of residence. But his professional reputation was founded more on his work as a private planner rather than as civil servant. By 1919, he had laid out the basic planning program for St Louis and had seen it through the preliminary effort toward the 1923 passage of a comprehensive bonding program for plan implementation. Now was the time to open his private office as a planner,[4] the professional format that was very much the rule rather than the exception in those days.

Private practice

To understand the impact that Bartholomew was to have on these developmental years of the profession, there are certain things about his office and his methods that need to be realized. Almost immediately after his debut as a private consultant, he came to occupy a special place in the hierarchy of American planners, and, apparently, in the affections of the nation's cities seeking solutions through planning for their problems of urbanism. The mode of expression for this has been by volume: the size of the Bartholomew operation quickly outranked those of his professional colleagues in numbers of contracts and populations served.

His move was made into an area already occupied by some prestigious planning personalities: John Nolen, credited with some twenty comprehensive plan reports between 1906 (date of his first, for Savannah, Georgia) and 1919; Edward H. Bennett, Daniel Burnham's associate on the Chicago Plan of 1909, whose comprehensive plans had been completed for such major cities as Portland, Oregon (1912) and Minneapolis (1917); two generations of Olmsteds with their coast-to-coast practice; and even his former employers, Goodrich and Ford (later to become the Technical Advisory Corporation) who had completed their work on the Newark Plan in 1913, prepared for Omaha, Nebraska, in 1917, and were moving on toward expanded planning services. Exact figures scaling the relative level of activities of the private planners of that time (or our own) are elusive, but some idea can be gained from the appendix John Nolen attached to his president's address to the nineteenth National Conference of City Planning in Washington, D.C., May 1927 (Nolen, 1927). Here

Nolen listed cities having comprehensive plans from 1905 through 1926 together with the date of the reports and their planners; an examination of this list indicates some interesting evidence of the nature of the services of the planning profession during those years. Of the 201 planning reports listed, only seven were not the product of a planner or planning firm brought in by the city to provide this special contract service. The days of the permanent municipal planning staff were still well ahead of the events Nolen was reporting. Bartholomew became a part of them as a consulting planner in 1919 with a report for Omaha (chiefly streets and parks). In 1920, however, his specialty in the preparation of comprehensive plans was under way, and the balance of the Nolen appendix scales his volume of work in this activity. (See Fig. 13.1.) The years from 1920 through 1926 include eighty-seven comprehensive plan reports by all planners (not included in this figure are fourteen reports indicated as something less than a comprehensive plan, e.g., "partial," "streets and parks," "streets"). These plans were the product of twenty-three different consulting firms, the total number of plans for each firm ranging from one to twenty. Of the twenty-three, only six consultants had prepared three or more plans during the seven-year period:

Table 13.1

Planner	Number of comprehensive plans
Lawrence V. Sheridan	3
Arthur A. Shurtleff	4
TAC (Goodrich and Ford)	9 (3 "preliminary")
M. H. West	10
John Nolen	12
Harland Bartholomew	20

It is also of some interest to rank the consultants by the numbers of people whom their planning recommendations were presumably to affect, the total populations whose municipal leaders had turned to the planner for assistance.[5]

Table 13.2

Planner	Population served
Lawrence V. Sheridan	74,618
M. H. West	356,886
Arthur A. Shurtleff	364,519
John Nolen	511,022
TAC	1,281,106
Harland Bartholomew	1,779,508[6]

Figure 13.1 Map of geographical spread of some Bartholomew comprehensive plans and zoning ordinances.
Based on records of the St Louis office of Harland Bartholomew and Associates for the years 1920–48.

In either case, Bartholomew's services are shown to have picked up remarkably quick professional momentum, and the size of his operations has since never been seriously challenged. All this had obvious contributions to make toward familiarizing the planning profession and American cities with the Bartholomew approach to the planning process. The distribution of its services has been at the broadest level, so that some portion of most of the nation's major population areas have been the subject at one time or another of Bartholomew's studied dismembering and diagnosis, and his equally studied proposals for their assembly. The fact also that these services were being provided at a time when few permanent municipal planning staffs were organized helped to fill an important functional vacuum – and with the Bartholomew image. Under these circumstances, one begins to understand the dissemination of the firm's influences by means of its reports for cities distributed throughout the nation.

Personnel colonization

There are other significant policies and practices of the firm and of its founder that deserve acknowledging in sensing the forces that contributed to the popularity among American cities of Bartholomew's services. One such policy was, in effect, that of personnel colonization.

From the beginning of his consulting activities, Bartholomew determined upon a relationship between the consultant and his contract city differing from the usual practice. He always committed himself to the goal of plan realization and saw an opportunity for organizing his work toward this end. Noting the usual practice of the ''expert'' who arrives in town for a survey visit, does a certain amount of leg work, basic data gathering, and public-appearing, and then disappears in the direction of his home office, to return some time later with a completed report, Bartholomew decided to establish a quite different footing on which to base his services in the city which had contracted for them.

How to enlist at the local level the interest and support of the people for whom the planning process was being pursued? Part of Bartholomew's answer (to this question still plaguing any planner today) was by means of his office personnel policy: his people did not just visit a city; they were assigned to and lived in it. A key man from the St Louis office would be selected to supervise the field work and take up residence in the contract city for a period that usually ran about three years, the normal amount of time required for completing its comprehensive plan. As part of the contract, office space would be arranged for directly under the noses of the local administration, in city hall itself if possible; and out of this office the gathering of the necessary basic data, preparation of statistics, field mapping, and so on would proceed.

Every effort was made to provide for this field operation the reality as well as the sense of decision-making at the local level. An advisory committee of perhaps one hundred of the city's citizens was organized into various working committees to assist the technical staff in gathering and interpreting basic data about the community and in clarifying the goals toward which it appeared suitable to go. As with today's municipal advisory planning commissions, this citizens' committee would have responsibility for reviewing the reports as they developed, reviewing the final comprehensive plan, and acting as the local vanguard for providing support and leadership for its adoption. Basic policies, key planning decisions, and final plan drafting were still the responsibility of Bartholomew in his St Louis office; but within this framework the maximum degree of autonomy was encouraged for the field man and the city to which he had been assigned. It was as close an approximation as possible – given the reality of a temporary contract relationship – of a permanent advisory city planning commission and its technical staff as parts of the municipal administration.

There is an additional policy practice here, and one that again was accepted from the founding as a result of Bartholomew's concern for plan realization. Extending the idea of colonization a step further, Bartholomew realized that the plan would more likely be implemented if his

Figure 13.2 Map of geographical spread of some of the personnel formerly associated with the Bartholomew firm.
Based on listing made in 1961 by Harry W. Alexander, retired partner of Harland Bartholomew and Associates.

field man were to become a permanent local fixture. Therefore his training policy and practice encouraged such a development, and although obviously expensive in terms of personnel costs for his office, if it was the wish of the contract city to retain its Bartholomew representative on a permanent basis (as it often was) and the latter was agreeable, Bartholomew acted as a kind of sponsor for the union and gave it his blessing. In terms of sustained planning momentum at the local level, this had obvious advantages. But there was another consequence of such a colonization: another area of the country was provided permanent personnel trained in the philosophy and techniques of Harland Bartholomew. (See Fig. 13.2.) And this same person would possibly return to Bartholomew for consulting services when circumstances at either his original city or another one to which he had moved suggested the need for aid in plan updating or an initial comprehensive plan study.

Personnel movement

The Bartholomew expertise was of course to be disseminated through more obvious channels than the above. One such means was through the normal come-and-go of employees through the office; and when that office has been a focal point in a profession for the number of years that Bartholomew's can claim, the ranks of employees, past and present, assume impressive proportions. Harry W. Alexander, one of the firm's retired partners, once listed names of planners he recalled who at one time or another had been associated with the firm; their distribution became nationwide. Another point of interest is the pivotal place that most of these ex-Bartholomew associates hold in the profession's hierarchy: most can claim rank among the leaders of planning, including retired partner Earl O. Mills, AIP's president in 1946–7.

Employee training

Training: this was actually the role the firm was providing in the pre-Second World War period. Following Harvard's 1912 initiative in offering city planning course work, similar service-course ambitions followed at the University of Illinois in 1913. These beginnings were later expanded by more extensive professional planning programs; but although some eighty colleges and universities were offering planning courses by 1929, the courses were still primarily designed to serve students enrolled in architecture, landscape architecture, or engineering degree work rather than as professional majors in planning (T. Adams, pp. 249–50). Even by 1940 there were only four universities in the United States granting professional planning degrees: Harvard, Massachusetts Institute of Technology, Cornell, and Columbia (F. J. Adams, p. 17)

Given the prevailing thinness of the professional curriculums of the period, Bartholomew turned to the resource from which he got his own training – experience – combining this with his developing methodology as he proceeded to organize his interpretations of the professional role into what he would call a systematized "science." Personnel would be drawn from various disciplines, especially from among engineering graduates and landscape architects, but they all then participated in a shared experience of the Bartholomew interpretation of the planning function. This was to be no intuitive process, but a kind of professional module within which each planner and planning contract found a basic order. It was out of this training experience that Bartholomew employees would come and go, some released to other positions by what was in effect the firm's colonization policy, others simply going on to new opportunities after they had served their professional apprenticeship. Although no diploma changed hands, in the scarcity of university curriculums in the field the new profession was being served by the firm's function as a training ground for new personnel.

A faculty role

Bartholomew was directly involved in planning education in the more common understanding of the phrase, for it was just before his emergence as a consultant that he accepted a university post as associate professor of civic design. This was at the University of Illinois. The original occupant of the position there had been Charles Mulford Robinson, who initiated the Illinois program in 1913 as a part of the College of Agriculture's Department of Landscape Gardening, and who became its (and the nation's) first professor of civic design. He gave lectures to the students on city planning and would also periodically organize a field trip that would bring them to St Louis to see the planning work there under Bartholomew's direction, incidentally introducing Bartholomew and Illinois to each other. Therefore, after the death of Robinson in the winter of 1917, the University turned to Bartholomew in the following year with a request that he assume the vacated post. He reacted to the suggestion with some misgivings, feeling that his obvious professional role was that of a practitioner rather than academician; but this entirely suited what Illinois' department head had in mind, and so Bartholomew agreed to teach the course on a non-residence basis for one year, beginning in the fall of 1919. The "one-year" experiment lasted until 1956.

The arrangement apparently suited the University, and it obviously suited Bartholomew. He enjoyed student contacts and stimulation, requiring as they did a constant examination of purposes and processes "from population to capital budgets" that he found provided a valuable kind of perspective not inherently available within the confines of a growing practice. Later more full-time personnel were added to the landscape faculty, combining both landscape and planning people, including Karl B. Lohmann, and he and Bartholomew came to share the planning seminar for many years. The course was called "Planning of towns and cities" and was required for landscape architecture majors, certain majors in civil engineering, and, Lohmann recalled, possibly majors in municipal administration. It was also available as an elective for others who cared to choose it.[7]

Lohmann was, of course, the professor in residence while Bartholomew, on his more or less once a month schedule of visits during the academic year, would come in "to explain what planning was and what we [his firm] were doing. I would take plans up with me, showing how principles applied in actual practice."[8] The two men thus shared a relationship and responsibility that they both recalled with warmth. Bartholomew would come up from St Louis by train the night before, arriving the next morning on campus always some thirty minutes ahead of the ten o'clock class time. Choice of subjects was left up to him, and these he would change from year to year, reviewing Lohmann's course outline and selecting those items on which he felt he had something to say and demonstrate; Lohmann carried the balance. From talking with either Lohmann or students who took the course one gets a sense of Bartholomew

Figure 13.3 Map of geographical spread of some of the personnel who were in the Lohmann–Bartholomew planning class at the University of Illinois.
Based on a listing made in 1961 by Professor Karl B. Lohmann.

as a teacher. Calm, serious, "practical," he used few notes, relying more on his experiences, an excellent memory, and a general depth of information including planning's prevailing legal and legislative atmosphere; these he supported with maps and reports from his current studies. Presentation was marked by its sense of clarity and, as Lohmann mentioned, his "emphasis on the positive. . . . Bartholomew was very positive in his expectations."[9] On one occasion, Professor Lohmann scanned the 1960–1 roster of the American Institute of Planners for names of former students who had been in the class, and he recalled forty-one who occupied various roles in the profession after having been prepared under the Lohmann–Bartholomew tutelage. (See Fig. 13.3.) Understandably, many of these students worked at one time or another for Bartholomew; one of them, Eldridge Lovelace, is now a principal partner in the firm.

If Bartholomew was then to be a partipant in the educational experience of generations of students, his academic influence can also be marked in another way, although its outline is less clearly defined: this is on Professor Lohmann himself. A graduate of the landscape architecture program at Harvard and then on the staff of the Bureau of Municipalities of the Pennsylvania Department of Internal Affairs, he joined the landscape architecture faculty at Illinois in 1921. Someone was needed to work with Bartholomew in the planning course; Lohmann expressed an interest and was chosen. So at the same time when he was sharing a teaching responsibility with Bartholomew he was also sharing a learning one, for he sat in on all of the sessions that Bartholomew conducted.

In 1931, Lohmann published what Henry Vincent Hubard at Harvard called the first textbook on planning, certainly the first introduction to planning for many people who subsequently moved into the profession as a career. This was his *Principles of City Planning*, a textbook used by the planning classes at Illinois as well as various other universities in the country, attaining a respectable circulation for its day. Lohmann has acknowledged that the chances are the book was "influenced a lot" by the Bartholomew lectures. Scanning the book, one senses this pattern of relationship: the subject matter and its treatment (for instance, the comprehensive plan, its preparation, role of the consultant, and so on; street and recreation planning; and housing) are both approached in terms reminiscent of Bartholomew practice, although specific details sometimes vary (Bartholomew and Lohmann differ somewhat as to organizational elements categorized as making up the comprehensive plan, a difference, however, more of nomenclature than spirit). Lohmann's book, then, became a primer for the professionals of that decade and the one that followed. And directly or indirectly, the Bartholomew viewpoint had been established in this prewar academic atmosphere out of which the American planning world sought a portion of its new professionals.

Professional leadership

In one final way, the impact of Harland Bartholomew on American planning has been reinforced, and this is through his role as a leader and spokesman for his profession. The American City Planning Institute (AIP's predecessor) had been founded in 1917 with Frederick Law Olmsted as its president. Bartholomew was one of its original members and the Institute's sixth president (1927–9), his predecessors having included one of his former employers, George B. Ford, and John Nolen whom he followed in office. One is struck again by a certain career precociousness; the average age of his predecessors was fifty-three, ranging from forty-four to sixty-three; Bartholomew ascended to the presidency at thirty-eight, the youngest ever to hold the office, then or since.

His role as spokesman for the developing science of planning is preserved in part by the proceedings of the National Conference on City Planning. His first appearance before that group and in the pages of its proceedings is his report on Newark progress in 1915, and this is followed with a 1918 report on the St Louis plan, in 1919 by one on residential zoning, and in 1921 by an updating of the St Louis report. All through the 1920s and into the 1930s, he continued to provide for the delegates a sequence of analyses and recommendations on aspects of the problems professionals were being asked to face, ranging from distributing the cost of street widening (1924) to St Louis metropolitan planning (1934).

These papers are paralleled and extended by those prepared for other forums such as articles for the *American Civic Annual* (now the *American Planning and Civic Annual*) as well as appearances and addresses before a wide spectrum of groups that called upon him as an after-dinner and convention speaker. Bartholomew has interpreted his responsibility as one calling not only for the development of a planning technology for the needs of his own practice but also for contributing that knowledge to the profession at large and for strengthening the general public's awareness of the planner's availability for using that knowledge in the search for solutions to the urban problems that all were finding increasingly about them. The combination of circumstances surrounding his practice and his supporting activities gave an unusually nationwide cast to his efforts.

Thus when one reviews Bartholomew's career and examines certain of its innovative characteristics, doing so provides not only details and dimensions to his record but to a remarkable extent similarly explains a whole milieu of the profession itself in the years before and, for a time, following the Second World War. Bartholomew would willingly acknowledge that he was not alone in developing certain characteristic ideas and practices, that others assisted him or worked independently along similar lines. Yet the ubiquity of his practice, the particularity of his means, and the personal stature which he came to realize in the profession gave his precedent special impact, a kind of semi-official cachet which both the literature and practice acknowledged and made their own.

After the how of the matter, what of the substance? Bartholomew's career covered the full range of the planning consultant's services of the times, ranging from complete comprehensive city plans through zoning ordinances to more specialized facets of service: traffic engineering studies, site plans, economic studies, various types of engineering reports, and so on. There were, however, certain themes which ranked high in his goals and, through the nature of his position in the profession, were by his examples to represent influences on contemporary practices or portend those just ahead.

Bartholomew and the comprehensive plan

Though the concept of the comprehensive plan was by 1912 no longer an innovation in the thinking or vocabulary of planners of that date, it was one whose specifics were by no means clarified; and this search was to be a central theme in Bartholomew's career:

My interest in city planning beginning with the Newark work was to produce for every city a true comprehensive plan. This feeling has so dominated my thinking that my family have jokingly remarked on numerous occasions that I should have a middle name, i.e. "C" for Comprehensive. This has seemed to me to be the basic essential in this field and my work was always oriented in this direction. . . . I still feel very strongly on this point. I feel that cities are woefully lacking in comprehensive city plans. . . .

I am as keenly interested as most people in many of the planning studies that are being produced today for unit areas, for cluster development, and for neighborhoods and such. I am far more interested, however, in whether there is a basic comprehensive plan which furnishes the framework and substance within which these individual designs can be made.[10]

The principles he was examining in the Newark Plan of 1915 continue to occupy him, in which any decision affecting the growth and development of the city – annexations, subdivisions, location and design of public buildings, street extensions, rapid transit and other franchises – were to be guided by the comprehensive plan. In the 1920s, he would arrive at a formula for his "science of planning" which, with variations through time, established the parameters that comprehensive planning had previously missed, aided by burgeoning opportunities as a planning consultant for him to pursue his search.

The prefatory and shakedown phases of the practice came to an end with a series of reports in the 1920s. Out of this emerged a prototype report which in program and content would continue to be the measure of the firm's service to a city in preparing its comprehensive plan.[11] After the report's acknowledging preliminaries, it would present a several-page introduction on the "Principles of city planning," in effect a kind of goals statement which guided the planner in his work and the reader in understanding it. He had written similarly in previous reports, but in these later reports it stands more independently as a general statement of principles, a central rationale in the development of Bartholomew's interpretation of his work.

In contrast to the planning preoccupations of the 1970s, the span backwards of fifty years permitted a more simplistic orientation: "City Planning is essentially concerned with the *physical* development of cities" (Bartholomew, 1924, p. 11). The "Principles" then list physical elements which "properly constitute the city plan," six in number: streets, transit, transportation (rail and water), public recreation, zoning, and civic art. (Housing had in earlier reports been included as an integral element, but in his consulting practice Bartholomew was finding that his clients would refuse to spend money for a housing survey.)

These are the physical elements which, when properly planned and correlated, make possible the creation of an attractive and orderly working organism out of the heterogeneous mass we now call the city (Bartholomew, 1924).

The explanations follow lines already established by earlier work. Streets are main arterial thoroughfares "like the spokes of a wheel" with at least 100-foot rights-of-way, secondary (crosstown) thoroughfares

(80–100-foot rights-of-way) spaced approximately one-half mile apart, and minor streets, chiefly for residential districts (50-foot rights-of-way). Supplementing these could be special service streets such as those serving industrial districts. Transit confines itself to route coordination with the street plan and population patterns. Under transportation the aim is to plan for rail terminal and route locations to expedite movements and serve industry with minimum friction between them and the other functions of the city. The section on recreation is also a restatement of ideas clarified in his earlier reports, a hierarchy of facilities using school plans where their location and offerings fit in with the comprehensive plan. Zoning follows in the planning, the ordinances based on typical use, height, area, and yard standards, all as part of the comprehensive city plan.

Closing with some rather elliptical attention to civic art, the "Principles" in their range and sequence established what the report would then examine in specific detail. Thus the methodology of the science was established, and the planner could now apply it step by step leading to planning proposals for the ultimate betterment of the community. Although an analytical framework, it was not a static one; without doing violence to the rationale, as the impact of changing forces such as the automobile and suburbanization became increasingly apparent, the "Principles" found their proper place within the science. Thus the firm became known for a reassuringly clear program of service – thorough, sound, and businesslike.

From scanning of contemporary evidence, whether the reports of other planners or the professional literature, while Bartholomew's comprehensive planning may not appear to be unique in its ideas and methods, it brought to the profession a refining of standards and a special sense of system and cohesiveness in which each step in the planning process assumed its logical place. In the Hubbards' national survey on planning and zoning (Hubbards, 1929), there is an implication that the systematism of Bartholomew's planning practice was, if not the universal prescription of the profession, then an admirable and respected criterion. The antecedents of his interest had emerged prior to his planning debut, but it was Bartholomew who was to formulate most rigorously the "capricious procedure" of planning into a "science." In the 1920s his work assumed a form and content which became recognizably his with its sense of professionalism and technical competence, a knowledgeability and clarified sequence of steps through which the planner took the commissioners in their search for an orderly and prosperous future of middle-class values as appropriate reflections of the type of clients and their ambitions. This was the portfolio of talents and techniques which, through the effectiveness of its methods and policies and its coast-to-coast applications, came to assume a kind of semi-official stature within the practice.

Urban land use data

The 1920s may have been formative in shaping professional methodology, but the research base on which the work was constructed was
notably insecure. In the 1930s, Bartholomew was to be central in developments leading to some repair of this weakness in his science. The firm's
work had resulted in the accumulation of a considerable body of material
on land uses in its contract cities, and Bartholomew realized that this
represented a valuable resource from which to draw. Here were the
means to make certain inferences of scale and ratio between the community and its areal needs for the various land use types, particularly helpful in zoning studies, and to bring a certain realism to the enthusiasm of
planning commissions in their manipulation of local zoning ordinances.
Bartholomew had discovered an interestingly constant ratio between
amounts of developed land uses among cities of differing character, size,
and location, and mentioned this to Henry Hubbard. Hubbard saw that
this material was sufficiently significant to call for its more general availability and suggested its preparation for publication as one of the Harvard
City Planning Studies.[12] This resulted the following year in Bartholomew's *Urban Land Uses* (1932), a study of the actual amounts of land
given over to the several land uses within the city limits of some twenty-
two different cities of varying sizes and types, based on surveys the firm
had made in them at various times.

   The objectives of the book as stated in the preface (by the editors of the
Harvard City Planning Series, Theodora K. and Henry V. Hubbard) were
to make generally available

a method for estimating the total area required for each particular urban use for
any given future population of between 5,000 and 300,000 persons. In addition, it
should aid municipalities confronted with the problem of determining the
desirable extent of city area and the location of future boundaries, since the
aggregation of amounts of land needed for each particular use will naturally
determine how much peripheral land can economically be absorbed. (Bartholomew, 1932: v)

This may sound oversimplified in light of present practices, but the place
this book occupies in the development of the science of planning must be
scaled against the vacuum of urban research then prevailing. By this contribution, Bartholomew was pioneering in a field untouched by any other
such ventures, public or private, and the material he here presented
would be a standard reference work, still cited as a source on the subject
of land use areal ratios a decade later in *Local Planning Administration*
(Segoe, 1941) (although, by then, with some reservations). Not until the
latter part of the 1930s with the figures coming out of the Real Property
Inventories of 1934–6 would there be any comparable additions to the
body of research on the urban characteristics of American cities. The first

census to include questions on housing on a nationwide scale was that of 1940. Thus urban research which had evolved out of the experience of Bartholomew's own practice and had come to serve him in it was made generally available to the profession and the public.

Urban land policy and renewal

The opportunity that the 1930s presented Bartholomew "to consider and study fundamental problems" was uniquely met in his work on *Urban Land Policy* for the City Plan Commission of St Louis. It was by this effort that research techniques were extended and major planning directions anticipated. It came about by the nature of the period: the Depression-induced lethargy of professional activities, assistance from federal work programs, a background of years of planning activities in St Louis, the city's need for area redevelopment, and the typical Bartholomew pragmatism which recognized that he could make his program against slums and blight more meaningful to the community and its leaders if he could give it a dollars-and-cents dimension. What were "the true costs to the community of slum areas?" The group he assembled consisted of St Louis Plan Commission staff, some of the "married employees of the largest St Louis architectural offices with little other active work," and a number of technicians whose employment was supported by the Works Progress Administration. The results were summarized in publication of *Urban Land Policy* in 1936.

Bartholomew examined land use and population shifts in St Louis from 1910 to 1935, and revealed the scale of some disturbing forces at work; he and his commission saw in its message the relationship of urban land policy to the city's social and economic future and hoped to convince the city administration of the situation's seriousness and the wisdom of their proposed policy. For the first time St Louis measured urban trends, and it found to what an extent it was headed toward economic and social collapse as the center city lost population and property values, deterioration at the center moved farther and farther out, and population abandoned the city's congestion for the suburbs.

The study also examined the record in terms of measured economics, an effort to determine the extent to which slums were costing the city money in dollar terms. It was a comparative analysis for 1930 through 1935 of municipal service costs against income for twenty different representative districts among the city's typical land use areas – downtown residential, midtown residential, newer residential, downtown business, industrial, and so on. From these figures, calculations were made which in summary demonstrated that St Louis "slums" paid to the city only about 40 per cent of what they received in costs of services, that "higher value residential districts" paid twice as much to the city as they received from it, the central business district two and a half times as much, and that the city as a whole annually was subsidizing its slum districts by $5,500,000.

The causes for this were in part planning's: excessive commercial and industrial zoning, declared the report. The ordinance had been designed when there had been no "scientific data" on actual area needs for land use types, but recent years had brought more knowledge of this relationship, including such a study for St Louis (more WPA-financed urban research) comparing actual land uses against amounts of land zoned for those uses. Excessive areas zoned for commerce and industry not only often faced unlikely development as such but discouraged appropriate residential use and thereby drove additional population to the suburbs. Similar overzoning for apartments (Bartholomew states by 149 per cent) encouraged speculative property development, while single-family residential areas were insufficiently safeguarded by the existing ordinance. Such policies added up to speculative exploitation, gradual neglect, and eventual abandonment.

The urban land policy proposed in their place was multifaceted:
1 Revised zoning ordinance scaled to "known laws of supply and demand" with more protection to residential uses.
2 Enforcement of sanitation and fire laws.
3 Elimination of smoke nuisance.
4 Enactment of a minimum housing standards ordinance.
5 Rehabilitation of structures where advisable.
6 Removal of unsafe, obsolete, and unfit structures.
7 Development of neighborhood units embracing all residential areas in the city for the improvement of the environment and elimination of nonconforming uses.
8 Construction of low-cost housing "in the older sections of the city."
9 Enforcement of building codes. (City Plan Commission of St Louis, 1936: 21, 23)

Also proposed was action toward encouraging rehabilitation and conservation programs in residential neighborhoods not yet requiring more drastic measures: rezoning as necessary; home maintenance; surveys for park, playground, and other community needs; code enforcement; deed restrictions; and the power to organize protective and improvement associations. This section was accompanied by a map organizing the city into "suggested neighborhood district boundaries." The policy statement closed by advocating passage of enabling legislation for the formation of a local housing authority to undertake reconstruction in neighborhoods requiring large-scale renewal and to accept federal grants for construction of low-cost housing for those income groups whose housing needs could not otherwise be provided.

What one reads in this report is an anticipation of the urban renewal program of the 1950s and 1960s. With other cities working along similar lines, this research work of Bartholomew and his St Louis staff would help move public opinion and national legislation toward placing federal and local governments in a new relationship with the forces responsible for urban environment. The subsequent United States Housing Act of 1937 with its commitment of federal money to the support of improved housing opportunities testified to the effectiveness of their message and is of course the antecedent of present-day federal involvement in urban concerns.

Housing policy

The matter of housing and responsibility for providing it in reasonable amounts based on decent standards had been an early area of Bartholomew's concerns, and one that in the 1930s was to resume its position in his priorities. The spirit of the 1930s was conducive to the social implications of a positive housing policy, and its possibilities for both work-producing activity and the satisfaction of human needs were obvious to the Roosevelt Administration. The previous administration had also made some effort to stimulate housing construction through the Reconstruction Finance Corporation. Even by 1933, however, a pattern was emerging with which Bartholomew could not agree. This was what appeared to him to be housing officials' disinclination to think in terms broader than the immediate project instead of "comprehensively."

At the twenty-fifth National Conference on City Planning in Baltimore in October 1933, he read a paper which he hoped would bring housing into the larger planning scene. Entitled "Technical problems in slum clearance" (Bartholomew, 1933, pp. 121–30) he sought to tie together the rebuilding and preservation of the city and discourage decentralization with housing as one phase of the total urban plan of action: reconstruction of slums would be meaningless unless linked with a broader plan of action getting at the heart of urban decay. Thus he indicated that the nation's housing program could not be separate from the larger planning scheme but must be intimately associated with it to succeed, reaffirming again his anticipation of the present-day renewal program. Coupled with limitations imposed on city size and standards of design excellence for the new residential environments, housing could hope to become meaningfully comprehensive for its own sake and that of the city and the public as investor. Bartholomew subsequently observed that his paper was not a critical success among the new housing officialdom, but eventually, through his membership on the national Slum Clearance Advisory Committee, his ideas helped shape the original Housing Act of 1937 and later that of 1949.[13]

Other contributions

Other facets of precedent for the profession come to mind: the approach of the firm's design team to its office and work production (as early as 1919); capital improvement programming backed by passage of successive supporting bond issues (St Louis beginning in 1923); and the incorporation of planned unit developments as standard zoning recommendations (from 1939). In all this Harland Bartholomew was central, and "while he would be the first to share any credit with people that worked with him, he is the one that was responsible."[14] Reviewing the output of that responsibility and noting the ranking of the firm in these formative years for planning, one comes to understand something of the nature of American planning policy through the years between the two World Wars and even into the 1950s.

Since then, quite different forces have been at work, revolutionizing in their effects on our cities and on the profession so directly charged with working with them. Seen from our present kaleidoscopic urban scene, this look backward may have a deceptively simplistic projection. Suitable, then, is a reminder that the crises of those days – expansionism, depression, experimentation, and initial postwar fragmentation – and Bartholomew's participation in them had their own sense of immediacy and urgency. When practitioners and precedents were few and techniques were largely intuitive, his work helped to define and clarify the planning process; when most universities failed to include planning education among their curriculums, his firm not only acted as a training center but encouraged the placing of its "graduates" throughout the country; when the basis of planning decision was made on the sketchiest of researched understanding, his investigations helped bring dimension to and clarify the American urban phenomenon; when legal concepts and tools were still rudimentary, his concerns and discoveries helped evolve them. These were no doubt some of the thoughts of the Board of Governors of the American Institute of Planners when in 1955 they awarded to Harland Bartholomew the Institute's Distinguished Service Award with the following citation:

Pioneer in the science and art of city planning, educator, public servant; through the practice of his profession he brought his skills and his understanding to the service of the people of our cities from coast to coast; his contributions in teaching and research, as well as in his practice, have helped to form standards of the profession of city planning.

Notes

1 See "An appreciation," AIP Newsletter, August, 1962, pp. 9–11.
2 Letter from Mr Bartholomew to the author, April 9, 1952.
3 His firm, Harland Bartholomew and Associates, continues, currently with

seven offices, a staff of 150, and a wide variety of planning and engineering activities. Bartholomew retired from active participation in the firm in the 1960s, though remaining in an advisory and consulting capacity.

4 He remained on a half-time basis as the city planning engineer until 1950 and as consultant for four more years.

5 US Census figures nearest to report date.

6 If one adds the 1917 *Problems of St Louis*, a comprehensive plan report for that city published under Bartholomew's direction by the St Louis Plan Commission, this population figure increases to 2,601,468.

7 Interview with Professor Lohmann, August 19, 1961.

8 Interview with Mr Bartholomew, April 23, 1960.

9 Lohmann interview, August 19, 1961.

10 Bartholomew letter, November 30, 1961.

11 His reports for Memphis (1924), Kenosha (1925), and Des Moines (1928) are typical.

12 Letter from Mr Bartholomew, July 15, 1963.

13 Interviews with Mr Bartholomew, June 14, 1960, and July 13, 1961, and with Mr Lovelace, July 25, 1961.

14 Letter from Mr Lovelace, February 22, 1971.

References

Adams, Frederick J. (1954) *Urban Planning Education in the United States*, Cincinnati, Ohio, The Alfred Bettman Foundation.

Adams, Thomas (1936) *Outline of Town and City Planning*, New York, Russell Sage Foundation.

Bartholomew, Harland (1924) *Memphis Plan*.

_____ (1932) *Urban Land Uses*, Cambridge, Mass., Harvard University Press. This book has been revised and reissued under his authorship in 1955 as *Land Uses in American Cities*, Cambridge, Mass., Harvard University Press.

_____ (1933) "Technical problems in slum clearance."

City Plan Commission of St Louis (1936) *Urban Land Policy* (Oct.).

Hubbard, Henry V., and Theodora K. Hubbard (1929) *Our Cities To-Day and To-Morrow*, Cambridge, Mass., Harvard University Press.

Lohmann, Karl B. (1931) *Principles of City Planning*, New York and London, McGraw-Hill.

Newark City Plan Commission (1911) *The City Plan Commission*, Newark.

Nolen, John (1927) "Twenty years of city planning progress in the United States," in *Planning Problems in Town, City and Region*, Philadelphia, National Conference on City Planning.

Segoe, Ladislas (ed.) (1941) *Local Planning Administration*, Chicago, International City Managers' Association (June).

14 The recollections of Ladislas Segoe

Edited by Donald A. Krueckeberg
from an interview conducted by
Sydney H. Williams

Introduction

What are the disappointments? The riverfront is a big one. What they have done down there – with the stadium and the coliseum – is a pain to my existence. Every self-respecting city in the world uses its waterfront as a parkway. The Serpentine is as much a central riverfront park as I'm Chinese.[1]

Segoe and Cincinnati are almost synonymous, but he pulls no punches on the city in which he established and operated, for fifty-two years, one of the most successful consulting firms in the history of American planning. And his strong Hungarian accent leaves no doubt – he is not Chinese.

Ladislas Segoe was born in Debrecen, Hungary, August 17, 1894. After military service in the First World, with the Central Powers, he finished his Diploma of Engineering from the Technical University of Budapest. He was then briefly employed with the Yugoslav government, planning new towns. In 1922 he came to the United States and joined the staff of the Technical Advisory Corporation of New York City, the pioneer planning firm of E. P. Goodrich and G. B. Ford. They sent him out to Cincinnati as resident planner. There he completed their work, briefly was employed by the city, then set up his own firm, continuing to do work for Cincinnati.

The other name in planning history so closely associated with Cincinnati is that of the famous zoning lawyer Alfred Bettman, best known for his brief before the US Supreme Court in the landmark case of *Eculid* v. *Ambler Realty* in 1926,[2] which won the constitutional test for zoning. Bettman and Segoe were, as Segoe puts it, almost like father and son – Bettman the legal and political reformer, Segoe the technical expert.

In addition to his association with Bettman, and their development of the technique of the capital budget for public works programming, Segoe discusses his consulting assignments with the Tennessee Valley Authority (TVA) and the City of Detroit.

Playing a role in the New Deal, Segoe was director of the Urbanism Committee of the National Resources Committee from 1936 to 1938 which produced the seminal document, *Our Cities – Their Role in the National Economy*.[3] He was also editor and principal author of the first edition of *Local Planning Administration* published in 1941 by the International City Manager's Association and presently in its fifth edition.

The Segoe firm of city planners and consulting engineers did work for 106 different American cities and counties, preparing comprehensive plans, zoning regulations, parking and traffic and transportation studies. While many of the clients were smaller towns and cities, they also included San Francisco, Chicago, Detroit, New York, Pittsburgh, Philadelphia, and Seattle among their number.

Segoe lectured widely in universities, from 1930 to 1942 at the University of Cincinnati, and also at Harvard, Carnegie Institute of Technology, and Northwestern. In 1957 he received the Distinguished Service Award of the American Institute of Planners, their special Fiftieth Anniversary Award in 1967, and several other medals and awards for his great contributions to the field.

The downtown offices of Ladislas Segoe and Associates were closed in the Fall of 1980. But he is still, with his wife Vilma, very much at home today in Cincinnati, Ohio.

The recollections

Budapest − 1919

My education in Budapest at the University was interrupted by the First World War, and I spent three and one-half years in the service. In 1919 I came back to the University. We were offered accelerated courses in recognition that we had given so much of our time. One day between certain classes, I had an hour or two and wasn't particularly busy in the studio, so I walked down a corridor and came across a hand-lettered sign saying that a Dr Forbath and somebody else were lecturing on town planning. And I went in there, and there were about a dozen boys sitting around so I joined them and I listened.

I found out later that this Dr Forbath was a lawyer. Lawyers abroad all have doctorates, you know. The other fellow was an architect. These two fellows were very active and very successful in entering competitions. In Europe when a large city or a medium size city was in the market for a town plan they had a national or international competition. This lawyer and architect combination had won two or three prizes during the two-year period that I followed them. As I understood it, the lawyer was the one who furnished the ideas and the architect was the one who translated them into graphics.

Well, I sat through this lecture and I liked it. They had the lecture once a week and I kept going to the lecture and along the way I asked, "Is there any literature available in this field?" Well, there was not in Hungarian

Plate 14.1 Cincinnati river front, inadequate use of the river front.
Source: *Official Plan of the City of Cincinnati*, 1925, p. 145.

Plate 14.2 The Danube through Budapest, river front used extensively for both commerce and for enjoyment.
Source: *Official Plan of the City of Cincinnati*, 1925, p. 150.

but I spoke fluent German at the time, so they gave me two names. One was Sitte, and I still have the book here, and another one. So I bought those books and I read them. This was of course an elective; you have no examination or any tests. For a period of a year and one-half I attended these lectures. They were usually lectures with not much theory but showing the way that they had evolved the plan for a competition in Belgrade, for example, with some explanation for why they proposed what they proposed.

My basic training does not quite correspond to civil engineering because we were getting a great deal of architecture. Not the design of monumental public buildings, but utilitarian ones, such as a railroad station, not regal but a division headquarters, something in connection with maybe the water works, an office building – utilitarian architecture. We got a lot of theory in engineering. I remember a structural engineering professor who said, "Now don't try to remember any of these formulas. What you have to remember are some of the fundamentals, the basics on which these formulas are founded, so that if you should be marooned on a desert island you would be able to develop these formulas by just doing." In other words, I found that this was a training that calls not for memory so much as for logic. It stood me in good stead.

Well, that was about the extent of my planning knowledge at the time that I graduated, about a year and one-half of these lectures, two or three books, and looking at some town plans. I graduated during the first communist regime in Hungary. I practically starved before I graduated because there was nothing to eat in Budapest. In the middle of summer we were living on sauerkraut and bread. My parents were living down in southern Hungary, which by that time was Yugoslavia, just on the border of Hungary, in the middle of Europe's bread-basket, the most fertile agricultural area in all of Europe, rolling in milk and honey. My problem was, after I graduated, how to get home. After having served in the Hungarian Army (mounted artillery) for almost four years, the communists kept their eyes on me because if they had to go to war they wanted to make use of the experienced soldiers and officers. I had to find a way of escaping. I couldn't just ask for a travel permit because I would never have gotten it.

So I went down to the railroad station and when I thought that no one could see me I jumped on a train. After it was going I hoped it was going south instead of north. Fortunately the train did go south but not to the city where my parents lived, however, close enough. So I went to the headquarters of the railroad administration and with the help of some friends of my father, who was one of the chief engineers in the Hungarian State Railroad and most everybody knew him, they put me on a handcar and gave me one of the railroad blouse/jacket combinations and a railroad cap and I managed to join my family.

First planning job: Yugoslavia

Pretty soon I heard that the Yugoslav government was looking for engineers who could help them with a program of agrarian reform.

Plate 14.3 Ladislas Segoe.

There was a time during the First World War when the whole Serbian Army was actually pushed off their country and they took them to some island in the Mediterranean to reorganize. At the same time the government sent out a call all over the world for young Yugoslav men who were emigrants, not Yugoslav but Serbians I'm talking about, to return and they promised them that they would get land after the war. They called them "Dobrojovac," which is a sort of good volunteer. So the program consisted of parceling up the estates of Hungarian landowners and designing and building farming villages.

The European farmers do not live on farms. They live in villages and they go to their small plots every day when they need to work them. They have small vegetable gardens right in the village behind their homes and then they have the farms some distance away. So, my first contract in the planning or engineering field was: here are so many thousands of acres of land and there are so many hundreds to benefit. Parcel them out and arrange them as best you can so that a reasonably centrally located village will permit this type of an operation. Find a location for the village, the best site of the village and lay out where the church goes, where the school goes, and so on.

So that was the job and I completed it in the Fall of 1921. At that time I had a very well-to-do American uncle who came for his first visit after the First World War, who asked me what I was going to do over the winter. I told him that I had just finished this one job and I had nothing else in view. He said, "Wouldn't you like to come over, we have a large home," which turned out to be quite an estate. "We'd like to have you and you might be interested in what is going on in your line in the

United States.'' So in due course I went on a boat and I came and arrived on the 22nd of February, George Washington's birthday. And then I attempted to find out what there was by way of planning courses at universities.

Looking for planning in America

First I went to Columbia, as I was in New York. I went to several universities and found no planning instruction as such. Nearest were some landscape architectural courses, and concurrently with that I also contacted the secretary of the ASCE, American Society of Civil Engineers, and asked him where could I find a firm that was engaged in planning operations. The secretary said he hadn't heard of anybody but if he did hear of anybody he would call me. So I gave him my telephone number. Several months went by and I was very discouraged because I had no leads. In the meantime I would be coming into New York from White Plains where my uncle's estate was, a beautiful place, and he went into town to his office on Wall Street and I went to the public library on 42nd Street and Fifth Avenue. I read awhile and wandered around. Finally I got a call: ''I have just heard of a firm that just got a job in East Orange, New Jersey – some sort of a planning job.'' ''The address,'' he says, ''is 132 Nassau Street,'' which is right down in the Wall Street district. So I went down to see them.

I told them, ''I am a visitor in this country, I don't think I am going to stay, but I will certainly stay another four or six months. Would you permit me to come to the office (and I won't disturb anybody), just to see what is going on, and if you wish I would be perfectly willing to do some work?'' I was not of course fluent in English, but I knew enough to be understood and after awhile I could understand the New York jargon. The English that I knew I had from a British lady who was teaching in Budapest and my ear took some time before I could understand the ''thoity-thoids,'' and so on.

Anyway, they wouldn't hear of it. They said no, they would not accept that but they would be interested in taking me on for a regular salary. But first they wanted to ask me a question, about my background and so on. I told them about it and the business head of the office who was not an engineer or a planner, but he managed the office, Campbell Scott, said, ''You know, this is only the second or third attempt of ours to get into the planning field so chances are that you have more of a planning background than we do.'' He offered me $25 a week and put me on. Well, I went to work for them and I found this East Orange job was maybe the third engagement of the firm in the territory and that they were also working on a reconnaissance in Cincinnati.

By that time Harland Bartholomew was in St Louis. He had been in their office, and left there just about a year or so before I went to work for them. Tracy Auger was not yet there but he, I think, was hired a week or two after I was. He was my closest colleague and has been over the years one of my dearest friends. He initiated me into the mysteries of some of the basement self-service cafeterias. He and I worked on East Orange. Our job was a land use map in black and white, india ink on tracing cloth, outlining every building by symbols indicating the size of the setback, sideyard, and the number of cars that would fit in the garage. It was something to look at. Poor Tracy, whose eyesight was never too good (he had a defect that he was born with) and I were working at two ends of a large drafting board.

The principals of that office included E. P. Goodrich. He was an engineer and he was the father of many of the traffic engineering principles and devices including the system on Fifth Avenue way back in the early 1920s. He and I are joint founders of the Institute of Traffic Engineers. He was designer of the Bush Terminal in New York, a very imaginative engineer. He was breaking ground in many different ways. The architect in the firm was George B. Ford, who I believe was responsible for the firm getting into planning. If you look back in the early National Conferences on City Planning you will find that half of the proceedings contain papers by him. The name of the firm was the Technical Advisory Corporation, known for many years as TAC. Ford was the architect. They also had a landscape architect, an industrial engineer whose last name was Ellis, one other fellow, and the head of the group was Campbell Scott. I'll give you a little background on how they came into being.

After the First World War, the federal government found itself owning a lot of war housing and they wanted to liquidate it. They also found themselves with some war bonds, municipal bonds, that they wanted to liquidate. So, they hired these same guys that I have mentioned to you and they called themselves the Technical Advisory Committee. They had the job of going around making the survey and then making appraisals, telling the government how much these installations were worth. When the job was finished apparently they managed to get along so well they decided to stay together. In the meantime, or shortly afterwards, George B. Ford was appointed to an international committee of architects to help France with the reconstruction of Rheims. So Ford, who was a Beaux Arts graduate, went over there and came into contact apparently with architects who had been engaged in town planning. As you know, you have to be an architect abroad before you can practice. Contacts with these architects opened his eyes that here was a field.

As I said, they already had a reconnaissance study underway, the purpose of which was to determine the state of health of Cincinnati in 1921–2 – What are its problems and what are the areas in which town planning could make a contribution? Cincinnati in those days was a very stodgy, dormant sort of community, quite aside from the fact that the whole country, during the period 1921–2, was in a depression. Now, they were not retained by the city. They were retained by the United City Planning Committee, of which Alfred Bettman was a founder and was the chairman. The city government of Cincinnati was considered at the time to be the most corrupt city government in the United States, and they would no more hear about spending money on planning than I don't know what.

Cincinnati had a reform administration, briefly, prior to the coming of the charter and city manager form of government in 1924. Under the first reform mayor, whose name was Hunt, they had elected a very short-lived, two year administration in 1912. Alfred Bettman was city solicitor. Can you imagine Alfred Bettman running for office? He did, and he got elected.

In that capacity he had a great deal to do with problems involving turnpikes, toll roads (which were then liquidating), interurban railroads (which were also discontinuing), and problems having to do with land and land use. Then I believe he also started going over to England to attend these summer courses in planning, which he kept up. He kept that up for I would say more than a dozen years. It was his interest in planning that made him organize this United City Planning Committee, and raise over $100,000 even though he had no assurance from the city administration that they would do anything with the result of the effort.

Even before that time, and I can't tell you how or why, he drafted and managed to get passed state enabling legislation. That must have been around 1919, or thereabouts. So there was a statute on the books, but the city would have had to make the appointments in order to make it official and the city administration then wasn't interested in even doing that. The most they would do was to assign the director of Public Works as one member of an unofficial planning commission. They called it that. It was not organized under the state law. The city did not have any charter at that time so this was an unofficial citizens' group with the director of Public Works and the secretary of the Park Board representing the city. The rest of them were prominent individuals. A couple of heads of industry, a retired industrialist, Irving Krohn who was chairman of the Park Board for innumerable years. That was the set-up of the commission that hired TAC for the study. The idea was that after the study was completed a program would be drawn up for the preparation of a city plan.

Looking for Cincinnati

About six months after I went to work for TAC they landed the contract for the Cincinnati plan. They came to me and asked me if I would go to Cincinnati and head the technical staff with Goodrich and Ford being joint consultants. Since the name Cincinnati meant nothing to me I asked my uncle. He had never heard of Cincinnati, being a typical New Yorker. He wasn't interested in anything west of the Hudson River. We went to a Rand-McNally atlas and we discovered that there was more than one Cincinnati in the United States but we figured that this was the Cincinnati that they had in mind. I hesitated, but they said I could always quit if I didn't like it. So I got on a train in the middle of summer. There happened to be a railroad strike so it took me two days to get from New York to Cincinnati.

We established the office and two years later we produced what eventually became the Official City Plan of Cincinnati of 1925. We had a staff but I couldn't hire any planners. There weren't any planners. We had co-op students from the University. That helped, and we had some draftsmen, one of them was an excellent map maker. And some clerks. The truth of the matter is, that not only did we have to train one or two fellows how to do things, but to be quite honest, I myself had to evolve some of the basic techniques, think through the kind of facts that were needed, what were the criteria and constraints, and so on. There was no precedent for making a citywide school plan, a citywide recreational plan, a citywide railroad plan (with seven different railroads) – how to determine where are the best locations for a union station, how to determine distribution of freight houses in the city, etc. I would say that a very substantial portion of the methods of how to do things were developed right·on the job.

The things that I learned through the courses that I attended at the University and the German books didn't include the concept of the community as an organic unit, or the social survey that Patrick Geddes has to his credit.

Each month either Goodrich or Ford would come out for a week to see what had been accomplished and what had been proposed and to help prepare a program for the period until their next visit. That was the way we operated. Ford took it upon himself to put the whole picture together, to take all of these functional plans, surveys, and what not, and produce a final document. After that I packed up and said goodbye to Cincinnati. I said goodbye to the TAC and I told them I enjoyed the experience and I felt that I had learned a great deal, and I was going back home.

Back and forth again

So I returned to Budapest. I had worked sixteen to eighteen hours a day to wrap up the Cincinnati job, so I was going to take a few months off and

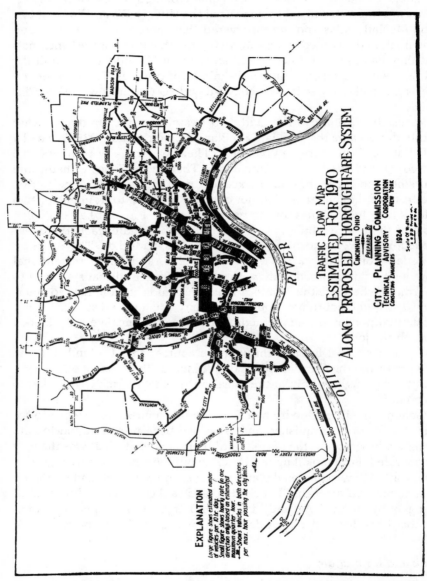

Figure 14.1 Traffic flow forecast, from the *Official Plan of the City of Cincinnati*, 1925, p. 62.

take it easy. I was getting $37.50 a week so I had accumulated enough money to take off for a little while.

Then I looked around in Hungary and went back to make contact with the University people. I went to see Dr Forbath, the planning professor, and he said that he definitely thought there would be enough work. Times were not bad. There was, worldwide, a sort of reasonably prosperous period, up until November 1929. So he encouraged me and I was looking round for office space to hang out my shingle, and then I began to get cables from the TAC. They had landed another job in Cincinnati, an industrial survey. They had a prospect for another plan in Louisville and they said that my Cincinnati friends would like me back and they offered me a junior membership in the firm. So, I decided to return to Cincinnati.

In due course the industrial survey was completed, that was for the Chamber of Commerce, and I moved on to Dayton to repeat the same kind of performance that we had here in Cincinnati. In the meantime, the Cincinnati people were getting fed up with the old city administration. Under the leadership of the Cincinnatus Association and Murray Seasongood, they started a drive to get rid of the large mayor council government with a lot of clowns on the council (and worse than clowns) and to draw up a charter. The move was on to establish a small council manager form of government.

As far as planning goes, they still only had the unofficial planning agency that was not organized under state law and therefore had no official role to play. After the charter was voted in and they had an election and got nine first rate people on the new council with Murray Seasongood as the mayor, they said, "Now we're ready to set up an official planning agency," which they proceeded to do. To my knowledge this was the first officially adopted plan for any major American city.[4] How Alfred Bettman managed to engineer that I do not know – the adoption. He wasn't even on the commission.

Then they said, "We need somebody to head the staff. Here is this guy in Dayton and he was the head of the staff that prepared the official city plan and he would be a wonderful guy to come back to Cincinnati and organize the planning office." So they offered me $6,000 a year, which was a lot of money for 1926.

In addition, I was unwilling to leave the private consulting field, and through the work that I had done in Cincinnati, Louisville, and in Dayton I had become well enough known and had enough contacts that I felt that I should nurse those contacts, as I did not intend to stay under a city hall roof forever. I made an arrangement under the contract. I wasn't a citizen yet, I had several months to go before I could get my papers. So they took me on under a contract that permitted me to devote one-fourth of my time to activities unrelated to my duties in the Cincinnati office. That was late in March 1926. I came on to Cincinnati and they found that the budget permitted me to hire one draftsman and one secretary. The planning office budget amounted to some $14,000. What happened next, I don't know if you want to take it down.

The old gang and the new planner

The old gang, the old Republican gang, was of course terribly hurt. Having lost out, they were looking around in every direction that they could for some way of attacking the new administration, hoping to find something that they had done that was illegal. So here is this guy Segoe who is not a citizen, and they put him head of a staff being paid tax monies.

There was a paper published at the time, by the organization, and one day the landlady of the small apartment house, a duplex where we lived, she came up and showed Vilma, my wife, the paper. The front page of it showed that a Hungarian Army officer, not a citizen, had a city job. Then they described the slaughter that he single-handedly perpetrated on American boys during the First World War.

I never was at the front where I faced any American boys. I was on the other fronts but not on the Western front. I was on the Russian front and the Romanian front. Vilma was flabbergasted of course. She didn't realize what this was all about. She had been here for only two weeks maybe. (Just a few months before I took the Cincinnati job Vilma came over and we got married.)

The newspaper was the *Hamilton County Republican*, or some such title as that. It was a scandal. The next thing we knew they brought suit against the city to stop paying my salary.

Now, it so happens that I was not paid by the city. Alfred Bettman apparently had enough foresight to know that something like this was likely to develop, so he had the Citizens' Planning Committee pay my salary for the first several months knowing that by July or August of that year I would get my final papers. Well, the city solicitor at the time didn't want to reveal this fact. He thought it would be more dramatic if we went to court and put me on the witness stand and then at the appropriate moment to spring this on the attackers. So we went through the charade. I was on the stand and the opposition was haranguing that I did this completely illegal, inexcusable, dastardly thing. Then the solicitor, when it came to him said, "Who is paying your salary?" Well, by coincidence I happened to have a check in my pocket which I handed him and he handed it to the judge. That was the end of the case. A few months later I got my papers and I stayed with the city until the middle of 1928. By that time I had a couple of jobs pending in Lexington and in Covington across the river – small towns with environs still being farmed. I set up my office and I was really fortunate. I already had a couple of these contracts when the bottom fell out of everything, in November of 1929.[5]

The terminal job

In addition, the union terminal projects were underway and the chief engineer, who was the first city manager in the United States, was Henry Waite. He felt that he needed somebody who could coordinate the planning of the terminal and accessory facilities, approaches, traffic schemes, etc. The location of it was recommended in the 1925 official city plan. The details had not been worked out. You see, these southern railroads and their miserable old stations were distributed all over the business area, and were all subject to flood (of the Ohio River). They were subject to the maximum flood of 71 feet or so, up until then. So the important features were not only a station, but an approach, track elevation, and to raise everything some feet above the then known flood level.

What happened then is that several viaducts that we had across the Mill Creek Valley (flowing into the Ohio) were too low to permit enough clearance above the 71-foot flood. So the problem thrown at me was what are we going to do with these viaducts? There were three of them. One of them was in such poor shape that every few months the city had a different sign on it reducing the permissible weight. One was not a viaduct at all but a level crossing that crossed more than twenty tracks. The problem was, should we arrange these old viaducts and build a long grade separation structure across the yard, or what would be the best solution. It seemed silly to repair those viaducts. They were very old.

I was told, "Here is our structural department, here is our real estate department, and so on. They can help you. They can tell you something about the viaducts, their condition, what it would cost to rehabilitate them, and so." The real estate man gave me an appraisal for the right of way for a new grade separation structure and approaches. So, I came up with what is known as the Western Hill Viaduct which is a double decker. The upper deck would be limited to passenger cars. The lower deck would carry the trucks and the streetcars, connecting with Springle Avenue which is a main street for the Mill Creek Valley industrial district.

Well, the selling of that viaduct was no small job. We were accused of selling the city down the river. Western Hills people were all opposed to it, and we had a time with the city too. The (railroad) terminal company felt that it would be justified to finance as much of this new viaduct structure as it would cost to reroute the existing structures and the grade separation. But if any more was needed it would have to be contributed by the city.

The problem was really this, from a planning point, aside from the financing and the economics, the Western Hills were dormant. There was no growth. The town was growing east and north. There were two reasons: one, driving east against the sun in the morning; and the other was these ramshackle viaducts barely above the railroad tracks. Anybody leaving the center of town couldn't help feeling he was passing through a railroad area. Bad orientation. The thought here of the double decker was some saving in the structure, but more importantly to get the second level so high that you wouldn't be aware there was any railroad anywhere. I felt that would revitalize the then dormant Western Hills.

One interesting little sidelight on this selling of the viaduct, in order for Waite to sell it to the city he would have to tell the city how much it would cost. We knew from the structural department what it would cost to repair the old crossings. But we didn't know how much for this substitute double decker. We felt that the committee of the heads of the seven railroads would never approve spending any more than we could justify.

Well anyway, here was the problem. We had to have some sort of estimate. So he (Waite) turns to the head of the very fine structural department (the department had maybe twenty structural engineers) whose name was Christiansen, a Swede. No he can't give him a preliminary estimate. To give him an estimate on a project of this nature he would have to have at least preliminary structural drawings. Waite said, "How long would that take?" He said, "Oh, maybe six months. Besides I don't really want to do it, because if they approve of this we would have to design and build it." Mind you this is at the depth of the depression, 1931, 1932, you know, when prices were at rock bottom. By the time the structure was designed and the contracts let, chances were that prices would be up and then Christiansen here would be blamed. So he refused.

My relationship to Henry Waite was personal as well as professional, so he called me into the office and said, "What am I going to do? We have to have some sort of an estimate to tell the city they will have to put in another million, or two million, or what." Well, after half an hour of complaining I said, "I'll give you an estimate; I won't have to build it." He said, "How?" I said, "Don't ask me how, but I'll give you an estimate."

Well it so happened that two or three years previous we had built a viaduct across the same Mill Creek Valley, the 8th Street Viaduct. So what I did, I went over to the engineering office and asked them for those plans and asked them for the cost figures and I started manipulating the things on a square foot basis, allowing for the supports to support both decks. Then I added on an ante and I came up with three and one-half million dollars. Waite just looked at me and he said, "Where did you get that figure, three and one-half millions dollars?"

So we went over to City Hall and told them that they would have to put in a million and one-half dollars. We talked a lot about our operation and our contacts and model building and exhibition and meetings and what not, and finally the city agreed.

Well I never thought to provide for lighting the viaduct and I never allowed anything for a complicated traffic signal system, especially on the west end. That was the first channelization; that was also my job. You see at the westerly end we had three streets all coming together and there was an upper deck and a lower deck so we needed the channels and we needed a dozen signals. We had a marvelous electrician in the city service and he worked it out. At any rate, I never thought of a lot of these things that should have been accounted in there. In the end, to make a long story short, it actually cost about $175,000 more, which was easy at that price level, you know. When he had spent all that money and were ready to cut the ribbons – there was no channelization job like that anywhere in the city – all the signals were blinking and I was standing alongside of Henry and he said, "You think this is going to work?"

This was the beginning of the New Deal, and what happened after the stock market break of course, was that year after year there had been retrenching, cities had been issuing script instead of checks, and the department easiest to cut, and justify, was the planning department. Cities were not building anything, private enterprise was not building anything, so there was nothing for them to do anyhow.

Many planning agencies went out of existence. Most planning agencies *existed* only, you know. Walter Blucher was the *only* employee of the planning department in Detroit. That was a characteristic of the situation at the time and the jobs were not much. I think I was four days a month with the terminal company, but by that time I told you I had this Covington, Lexington thing.

Alfred Bettman and the programming of public works

Ever since I came to Cincinnati to work for the unofficial planning agency my relationship with Alfred Bettman was very close, almost a father and son relationship. We spent some weekends, picnicing together, we went to the conferences, traveled together, we spent summer vacation on Georgian Bay fishing (feeding them worms), gathering berries and canoeing together. Much of the time we were talking about planning. He was born in 1873 and I was born in 1894, so we were almost twenty years apart. Twenty-one years, so not quite father and son but very close.

He was a stickler for excellence. Don't do anything unless you have a good reason for doing it. If you are convinced that you are doing the right thing, that it is in the public interest, don't pay any attention to the legal aspect. Get yourself a good lawyer. The emphasis has always been on the public interest as the end rule, and the only thing that can basically justify any proposal or action that is made on behalf of planning. I suspect his original contact with land use problems and somewhat with transportation had to do with the original subway in Cincinnati which, as you know, was a complete failure from every point of view. And, of course, the legal aspect of it concerned him. He did not hesitate to make speeches on such subjects as "The city engineer's role in planning," or "The real estate profession's contribution to planning."

Now, during the time that I was in the city hall, he kept in very close contact with what was going on and he was also a mover in the bureau of governmental research. At the same time when I was brought back by the charter people they also brought a fellow by the name of John Blandford to head the Bureau of Governmental Research, which was a privately supported organization. John along the way became the Director of Public Safety, then he became the manager of the TVA, and then he became head of the Bureau of the Budget in Washington. In those days, Alfred's interest was in both of these operations, planning and governmental affairs, and in how to begin to rehabilitate the city. He felt that there ought to be some system for the city's public works operations. He also felt that it would be difficult to do this if the city and the county and the school board are each going along with their separate programs.

So, he and John Blandford and I had a number of sessions discussing what has evolved into the programming of public works, based on the combination of recommendations from the operating departments and the planning commission. We felt that the city, county, and schools ought to get together because the money is all coming from the same pocket. If they could somehow reconcile themselves and each of them get going after the most important things at any given time and not overloading the bond request, that would improve the chances of having the bond issues approved. And, believe it or not the city, county, and schools adopted an official policy for the preparation, each year, of a five year medium or long-range coordinated public works program and the one year capital budget, the companion of their operating budget. Up until that time, to my knowledge, there was no recognition, at least not in the cities that I knew, of separating the operating budget from the capital outlay budget. There was a tendency to use bond issue monies, that of course had to be serviced for twenty-five years, on buying automobiles for the police department that wore out in eighteen or twenty-four months.

So, I feel that that was a very long step and I say that I would credit the planners, not only Alfred, myself, and Blandford. That idea spread among the planners. It became national. And when the National Planning Board came along they started national long-range capital improvement programming.

It caught on, nobody can say why or how it but it caught on. You might be interested to know that in the plans for Covington and Lexington which were evolving just about the same time, that idea was carried even further. I could show you graphs that showed how many cents per hundred dollar valuation over what period it would take to accomplish the improvements that are proposed over a corresponding period. The plan not only took stock of all the things that were needed. It had a system of priorities and put a price tag on them. It provided the ammunition for the promoters of the program to sell the plan. It showed the assessed valuation, the stock operating expenses, projections of the operating expenses, and that to do these things, for example, would require 7.25 cents per hundred of property valuation for a period of ten years.

These were innovations. I remember I had some of these graphs at one of the Institute meetings. There was a time, you know, when the consultants and some of the cities that were producing plans felt that they had something novel to show and exhibited them.

Consultant to the Tennessee Valley Authority

The TVA, of course, was created a year or so after FDR took office. I acted as a consultant to the TVA planning department for six or eight years. Among other duties, the planning department was given an assignment somewhat unique; namely, the economic salvaging of some of the communities that either physically or economically had been impacted by the TVA program. Now, there was one community, Gunthersville, Alabama, that itself was not touched by the lake. But being a trade and service center to a very rich agricultural area consisting of bottom land that was to be flooded, it was going to lose all that business in agricultural implements and repairs, gasoline for their machinery, and all of the other things. We had to find some kind of an economic activity that would make up in part for this loss because without it the town wouldn't be able to exist. So, after a study we found that the only feature in the new situation that could furnish this would be boating and river traffic. So, the plan that we prepared provided for commercial and recreational navigation.

Now it so happened that a couple of years after these facilities had been built the TVA promoted a boat show and boat races, and we thought that it was going to attract two or three thousand people and that it would be successful. Lo and behold, by 11.00 in the morning there were over 10,000 people there and by 1.00 the restaurants were out of food and they were sending kids out to private households to pick up any canned goods they could spare. It was a huge success, and since then the town not only recovered from the loss of all this trade related to agriculture but has become a veritable boom town, principally because it is the nearest place with any water to Birmingham, and a lot of the well-to-do Birmingham people have their yachts up there, etc.

Another interesting experience in the same line, but totally different, was a small town, I have forgotten its name, but farther down the river, which subsisted primarily on two things. They had a ferry which transported cars and another which transported railroad cars, and while waiting for the ferry to return from a trip people usually sauntered into a restaurant or store or what not, and they derived quite a bit of trade. The other source of income was pearl buttons, shirt buttons, made from the mussels in the river. The name Mussel Shoals down there derives from this. They fished for those mussels and they had a small plant where they had made these buttons. Now the mussels, they don't swim around, they just stay in one place and they depend on the river to bring the food to them. But with a lake and with still water they would be deprived of their food, so they would die and therefore there would be no mussels and no material for the buttons. So the economy of that town was completely destroyed. Not a drop of water would be left in the town itself. The only answer in that case was to relocate the two or three hundred households. So that was our recommendation, and the TVA expropriated the town and built a new small town just for the few families that remained, because most of them took the money and moved to Florida.

The Detroit Master Plan

I was so fortunate as to be selected as consultant for Detroit's Master Plan Program. I got the job there in 1941, just about as bad a time as possible.

A lot of the planning fellows were drafted or joined the Armed Forces, and the planners who had any kind of experience or educational background were almost impossible to get. I managed somehow to get a staff together including Bryant Hall, who didn't stay very long, Donald Monson, who was fresh out of school, and a few others. They represented all of the people with some planning background or experience in a staff of about thirty-six. So we had a very difficult job trying to produce what was expected of us and at the same time train these other people.

It was a veritable planning school. I usually went one week a month and spent the first two and one-half to three days looking over what had been accomplished under a previous assignment and then another day or so educating them to do their new assignment, which I left with them for the next three weeks. It took seven years under those conditions to produce the Detroit Plan, published in 1951. Actually the job was finished in 1948 or 1949. The director of planning, upon completion of this job, wrote me a letter, which is very rare for a consultant, telling me that without my efforts and dedication, the plan could never have been brought into being.

Two things stand out about this experience. One is our effort to assure that the operating departments, who were not too friendly at the beginning, were going to make some use of the plan after it was finished. As soon as we had the preliminary functional plans in some sort of shape, we invited the heads of various operating departments, the police, the fire, the building department, and the school people, over to the office and spent a morning with them. They didn't know at the time what we expected them to do after the plan was finished; namely, that they sign those plans and have some responsibility to use those plans in their operation. So we had each functional plan bear the signature, in addition to the planning agency, of the head of an operating department.

The second thing worth mentioning is that this is the first time I had the opportunity, because it was the largest city where I had had an engagement for a complete overall plan, to develop the concept of the subcommunity. Now of course the neighborhood concept was old. Clarence Perry of New York was the first to be credited with the original idea. And then we had the problem that the "neighborhood" is so kind of loaded up. We wanted something a little more neutral. Let me tell you what it is, because it is not simply a large neighborhood. Neighborhoods are characteristically residential as far as the land use is concerned, with the associated mixed facilities serving them, the elementary school, the small neighborhood center, and so on. The subcommunity is a combination of neighborhoods, of a population anywhere from 50,000 to 100,000, including the industrial work places, a high school, a civic center of sorts, recreational facilities for people beyond high school age, and a subcity hall, where you could get a dog licence, pay taxes, and get other types of licenses – the plumber can go here, the electrician, etc. It becomes a decentralization of some of the most common municipal functions – a municipal subcity hall.

Detroit was especially favorable for this type of organization, because it had a railroad network which induced the distribution of places of employment. The concept was to somehow reestablish the advantages of a city of minor size, about 100,000, and develop a sense of identity. Otherwise, with a town like Detroit where about 30 per cent of the labor force goes back to Kentucky and Tennessee while the model is being changed by the automobile industry, there is no identification by the people with Detroit. As a matter of fact, until very recently the automobile industry there had done very little for Detroit. In the end this would make possible the combined advantages of living in a medium size city and having available the institutions of a metropolitan area.

Of course the other implication, besides the social aspect, is a minimizing of the need for transportation. My answer to the traffic problem has always been to do what you can by the proper distribution of the economic activities in the community to minimize the need for transportation. This kind of organization that I have just described, hopefully providing employment for a reasonable portion of the inhabitants within their sub-communities, would call for daily trips of only a mile or two, and maybe once a week or so to the center of the city, to the main library or to go to the symphony.

The first edition of Local Planning Administration

I'm going to tell you about how it all started, which will explain to you why it starts out just like a cookbook does: "First you have to light the oven or put on the burner, etc." The director of the City Managers Association was Clarence Ridley. He was on the 'phone and he said they had been discussing the problem that we are going to have at the war's end, with no construction whatsoever going on in the cities during the war. Boys will be coming back from the service, they will need jobs, the cities will have to make up for their inability to build anything, and in order to provide the jobs they will have to accelerate their building. Everybody is urging the public agencies and also private enterprise to have blueprints on the shelf so that when they come back they can be put to work in short order. Now, most of it is going to be done without any consideration of the planning aspects. If planning considerations are to bear on this large public works program, then those who will be in charge of the programs ought to somehow become a little familiar with what planning is all about. Hopefully they might take the time to acquaint themselves sufficiently with planning, so that without any direct participation of professional planners they will be able to give some consideration to the broader aspects of locating and designing and building these facilities. The thing that they thought would be helpful was some sort of a manual that they could put in the hands of the director of Public Works, city engineers, directors of the park board, and the heads of the operating departments who will be responsible for designing, locating, and building these facilities. They had very little money to pay for my efforts. They were willing to compensate the other participants for stenographic services and they wanted me to be the editor and furnish the guidance to put together a document of this nature.

He wouldn't take "no" for an answer, even though I tried to get out of it because I had a number of jobs on my hands including Detroit, and the same shortage that handicapped us in Detroit, handicapped me to get help. I couldn't get any. Well, as you know from the book, I had collaborators. Unfortunately some of them didn't deliver their goods, so I had to pinch hit for some of them, as the introduction says. Instead of being just the editor, I had to actually attend to putting the thing together.

I managed to do it on trains, on buses, and over the weekends. Pressure was brought on me by referring to my patriotic duty, to prepare for the returning veterans.

The typical start of a planning program

In those times we had a lot to do pioneering, crusading, and educating. The typical start of a planning program in a community had its origin in some members of a garden club, who read something maybe in a foreign publication about something called planning and next, taking the Cincinnati newspaper, found out that there is a guy called Segoe in Cincinnati who is a planner. Now we have to have some speaker at the garden club from time to time, so why not call up this Segoe guy and see whether he is willing to come to Marietta and talk to us about planning? Well, the date had been agreed upon, the speech was dutifully made, and then nothing happened for several months, and then you got a call from the League of Women Voters (you graduated to the League of Women Voters) and after that stage, maybe a half year is gone and then came a call from the members of some other luncheon club or service club. Then, after a year and a half or two years, somebody down in Marietta suggested that if I came down for a day that he could introduce me to somebody in the city hall who is willing to listen to me, with a possibility of planning. Now by that time the local papers carried the speech and three or four of these club members have heard about planning, some groundwork had been laid so that by the time you got to city hall and went through some preparation, with occasional publicity and occasional town meetings with various town organizations along the way, planning had managed to take root, after a fashion, with the prospect of being implemented sometime after the plan is completed and the planner has left.

Now, let me just mention a couple of aspects of my operation which I have persistently pursued, because it is related to this problem. It is easy enough to prepare the plan, but how to accomplish it? Well, one technique in a city was the Detroit technique. Have the operating department be a party, joint authorship, as it were. The other, which I pursued in every community which was reasonably large, was to insist, before taking on a planning job, that the planning commission hire a young planner, and if they couldn't afford that, see that someone in the city engineering department be assigned to become the full time planner for the commission. He would then participate from the ground up in the preparation of the plan and would be fully conversant with it after it was finished. He would continue on with it, he would have responsibility for zoning administration and for all the other functions of the staff of the planning office. That was the way that I operated in communities of, of I would say, 25,000 and up. Get a local employee full time assigned to planning. Another aspect of it, I mentioned without, I hope, seeming too proud, I never took on more engagements than I myself had time to participate in, at least in the major decisions that had to be made along the way. Knowing enough of the city and knowing enough of the work so I might go in as the planner assigned in the office to handle the job.

Notes

1 Ruth Knack (1980) "Segoe on Cincinnati," *Planning*, 46(10), 25.
2 For a brief but lively résumé of Alfred Bettman in Cincinnati, see Laurence C. Gerkens (1980) "Glancing back," *Planning*, 46(10), 23–6.
3 National Resources Committee (1937) *Our Cities – Their Role in the National Economy*, Washington, D.C., US Government Printing Office.
4 The City Planning Commission (1925) *The Official City Plan of Cincinnati, Ohio*, Cincinnati, The City Planning Commission.
5 In 1953, during the McCarthy era, Sydney Williams, who conducted this interview, was an associate professor of planning at the University of California, Berkeley, and became aware that brief association with presumed radical organizations, early in his career, might become a problem. He considered leaving California. His professional biography says only that: "During this period (1953–1956) I left California for a new environment in the Middle West. I became the first new Director of Planning for Cincinnati in over twenty years." But sensitive of a still growing wave of McCarthyism a year later it seemed prudent to resign the Cincinnati job and accept a position, offered in sympathy by the well-known Cincinnati consultant, Ladislas Segoe. Segoe understood.

15 Between the housers and the planners: the recollections of Coleman Woodbury

Recorded and edited by Donald A. Krueckeberg

Introduction

In 1953 the University of Chicago Press published a two-volume work entitled *The Future of Cities and Urban Redevelopment* and *Urban Redevelopment: Problems and Practices*, edited by Coleman Woodbury. In the following year and one-half the *Journal of the American Institute of Planners* published three separate and complete reviews of the work. Never before in the history of the professional journal, and rarely since, had one publication earned so much attention.

"Brilliant" was the acclaim for Woodbury's contribution. Special accolades were given to the work included in it by Catherine Bauer on historical redevelopment strategy, Woodbury on industrial location, Slayton and Dewey on community attitudes, Ludlow on densities, Meltzer on displacement. One critic, Lloyd Rodwin of MIT, never known to exaggerate his praise, acknowledged Coleman Woodbury as "one of the ablest and most respected of this country's housing and planning experts."[1]

These events were neither the first nor the last of Woodbury's distinguished intellectual and professional accomplishments. In the recollections below he describes his career, in the two decades preceding the Urban Redevelopment Study, concentrating between 1922 and 1942. He entered Northwestern University in Evanston, Illinois, in 1922, fresh out of the small Midwestern town of Sandwich, Illinois. He had earned his Ph.D. in economics by 1927. He stayed on for the next five years to teach and conduct research with his mentor, one of the giants of American economics, Richard T. Ely, at Ely's Institute for Research in Land Economics and Public Utilities.

From 1933 to 1934 Woodbury served as executive secretary to the Illinois State Housing Board. In 1934 he assumed the post of executive director of the National Association of Housing Officials. NAHO was one of a new cluster of national associations headquartered at the Public Administration Clearing House in Chicago, more familiarly known by its street number "1313" (East 60th Street).

With time, various activities in Washington, D.C. gradually drew him into the federal orbit, eventually as Assistant Administrator of the National Housing Agency in 1942 . This agency was the direct ancestor of the present cabinet level Department of Housing and Urban Development. Woodbury's position in national policy then, from 1942 to 1946, was roughly equivalent to Assistant Secretary of HUD.

The recollections

The very beginning

Well, to start, I was born in a little country town in northern Illinois by the name of Sandwich, just sixty miles or so west of Chicago on the Burlington Railroad, a little country town of retired farmers, a little farming, and a little manufacturing company. My father was the superintendent of schools. He spent 58 years in that school system. I went as an undergraduate to Northwestern, for no particular reason except that I got a fellowship, $500, a lot of money. There I majored in economics.

At that time, at Northwestern, the Department was Economics and Sociology. I took quite a bit of work on the sociology side of things. Northwestern didn't have very much in the way of graduate work. They had good professional schools. They always had a good law school, good medical school, dental school, and they had some graduate work, but not very much. In those days the traditional route was that you took your graduate work at another institution than the one in which you did your undergraduate work, but I didn't know that. I had gone to Northwestern partly because I thought I was going to law school. Yet the more I saw of the practice of the law, the less attractive that became.

I'd become very much interested in economics and sociology, and I had minors in political science and philosophy. Along toward the end of my senior year (1925), the chairman of the Economics Department called me in and said, "By the way, what do you plan to do next year?" And I said, "I haven't really decided. I'd hoped I might go on for some graduate work, but I'd need some help." And he said, "Well I just got a letter from old Uncle Vic T. Ely [Richard T. Ely]" – who had spent long years at this place [Madison, Wisconsin] and was one of the founding fathers of the American Economic Association. He had a lot of publicity as a young man for a trial for teaching socialism here. He was locally very famous. The University Trustees exonerated him and there's a phrase from their report on the matter which was written by the then president of the University, a man by the name of Adams, that says, "Whatever may be the limitations which trammel inquiry elsewhere we believe the great state University of Wisconsin should ever encourage that continual and fearless sifting and winnowing by which alone the truth can be found." That phrase has gotten into people's consciousness.

Plate 15.1 Coleman Woodbury, 1935.
Source: The Walter Blucher Papers, Olin Library, Cornell University.

Well, anyhow, Ely was something of a figure, had written one of the most popular texts, until Samuelson came along, on economics and had been here at Wisconsin . . . well, he was well past retirement age. But, things were pretty easy in such matters in those days, and he was still vigorous. He had become interested a few years before that, in the developing speciality within the general field of economics which he labeled land economics. Well, this began originally as being concerned with agricultural land and to some extent with crops, marketing, and so forth. The 1920s was a decade, despite the boom, so called, in which agriculture was depressed as a result of over expansion for a very short period during the First World War. Land economics was concerned with that. It was also concerned with land tenure, land taxation, forest taxation, yield taxation, things of that sort. There were two or three very good men.

Ely had been notable, not so much for his scholarship, but for his ability to pick people and get them started on the fields in which they later became internationally known. John R. Commons was one of them. Ely rescued him from some old jerkwater teacher's college down in southern Indiana. He had been turned down on his Ph.D. thesis at the University of Chicago. Had just been drifting around. Well, anyhow, Ely had started this Land Economics Institute, and as a result of his long tenure, long life, and the fact that his department here in this University [Wisconsin] was for many years one of the top two or three in the country, he had accumulated quite a whole list of friends, many of whom as the years went on, made more than a little money. So the old Doctor put the arm on the contributors. In the 1920s it was, as you know, easy come, easy go, and he built up quite a little budget for his Land Economics Institute. And then a curious thing happened. (It sounds curious today, it wouldn't sound so curious then.) He also asked for and accepted some money from the Rockefeller Foundation. Not a large amount. A few thousand dollars, twenty thousand dollars, or something like that. And the Regents of the University took exception to this, these predators of great wealth and so on. The Regents, at that time, had people like Zane Grey, the novelist, and a lot of other populist characters, to whom Rockefeller, even then (and that was many years after the old man had been passing out the shanty dimes to kids), was the man who drove the small businessmen to the wall. So they formally objected to his taking the money. If there were merit in his ideas, and they weren't passing judgment on that, but if there were, he should put forward his case, and if this work was desirable, why the state would find some way to finance it.

Well, the old man, who'd had his troubles every off and on as who hasn't who stays around at a university very long, he got his dander up. I think aided some by the fact that his wife, who was a very — I never met her, but by all accounts a charming and gracious lady, died, and this kind of loosened his hold here. But, anyhow, he picked up his Institute and left. Northwestern at that time was on the way up, in size and money and so forth, and so he found a new home. The arrangement was that the Institute was a separate corporation, with its own board, and Northwestern University provided free office space in one of their new buildings on the downtown campus, and a very sizable additional area for Ely's library – he had one of the finest private economics libraries in the country – and appointments in the department of the University, mostly in economics for which they required a minimum amount of teaching, never more than one course a semester, and usually one course a year.

A graduate student in land economics

Well, to get back to my story, Geiger, head of the Economics Department at Northwestern, who had spoken to me, was a University of Wisconsin Ph.D., and he said,

The old man says that he has five scholarships that are offered in something he calls urban land economics, and he's held one of them out for me to fill . . . as a gesture toward his new home. And I don't know what he means by urban land economics, but he's a very interesting old man, with a lot of influence around the evolution of economics in this country. He's a delightful old fellow. You certainly can't go very far wrong with a year with him, and if you want me to, I'll recommend you.

So he did, and I was accepted and joined the Ely staff for my masters work.

Curiously enough, there was another young buck that came in at the same time from Ohio State by the name of Morton Godfish. Beginning about the time of the New Deal, up until the 1950s, he was the executive vice-president of the United States Building and Loan Association and one of *the* most influential lobbyists in Washington. Well, Godfish and I kind of split up this new field just by natural inclination. He was interested in the real estate side of things and I very soon became interested in, well, say the public sector. I wrote my master's thesis on the comparison of zoning ordinances in the Chicago metropolitan area. There had been a great burst of zoning activity going on at that time. I made a comparative study of two or three dozen of those ordinances. The end of that year I got a Rhodes Scholarship and went off to England where I read, as they say in the school, modern philosophy, politics, and economics.

The summer before I went to England, I did some work for the Chicago Regional Planning Commission. They had been organized two or three years before. It was headed then by Daniel Burnham, Jr, the son of the old man of the Chicago Planning Commission, an architect, an awfully nice guy, but not a very effective man. The man that made this show go was named Robert Kingery. He had been an engineer and was a first rate administrator. This commission concerned itself with the Chicago metropolitan area which they defined as roughly a 50-mile radius from the Loop. That took them up into part of Kenosha County and clear down around the end of the lake and to Gary and other towns in Lake County, Indiana.

Well, the Regional Planning Commission was really a suburban planning commission because they didn't address themselves to the city. In fact, their relations with the City Commission were not very good. But it was a membership organization which included businesses, particularly those with a direct immediate personal interest in the development of the area, notably utility companies and some of the big department stores, and so on. (Most people don't realize that Marshall Field had suburban branches in the 1920s – they had one in Oak Park and one in Evanston.) They also had membership of counties and cities and villages, and so on (incorporated places), and quite a few of those governmental units paid dues to the association. I never knew what their budget was. A dollar amount wouldn't mean very much today. But, they had a staff of about four or five professional people, and they operated through a series of committees, in transportation, in recreational uses, and so on, and then they had one on zoning and subdivision control. That was the one that I worked for during the school year, kind of part time and full time in the summer when I did that study. I find some people think that is the only piece of research I ever did – on account of the publicity at the time. It was simply because it was somewhat new.

I measured the front footage of commercial space in suburban localities, forty or fifty of them, around the area; and expressed it as so many feet per thousand inhabitants of the locality. I found that the farther away one went from the metropolitan center, the larger the proportion of local commercial space to local populations. Well, naturally, fewer people would come into the "Loop" to shop, presumably, and more people from the surrounding countryside would go to local shopping areas. This was useful because the great hassle in zoning in those days and for a long time thereafter, was holding down the horribly overzoned commercials.

When I was in England they were in quite a turmoil then on the homesteads-for-heroes business after the First World War, a phrase that Lloyd George invented. They were experimenting with various forms of subsidy for low-income people. So I poked around in that for quite a bit and also got introduced to the Garden City movement. Howard was still alive. There was a Garden Cities and Town Planning Association, and an International Federation for Housing and Town Planning which dominated and which was largely concerned with propagandizing Howard's ideas. One of the garden cities had been started, oh, well before the war; and then after the war, Welwyn was started. And that was under construction. I remember going out to see it.

Back with Ely after England

When I came back, Ely offered me a job in his Institute so I did my graduate work there and headed up the work in urban land economics. Then came the Depression and the Institute came upon evil days. A lot of these wealthy people that Ely had been getting money from found themselves very poor all of a sudden. Stocks went down. Also, about the time that he came to Northwestern, immediately thereafter, he had branched out his Institute. It became the Institute for Research in Land Economics and Public Utilities. His argument, and I think this was genuine on his part, was that utilities were essential to the utilization of land and had great influence on land use patterns even in rural areas, let alone in urban areas.

But, there was something called the . . . well, it was the utility lobby. They renamed it later the Edison Institute, but it had a less fancy name originally. They were putting out money to universities for courses in utilities and studies of one thing or another. At that time, public ownership of electric light and power plants was quite an issue. And, of course, the old question of rural electrification was being formulated, and Ely took money from them, at the time of the Depression when the witch hunts started. The utility lobby group was one of the prime targets. His name got dragged into it simply as one of the people whom its money supported. But there was a lot of rumor and innuendo that he had just stuck the name "utilities" onto his Institute in order to get that money. Then, of course, the utilities had built up a very shaky structure of holding companies. Insull, who operated out of Chicago, was one of the principal malefactors. What supported the superstructure was some operating companies selling power and gas to homeowners and the industries. Once that income stream became diminished, the whole thing came tumbling down. Insull was the dominant figure in the city life in Chicago, in the whole area as a matter of fact, in the 1920s. He was indicted for various alleged crimes of financial shenanigans of one sort of another. It was a great scandal, and by implication he (Ely) was allied. So the Institute, for all purposes, was bankrupt.

This would have been 1932, roughly, give or take a year. To make matters worse, Northwestern had also been expanding pretty rapidly and had taken on a number of perfectly proper, but nevertheless financially not very strong operations like the Institute. They had one in crime and police, one of the first of them. They had a traffic institute, run by a fellow by the name of McClintock who was later at Harvard for a short time. And the University's benefactors were also feeling poor. So the first year that Ely was without income, the University said, "Well you go ahead and raise as much as you can and we'll underwrite your budget at the level of last year." Well, that year, the poor old man . . . he had hardly anything. And, the University had to pick up the tab, practically the whole amount. Then they said, "Well, we're sorry, but we're hard pressed too, and we can't continue this arrangement. If you want to keep working it on your own, you can stay here under the arrangements we've had before, but we can't underwrite your budget."

One of the curious things about this was that in a matter of some months, not a year let us say, before the real crunch came, there was a move afoot to take the Institute from Northwestern and move it to a similar arrangement with Columbia in New York. The old man was an alumnus of Columbia. He always had kind of a yen to get back to the East, and went into negotiations quite seriously for the move to Columbia. The old man bucked at the last moment because the Columbia officials insisted that if he became affiliated with them, he would have to make himself amenable to their rather highly organized money-raising machinery. They had a high-powered committee representing various schools of the University, their governing body, the president, and so forth, who were kind of a tracking device so that two or three Columbia units were not out after the same money at the same time. And they offered Ely a position on that committee and assured him that the purpose of the committee was simply, in the first place, to help dig up prospects and, in the second place, to avoid embarrassing doubling up. It was not an attempt to censor or control the subject matter for which money was being asked. But the old man turned it down. He wanted to have a free hand, the same old issues as some years before here.

Ely moves to New York anyway

Ely, after a couple of years of failure here, then tried to move the Institute to New York and run it independently. He was then a man about 80. He had married, just a few years before that, the second wife, a contemporary of mine at Northwestern. We were on the debate team together, she was a year ahead of me in college, and by her he had two children. He had almost adopted me. I lived in his home in Evanston for two or three years. He had two sons who were grave disappointments to him. Ely had a very fine daughter who married Ed Morehouse, who was one of the chief utility economists of the Institute and the first editor of the *Journal of Land & Public Utility Economics*, a close friend of Dave Lilienthal's who, when the bustup came of the Institute, came back up here to Madison. Dave had been appointed to what was then the Railroad Commission, the Utility Commission in this state, and Ed came up to be the chief economist of that outfit.

Well, Ely wanted me to go to New York and help him there and be a kind of heir apparent. I remember going down to New York. He said he was interested in some new people, younger people and so forth. He was then living over in Radburn, which had just gotten started, you know. I remember visiting him over there and meeting some of these people he was talking about. I came to the conclusion it just wouldn't work. One of the hardest things I ever did in my life was to write him a note to that effect.

To finish up on Dr Ely, he stayed on in that area. Of course, he wasn't getting any money. In my place he took a young fellow from the staff who was my junior a little bit in years by the name of John Burton. Burton was a tax man, and for awhile they had some contracts with an outfit, forgotten what it was called, New York State Commission on Mortgage Finance or something of the sort. An enormous proportion of recent apartment house construction in the old New York City and other parts of the State was bankrupt. They had various relief measures and John did work for that commission. This was a bipartisan commission, and the Republican member took quite a shine to John and got him some work with the Republican party of the State. It was then, when Dewey became governor of the State, that he made John Director of the Budget, a job of no mean proportions. John stayed at that until well after Dewey left, and later became Business Manager of Cornell.

Anyhow, Ely was in a bad way. Henry Taylor, the chief agriculture economist, and some of his older friends were passing the hat for him one year. And then old Nicholas "miraculous" Butler (Nicholas Murray Butler – president of Columbia for quite a while – a pompous old guy and quite a power in the Republican party) heard of Ely's plight somehow or other. And damned if the old man Butler didn't wrangle an offer to Ely of some such post as university associate and that got him an extra something, maybe $3500 a year. The only duties of it were that he held himself open to graduate students or others who might seek him out for advice on their work. But it made the difference in his latter years between just being almost a pauper and living with his new found reasonable dignity. He lived on about another ten years. During the War he died. He was approaching his nintieth birthday at the time. He was eighty-nine.[2]

The furthest thing north – limited divided housing

Well, let's switch back to when the Institute left Chicago. I knew it wasn't going to work in New York. I needed a job too. About that time, I guess it was actually during the last year of the Institute in Chicago, which had been probably the year 1931, academic year 1931–2, there was a move under foot to set up a Temporary State Housing Commission.

In the period after I came back from England, old Dr Ely got some money for developing course work and starting a research program on housing. I think he got it from the Carnegie Foundation, if I remember correctly. And, he really kicked this over to me. We offered a course or two and I wrote my doctoral dissertation on the trend toward multifamily housing construction during the 1920s, a very interesting phenomenon which I never really got to the bottom of, but I got a degree out of it. It's very interesting because you see some recurrences today; that is, the building boom continues for a while (of course this one has gone much, much longer than we've ever seen before), but when the house building boom begins to taper off, the rental stuff takes off. That was what I was trying to study in the 1920s. You see much the same thing today.

This temporary commission had a funny origin. During the 1920s the furthest thing north in housing in this country was the state program in New York, the state-supervised limited dividend corporation which had been set up following a study commission in the early 1920s. Al Smith was the Governor, and this was the Commission of Housing and Regional Planning, I think it was called. Clarence Stein was the chairman of it and Henry Wright was one of the principal staff people. They had a series of reports, and on housing they recommended state-regulated limited dividend corporations. They had a state bank that was going to lend money to these limited dividend corporations at low interest rates. If I remember correctly, the properties of the limited dividend companies were to be, I don't know if they were to be exempted from local taxes, but they had a tax break. Well, when the bills emerged from the Legislature about 1924 they cut out the state bank and Smith was disgusted. His first inclination, and it was a strong one, was to veto it. But Stein and others stayed his hand, and so the State Board of Housing was set up. A few projects were started, some eight or ten, mostly in New York City. I think there was one in Buffalo, maybe two.

Well anyway that was looked upon as kind of the furthest thing north in governmental intervention in the housing business. Curiously enough the word housing was very little used in those days. It wasn't in most people's vocabulary. And if you used the term, and found anybody who could attach any meaning to it at all, it meant to him tenement house regulation in big cities in the East, and possibly in Chicago, the sort of thing that old Lawrence Veiller and DeForest had pushed in the early years of the century.

Anyhow, there was a little spill-over of that kind of housing in Chicago without any governmental framework. Of course you could set up a limited dividend corporation if you wanted to. In Chicago there were, I guess, only two examples of that. One was the Marshall Field estate. There were these trustees of the estate. One of them was a very fine guy by the name of George Richardson. He got interested in housing and they put several million dollars into an apartment development up in the near northside of Chicago. It was up about Division Street or so, a mile, mile and a half north of the Loop. Julius Rosenwald actually did the other one on the southside, on State Street and about 30th or 39th I should think. And these were started almost the same time, as a matter of fact, in the late 1920s, and were finished up. They were filled, of course, and all right.

During the late 1920s, there was a semi-reform mayor of Chicago. He only had one term, but someone talked him into establishing a state or a city investigating committee on housing. It was established, raised some money, but never did very much. Went out of existence when his term expired. There was some money lying around somewhere. About 1932 or so, one of the Rosenwald sons-in-law, whose name was Al Stern, Alfred K. Stern, was, putting it bluntly and maybe cruelly, looking around for something to do. The old Father Rosenwald had obviously been trying to find something that Al could do that was in keeping with the traditions of the family and where he couldn't do very much harm. He had him on the Rosenwald Fund which had been established and was getting into high gear at that time. The old man set up quite an operation. They did a lot of work in the South. The Fund was then in the hands of a very intelligent and ambitious man who did a very good job with the Fund, and he didn't want Al underfoot. Al was in on the construction of the Rosenwald apartments. They were operating and filled and had a very excellent black man as the manager, Robert Taylor, who later was on the Housing Authority of Chicago. For a short time he was the chairman of it, and later became a figure of some importance in Negro affairs. A close friend of mine. Died, unfortunately, while he was still quite a young man.

Bob Taylor, a leader of his people

Taylor, I first met when he was the manager of those Rosenwald apartments on South State Street in Chicago. I felt Bob was an easy man for me to know. He was a very soft-spoken, gentle sort of person with a nice sense of humor, quiet humor. I learned that he came from one of the Carolinas. His father was apparently a man of some little means. He was a landowner, among other things. I don't know how much land, but up the scale quite a bit from the run of the black people in that area at that time. Bob went to the University of Illinois and got a bachelor of science degree there. He came to Chicago after his graduation to work in a real estate office – a black real estate office on the South side of Chicago. He was so appalled and outraged by what went on there that he wanted to get the hell out. It was about that time that somebody approached him for the Rosenwald apartment bit. I remember him telling me that Mr Rosenwald himself, who was an elderly gentleman, interviewed him. He was offered the job and jumped at it. He stayed with that job, as far as I can recall, all the rest of his life which wasn't too long.

He would have considered himself a houser, and secondarily a moderate liberal leader of his people. He was not belligerent at all, but he looked upon himself as a spokesman for an oppressed and downtrodden group. While he was manager of those apartments, I remember, he established some sort of a savings and loan association. He was the president of it. I think it was a federal association, when they were chartering federal associations at that time in the early 1930s.

He felt this was not anything world-shaking but was giving the opportunity first to provide some mortgage money for people who might find it difficult otherwise to get it at decent rates. It would also be somewhat of an offset to the impression that a lot of white people had – and the white people who were not nasty people at all, but well-disposed to Negroes, but nevertheless had – the impression that Negroes can't handle money and can't take care of themselves in an urban setting.

He and I never overlapped on the Housing Authority. I had a three year term, as I recall, starting 1937 and running to 1940. I was always unhappy about my term on that commission because I had this job with the National Association of Housing Officials (NAHO), and I was gone a lot and I missed meetings that I didn't want to miss. When my term was up in 1940, things were really hopping with the defense period and this office of Housing Defense Coordinator. Mayor Kelly offered to reappoint me and talked with me about it, but I turned it down. Then Bob Taylor who was coming on the Board in place of someone else, came and asked me if I would stay on to help him get started. But, I told him he didn't need any help. Elizabeth Wood was the director of the Authority, and Elizabeth was a red-hot champion of the black people then. In fact she went way out on a limb on that long before anybody else in the housing business in any responsible administrative position did. She made herself very unpopular with some members of the Commission. For a while she developed something of a persecution complex, I think. Much of that time was while Bob was chairman of the Authority.

The temporary Illinois State Housing Commission

So, Al Stern hit upon the idea of getting a state commission to look into housing. And, he was encouraged by some people on this and we got a resolution through the state legislature, sometime in 1931 or 1932.

No state appropriation (no money). Incidentally, that resolution was handled in the House of Representatives in Springfield by Harold Ickes' wife, then a member of the Legislature from the North Shore of Chicago. A wonderful person. A woman of considerable means in her own right, and she dressed like my grandmother did, always in dark clothes, usually black. Real stays, you know, to hold up the lace around your neck. That was very interesting to me – strange person. And she won the respect of the members of that Legislature, just by being what she was and not trying to fake anything or doing anything different. I remember going down. My first testimony before a public body was the airport resolution that was about to pass, and several appropriations.

One of the members of the temporary State Housing Commission was a man by the name of Webolt. The Webolts were not in the Rosenwald class of money, but they were rich people, construction company of considerable parts, and then they were starting a chain of department stores at that time in the outlying sections of Chicago. A very interesting bit, and they made quite a go of it. George Richardson of the Marshall Field estate was on it, and he coughed up some money, too, I'm sure, from the estate. We had a commission of about eight or nine people.

The commission held its hearings and, it was operated on a shoestring, but we came out with recommendations which were essentially the same as in New York State. We had some features that we thought were improvements, but it was essentially copying the New York procedure with supervised limited dividend corporations. A bill to that effect was introduced into the Legislature, was passed, and a permanent Board was set up. Stern was made the chairman of it .

We were beginning to talk about housing authorities. The first enabling legislation, I think, was in 1933, in Ohio. (Well, Ohio and New York used to argue as to who got it through first, but I think Ernie Bohn got it through the Ohio Legislature first.) I became the executive secretary. We couldn't get any limited dividend housing going in those days because the Depression was deepening all the time.

A little bit later when the work programs were going, we actually did what I think was pioneering in the use of WPA labor. This was before the WPA was set up actually, but it was that kind of labor – fellows on public assistance, doing work under wrecking contractors, wrecking the unlivable. We tore down quite a chunk of the worst housing in Chicago; much of it, not all of it, but much of it abandoned. What the Board did, or the staff of the Board did, was to package these demolition jobs. Otherwise the brick buildings which had some salvage value (some of them quite a bit) would have been torn down and the old wooden shacks which were some of the worst, wouldn't have been touched, because they had practically no salvage value. So what we did was to package them, and the contractors had to bid on the package with the understanding that so much of the unskilled labor would be provided from the welfare rolls. There were certain skilled jobs that they had to provide their own men on. I remember one of them. We used to call them "wall men." They stood on the walls and knocked the bricks off. But there was a lot of unskilled labor. They had to carry insurance on their whole work force; not only their own men, but also the welfare guys. But, it made it a make-work project, and not too bad.

Then we eventually put forward the enabling legislation for the Housing Authority in Illinois. After a wait, that was through, and that was where we put in the provision of the State Board reviewing and passing appointments. To follow that one up, Ed Kelly had become the Mayor of Chicago during the depth of the Depression. The curious thing was that he had been a so-called engineer, although he had no real formal training in engineering. He came up the political route, through the park districts in Chicago. He had been making a living all right, and was a sort of second or third string guy in the political machine.

About 1932 a more prominent politician by the name of Tony Cermack who had been for a long time the chairman of the Cook County Board, had gotten himself elected Mayor of Chicago. It was after Roosevelt was elected. At that time you see, the election was in November and the President did not take office until March, and sometime in that interim Roosevelt was down in Miami, resting and scheduled to make some outdoor appearance where the fellow attempted to assassinate him and actually got off a couple of shots which hit Cermack who was also down there, recuperating from his election, and killed him. Didn't kill him outright. He lived, oh, three or four weeks, but eventually succumbed.

Chicago was in a desperate situation financially, and there they were, without a mayor – had a special election and what not. Kelly got the job, partly because of the support of the *Chicago Tribune*. Curiously enough, the *Chicago Tribune* used to climb all over the City of Chicago, you know, all sorts of allegations of corruption, some of which were true, many of which were not in my opinion. But, somewhere in his early days, old Colonel Robert R. McCormick, who was then old and ran the *Tribune*, had been a member of the South Parks Board. He had met Kelly as a young staff guy and they struck up a friendship which had endured all those years. So the *Tribune* came down hard for Kelly as just the man for the City, and he got the job. He was also with a man by the name of Nash – they both inherited Cermack's role as the boss of the Cook County machine – chairman of the Cook County Democratic Committee, technically. Kelly turned out to be not a bad mayor.

To follow through on the Housing Authority, Kelly didn't have much use for that sort of thing. It was new, and untried, and as he told me once,

"You people think that a politician like me would jump at this public housing, but it scares the hell out of me. I can't imagine anything in which you could make more enemies than a handful of ingrates of the County." But, Roosevelt wanted housing authorities eventually and, so, Kelly undertook to appoint one.

Al Stern was still on the State Housing Board at that time. It was early on, it must have been about 1934 or early 1935. Al got the Board to turn down the appointments made by Kelly. There was one guy they objected to particularly. He was a small store owner down in the extreme south-side of Chicago, in a white area, and he was a white man. I doubt that he had very much ability to act as a commissioner, but he wouldn't have been the worst one around. But, Stern and some of the other members of the Board didn't like him. Well, anyhow, they turned that down and Kelly was madder than hell and just refused to do anything about it for some time thereafter. Finally, in 1937, about the time that the United States Housing Authority Act was going through the Congress the story is that Roosevelt personally mentioned the absence of a Housing Authority in Chicago to Kelly. And Kelly said, well, he'd see that there was one. "When it was up before," he said, "there really wasn't enough for it to do. Now that its going to have some money for financing and so forth, I'll get you one." So he did. And, strangely, he put me on the Authority. I'm sure he didn't know that I had been the secretary of the State Board at the time that it had turned him down. But he didn't know me from any old fox in those days and very little more about me in 1937. Anyhow, I went into the Authority.

The Committee on Large-Scale Operations

1931 and 1932, was the time in which the temporary State Commission was just being formed. Herbert Hoover was President of the United States, and when he was Secretary of Commerce he had shown some interest in something he called housing and set up a unit within the Department of Commerce – The Bureau of Building and Housing or something of that sort. It was headed by a man by the name of John M. Gries. For some reason that name sticks in my mind. Gries, who was a personal friend of Hoover and a very intelligent and likable guy. One of the things that they did was to set up a committee of essentially planners, particularly the element in the planning fraternity at that time which was legally and regulatory oriented. There were such people on that commission as old Edward Bassett and Alfred Bettman. They put out, among other things, a model state zoning enabling act, and those things had an enormous influence. They were copied, particularly the one on zoning, sometimes straight out and sometimes with minor variations, in lots and lots of states. Well, they'd done some other things. They'd done some studies looking toward the notoriously inefficient operations of the house building business. And about half-way through Hoover's term, from 1928 to 1932, they talked him into sponsoring the President's Conference on Home Building and Homeownership. That conference was held in Washington, it was probably in the late winter of 1931 or the spring of 1932.

The conference operated through a series of committees. The committee reports were published in a series of volumes, some eight or ten of them.[3] Well, Al Stern, with some other people talked Gries into creating a committee which was labeled "Large-Scale Operations," which wasn't too happy a label. But the primary orientation of the whole conference was towards small house construction, homeownership, and so on, and this Large-Scale Operations addressed at least some of the problems of rental housing and also the Stein–Wright thesis that rebuilding cities had to be undertaken on large scale. The argument was that in a blighted or declining area it couldn't proceed on a lot-by-lot basis – it would mean just throwing good money after bad. Of course all the architects jumped at this – this was wonderful, you see.

One of the few inducements in the early state enabling acts for limited dividend housing was that the limited dividend corporation could have the power, under rather strict conditions, to exercise eminent domain to assemble a sizeable, contiguous site. I've forgotten whether Clarence Stein was on that committee, but Al got himself made the chairman, and Henry Wright was the chief staffman. I was more or less his assistant. We worked together on the report. Actually I did more work on the report than Henry did, but he was the primary educator of the commissioners. I guess that was about the first time I had been in on anything that was not Chicago or Illinois oriented. After Roosevelt was elected and the housing division of the PWA was set up, I was one of a group of the Advisory Committee. I remember my first incursion into Washington, the month of June of 1933. It was summer and hotter than the hinges of hell. In those days they didn't even have air conditioning on the trains. You slept in those berths, either closed, or you could open up the window some, there was a screen there, and you woke up in the morning with the cinders all over you.

The National Association of Housing Officials and PACH

Meantime, another stream comes in, one that was more influential in my career than the others. In the 1930s, 1931, the Public Administration Clearing House (PACH) was born. And it was the brainchild of three people – Merriam, Brownlow, and Beardsley Rummell. Charles Merriam was chairman of the Political Science Department at the University of Chicago. Louis Brownlow was there too. Rummell was an amazing character. He had been in the Rockefeller stable in various staff jobs con-nected with their philanthropies. One of the things he inherited was to clean up the residue of Mrs John D. Rockefeller's personal philan-thropies. Like the wives of many horribly rich people, she had gone into philanthropy on her own in kind of a hit or miss way. Committed quite a lot of money to Baptist missionaries' societies, various things, some of them very worthwhile. She died at a very old age. And there were various problems, of course. They couldn't just cut all this off, cold. They had to kind of sort it out and give declining grants to some, and try to get the others into the Rockefeller Foundations' orbit, or what not. Well, he had done that, and somewhere in that operation had established something called the Laura Spelman Fund of New York, as part of this cleaning up job of Mrs Rockefeller's personal philanthropies. Eventually it was to give several million dollars to help in the improvement of public adminis-tration on all levels of government. And this was largely Rummell's doing. Rummell was an idea man.

The University of Chicago wasn't exactly dumb in matters of money. Certainly not Charles E. Merriam. Merriam and Rummell decided to establish this Public Administration Clearing House and to assemble in it, in Chicago, a number of associations of public officials. Now, there has been quite a lot of misunderstanding – the Clearing House did not control those other agencies. They were independent agencies. Many of them had been in existence for some time, such as the City Managers Association and the Civil Service Assembly of the United States and Canada, which was mainly personnel officers. A number of them had been in existence for quite a while, but they had been kind of struggling along on inadequate budgets. Some of them did very little except hold an annual meeting to elect officers and talk and some of them had little pub-lications, house organs.

Brownlow organized the Spelman money to get them into one place, provide certain common services, particularly the joint reference library, and encourage them to undertake some joint doings, projects of one sort or another. For example, NAHO, the outfit that I was with, had a very useful joint committee with the American Public Welfare Association. Well, this grew out of an initiative, as we would say today, from Brown-low who assembled representatives of the two associations. The other thing that he did, Brownlow, was to form several new associations with the Spelman Fund money as bait. He undertook at first to bring in the old National Housing Association. That was the Veiller outfit that had been established back at the turn of the century. But it concerned itself only with tenement house regulations. Old Veiller was still alive, but he didn't want any part of Brownlow and his doings. So Brownlow set up the

National Association of Housing Officials. ASPO (The American Society of Planning Officials) was created at that time, shortly after NAHO, as a matter of fact, and Walter Blucher, then in Detroit, was brought in as the first director of it. What has become the Council of State Governments was started then as the American Legislators Association. Well, for anybody who wants details on that, Brownlow wrote quite a captivating autobiography, a two-volume work, which I think is worth anybody's reading who is interested at all in public affairs in this country.[4] He had an amazing career.

There are two volumes. One is called *A Passion for Politics*. The second was called *A Passion for Anonymity*. This title came from the report of the President's Commission on Administrative Management which Roosevelt set up, 1936–7, in his second Administration. Newspapers played it as a reorganization of the federal government. It really wasn't. It wasn't intended to be. It was a three-man commission. Brownlow was the chairman. Merriam and Luther Gulick were the members. And what they were trying to do was to reform the presidency, the executive office of the president, and give him the kind of tools and the kinds of authorizations so that he could manage the federal establishment. That's what it was about. Well, in their report, which was given quite a bit of attention, they recommended the establishment of six assistants to the president and it said something to the effect that they should be people of high intelligence, experienced in public administration, of great physical and intellectual vigor, and a passion for anonymity. Of course the newspaper guys got onto that and there was a lot of talk about the passionate anonyms and so on. Brownlow took this as the title of the second volume of his autobiography. And then more recently, there's been a fairly good biography of Merriam called just *Charles E. Merriam*, written by the man who helped Brownlow edit his autobiography. The guy is now in the History Department of the University of Chicago, Barry D. Karl.[5]

Brownlow had been interested in housing for some time, going way back to his newspaper days. He took a junket to England and Scotland and to various other European spots, and became interested in the very early attempts in what we call public housing. There weren't very many, even in Europe in those days. He was particularly impressed with one or two of the projects he saw in Scotland. I happened to be there in Chicago working on this commission and also part time on the Committee on Large-Scale Operations. Veiller wouldn't listen to joining in, and he was probably right. I'm sure Brownlow didn't press him very hard because Veiller himself would have been a great trial for anybody. He was then quite an old man, a very opinionated guy, a man of real ability actually in many ways, but opinionated and in some respects a bitter man at that time.

But anyhow, we decided to have an organization meeting of Housing Officials from the State Boards that I mentioned. We had one in New York, we had one just getting going in Chicago. Yes, it had just been established. This was in 1933. I remember that date. It was in November 1933 that the organization committee for NAHO was set up. A young alderman from Cleveland, Ohio, name of Ernie Bohn, had been a boy wonder in the Legislature in his twenties, was then around 30, a city councilman. He'd become interested in this, even before he knew about us, and had established a committee of the council. The PWA Housing Commission, you see, was just being established in the fall of 1933. So, scratching around in one way or another we got together about thirty-three people for an organization meeting in Chicago. There was an agreement that there should be such an association, and an organization committee was established, authorized to go ahead with the incorporation of such an outfit and to apply to the Spelman Fund for money. And this was done. The money was forthcoming, and we opened up the office on January 2, 1934.

Well, by that time I was secretary to the State Board. Brownlow wanted me to be the director of the association. So did Ernie Bohn. But Al Stern didn't want me to leave the State Board. He wanted to be the first president of NAHO. Ernie outsmarted him which was fortunate, because Ernie was a superb president and Al would have been a terrible president. But, anyhow, it worked out so far as I was concerned. For the first six months or so, I would split my time between the State Board and NAHO, to see that the association got started and give Al a chance to get a successor for me. Charles Ascher, who was an assistant administrator, or assistant director, of PACH, became the acting director of NAHO for the first six months or so. Then I took it over. So it was in that rather circuitous way that I got into the housing business so strongly.

Housers and planners

Curiously enough, if you look back on it, while I got involved in the legislative, financial, and subsidy aspects which were the great bones of contention in those times, my initial interest was not in housing but in urban land economics and urban planning. This became useful later because in the late 1930s, after the public housing movement was more or less underway, there was a growing group who got to be called housers. There grew up a very sharp, and in some ways, unpleasant antagonism between the housers and the planners. The housers claimed that the planners were just a lot of fuzzy guys whose livelihood was dependent upon the more conservative elements of the community – members of planning boards and commissions and so on, and who were reluctant to give aid and comfort even let alone take any active part in anything that would look so radical and socialistic and so forth as public housing. To the extent that individual planners might get a little ways into the housing activity about all they did was to bleed about comprehensiveness. That's the great slogan. Well, there was something in that without any question. It did apply to quite a few people I remember.

In 1933, I spoke at this meeting of the advisory group in Washington. The PWA Housing Division was just being formed. It was taken more or less for granted that the money would go from the PWA to limited dividend corporations. Not many people recall, but it's a fact that the Reconstruction Finance Corporation which was a great rescue agency for banks and other hard-pressed business corporations, was set up in Hoover's Administration. There was provision for the Reconstruction Finance Corporation to lend money for limited dividend housing. It was not a part of the Hoover Administration's bill, it was put in on the floor by Senator Wagner of New York. Brownlow claims he wrote that language out on the back of an envelope because Wagner ran into him somewhere in the Capital and asked him, ''Well, we've got to get something in that bill. What do you suggest?'' So Brownlow wrote the language out and Wagner introduced it and it was passed.

I came out of that meeting with the understanding that when applications came, as they expected some would from Chicago, and as some indeed did, I would be asked to make reports on the projects, particularly on the location. I looked at a very considerable portion of the vacant industrial land in the city of Chicago during the next six months to a year.That you could get in fairly large chunks, you see. Most of it wasn't fit for housing and I said so. But as it became apparent that this limited dividend device was not going to work, Old Ickes fired Robert Kohn, the New York architect who had been the first head of the division, a fine gentleman who was put in by the Stein/Wright faction but had no administrative ability whatsoever. He couldn't get along with Ickes, and was trying to get a program started which with the best skill and luck would have been a slow-starting operation. Well, Ickes fired him and brought in a man by the name of Colonel Horatio B. Hackett. Hackett was a West Pointer, all-American halfback at the military academy about 1904 or so. He was then nominally a member of the architectural firm of Oliver and Root in Chicago and in the 1920s Oliver and Root was one of the two architectural firms that dominated the big building in Chicago – the skyscrapers in the Loop development. (The other one I remember was named Grant, Anderson, Probst, and White.)

Colonel Hackett was a business-getter and a wonderful character. I'd heard of him before, not in connection with housing of which he was entirely innocent, but following his distinguished football career. He had been a big ten football official and I'd seen him on the football field many times during games. He was a bullet-like man with enormous energy. He was a superb administrator. He had enough intellect, quite a bit of it as a matter of fact, that he could get to the essence of a thing, its major line-aments, and pick out people to run it. He had the ability, in his manner and his enthusiasm, physical and intellectual vigor, to motivate people. And he never let any of his subordinates down. If they pulled the worst boner in the world, the Colonel was in their corner when they came under fire and would take most, or all if necessary, of the blame. And he built the morale in that place enormously.

When this transition was clear, I was asked, and I am pretty sure this was before Hackett came in, to pick out three sites in Chicago for federally built low-income housing. I got two people to help me. One was Jake Crane who had been one of the leading planning consultants in Chicago in the late 1920s. And a wonderful guy down at the University of Chicago by the name of Charlie, can't think of his last name, he had been in charge of a lot of the survey work that had been going on in the University on various neighborhoods of Chicago. Charlie made this available to me. They had the first breakdown of census material by what later became known as census tracts. They'd worked out the tract system themselves and paid for the census breakdown for, I think, two maybe three censuses back. Wonderful stuff and unmatched anywhere else in the country as far as I ever found out. Well, anyhow, the three of us worked over this census material and drove around the city. Fortunately, we were very compatible. Personally I was very fond of both of them. The report was made.

Now I'm getting back to the point that I made about the antagonism between the planners and the housers, because one of the things I wanted for this site selection process was in the possession of the Chicago Planning Commission. They had gotten some money under some make-work scheme, and they had done some special work. I've forgotten now exactly what it was, but they had mapped land use on a fairly intricate scale, for practically all the then blighted areas of Chicago. So I approached the head of the staff. I told him what I was up to, what I had been asked to do and told him what I heard about their study on these blighted areas, and I would like to have the benefit of their information, their judgment and so forth for this job. He kind of backed off. He admitted that they had the information, but he didn't know about this public housing move and the federal government coming in and building houses and what not. But he would arrange, if I wanted, for me to appear before an executive committee of the Planning Commission. The Planning Commission then was a great unwieldly thing – oh, dozens and dozens of people.

I said okay and a meeting was arranged. It was chaired by a guy by the name of Wilson who was the descendant of the Wilson Packing family, one of the wealthy families of Chicago. Well, the string had run pretty thin before they got down to this guy. I mean he was a rather slow but pleasantly mannered man. We talked about the thing and I explained what I was about. They hemmed and hawed, and finally somebody proposed that I should be given access to the data in the files of the office, *in* the office. I was not allowed to take it out. But that was all. Nobody on the staff, not this managing director or anybody else, was to take part in my deliberations or do more than simply point stuff out to me, where it was, and what I might want to know about the method of its collection. Well, as I say, it may be an extreme example, but maybe in some ways typical of attitudes of too many of the planning people. Not only members of the commission, but the fact was that this staff guy was just too scared – and personally, I'm sure, he didn't want any part of it. That was the view the public housers had of the planners.

The planners on the other hand looked upon the housers as a kind of Johnnies-come-lately, you know, rushing in with all this hoopla and the federal money behind them and so forth. Remember this was in the time when the planning profession, as far as local agencies were concerned (and practically nothing had existed on state planning in those days under that name) were flat on their backs. Some of them were just cut off completely and others were down to an office and themselves and one girl or something of that sort. Here are these other guys coming in with all of this money and all this hoopla and how they're going to remake cities and clear slums. It is true that a lot of the people who got some prominence and influence were ill-prepared for it. I think it's probably true that a lot of them didn't even know that there was a planning office in their city. And if so, they didn't have any use or any respect for it. So, there was the makings of a split. And the antagonism was taken up by some fairly considerable people on both sides.

One of the sharpest critics of the planners' attitudes toward public housing was Catherine Bauer. Catherine outgrew that completely, but she had no use for them in those days, the early 1930s. She was coming off a radical bent. Well, I mentioned that antagonism because one of the advantages I had was that I had started out primarily concerned with the broader stuff. Then I got into the housing, and got into it very far with the NAHO, particularly. So I undertook to do what I could to try to dampen this antagonism in an effort in which very considerable help was given by Walter Blucher. In fact, that isn't stating it quite fairly, because I can't recall that Walter and I ever talked about this explicitly, in so many words, and agreed we ought to do something about it. But, as I say, he operated more or less independently as I did, but to the same effect. A few years later the two associations did collaborate on two or three pamphlets. We wrote one called *Planning for Public Housing*. Walter sat in on some of the meetings and distributed the product, and I think we had one or two joint committees. At the time of this antagonism and so forth that I was trying to overcome, I thought I ought to join the AIP (American Institute of Planners). I hadn't been in before. With the Depression and then my absorption in housing, I just hadn't gotten around to it. Well, they were perfectly open for membership applications in 1934 or whenever it was. But, the affiliate route was faster and easier. You had to have some sponsors and you had to submit some information and whatnot for the other. So I just put it down as an affiliate member and that would show my alignment, to some degree, with the planning approach and emphasis on things. Subsequently I just never got around to changing it.

Coordination of federal housing policy

In housing, back in the 1930s, the chief issue that developed was the respective roles of the federal government and local governments and incidentally of the states in the financing of public housing. Everyone claimed that he was all for getting the federal government out of the house building business, having the federal government simply as financier and subsidizer. But, the question was *when*, and *how* this transition was to take place. There was an enormous amount of ill-will expended on that, generated to a very considerable extent by the New Yorkers. Charlie Abrams and Lang Post were good friends of mine and their ways had been very useful in the public housing movement. Langdon wanted to make a big political haul out of it, and Charlie wanted to be king-maker, putting that as bluntly as possible. Eventually that was pretty well resolved in the Housing Act of 1937 which not only took the federal government out of housing construction business, and made them a subsidizer and a financier of housing authorities ("Local Public Agencies," as they were called), but also mandated the turning over of the PWA housing as fast as feasible to local agencies.

With that more or less resolved, the attention began to turn to the question of "coordination" – the accurate word (although an unfortunate one) – of the federal government's activities in the whole housing field. They had the FHA in insurance business, the home loan bank, which of course ran the HOLC (Home Owners Loan Corporation) during the depth of the Depression. At one time I think I figured that at the height of this program, the HOLC held one in six of all small house mortgages in the United States. They had millions of them. Then, of course, they had an insurance corporation, too. There was the USHA, after the PWA housing division, and the Subsistence Homestead Division of Hopkins' Rural Industrial Communities, which was also a subsistence homestead sort of thing. But all these agencies were headed by presidential appointees. They were jealous of their prerogatives.

I learned that the real difficulty in getting so-called independent agencies to work together, or even to hold still for a certain amount of linkage usually is not with the head guys. It's usually with their assistants and braintrusters. This is not because the head guys are necessarily more broadminded or more public spirited. They usually are men with some personal security, shall we say. They'd gotten appointed by the President and confirmed by the Senate of the United States and so forth, and they usually have something that looks like a constituency behind them, some groups in which they're known or respected and so on. These other guys usually have been selected by them, and are dependent upon them almost exclusively. Therefore, anything that looks like it might threaten a little diminution of these parts is taken more seriously by the second and third string than it is by the nominal heads.

From the Central Housing Committee to the War

Around about 1937, I think it was, Old Uncle Fred Delano who was the chairman of the National Resources Committee under the various names became interested in housing. He wanted to build up some support on the part of the bureaucracy for the committee. Up to that time the Resources Committee had some pretty active detractors, notably the Army engineers, but mostly a kind of complacent indifference on the part of most of the bureaucracy which was involved in New Deal programs of one sort of another. Therefore, they weren't going to disparage or go out of their way to run down something that the great white father obviously had some use for. But, what the hell were they doing? They were busy then, jobs to do and people to hire and fire. And so there was this kind of attitude of indifference. Delano thought, I am sure, that he could overcome this if he could find some way of establishing linkages between the committee and at least some of the activities of the New Deal bureaucracy. I think housing appealed to him on that ground, but I think the old man also had a genuine interest in housing.

Anyhow, sometime along in 1937 he called me in one day, and said that he wanted to try to do something under housing. He mentioned that the President had encouraged him, but they hadn't talked about it very much. He was proposing to establish something called the Central Housing Committee which would be made up of the heads of the major federal housing agencies. He, Delano, would be the chairman of this, by presidential designation. The central committee would operate through a series of subcommittees on various aspects of the housing problem.

Would I be able to help them get it started? Well, I thought it was worth doing. I told him I had a job that was keeping me more than busy, but I'd like to. So an arrangement was made for I guess it was six months and

I spent a very considerable portion of my time in Washington on that. We had committees on a number of different things. We had committees on local taxation policy, which went all the way from the usual gripes that the FHA passed on from builders to the questions of tax remission, tax exemption, payment in lieu of taxes as a form of public housing subsidy. I remember one on land acquisition. We had one that tried to deal with the question of income and different levels of income indicating eligibility for certain types of housing – not only a question of limitations of the public program, but the question of what income various types of families could afford in the FHA, for example. Interestingly enough, the FHA was not only willing to play ball on that, but was looking for some help. They felt that they were kind of stumbling around. Well, anyhow, that was done. The War came, after a year or two. The "arsenal of democracy" business, you know, from June of 1940 on was just as much a disrupter or maybe more of a domestic program as the actual entrance into the War eighteen months later.

In the summer of 1941, I think, or maybe the preceeding winter – they set up this National Defense Advisory Committee, a curious arrangement, one that Brownlow had quite a bit to do with. Nominally it was a committee of cabinet officers. And then each one had a more or less alter ego on this Advisory Committee, who were civilians. They were the boys who were in charge. Oh, they were called Advisory Committee, but they didn't advise anybody very much. They went ahead and tried to prepare a war economy with such fellows as Knudson who was then chairman of the Board of General Motors, and the pretty boy who was chairman of the Board of United States Steel, later Secretary of State, and Sidney Hillman with the Amalgamated Clothing Workers. These are national figures and authoritative figures in their own right. And, they were operating under a statute of First World War vintage that had never been repealed. But it's a curious use of the English language to call these people advisors. Of course they kept in touch with their political opposite numbers in the Cabinet. In many cases there weren't opposite numbers really. Take Knudson, for example. He was in charge of defense production, and in his case there was no opposite number in the cabinet for that.

Shortly after this Advisory Committee was set up, they added a job which was called the Housing Coordinator. He was not technically a member of the committee, but he was supposed to have the powers of co-ordination with the Housing Programs to get housing into areas where it was needed for defense production purposes. The first guy, I guess the only man who held that job, was NAHO president at the time in 1940, his name was Chuck Palmer. Personally, a very likable guy. Good friend of mine. But, a little egotistic, I should think. He put on a good front. He wasn't a dummy by any manner of means, but he didn't have much caliber or substance and he messed it up pretty badly. Then in January or February of 1942, right after we were in the War formally, Roosevelt exercised his war powers and created something called the National Housing Agency. He swept into it all the urban programs and set up over them an Administrator of the National Housing Agency – and an Office of the Administrator (John B. Blanford, Jr was the appointee). The following summer, I resigned my NAHO job and went to Washington full time as Assistant Administrator for housing programs in the Office of the Administrator. I spent the War at that. After the War it was continued for some time and then was given the name Housing and Home Finance Agency and in 1965 was transformed into the cabinet-rank US Department of Housing and Urban Development.

Editor's postscript

In 1946 Woodbury returned to the University of Wisconsin-Madison, an association he subsequently maintained, in various forms, almost continuously until 1974. From 1948 to 1951 he directed the Urban Development Study, made possible by a grant of $100,000 from the Spelman Fund of New York to the Public Administration Clearing House.

Woodbury spent 1951 to 1953 at Harvard as Charles D. Norton Professor of Regional Planning. Back at Wisconsin he chaired the Department of Urban and Regional Planning from 1962 to 1965. He also held various visiting appointments at Cornell, Yale, Princeton, and Salzburg. He has received numerous honors and awards, including presidential appointment in 1967 to the National Commission on Urban Problems to which he contributed much energy.[6] The commission was chaired by an old friend, Senator Paul H. Douglas, who had sat on the first commission Woodbury ever worked for, the Illinois Temporary State Housing Commission.

These recollections, at the age of 75, of his early years of leadership and action in American planning were recorded on December 11, 1978, in Madison, Wisconsin, where Coleman Woodbury now resides.

Notes

1 Lloyd Rodwin (1953) "Review of *The Future of Cities and Urban Redevelopment* and *Urban Redevelopment: Problems and Practices,*" *Journal of the American Institute of Planners*, 19(4), 244. The other reviews were by Francis L. Hauser (1953) (*JAIP*, 19(3), 176–9) from the perspective of civil defense and by James E. Lash (1954) (*JAIP*, 20(1), 39–41) from the perspective of a redevelopment agency.
2 Ely's autobiography, *Ground Under Our Feet* (1938), New York, Macmillan, makes very favorable mention of Woodbury. A fuller biography of Ely is presented in Benjamin G. Rader (1966) *The Academic Mind and Reform: The Influence of Richard T. Ely in American Life*, Lexington, University of Kentucky Press.

3 John M. Gries and James Ford (eds) (1932) *The President's Conference on Home Building and Home Ownership*, 11 vols, Washington D.C., National Capital Press, Inc.

4 Louis Brownlow (1958) *A Passion for Politics* and *A Passion for Anonymity*, 2 vols, Chicago, University of Chicago Press. Also see Barry D. Karl (1979) ''From the professional stream: Louis Brownlow,'' *Public Administration Review*, pp. 511–16.

5 Barry D. Karl (1972) *Charles E. Merriam and the Study of Politics*, Chicago, University of Chicago Press.

6 US National Commission on Urban Problems (1969) *Building the American City*.

16 From the backyard garden to the whole USA: a conversation with Charles W. Eliot, 2nd

Donald A. Krueckeberg

Charles W. Eliot, 2nd, was born on November 5, 1899. He was
steered into landscape architecture and city planning by his
grandfather along the path of his uncle who had died in the prime of
his career as a landscape architect. After graduation from Harvard
and a brief practice in Boston, young Eliot went to Washington, D.C.,
to work for the National Capital Park and Planning Commission,
soon serving as its director. In 1933 he became the executive officer
of Roosevelt's National Planning Board (successively renamed
National Resources Board, National Resources Committee, and
National Resources Planning Board) where he served until it was
abolished by Congress in 1943. Then, after several years in California
as a lecturer at UCLA and a planning consultant to various
communities and foundations, he returned to Cambridge,
Massachusetts, in 1954, to teach planning at Harvard as Charles Eliot
Professor of Landscape Architecture and later as professor of city and
regional planning, and to continue private practice. It is clear from
what follows that he is, at the age of eighty, still an active force in
planning affairs in greater Boston and that he cares very deeply about
his field of service. This conversation of March 23, 1979, is part of a
series recorded while conducting research on the history of the *APA
Journal*. (See *JAPA*, January 1980.)

Getting started

K. Did you study landscape architecture as an undergraduate?

E. Oh yes. When I was a freshman I lined up my courses – all directly
related to landscape architecture. Then I had a message from my
grandfather, who was then retired from being president of the
university and living up here on Fresh Pond Parkway, to come and
see him.[1] So I went, and he wanted to know, "What courses are you
going to take, Charles?" So I told him. I thought he would be pleased,
but instead, "Absolutely wrong, Charles! There is enough time to
specialize when you get into Graduate School. Your responsibility
now is to get a *broad* general education." So part of this story that I am
able to tell you now begins with my grandfather's intent that I should
be a landscape architect and continue the work of my uncle

Charles Eliot.[2] He, my grandfather, followed through all the way along as I was growing up. He took me to a meeting in Boston before the ACPI was first organized – the American City Planning Institute. It was a lunch occasion, and F. L. Olmsted, Jr, Alfred Bettman, George Ford, and all those original founders were there, and it was at that session – I don't know if it was that day or the next – that they decided that they were going to have a professional organization.

K. What year was that?

E. 1917.

Well then, you wanted to know in particular about how I got involved with the *Journal*, so I got out these first volumes, 1 to 6, that I had bound years ago and was looking them over in preparation. My professor at Harvard who was really the inspiration for my enthusiasm about the planning aspects of the landscape profession was Henry Vincent Hubbard. In the Fall of 1924, when I came back from a traveling fellowship in Europe, instead of going to work for another professional office I set up for myself, with my grandfather's help, in the same building where my uncle had had his office, 9 Park Street, Boston. I had very little to do at first. I did work for the Trustees of Reservations that my uncle (Charles Eliot) had founded, as kind of a field secretary with my expenses paid, and I did a lot of small jobs that I got because of family, and things like that. Prof. Hubbard said, "Well, you've got lots of time on your hands, why don't you join me now and see what we can do on a magazine?" So the headquarters of the magazine was established in my 9 Park Street Office. He gave me very free rein. I can't find any files and think they are probably at the Graduate School of Design because the files when Brad Williams died were sent out here in a big file cabinet and dumped in the basement. Later I turned them over to the Harvard School of Design Library. At least that's the best that I can recollect as to what I did because I searched upstairs in my so-called drafting room and study and I know that they are not there. So I think they are at the library because I have given most of my things to them and because that was the appropriate place for them, considering Hubbard's relationship to it. So for the first volume in 1925 I did almost all of the correspondence. For the contents, Hubbard must have suggested, "Why don't you write to so and so." I assembled most of the materials; that was my role.

K. Why was it published by a company, separate from the Institute?

E. Darned if I know. On the title page here is the City Planning Publishing Company. I do know that Carl Parker was a partner of Hubbard's over at the Olmsted office, and Brad Williams, who shared the office with me and later took over the office when I went to Washington, was a year behind me at the graduate school at Harvard.[3]

Plate 16.1 Charles W. Eliot, 2nd, as a young man.

Now these other people here are contributing editors; you know of course who all of those are. TK (Theodora Kimball Hubbard), as we always called her, was the librarian of the school before she married Hub. Looking at these early editors I was delighted to have some of these things recalled, but that's about the extent of what I can tell you about the origins. I don't know why they set up a special separate publishing company.

K. Were Carl Parker and Brad Williams both landscape planners?

E. Yes, they were landscape architects. Parker was definitely a partner of the Olmsted brothers' firm of landscape architects and Brad – there was no instruction or degree in planning at that time, that didn't come until 1929 – Brad Williams was a landscape architect all of his life. When I went to Washington he took over several of my activities – as with the Trustees of Reservations and so on. My other office sharer

CITY PLANNING

Regional Planning—Rural Planning—Town Planning

OFFICIAL ORGAN
AMERICAN CITY PLANNING INSTITUTE
NATIONAL CONFERENCE ON CITY PLANNING

QUARTERLY

Vol. I   **APRIL, 1925**   No. 1

CONTENTS

Published Quarterly at Augusta, Maine, by
CITY PLANNING PUBLISHING CO.
BUSINESS OFFICE: 9 PARK ST., BOSTON, MASS.

HENRY VINCENT HUBBARD, Editor.   CHARLES W. ELIOT, 2ND, Assistant Editor

CONTRIBUTING EDITORS
EDWARD M. BASSETT   FRANK B. WILLIAMS   GEORGE B. FORD
FLAVEL SHURTLEFF   THEODORA KIMBALL HUBBARD

CARL RUST PARKER, *Business Manager*
BRADFORD WILLIAMS, *Advertising and Circulation Manager*

75 cents a copy, $3.00 a year (Foreign $1.00 a copy, $3.50 a year)

Plate 16.2 Contents, *City Planning*, vol. 1, no. 1.

was Robert N. Cram who was definitely a landscape architect. My first planning activity from that office was in 1925, same year that this [*Journal*] got going. It was to prepare a plan for the Town of Arlington – just west of here. That came about because I read in the newspaper that the Arlington Town Meeting had appropriated a sum of money for the preparation of a town plan. I found that the chairman of the Planning Board was Cyrus Dalin, the famous sculptor. His son was a classmate of mine at school. So I went out to see Mr Dalin and said,

You know, for this amount of money you are not going to get much of anything. But if you will employ me, I am more than willing to devote my *full* energies to it, and you will get everything that I can possibly give you for this particular sum of money. Furthermore, I used as my thesis for my MLA degree the park treatment of the part of Arlington adjoining Cambridge – Alewife Brook, Spy Pond, etc., so you've got the park plan for eastern Arlington already done!

I got the job!

K. You started your office here in what year?

E. 1924. I had one summer at the Olmsted office in the summer of 1922, and then when I came back from a year and a half in Europe on a Sheldon Traveling Fellowship I started my own shop.

"Job here" – Washington, D.C.

E. The family relationship with the Olmsteds was always there in the background, and in the summer of 1926 I had a telegram (I was living here with my parents) from Washington. "Job here. Would have jumped at your age. Meet me Cosmos Club, breakfast, Monday morning," signed Frederick Law Olmsted, Jr. So I borrowed some money from neighbors and got on the Federal Express and went down. He met me at the door of the club and said, "I suppose you want to wash up?" I said, "Yes, sir." So we went into the men's room and he immediately launched with,

I don't want any misunderstanding about this thing. Congress has just authorized the establishment of a National Capital Park and Planning Commission. The President has appointed me as one of the members of that commission. We've had our first meeting. The law authorizes the Commission to employ a "Director" for this new commission. We have offered it to all the people that we think are qualified and they've all turned it down on the grounds that it doesn't pay enough. So, we have decided to change the title, cut the salary in half, and offer it to you.

I said "Accepted, Mr Olmsted!"

So I went to Washington. A very extraordinary experience. After breakfast we went down to the office that they had just established. The executive officer as he was called, was a major with the name of U.S. Grant, III. He was in charge of public buildings and grounds for

Washington, assigned from the Corps of Engineers. So we went to his office and he said,

Well, there is no such thing as your position in the civil service, so we have got to invent a new position and we will just call it city planner. You go down the hall and there is a door on the left and a private room there. You sit down there and you compose a civil service exam that you are sure to pass among the top three.

Which is what I did!

K. Did you take it?

E. Those were the days! Yes, I think I had the second best score, but they could choose from the top three. That was the reason I had to be sure to pass among the top three. So I was city planner for a couple of years and then they made me director. I had that job until the New Deal under Roosevelt, and then I decided that I wanted to expand and get into the field of national planning. I felt that a lot of the principles of planning that we had been working with were applicable in a much bigger field. So I got hold of my father-in-law who was an old friend of Harold Ickes who, it had just been announced, was going to be the Secretary of the Interior, and asked him for a letter of introduction. When I went to the Secretary's office, I told Mr Ickes that I would like to be Assistant Secretary of the Interior in charge of planning for the public domain. Do you really want all these stories?

K. Sure! Yes.

E. O.K. When you get an old man going, it's dangerous. He (Mr Ickes) looked at me and he said, "Do you realize that I am the first Secretary of the Interior from East of the Mississippi, and I come from Illinois! You couldn't be confirmed! You come from Massachusetts!" I said, "Well, I think I could be confirmed." He said, "Of course you couldn't!" I said, "Well, do you mind, Mr Secretary, if I go up to the Hill and see what chances I might have?" So I went up and I sent in my card to one senator after another from the anteroom of the Senate, and I got thirty senators to say that, yes, they would endorse my nomination. Of course that wasn't enough, but that was just one afternoon. So I went back to see Mr Ickes and told him. And he said, "Too late. Too late. Yesterday I appointed Oscar Chapman."

So instead I got to work with the so-called "Brain Trust" – Ray Moley and Rex Tugwell and the rest of them – when we were involved in the NRA, the PWA, WPA, and all of the rest of the New Deal alphabetical agencies. The next thing was that Ickes was named head of the PWA, the Public Works Administration. So I thought, well, they need planning, certainly, checking all of these project applications from the cities and states all over the place. So I got hold of Mr Delano (Frederick A. Delano, who was chairman of the National Capital Park and Planning Commission) for whom I had been working, and he arranged for us to see Ickes again, and propose a planning process. So it was that the National Planning Board was established as part of the Public Works Administration. From there on it was national planning.

Planning the nation

K. For about ten years?

E. Yes, ten years. Until I was fired by an Act of Congress in 1943. One of the reasons that the Board was abolished and I got fired in 1943 was that the board was attacked for three or four different reasons by different groups, politically. Of course there were always the extreme conservatives among Republicans and Southern Democrats who were edgy about this being a wicked, socialist-communist activity and all of that kind of junk, and they were particularly thrown off because our Board actually advocated national health insurance in 1942. Now just think of that! It was just, oh, so absolutely outrageous! And we also were putting out reports saying that it was absolutely essential that the federal government support various educational kinds of programs and grants. That was interference with, I don't know, religion or something. It was awful! And then the main opposition came from the rivers and harbors block in the Congress because in our plans for the wise use of land and water resources we had made it essential for the Corps of Engineers to justify every dam project in terms of its relation to the whole river basin, not just to the congressional district in which it was located. Of course, what tickles me now is that here is President Carter in the same boat exactly. And some of the candidates are still advocating national health insurance!

K. Well, it must have been an exciting place to be at the time.

E. It was indeed. Another aspect of the attack was that in wartime this was an absolutely unnecessary organization and all efforts of the nation should be put on winning the war and not on some kind of planning stuff. So of course our response was – what's going to happen when the war is over? Are we going to have another depression when all of the defense industries close down? We were working on postwar planning. Well, that didn't matter. And the final real background element, that I think was one of the significant causes of the reason for our defeat, was that Frederick A. Delano was the chairman of this National Planning Agency. He was the uncle of the President and here was a way for those ''hate Roosevelt'' people to attack the President and hurt him personally, which it did. There is no question about that. I was in a very difficult situation because, yes, Delano was President Roosevelt's uncle, but he was also ''Uncle Fred'' to me. He was a classmate of my father's in college and a fraternity mate, and when I went to Washington at Olmsted's telegram I stayed with Uncle Fred at his house. Frederic. A. Delano was an important proponent of planning, as you perhaps know, from way back in Chicago in 1908–9 and then with the Regional Plan in New York. More than anybody but Norton and Adams, he was really the person responsible for getting it going. He did the same, when he was chairman of the Committee of 100 for the national capital, in getting the legislation for planning of the national capital. I was very devoted to him. We had a wonderful thing to remember. At one of the White House receptions he took my wife; I couldn't go for some reason. And when the reception line reached Eleanor Roosevelt, Uncle Fred said, "Eleanor, I want you to meet another niece of mine," and then didn't give her name. Eleanor was nonplussed, but when they got to FDR, he said, "And who *are* you young lady?" And she said "Regina Eliot," "Oh," said FDR, with a hearty laugh.

K. Well, there's no doubt about the great contribution that decade of work made to planning.

E. Yes, when the Board was abolished I was one of about six people in the history of the country that were fired by an Act of Congress. That was in August 1943 and I was instructed to dispose of all of the records and personnel and everything of the organization before the end of the year. They meant that I should really dispose of them. Of course, all the official files, records, minutes, reports, etc. went to the National Archives, but I did what I could to get the extra copies of our reports to the university libraries all over the country! So then I had to get another job and this opportunity came in California.

Moving west

K. To teach at UCLA?

E. Yes. So on January 1, 1944, my wife and I packed the four kids, the nurse, and the dog in the station wagon and drove across the continent. That also has a silly story attached. Of course there was a war on, and we had to have gas rations. So in preparation I went to the ration board and said that I needed to go across the continent and we thought the best way to do it was to take the whole family in the car. The woman said, "You have to prove to me that you have a job at the other end. This is wartime!" I said, "Will this letter from the Chancellor of the University do?" She said, "Yes, but you also need a letter saying that you are no longer necessary for your job in Washington," I said, "Will an Act of Congress do?" She said, "You don't understand. All you have to do is get a letter from your boss saying that your services are no longer necessary.'' ''But,'' I said ''that's not exactly practical. My only boss at the moment is named Franklin Delano Roosevelt and I don't think in the middle of a war it is appropriate for me to go and ask him for such a letter.'' She persisted, ''You don't understand, young man, all you have to do is get a letter from your boss.'' So I went back to the office and dictated: ''Dear Mr Eliot: Your services are no longer necessary in Washington,'' signed it Charles W. Eliot, and when I took that back, I got my gas rations. Whoo – red tape!

K. Let me follow through on what happened after you were out in California. Was it then that you set up practice in Los Angeles?

E. At first, while I was lecturing at UCLA, I served as director for the Haynes Foundation. Then I opened my office for private practice, operating out of Pasadena but in the Los Angeles area. I had quite a variety of experiences, including planning for Old Town San Diego, Riverside, Upland Claremont, Coachella Valley, etc. I was doing so-called Master Plans. Then in 1951 or 1952 Paul Hoffman, who lived in Pasadena, was named as first head of the Ford Foundation and he asked me to join the original Ford Foundation staff as director of Resources Programs, as it was called, with the idea that we would try to solicit requests for grants from people concerned with conservation and with planning and all of this kind of thing. Through that I got Resources for the Future organized. I did most of the organizing.

K. When was that?

E. 1952 or 1953, I don't remember. Then the Foundation moved to New York and I was left back there. I was on a part time basis with the Foundation, so I was still carrying on some of my professional jobs.

K. This was still in California?

E. Yes, Pasadena. I had a contract that went for a couple of more years, but they did the old business trick. First, they removed the rug from my office. Then they moved something else and then they moved my office to a very small little cubby hole. Then they took away my secretary, you know, and they just got rid of me. I could stand it no longer. Bob Hutchins was also left behind. I don't know why; he didn't want to move. He stuck it out until he got a major grant for his Santa Barbara Center for the Study of Democratic Institutions. So then the Eliots moved back East because our four children were in college or school hereabout. A few months after we took over this house (in which I grew up seventy years ago), Harvard offered me the Charles Eliot Professorship in Landscape Architecture at the Graduate School of Design.

Teaching planners to plan

E. I insisted on a half-time basis at Harvard, on the grounds that when teaching a profession you have to keep in touch with current activities. This has been a major issue at Harvard in the last year with the present dean insisting that people should be full time. I think it is absolutely wrong. In fact, I heartily disapprove of much that has been going on in the planning department at the school.[4]

K. Do you have primarily studio kind of teaching?

E. Not primarily, but we have studios. We don't have a school of design or architecture so it is more difficult to teach design under those conditions.

You have to have some kind of "design." I had never done any teaching except being an assistant to Professor Pray in the city planning course, in the third year of graduate school but I came, of course, from a teaching family. So when I started here in 1955, I ran my studio course on the basis that we would take a project that is a possible actual planning project in some community near Boston. The students would collect the basic background material and then, in rival teams, prepare alternate solutions. Then I would arrange in the community – with the board of selectmen or the city council or the planning board – to allow them to make a public presentation, with the public invited, so they had to explain and go through the kind of thing that a consultant has to do, *in school.* They would have the actual experience of doing this. I still think, and many of my students still say, that this was a major contribution.

K. Yes, most of our studios do that. I just taught one this last semester, which I had not done for a while, and it was very stimulating to me as well as to the students.

E. Yes, it is quite exciting. In a local community we get the reactions and see which students are able to get their ideas across and what particular kinds of maneuvers and ways of expressing things register and which don't. It's quite fascinating.

K. It really is.

The Hubbard Education Trust

K. Do you know why Hubbard stopped editing the *Journal* in 1935?

E. No I don't.

K. The one thing that occurred to me is that I noticed that that is about the time . . .

E. That T.K. died?

K. I thought that maybe that was part of the reason.

Plate 16.3 Charles W. Eliot, 2nd, about 1960.

E. Well, I wouldn't be surprised.

By the way, I was at a meeting yesterday of the Hubbard Educational Trust which was founded in his memory and which now finances, with very limited income, various projects about the profession, particularly a series of audio-visual recordings. Have you heard of them? You might be interested in some of them. They made one of me that goes for two hours, unfortunately. They set up the lights over there and Sidney Shurcliff sat where you are and I sat here and it was an interview such as we are having now but with all the bright lights and visual business as well. That was the first of a series. We have Gilmore Clarke (landscape architect, primarily), Frank Church of California, and Norman Newton (who used to be president of the ASLA), and various others now on tape with the stories of their careers. The idea is to try and give students in the field some idea of the variety and kinds of work that a career in landscape architecture and planning can involve.

K. That's a nice idea.

I ran across a copy recently of the Hubbards' textbook on landscape architecture published by the Foundation.

E. Which we reprinted. Yesterday they were talking about reprinting *Charles Eliot, Landscape Architect*. They say now that copies are hard to get and sell for about $70.

K. Is that right? Fortunately I already have one.

E. I have only one, over there. I've got to give a lecture on his work May 3rd before the Society for the Preservation of New England Antiquities, which is suddenly getting interested, quite appropriately I guess, in the preservation of outdoors as well as structures, which is good. That was one of the things about the tape of my career that caused some of the people to raise their eyebrows, because of course I stressed in the tape that I had expanded the idea of the role of the landscape architect to planning for the whole United States. They thought that was extreme – going from the backyard garden to the whole USA.

Father and family

K. What did your father do?

E. My father was a Unitarian Minister, president of the American Unitarian Association for twenty-seven years, and minister of Arlington Street Church after that. He and my mother had seven children. That is why we had such a big house as this. He was off every Sunday somewhere preaching, although he didn't have his own parish because he was working for the association, as head of it.

K. What was his first name?

E. Samuel.' Same as his grandfather and great grandfather. You are sitting in the chair that was in my grandfather's college room in 1851.

K. What was your grandfather's training?

E. He was a chemist and, right out of college, was an instructor and assistant professor here (at Harvard). And then, when he was denied promotion, he went to Europe. When he came back they were just starting the Massachusetts Institute of Technology, where he was made a professor of Chemistry as MIT began. Shortly after that Harvard needed a new president and they elected him.

K. After not giving him tenure?

E. Yes!

K. Isn't that ironic.

E. So he was president for forty years. Too long! My younger brother Thomas H. Eliot was chancellor at Washington University in Saint Louis, and when ten years rolled around, although he was still under retirement age, he resigned.

We are a teaching family, all right. All of my brothers and brothers-in-law, except one, somehow or other are professors or college presidents or something.

Thoughts on Planning
from Fifty Years of Active Practice and Teaching
Charles W. Eliot 2nd
June 1979

Planning is Design — The interrelation of forces to produce a desired result. Every program or project for which a Plan is designed involves many forces or ingredients; each with its own measure of values or importance. There are always physical or natural forces, social considerations, economic factors, and aesthetic or spiritual aspects to be evaluated, as well as purpose, timing and other considerations. Different individuals, groups and peoples, in different times and countries measure each of these forces in different ways. And for each project, each of the forces involved has a different value, weight or significance.

Furthermore — time and "inevitable change" cause whatever relative values may have been assigned to different forces to also change, — so that what was once a "good" plan becomes "out-dated" and inappropriate. Almost all of the "forces" involved in planning follow the giant syndrome of Life — 1) Birth or Beginnings, 2) Growth and Development, 3) Fulfillment, 4) Decay — partially off-set by care and rehabilitation, but finally 5) death or destruction. Values reflect the stage in this syndrome of each of those forces. Planning, therefore, requires understanding and projection of trends in value changes in and among the forces involved in any particular project or program. Only then can a plan fulfill another definition — Planning is The Guidance of Change.

Planning is Proposing. Start by proposing the Best (not the "practical" or what has the best chance of approval and early accomplishment — as too many planners now consider the mark of success). There are certain to be compromises, reductions and limitations on any proposal during its review and before its approval and implementation, — and, if a minimum or "practical" proposal is presented, those inevitable compromises may turn a "good" project into a bad one. To mobilize support for any Plan the Proposal must be worth fighting for — and, if it doesn't attract support, it probably doesn't deserve approval. People respond to a Challenge — not to a whimper.

Plate 16.4 Thoughts on Planning.

K. Did you teach from the time you came back from California?

E. While my grandfather was president of Harvard they established the rule that the year in which you become sixty-six is your last year of full time teaching. You can be continued on a kind of a part time arrangement after that. I am always as old as the year, so in 1966 I was "out" at the end of that college year. Yes, I went back to give lectures and things but that was the end of that. So from there on I devoted myself to private practice. But it has gotten thinner and thinner, with fewer and fewer jobs.

Being practical

E. But I have all that I can do. I am very, very busy with the Trustees of Reservations and historical things and the Metropolitan Area Planning Council, of which I am one of the founders and have been a gubernatorial appointee from the beginning. It was established as an independent agency. It is very important that a planning agency should have some degree of independence. Another trouble is (maybe you have run into some of this in your teaching) I find that more and more planners are interested only in planning things for immediate action. That the things that are going to happen must be

Plate 16.5 Charles W. Eliot, 2nd, at home on his eightieth birthday.

planned, yes; but the idea of the long range, or the idealistic, is pretty much out and everyone seems to be concentrating on only working on things that might get done in the next five years. Well, that leads to these complications with people like the governor wanting more and more control, if that is what they are going to be doing. Instead, all of the so-called master plans of these cities that I have ever worked on – some done years ago – contain recommendations, many or most of which are still to be done.

K. Yes. I think that you are right. That is very characteristic of the times.

E. Trying to be "practical," as they say. But I don't think that it is practical, in the long run. I think that we have to nail a flag at the top of the mast, something to shoot for, not something that is just going to get done next week.

K. Do you still follow the *Journal*? Do you read it?

E. Oh yes, sure! There is too much on statistics for my taste. And it is very difficult for an outsider to understand the significance of it. There is a Board of Review?

K. Oh yes. At least two other people in addition to the editor read the papers.

E. I think that is the only real criticism that I have of it. The statistics. That kind of material isn't adequately interpreted in the articles to make it really useful.

K. I think that is fair enough.

E. Of course I am delighted that finally we have got the various organizations united because I tried hard to have it happen long, long ago. In fact, when ASPO was first set up – working with Brownlow and the people at Chicago, who were chiefly responsible – I protested then that they ought to be combined with the existing AIP. So I am delighted that this has finally come about.

I do think that there ought to be a strictly professional kind of sub-organization that has strictly professional aspects.

K. Yes, there will be the American Institute of Certified Planners as it is going to be called.

E. On the other hand, I've vigorously opposed these bills for "registration" of planners because to segregate out people who are called "certified planners" is a denial of the very purpose of planning. The whole thrust of our profession should be to bring together the engineers, the landscape architects and the architects, the real estate experts, and all kinds of other economic and social people. It isn't a kind of speciality in which competence can be judged by an exam.

K. No, it is very difficult.

Saying goodbye

E. Where are you going next?

K. This afternoon I am going to Lexington to see Roland Greeley.[5]

E. Roly Greeley, oh good! Roly serves with me in the work of the Trustees. He is head of our Reservation Management Committee and I see him at least once a month that way. But he also worked for the National Resources Planning Board as head of the staff for the regional office here in New England, so my association with him goes back then. And his father had the office next to mine on the top floor of 9 Park Street when I started out. He was very kind to me – William Roger Greeley. And his older brother Dana Greeley succeeded my father at the Arlington Street Church and the American Unitarian Association. A very close family. I think that you will enjoy him.

K. Well, you certainly have a full life.

E. Well, at the moment I'm absolutely swamped with the details of my wife's estate.[6]

K. I do appreciate your taking the time. I have enjoyed your company very much.

E. Well, It is a relief for me to think about something else.

Author's note

The author wishes to thank Marilyn Watterson and Vera Lee for their kind and able assistance in preparing the interview for publication. Thanks also, of course, to the generosity of Charles W. Eliot, 2nd, for his timely thoughts and careful review of the finished product.

Notes

1 Eliot's grandfather Charles W. Eliot was president of Harvard University from 1869 to 1909.

2 Eliot's uncle died in the prime of his career. His work is memorialized in a biography mentioned later in this conversation, *Charles Eliot, Landscape Architect*, Boston, Houghton, Mifflin & Co., 1902, written by the father, Charles W. Eliot.

3 Eliot is commenting on the masthead of the magazine which shows that Carl Parker was its business manager and Bradford Williams was its advertising and circulation manager. Eliot himself was the assistant editor.

4 On October 15, 1979, seven months after this conversation took place, Harvard's President Bok announced the appointment of a new dean of the Graduate School of Design, and on December 5, 1979 recommended the transfer of the City and Regional Planning Program from the School of Design to the Kennedy School of Government.

5 Roland Greeley was managing editor of the *AIP Journal* from 1944 to 1952 while serving on the planning faculty at MIT. He then served MIT as Director of Admissions until his retirement.

6 Eliot's wife of fifty years, Regina, died in January, 1979, just two months before this interview.

17 Charles Abrams: a lover of cities

Bernard Taper

Preface

Charles Abrams once said that any housing expert worth his salt should have a thorough grasp of economics, law, urban land policies, real estate practices, architecture, construction methods, sociology, politics, administration, and public relations. Upon being apprised of this definition, his friend and colleague Lloyd Rodwin, then chairman of the Faculty Committee of the MIT–Harvard Joint Center for Urban Studies, observed, "Wouldn't you know it? Abrams has come up with a definition that fits only himself. No housing expert in the world that I know of besides him comes even close to possessing all those qualifications."

How Abrams developed his range of expertise remains a wonder. He was very much a self-made man. Just as he made his own considerable fortune, so he made his own education. Though, at one time or other, he was on the faculty of MIT, the University of Pennsylvania, City College, the New School, and ultimately Columbia University, where he headed the Division of Urban Planning, he himself never went to college. His only degree was one in law, which he earned at night school, while working days. When, toward the end of his life, he was asked how he acquired the background to become a professor, he would reply in a matter-of-fact way, "By teaching courses and writing books."

The account of Charles Abrams' life and career published in this volume is a slightly abridged version of the second part of a two-part *New Yorker* Profile that originally appeared under the title of "A Lover of Cities" on February 4 and 11, 1967, three years before Abrams' death at the age of 68. The first part of the Profile dealt in considerable measure with Abrams' career as a United Nations adviser on housing problems of developing countries and with his articulation of issues involved in the unprecedented urbanization taking place throughout the Third World. Space does not permit inclusion of that part of the Profile in this volume; therefore, some summary acknowledgment needs to be made here of this phase of his life, since it was of special importance and satisfaction to Abrams and produced noteworthy achievements.

Beginning in 1952, Abrams participated in UN missions to over a score of countries, leaving his recognizable impact on many of them through the quality of his personality as well as his insights. Ernest Weissman, who headed the United Nations housing branch, commented at the time:

The impact that Abrams' missions make has amazed us . . . Twenty-four hours after he arrives in a country, housing suddenly becomes a front-page topic. Somehow he makes the leaders aware of the importance of problems they had been taking for granted or else had considered hopeless. He shows them possible solutions that are right under their noses, and he convinces them that they have to drop everything else and get going on the solution right then and there. Wherever he goes, he foments reform.

Barbara Ward summed up this aspect of Abrams' career well in a tribute she wrote for *Habitat*'s special Abrams *Festschrift* issue, 1980. She wrote:

Drawing on his profound knowledge of urban problems in America and seeking to apply this experience to the emerging cities of the Third World, he was a pioneer in bringing to governments and ministries and to the new professional groups some sense of the scale of urban disorder and deprivation they would have to confront and some outlines of the strategies they would need for effective action. He could advise all the more early and successfully because he combined a very wide range of experience with great humour, immense good will and no trace of that "white man's arrogance" which, as the activity of giving advice on development grew on an ever greater scale, became all too often a source of extreme annoyance and even a block to otherwise useful plans and ideas. But Charles Abrams saw everyone as an equal and honourable member of the human family. No one could mistake his basic common sense and humility. He gave counsel. He received in return not only a ready hearing but lasting friendship as well.

Charles Abrams: A Lover of Cities

Three years ago, a high-level team of French officials, architects, and city planners, charged with drawing up France's Fifth National Plan on Urbanism, made a month-long tour of the United States to see how we were handling our urban problems. During their stay here, they conferred with numerous American authorities and were shown significant projects and developments – Lincoln Center, various high-rise housing projects, the gleaming new business center of New Haven, the urban-renewal transformations in Philadelphia, the San Francisco slum-clearance projects, the Los Angeles freeways. Returning to New York, just before their departure for France, they met with Charles Abrams, the chairman of the Division of Urban Planning of Columbia University and one of the world's leading consultants on housing and city planning, and spent a Sunday morning taking a guided tour with him. Abrams, who is in his sixties, has a round, usually amiable face and a leisurely, rather shambling gait, which scarcely suggests that he is a person of remarkable drive and energy. As experts in his field go, Abrams is an unconventional figure, with a personality pungently compounded of zeal, shrewdness, ingenuity, and ebullient humor. His guided tour that Sunday was not a conventional one, either. He did not take the French planners to view a single new project, or even the site of a future development. Instead, he took them on one of his favorite walks – a walk with which many of his planning students at Columbia had become familiar. It was a perambulation through the Lower East Side: through the noisy, crooked, narrow streets of Chinatown; along the Bowery, past a group of jewelry shops that Abrams characterized as "the Off Broadway diamond center;" down Grand Street, with its cluster of bridal-gown shops, for a pause at an aromatic bakery, where Abrams bought some pumpernickel and from which the wife of one of the French officials emerged with a string of bagels around her neck like a *lei*; up teeming Orchard Street, past pushcarts heaped with bargain wearing apparel, where one of the French planners, on an unplanned impulse, bought a trunk, which he then had to lug along with him; on to East Houston Street, for a stop at the delicatessen of Russ & Daughters, whose proprietors greeted Abrams heartily, asked after his family, and boned a whitefish for him; then across the street, where the party paused again, this time to watch a game of boccie; up Second Avenue, where the Yiddish theatre once flourished, and past McSorley's Old Ale House, regrettably closed at that hour; on to visit a Ukrainian shop on Seventh Street to buy some honey; south from Astor Place, past a nondescript building that Abrams identified, with a wave of his hand, as the largest birdseed factory in the United States, to Waverly Place, with elegant, ornamented lofts that have so far escaped the wrecking ball; across Washington Square; and, at last, after a brief pause to savor Washington Mews, on to Abrams' residence, a spacious house on Tenth Street, just off Fifth Avenue, where they lunched on the whitefish, pastrami, lox, pumpernickel, pickles, bagels, honey, and candies they had garnered along the route, feeling as pleased about this as do fishermen when they make a meal from their catch.

Abrams' purpose in taking the French group on this walk was partly admonitory. The chaotic, crowded, vivid neighborhoods they had toured with such fascination were not the design of any planner. No planner could ever have created a scene so varied, so full of enterprise and vitality. Yet planners are perfectly capable of destroying or homogenizing such a scene – and all too often do so. Instead of identifying and appreciating the innate values that have spontaneously grown up in a neighborhood, and attempting to reinforce and build on these values, the planner's approach is apt to be one of distaste for all the messiness that life has generated without his assistance; he tends to want to raze neighborhoods like these and replace them with large, costly, sterile projects. Abrams was warning the French planners that they had to be on their guard against forming such a mistaken conception of their role, and

Plate 17.1 Charles Abrams.
Source: Department of Manuscripts and University Archives, Olin Library, Cornell
University.

urging them to make plans that would cherish and foster spontaneity and
diversity – even, to use a phrase he is fond of, "a diversity of diversities."
It was a message whose cogency the French planners were well prepared
to acknowledge by the end of their walk.[1]

Most of the world's housing and planning experts and reformers, it
happens, háve been people of middle-class or wealthy backgrounds; to
learn about slums, they have had to make field trips and pore over
surveys. Abrams acquired his knowledge of what life in a slum is like by

being brought up in one. Born in Poland, he arrived in this country at the age of two, when his family immigrated and settled in the Williamsburg district of Brooklyn, which was, in those days before the First World War, more or less an extension of the Lower East Side – a polyglot neighborhood of cobblestone streets that were never cleaned and that teemed day and night with people and pushcarts, and of rat-infested, highly combustible wooden tenements, which were scientifically designed to compress the greatest number of human beings into the smallest tolerable living space. The Abramses' apartment was a three-room flat in a six-story walkup. There were four children in the family – three sons, of whom Charles was the youngest, and a daughter – which meant that six people lived in the apartment's three small rooms. Charles and his brother Ralph slept in a windowless cubicle, not much bigger than a respectable closet, the two of them sharing a bed so narrow that, no matter what furious quarrels they may have had during the day, they always had to sleep with their arms wrapped around each other to keep from falling to the floor. The apartment had no hot water and no heat, except what was given off by a coal-burning cookstove in the kitchen; on each floor of the building was a single toilet, for the use of all the families; there wasn't a bathtub in the building – or, for that matter, in the entire neighborhood, except those at a public bathhouse a few blocks away. Today, Abrams jestingly gives credit for the resilient health that permits him to take the tropics in stride on his overseas missions to his boyhood patronage of the neighborhood public bathhouse; he surmises that there are probably very few pestilences lurking in the tropics that he did not encounter, and develop an immunity to, during those weekly immersions at Bershadsky's Baths.

In Poland, Abrams' father had worked on a communal farm. In Brooklyn, he set himself up as a sidewalk vender of herrings and pickles – a precarious business from which he was barely able to squeeze out a living, though he worked punishing hours. Some days, there wasn't enough money for a proper meal, but Charles' mother never dreamed of admitting this to anybody outside the family. On those days, she used to keep covered pots of water boiling on the stove, so that neighbors who dropped in would not guess the family's desperate situation. Mrs Abrams, the daughter of a Vilna book-keeper, was a delicate-featured woman whose entire life was centered on her children and her concern that they must "make something of themselves." Her husband was a figure whose prototype one often encounters in stories of Jewish slums and ghettos – a man who, despite the squalor around him, managed to convey an impression of dignity, grave humor, and even wisdom. Today, Abrams says of his father, "There was something noble about everything he did. The way he comported himself, even the sale of a miserable pickled herring became somehow a courtly and humane transaction.'' Abrams' father had his sidewalk stand across the street from their tenement. Above Mr Abrams' head hung a large sign belonging to the store from which he rented his few feet of space; in stormy weather, the sign used to swing and creak perilously, and the family feared that at any moment it might crash down on Mr Abrams' head – a worry that Abrams remembers as being for some reason one of the abiding anxieties of his childhood. Yet none of the family seems to have considered it possible to cope with the problem in any way – to move the stand elsewhere, or persuade the storekeeper to take down or repair the sign. It was simply fate, and when fate hung over one's head, there was nothing that an ordinary mortal could do about it, except perhaps wear a hat, and this Mr Abrams always did anyway, being an Orthodox Jew. Young Charles was very close to his father. From the time he was seven or eight years old, it was his habit to wake up when his father returned home for the night, sometimes as late as one o'clock. Charles would put on his bathrobe and make a pot of tea, and then he and his father would sit together at the kitchen table, sipping their tea and discussing all sorts of things. Abrams says he got the greater part of his education during those sessions.

Those who don't know Abrams might picture the future reformer as a sensitive boy who vowed that when he grew up he would dedicate himself to the task of wiping out the slums that had blighted his childhood. Actually, Abrams remembers his childhood as quite happy, on the whole. If the slums were damaging him, he wasn't aware of it at the time. He simply accepted his environment as the conditions that prevailed, being unaware that it was possible for people to live in any other way. He was ultimately moved to work for better housing not so much by a feeling of personal grievance as by intellectual exasperation at what he considered the utter illogicality of the nation's housing situation. He says that when he first became active in the field, in the early 1930s, it never occurred to him to think of his own old neighborhood as an example of the slums he was inveighing against, or to think of his childhood neighbors and friends as the miserable wretches evoked by the phrase ''slum dwellers.'' Not until one day in 1933 did these words take on reality for him. As one of three lawyers drafting the basic state housing legislation under which the New York City Housing Authority was established, he was called upon to draw up a legal definition of a slum area, and as he was working on this, it dawned on him that the definition fitted his own old home and neighborhood perfectly. Abrams was almost as surprised by this discovery as Molière's M. Jourdain was to learn that he had been talking prose all his life.

Abrams may have had a happy enough childhood, but it was hardly a carefree one. He has only a dim memory of a time in his life when he did not work. "My first job was as lookout man for a gang of herring boot-leggers," he recalls, half seriously. As a tot in short pants, he was given the assignment of standing watch at the front of the tenement house on Sundays while other members of his family wrapped herrings, kosher dill pickles, pickled onions, and other such snacks in a back hallway and smuggled them to customers throughout the building, in violation ("fragrant violation," Abrams, a pun fancier, now calls it) of the Sunday work laws. To be caught at these activities meant a fine of as much as ten dollars – a punishment that the Abrams family could ill afford but that they suffered more often than the former lookout man cares to remem-ber. By the time Abrams was nine, he was taking on outside jobs to sup-plement the family income. While he was in high school, he worked as a lamplighter, tending the street lights on Lafayette Avenue. He was a very small lamplighter, being the shortest boy in his class. Every evening, he strapped on a pair of roller skates and went rolling along Lafayette over to Myrtle Avenue and down to Fort Greene Park, lighting up the neigh-borhood, pole by pole, as he went; every morning he skated off at dawn and turned the lamps out. As he rolled along, he could be heard declaim-ing resonantly into the Brooklyn twilight, "If you have tears, prepare to shed them now." He was possessed of a wonderfully loud voice, and by then he had achieved some fame in school as an orator; whenever the superintendent or some other dignitary visited his school, Abrams was called on to get up in front of the assembly and tear Mark Antony's funeral oration to tatters. For his lamplighting, he was paid four dollars a week by the Brooklyn Edison Company. After a year or so, however, he began to feel that he was something of a slacker, having what amounted to only a half-time job outside of school, so he quit his work for Brooklyn Edison to become a message clerk at the main office of Western Union in Manhattan. At this job, which paid twelve dollars a week, he worked a full eight-hour shift after high school, starting at 5 p.m. By the time he got back home to Brooklyn, it would be nearly 2 a.m., and then, after a cup of tea with his father, he would settle down to his homework. He was fourteen at the time, and had attained a lifelong ambition – to be completely self-supporting.

When he finished high school, he chose to study law, mainly because that seemed to him the profession that could be most easily learned at night school. He signed up for evening classes at Brooklyn Law School, and by day he worked – first as an office boy and later as a clerk – for a succession of law firms. The first of these was McLaughlin & Stern, which had offices on William Street, and his first day with them remains memorable because he was sent uptown to pick up a payment in settle-ment of a case and found himself being handed sixty thousand dollars in five-hundred- and thousand-dollar bills. He had never before even seen anything larger than a ten. Rising to the occasion, young Abrams behaved in the way he assumed was expected of him as the sophisticated representative of a great law firm. He signed the receipt coolly, giving no indication that to be handed such a sum of money was in any way unusual, or even interesting, and, stuffing the money casually into his pockets, rode the subway back downtown. When he walked into the office and began counting out the sixty thousand dollars, the office manager who had sent him on the errand appeared about to faint; she had taken it for granted that the settlement would be made in the customary form of a certified check. The event created quite a stir at McLaughlin & Stern, none of the partners responding at all coolly or casually to the idea of their new teenage office boy riding the subway with sixty thousand dollars in his pockets.

Abrams learned less law from his classes than he did from his clerkships – by far the most important of which was a three-year stint in the law offices of Arthur Garfield Hays. The apprenticeship he served under Hays not only educated but inspired him, and probably did as much to determine the direction of his life as anything else that happened to him. Hays was general counsel for the recently formed American Civil Liberties Union, was associated with Clarence Darrow in the famous Scopes evolution trial in Tennessee, and was involved in a number of significant civil liberties campaigns. In the course of one such campaign (to establish constitutional freedoms and individual rights in the tough coal-mining company town of Vintondale, Pennsylvania), Hays – much to his young law clerk's admiration – succeeded in establishing his inalienable right as a citizen to get himself arrested and thrown in jail. (The right to be arrested, Abrams remembers Hays explaining shortly before he set off for Vintondale, should be valued as one of the most important of all civil rights, for if a man can't get himself officially taken into custody – and instead is, say, simply hustled out of town – he has no way of legally challenging a despotic situation.) Such battles, as Hays waged them, were undertaken not in a stodgily righteous spirit but with considerable verve and drama, and Abrams recalls the atmosphere in Hays' office when civil liberties cases were being worked on as a rousing one of derring-do in the quest for social justice – something that the youthful Abrams found both stimulating to his conscience and congenial to his temperament.

In addition to his work for the Civil Liberties Union, Hays carried on an extraordinary diverse private practice; he had labor unions, huge corporations, and foreign governments among his clients, and he did not hesitate to accept spectacular criminal and divorce cases. It was a highly lucrative practice (Hays once got a fee in excess of two hundred thousand dollars for a single case), and this was a circumstance that young Abrams – who had never equated poverty with virtue – also found inspirational. For Abrams, Hays was a model as well as a mentor. He held Hays in such fervent esteem that for a while he even walked with a limp because Hays had a game leg, and he also took to smoking a pipe in what he hoped was a convincing imitation of Hays' profound, brooding manner. It was during this period that Abrams began to form some idea of what he wanted to make of his life. Like Hays, he wanted to be a fighter for unpopular social causes, and, also like Hays, not an impecunious one.

While Abrams was in Hays' office, he was given ample opportunity, though a mere clerk, to poke his nose into a variety of legal matters. He worked, for example, on the briefs of an important free speech case, preparing all the necessary papers as it went up through the courts to the United States Supreme Court, and, at the other end of the scale of social significance, he did the law research on one aspect of Hays' vain defense of a couple of crooked stockbrokers in the lurid Fuller–McGee bucket-shop case, coming up with a bright idea about the strategy Hays might follow in developing that aspect. The idea caught Hays' fancy, and, in general, Hays seems to have taken a special liking to Abrams; later they became close friends and ardent chess adversaries. Abrams kept a big meerschaum pipe handy for these chess encounters. As his own reputation grew, he gradually learned to puff on it with an authoritative profundity that fully matched Hays'; the only trouble was that the more solemn his pipe-smoking became, the harder he found it to keep from laughing at himself.

Shortly after being admitted to the bar, in 1923, Abrams, with six hundred dollars he had borrowed from Hays, set up a law office of his own on lower Broadway, in partnership with another young lawyer fresh from the slums, Bernard Botein (who has since gone on to become Presiding Justice of the Appellate Division for the First Department – New York and Bronx Counties – of the New York State Supreme Court). Their practice flourished, and by 1928 Abrams was earning twenty-five thousand dollars a year in fees – a sum that is considered fairly good going for a fledgling lawyer even now. In that year, he married Ruth Davidson, whom he had met through an improbable chain of circumstances. A friend of his, who did not know Miss Davidson, was arranging a blind date for Abrams, but the girl he had in mind did not answer when he telephoned her. Something seemed to be wrong with her phone, but just as the friend was about to hang up, he heard a puzzled voice saying, "Hello? Hello?" It was Miss Davidson, who at that moment happened to be phoning the same girl, and whose line the Telephone Company had somehow connected with that of Abrams' friend. They got to talking. The friend was a persuasive man, and Miss Davidson was of an impetuous nature. Before they hung up, she had agreed to go out with Abrams that evening. The two hit it off right away.

The Abramses began their married life in an apartment in Greenwich Village, and they have lived in that part of town ever since. The heterogeneity of the Village, and its constant ferment, proved to be perfectly suited to Abrams' restless, adventurous spirit. He soon became a member of a circle of radical intellectuals, social critics, and literati who used to gather every Wednesday evening at the Morton Street apartment of V. F. Calverton, the editor of the *Modern Monthly*, to discuss social and literary issues. At the same time, he became a member of a wisecracking theatre and Tin Pan Alley crowd. He was stagestruck in those days, as he still is; he and his wife used to attend nearly every opening night, and were often included in the party that the show's writers or producers gave afterward. Sometimes, while still mulling over the lofty statements he had heard at Calverton's a couple of evenings before, he would drop in at the Ira Gershwins' apartment on Riverside Drive for the Friday night poker game there. Before the game got started, some of those who had shown up – among them such songwriters as B. G. De Silva, Oscar Levant, and E. Y. (Yip) Harburg – would gather around the piano and try out their latest tunes on each other. Abrams, listening, was stirred to emulation. High on a list of secret ambitions that he drew up in 1929 appeared the exhortation "Write a great song hit!"

When Abrams had known the Gershwins for several years, Ira Gershwin phoned him one day at his law office and said mysteriously, "Charlie, it appears that a President of the United States is going to have to be impeached. Do you think you could draw up a bill of impeachment?" Startled, Abrams began to question him. Gershwin said, "Never mind why, or anything else, Charlie – just go ahead and impeach the rascal." So Abrams looked up the proceedings against President Andrew Johnson, drafted a bill modeled on them, and sent it off to Ira Gershwin. In due course, Gershwin responded with a check for a hundred dollars as a fee for his effort. Not until he went to the opening of the Gershwins' "Of Thee I Sing" and heard the chorus launched into the "Whereas" song did he discover the use that had been made of his legal work; the President he had helped impeach was that jilter of the illegitimate daughter of an illegitimate son of an illegitimate nephew of Napoleon – John P. Wintergreen. Though there wasn't much left of the tedious legal paragraphs he had sent Gershwin – little but the "whereas"es and the "hereby"s – Abrams sat back in his seat glowing with the pride of authorship. So far, this is the closest Abrams has come to realizing his ambition of writing a song hit.

Some of Abrams' clients in those days were making mortgage loans on Greenwich Village property, and soon he began to follow their example. Then he grew restless at remaining on the sidelines, and, while still keeping up his law practice, threw himself headlong into real estate – not as a broker but as an entrepreneur, a sort of freelance capitalist without any capital to speak of, embarking on shoestring operations of a wildly speculative character. Before long, he was up to his ears in deals and was becoming known among real estate men as a shrewd operator and a formidable negotiator. "Those Indians who sold Manhattan were lucky they didn't have to negotiate with Abrams," one real estate man remarked after a bargaining session with him. "I'll bet they'd never have got *him* to go as high as twenty-four dollars." Nowadays, Greenwich Village, having become one of the city's high-rent districts, is considered a prime investment area, but in the 1920s banks and other financial institutions looked down their noses at it as a shabby and disreputable bohemian quarter and, not perceiving that quaintness could be turned into a capital asset, were reluctant to put mortgage money into Village property. In order to raise funds for his dealings, Abrams had to scurry around to loan sharks and shady mortgage-discount operators, and to engage in complicated and ingenious transactions, piling one mortgage on top of another – occasionally as high as a fourth mortgage – and ending up with fantastic financial structures as precarious as a child's tower of blocks. He repeatedly got himself into tight and potentially ruinous situations, but he usually managed to devise some profitable way out. More than thirty years later, Abrams can still recall in detail, and recount with zest, the improbable details of some of those transactions. It was during that period, he says, that he lost most of his hair.

During the six or seven years of his speculative heyday, he acquired, all told, perhaps seventy or eighty pieces of Village property. Some he refinanced and sold. Others he remodeled and rented, turning stables into studios, transforming loft buildings into avant-garde shops, and making many of the other ingenious conversions that eventually helped bring Greenwich Village to its present curious state. He had a hand in making Eighth Street the Village's main drag, by tearing down a number of old shacks and erecting in their places shops, a night club, and a motion-picture theatre – the last designed by the unorthodox Viennese architect Frederick Kiesler and heralded at the time as a great advance in movie-house design. The tenant for whom Abrams built this was Symon Gould, who was later to be a candidate for President of the United States on the Vegetarian ticket. Gould was certain that talkies were just a passing fad (like meat eating), and he called his cinema the House of Shadowed Silence. Gould was to have bad luck all around. He lost his lease on the movie house, giving way to a more practical entrepreneur, and his political party, up against such slogans as "A Chicken in Every Pot," has never carried a single precinct. The building that contains the movie house, now called the Eighth Street Playhouse, at street level and the Village Barn in the basement is one of the properties from Abrams' early real estate days that he has held on to. In partnership with his brother Ralph, he has since invested in some other movie houses, including Cinema I and Cinema II, on Third Avenue. The theatres not only bring him in a good return but give him the privilege, any time he likes, of strolling in to see a movie without paying, which he does with the conspicuously nonchalant air of a small boy who half expects to be picked up by the scruff of the neck and tossed out.

All this real estate speculation may have been an unlikely form of preparation for a career as a reformer, but Abrams values it as having been fundamental to his education, as well as to his financial security His real estate transactions gave him a worm's-eye view of the housing picture and an intimate acquaintance with what are generally called practical affairs – two credentials that few of his colleagues in the reform camp possess – and thus made it possible for him to move on to the activity he likes to call "finagling for society." His first opportunity for this sort of finagling came in 1933. As that rarity, a lawyer who combined a detailed knowledge of real estate with a liberal social outlook, he was named by Mayor Fiorello LaGuardia as one of a team of three lawyers who were to draft a new state housing bill. This bill, which ultimately became known as the Municipal Housing Authorities Law, was the basic legislation under which the New York City Housing Authority was established, and it became the model enabling act for the country as a whole, on the basis of which a total of more than two thousand local housing authorities have since been formed. It was a piece of legislation asserting a social principle that was new to the United States – that since private enterprise manifestly could not clear slums and provide decent housing for people of low incomes, some government agency would have to do it if it was to be done at all. Nowadays, Abrams, after more than thirty years of worldwide experience, can bat out a complicated housing or city-planning law in short order; a lengthy, detailed bill that he and Dr Otto Koenigsberger, a tropical-housing expert, prepared for Pakistan in 1957 while on a UN mission to that country took them only ten days to draft. But it took Abrams and his two colleagues on the 1933 committee – Carl Stern and Ira Robbins – nearly three months to draw up the much shorter Municipal Housing Authorities Law. They were aware that although the concept of public housing had been accepted in Europe for thirty or forty years, its introduction into the United States was bound to be attacked as a dangerous heresy, a forerunner of Socialism, a threat to the American Home and the American Way of Life. Inevitably, they knew, the law's constitutionality would be challenged, and they were determined that there should be no technical flaws in it. "We agonized over every comma of that law," Abrams recalls.

The housing problem as we know it is a product of the industrial revolution and the complex cities that it required and engendered. Almost everywhere, as industrialization has progressed, the state has felt compelled, for the sake of the public welfare, to show an increasing concern and assume an increasing responsibility for the habitations of its populace. This change in governmental attitude constitutes one of the dramatic historical changes of our era, Abrams notes in a volume called *Urban Land Problems and Policies*. He wrote,

In the eighteenth century the elder Pitt, Earl of Chatham, could declaim that "the poorest man in his cottage could defy the King – the storms may enter; the rain may enter – but the King of England cannot enter; all his forces dare not cross the threshold of the ruined tenement." But in the twentieth century, the king (or his counterpart, the state) may enter for the very purpose of keeping the wind and rain from entering. The "ruined tenement" has become a matter of state concern.[2]

The most important housing legislation in the US prior to the Municipal Housing Authorities Law had been the Tenement House Act of 1901, brought into being by disclosures of slum life horrors by such crusading humanitarians as Jacob Riis and Felix Adler. Humane and enlightened as the 1901 regulations and restrictions were, the Act itself brought no new housing into being. The slums continued to grow, and the need for decent new housing increased. By 1933, therefore, when Abrams, Stern, and Robbins sat down to draft the Municipal Housing Authorities Law, reformers were ready to turn from restrictive to constructive legislation. It was time, they felt, for the city itself, or some other agency, to build the housing that private enterprise could not supply. And because this moment – the first year of the New Deal after three years of depression – was a time of social experimentation, the new doctrine stood a good chance of acceptance. To many New Dealers, public housing was an appealing idea not only on humanitarian grounds but as a means of pumping life back into the economy. The very inefficiency of the home-construction industry, the country's most backward in its methods, appeared a virtue in the eyes of some Brain Trusters; a public housing program, they believed, would be a dandy way of creating a lot of jobs and spending a lot of public money. In retrospect, Abrams thinks that the public housing program has suffered from this initial confusion of purposes; it still operates under fossilized principles that were well suited to a time of depression but are not at all appropriate in today's inflationary, expansionist economy. "There are Newtonian laws in politics as well as in physics," he says. "A reform set in motion continues in motion long beyond the time when the reform itself needs reforming."

Early in 1934, shortly after the bill that Abrams worked on had been passed and the New York City Housing Authority had officially come into being, the Authority's chairman, Langdon Post, asked Abrams to serve as legal counsel in getting the agency started on its program. In that capacity, he devoted himself ardently to the work of the Housing Authority during its first three years – years that he recalls as in some ways the most exciting period of his life. Age-old prejudices were dissolving, injustices were being corrected, and a better, fairer, more humane world was in the making – or so, at any rate it seemed to him, and to many another idealistic young man inspired by the New Deal. There were innumerable things, large and small, to be done in getting the Housing Authority under way, and Abrams was involved in most of them. There were hearings to be held, surveys to be made, policies to be determined, contracts to be negotiated, opponents to be debated, impatient tenants' groups to be placated or exhorted, budgets to be drawn up, and interminable conferences with governmental officials to be attended. There were hasty trips to Washington for sessions with Senator Robert F. Wagner, with Harry Hopkins (who was to become Works Progress Administrator), with Secretary of the Treasury Henry Morgenthau, and with Secretary of the Interior Harold Ickes, among others – sometimes to solve New York City problems and sometimes to discuss the content and strategy of the national public housing bill that Senator Wagner was introducing, and plan strategy for getting it through Congress.

Throughout the New York City Housing Authority's early days, millions of dollars were allocated to it on paper, but it had no cash to speak of. Early in January 1934, Secretary Ickes, who was in charge of the Public Works Administration, sent a telegram to Mayor LaGuardia saying that he had earmarked twenty-five million dollars for the New York City Housing Authority; unfortunately, it took two and a half years to extract these funds from him. If ever a man was out of place as head of an emergency agency whose job was to pour out money like water in order to prime the economic pump, it was Ickes. An honest and fearless tightwad, Ickes had risen to prominence battling the graft and corruption of the Chicago city machine, and now that power had been put in his hands, he trusted nobody in the world except himself, acted on the theory that all local officials were crooks, suspected the other cabinet members of plotting against him, and tapped the telephone wires of his subordinates. Abrams and Post battled Ickes desperately for the funds the New York City Housing Authority had been promised, but Ickes, hating to part with even a penny of the tremendous amount he had been given to spend, kept setting new requirements and finding other new reasons for delay. Meanwhile, the Housing Authority, itself ill-housed in some cramped offices at 10 East Fortieth Street, was trying at least to draw up some grand plans on a pittance of twelve thousand dollars that the city administration had lent it.

Obviously, this sum wasn't going to go very far, even though Abrams and other officials volunteered to work without recompense until the

Housing Authority became solvent. After a few months, Post and Abrams decided that the Authority had better get going somehow on its own, without waiting for Ickes' largesse. Putting their heads together, they contrived (or perhaps Abrams' word "finagled" is the perfect one here) a financing scheme as unorthodox as any public body ever employed – one that provided certain poetic satisfactions as well as badly needed cash. Post, a man of inherited wealth that derived from real estate (including, as he was regretfully aware, some slum properties), was a dashing, idealistic figure of patrician bearing. As it happened, he was Tenement House Commissioner as well as chairman of the City Housing Authority. At the time he assumed the former office, in January, the city had suffered a number of disastrous tenement fires, and he set to work to apply the provisions of the law more rigorously than previous commissioners had. The owners of many of the most dilapidated tenements thereupon chose to close up their buildings rather than go to the expense of fireproofing them and otherwise bringing them into conformity with the law, and soon nearly two thousand tenement houses, many of them on the Lower East Side, were standing boarded up and vacant. The idea that Post and Abrams conceived was to offer to tear down these buildings free of charge if the owners would let the Housing Authority have whatever proceeds could be realized from the sale of the bricks, plumbing, and other scrap that was salvaged. Most of the owners were only too glad to accept the offer, because the vacant tenements presented a serious hazard for which the landlords remained legally liable. A force of WPA workers recruited from Harry Hopkins' agency by Post, a man with a good many friends in the Roosevelt inner circle, performed the labor of demolition and salvage, tearing down well over a thousand slum tenements during the next two years. This form of slum clearance, in itself a satisfaction to housing reformers, ultimately brought the Housing Authority more than half a million dollars, and was its only source of funds, aside from the city's loan, until 1937. Not only did this money permit the Authority to go ahead and prepare the housing program it planned to put into effect when it finally received its federal allocation but it made possible the actual construction of a small housing project on the Lower East Side at Avenue A and East Third Street. Called First Houses, this group of buildings was opened with great ceremony on December 3, 1935 – the first public housing project in America.

This whole financing operation was, of course, a highly irregular demonstration of public enterprise. Shortly after First Houses was opened, the City Comptroller, awakened to the situation by the fanfare, sent the Authority a letter saying that the funds from the salvaged materials should have gone to the city treasury and peremptorily demanding that the Authority make good the treasury's loss. Abrams, worried, set to work on a tortured brief, attempting to justify, with solemn citations and footnotes, the Authority's right to the money. As he was going over his arguments with the Authority's commissioners before sending off the brief, he was interrupted by one of them – B. Charney Vladeck, the general manager of the *Jewish Daily Forward* and New York's first Socialist city councilman. Vladeck, as a young man in Russia, had once been under a sentence of death for revolutionary activities, and he was not much frightened by the fulminations of the City Comptroller. "So he says we stole the money?" Vladeck asked, with a shrug. "So all right. What are you worrying about? Did we use it for ourselves? Don't you know that as long as you act in the public interest who cares which pocket the money goes into? Forget it. The public wants decent housing."

Of all the matters that Abrams was involved in during his years as counsel to the Authority, undoubtedly the most important was the Muller case, which was the major legal test of the Municipal Housing Authorities Law and the one that established beyond question the city's right to institute eminent-domain proceedings when balked by unwilling property owners in acquiring housing sites. This right is taken for granted now, but in the early days nobody was sure that the courts would uphold it. The case involved two pieces of property owned by one Andrew Muller on the run-down block selected for First Houses. The rest of the site had belonged to Vincent Astor, who had willingly sold his holdings to the Authority. Muller refused to come to terms. When it became apparent that negotiations would get nowhere, Abrams suggested to the Authority that the time had come for a test case. Some of the commissioners were dubious, fearing that loss of the case would jeopardize the whole public housing program. Mayor LaGuardia flatly advised against it, thinking it was too big a gamble. Abrams nevertheless got permission to go ahead, and, having done a notable job of preparing his argument, was victorious both in the lower courts and in the appellate division. "If Abrams hadn't pressed the Muller case and won it, there would be no public housing today," Post said later. For that matter, there might be no Stuyvesant Town, no Coliseum, and no Lincoln Center, either, for all these developments involved the exercise of eminent domain to acquire property for an avowed public purpose. And whenever this purpose was challenged in the courts, lawyers defending the developments cited the Muller case as the precedent.

After First Houses, large projects were constructed in Harlem and in Abrams' own boyhood neighborhood of Williamsburg, and, as more federal funds were pried loose from Mr Ickes, a number of other projects were started. In 1937, Congress passed the Wagner–Steagall housing bill, and the United States Housing Administration was established, under the direction of Nathan Straus, who said that just about everything that he knew about housing at the time he had learned from Abrams. By the end of that year, when Abrams left the Housing Authority – doing so, typically, in a blaze of public fireworks as a result of a policy disagreement with LaGuardia – the wild, freewheeling days were over and the form that public housing was to take from then on had been pretty well determined. Since those tentative beginnings, the New York City Housing Authority has changed the face of the city drastically, becoming in the process the nation's largest landlord, with assets of almost two billion dollars, and with about half a million tenants living in the hundred and forty-three thousand apartments it has constructed.

Despite such statistics, it is now generally recognized that the public housing program in the United States has not fulfilled the perhaps over-enthusiastic expectations of its early advocates. In terms of such amenities as yard space, sunlight, and ventilation, the public projects are undoubtedly more salubrious than the rotting tenements they replaced – indeed, as Lewis Mumford has often pointed out, they are probably superior in these respects to most Park Avenue luxury apartments – but the majority of them are stamped with a dreary, institutionalized look, and all of them are administered under a rigid code of petty regulations calculated to distress any self-respecting tenant. Furthermore, the social benefits of housing project occupancy have not been all that the reformers had hoped for; changing the physical environment of onetime slum dwellers has not reduced the incidence of crime, delinquency, and disease to the extent anticipated. Throughout the years since the program came into existence, Abrams, while devoting energy and ingenuity to furthering the cause of public housing in this country, has at the same time been one of the most persistent critics of the direction that the program has taken. He deplores the poorhouse atmosphere and stigma that have become attached to the projects. "Why do housing projects all have to look like housing projects?" he asks. If he had his way, public housing developments would not bear distinguishing names, on the order of George Washington Carver Houses, but would simply have street addresses like all other apartment buildings. They would be smaller structures, too – "vest-pocket projects" – which would not dominate their neighborhoods. A more fundamental change that Abrams would like to make would be to do away with the government's present policy of evicting tenants whose incomes rise above the modest amount that is now stipulated as the maximum income for project tenants:

No penalty should be put upon ambition so that the moment a family improves its income, it is forced to pull the children out of school, give up neighborhood associations, and move back to a slum. If the tenant earns more money, he should be required to pay a higher rent, at which time he ceases to be subsidized. He should be looked upon as a potential prospect for a non-subsidized dwelling unit,

Charles Abrams 383

not as a permanent charity case whose ascent from poverty is regarded as a violation of lease. Projects should be built not as almshouses but as attractive additions
to the urban scene, fit for families of improved income. The misassumption of
public housing has been that there will always be stratified classes in the United
States and that stratified projects must be their permanent habitat.

Actually, Abrams would go beyond merely permitting tenants to keep
their apartments and pay increased rent as their incomes rose. One of his
more unorthodox proposals – which has nevertheless begun to win favor
recently – is that tenants who improve themselves economically should
be permitted to buy their apartments from the government if they wish,
so that over a period of time many projects could become private coopera-
tives. Though Abrams believes as strongly as ever that a government
concerned about the welfare of its people is duty bound to supply housing
for those whom private enterprise has neglected, he sees no inherent
virtue in the government's continuing to own and manage all the housing
once it is built. In fact, he thinks it would be better all around if the
government did not continue to play the role of landlord. "To accomplish
certain ends in a complex modern civilization we have to use the methods
of socialism, but we should also be continually de-socializing as we go
along," he says. It is propositions like this that have given Abrams his
reputation as perhaps the most flexible and original mind in his field.
Catherine Bauer Wurster, one of the crew of New Dealers who conceived
the first federal public housing legislation, once said of him, in a tone of
exasperated admiration, "Charlie has always kept all his friends and
allies off balance. He is continually questioning and rethinking the ideas
and fundamental beliefs for which all of us, including him, have fought
and bled."

When the United States public housing law was drawn up, one of its
essential components was the slum-clearance requirement; one slum
dwelling unit had to be destroyed for every public dwelling unit built.
Abrams took great satisfaction in that provision at the time, but he now
regrets that it has stayed on the books, virtually unchanged, ever since.
He sees its persistence as another illustration of his political Newtonian
law. "The slum-clearance policy made sense during the Depression,
when there were many apartment vacancies, but it is unworkable in a
period of housing shortage," he says. Since the Second World War, when
the shortage first became acute, he has been trying with no success to get
the United States to alter its policy sufficiently to build primarily on
vacant or underdeveloped land. Unfortunately, he and his fellow-
reformers made such a powerful impression in the old days that he has
found it all but impossible to change the course of the program he and
they helped set in motion. He's had much more luck at getting across-the-
board slum-clearance operations suspended in Africa, South America,

and Asia than in the United States. The painfulness of the whole operation here at home is exacerbated for him by the fact that slum clearance
has nowadays become almost synonymous with Negro clearance, since it
is Negroes who currently occupy most of the urban slums.

As a matter of fact, Abrams sometimes wishes that the concept of the
slum had never been formulated, for he has come to regard it as a misleading one. "I'm no longer as sure as I once was that I know what I'm
talking about when I describe some district as a 'slum,'" he says. In
drafting housing legislation in the New Deal era, he and his colleagues
tended to define slum housing or substandard housing according to
specific physical criteria — windowless rooms, inadequate toilet
facilities, sagging ceilings, wooden stairways that had not been made fire-
resistant, and the like — and slum-clearance agencies throughout the
nation are still using these criteria, almost unchanged, in determining
which houses and neighborhoods are to be demolished as slums. But
Abrams, with long years of experience under his belt, now prefers to
judge a housing situation according to much broader and subtler considerations. He said recently to the students in one of his Columbia
seminars,

You can't necessarily tell whether a family is happily or wretchedly housed by
using a standard that takes account only of the physical attributes of the building
it's living in. A family may dwell in contentment in a rickety shack without
plumbing if the shack happens to be in a lovely rural setting. An ex-urbanite's
mansion on a five-acre plot may have all the latest conveniences and gadgets and
yet be basically a miserable housing situation if the owner finds himself having to
commute for an hour and a half every morning to his work through snarled-up
traffic, and if his wife and children are pining for diversion and company. In the
city, a banker's family may be considered ill-housed in a thousand-dollar-a-month
apartment if jackhammers and steam shovels are everlastingly shattering their
peace or if they have disagreeable relations with their neighbors, while for the
family of a [—Abrams paused and grinned—] of a pickled-herring vender in a
tenement apartment on the Lower East Side amid neighbors and friends who care
about them and share their troubles and triumphs, and with all sorts of shops and
lively activities right at hand, such a tenement, despite the bathtub in the kitchen
and the railroad layout of the place and the insufficiency of sunshine and fresh air,
may be (I say, *may* be, mind you) a better, richer housing situation than anything
that city planners and bureaucrats are apt to provide as a substitute.

When Abrams resigned from the New York City Housing Authority in
1937 after clashing with LaGuardia, he was given a demonstration of how
rough the Little Flower could play when crossed. From the start, the
strong-willed Mayor had been annoyed with Abrams for daring to have a
mind of his own about housing matters. They had disagreed over whether
the Housing Authority should be dominated by the Mayor or should be,
as Abrams advocated (and as it later became), a semi-autonomous municipal corporation. And LaGuardia, who had made his peace with Ickes,

had been exceedingly annoyed when Adams continued to push for a federal housing program that was independent of Ickes (a campaign that was ultimately successful). After Abrams' ouster, the Mayor got further steamed up when the press lambasted him for forcing Abrams' resignation, and his volatile temper boiled over when Abrams, defending himself during a radio interview against disparaging comments by the Mayor, pointed out that the Housing Authority had been forced to resort to all sorts of expedients during most of its existence because its only support from the LaGuardia administration had been a measly twelve-thousand-dollar loan. No reactionary can aggravate a reformer more than can a fellow-reformer who is accusing him of being less than wholehearted about his reform efforts; no battles in public life are apt to be more sanguinary than those between two fervent liberals, differing over aspects of policy and tactics that to the public appear trivial but that to those concerned loom as irreconcilable. Vowing that he would teach Abrams a lesson, the Mayor had his subordinates draw up a list of the buildings that Abrams owned, and he took this list over to the Buildings Department himself and ordered, "Slap these places with every violation you can find!" The man who was then Deputy Buildings Commissioner, Harry Prince, has said that this was the only time he ever saw LaGuardia use this particular kind of roughhouse tactics against a political foe. Over the next few days, inspectors swarmed through Abrams' buildings, listing one transgression after another. Some of the buildings had been given routine inspections just a short while before and had been declared satisfactory, but the New York City building code is such a hodgepodge that an inspector who puts his mind to it can find violations in any building. This was comically illustrated during the LaGuardia blitz of Abrams' properties. By mistake, LaGuardia's avenging inspectors had 29 Washington Square West, an imposing, deluxe apartment house, listed as belonging to Abrams, so they descended upon it. The actual owner was flabbergasted when the inspectors began combing it as if it were a festering menace to the city's health and welfare. It was then virtually a new building, had passed a complete inspection not long before, and subsequently became the New York address of Mrs Franklin Delano Roosevelt.

This experience cost Abrams several thousand dollars and some of his idealism – or, at any rate, his political innocence. For all his disagreements with LaGuardia, he had admired the Mayor immensely as a fighter for human rights, and had not been in the least prepared for such a demonstration of political ruthlessness. In his distress, Abrams decided to wash his hands of public affairs forever and concentrate on the private practice of law. This resolve lasted for four days – until the first private client came into his office. As the client began detailing his petty grievances, Abrams' heart sank. He realized at that moment that, having been stirred by great public issues and having known the satisfaction of helping to determine public policy and thus affect the lives of great numbers of people, he could never be content to serve only narrow private interests. But since he also realized that his high-spirited nature was ill suited to the routines of bureaucracy, he decided that he would have to serve the public privately – that is, in his own way. He thereupon began carving out his special niche as a freelance, freewheeling combination of reformer and expert. He started writing his first book, *Revolution in Land*, which, on its publication in 1939, Lewis Mumford described as the first really important word on the subject of the social occupancy and control of land since the writings of Henry George, and which sold a thousand and nine copies. He began teaching courses in housing and land economics at the New School for Social Research, and later at other institutions, including MIT. He turned out pamphlets, made speeches, wrote articles for the *Nation* and the *New Leader*, appeared as an expert witness before congressional committees, showered advice on government agencies that would have been just as happy without it, criticized most of what was being done about housing in this country, and, upon being challenged to make constructive proposals instead of merely sniping from the sidelines, went ahead and, to the annoyance of his challengers, drew up detailed plans for what he believed should be done.

In 1942, Local 32-B of the Building Service Employees Union sought a wage increase, and when the members of the New York Real Estate Board pleaded that they couldn't afford to grant it, the union got Abrams to testify before an arbitration board, as an expert real estate operator, that real estate management was making ample profits. The Real Estate Board countered with a surprise witness – Abrams' own business manager, who testified that Abrams' buildings were losing money. It was a blow aimed at discrediting both Abrams' acumen as an operator and his repute as an expert. Abrams sought and got permission to cross-examine his manager, and by the time he had finished, he had elicited information that showed his buildings to be, in fact, making a handsome profit of thirty per cent. The building employees got their raise.

Through the years, whenever housing, racial discrimination, or a similar cause has been at issue, and a worthy organization concerned with such matters has needed someone to address a meeting, the organization has been able to count on Abrams no matter how short the notice or how far away he might be.

The only problem is that you can never count on him to say just what you want him to [the director of one such organization says]. Most of the time he's magnificent – rousing, informed, warm, humorous, challenging, constructive. But every once in a while he'll come up with some odd idea out of nowhere – something he is probably mulling over tentatively. He'll present it as if it were gospel and derail everything. That's the chance you take, but it's worth it.

An architect who has known Abrams for a long time has found that whenever he runs into Abrams, the effect on him is always unsettling. "Charlie is always doing something new," the architect said. "He's always blithely taking on some huge new project or campaign, or decrying some new outrage. And as he goes off, at that ambling gait of his, I just stand there, saying to myself, 'Brother, I'm sure in a rut.'" In whatever Abrams has undertaken, he has seldom been content to play just one role. More often, like a gabby Marcel Marceau, he has played all, or nearly all, the parts there were. For instance, in 1949, when a major federal housing bill – what became the Taft–Ellender–Wagner Act – was being considered, Abrams played the parts of the sober expert, giving legal and technical advice to the framers of the legislation; of the passionate agitator, delivering speeches and writing articles in support of the bill; and then, after it was passed by Congress, he played the part of minstrel. He wrote songs, skits, and lampoons for a victory celebration that was held at the Mayflower Hotel in Washington, and himself gleefully breezed out on the ballroom floor and performed them for his audience. One of his comic songs caused the usually dour Senator Robert Taft to roar with laughter, and Abrams still cherishes that moment. "I'll bet there aren't many people who can say they made Senator Taft laugh," he likes to boast.

Shortly after the Second World War, Abrams embarked on a new enterprise, becoming a special reporter and housing expert for the New York *Post*. Having been given a free hand by the paper, he was able to keep City Hall in a gratifying turmoil with his denunciations of slums and segregation, and he had a fine time thinking up vast city housing programs, providing handy instructions for financing, legislating, and administering them, and then agitating for their adoption in article after article – exhorting the public, badgering Mayor William O'Dwyer, and lambasting that grand panjandrum, Robert Moses, who was then the city's housing coordinator, for being picayune. ("Moses – Or Houses?" was the title of one article.) His campaigns succeeded surprisingly often, ending sometimes with Mayor O'Dwyer telephoning the *Post*'s publisher and saying wearily, "Tell Charlie he can lay off now – we're going to come through on that idea of his." In 1948, he pushed through in this way a public housing scheme for middle-income families, under which about thirty thousand apartments, with a total value of five hundred million dollars, have been built so far; the scheme, which is self-supporting and requires no cash subsidies, is nowadays regarded as one of the more successful elements of the city's housing program. After his middle-income housing campaign was put across, Abrams started in on a campaign to get the city to put up a hundred thousand dollars for rat control in the tenement districts. Around this time, O'Dwyer, fed up with Abrams' articles, offered to create a cushy position for him as special housing consultant to the Mayor; all Abrams would be expected to do would be to drop in at Gracie Mansion now and then and give the Mayor the benefit of his advice in a friendly chat instead of splashing it before the public. "Would I be expected to give up my column?" Abrams asked O'Dwyer suspiciously. "Well, that goes without saying," O'Dwyer replied. Abrams declined, with thanks, and went back to writing for the *Post*, which he continued to do for another year, leaving after the paper's ownership changed hands.

Yet another of Abrams' activities, utilizing yet another of his talents, was, from time to time, to take on socially significant court cases without fee. Unquestionably the most significant of these was the one known as *Dorsey* v. *Stuyvesant Town*, which was initiated in 1947. At issue was a decision by the Metropolitan Life Insurance Company to rent apartments in its Stuyvesant Town development only to whites. Abrams, representing three Negroes who had been turned down as tenants, argued that this was unconstitutional. To encourage the construction of Stuyvesant Town, the city had granted Metropolitan Life tax concessions worth an estimated seventy-five million dollars and had also used its condemnation and eviction powers to help the corporation acquire the site. While the case was being argued, the insurance company's attorney, Samuel Seabury, confronted Abrams with the precedent of Abrams' own Muller case, saying that it provided the legal basis for Metropolitan's development of Stuyvesant Town, and that he was therefore nonplussed to find Abrams challenging the project. Abrams replied that he was challenging the project's policy of selecting tenants, not its policy of acquiring land. Since the corporation had accepted extraordinary public assistance, Abrams argued, it had no right to describe itself as just an ordinary landlord, whose tenant-selection policy was a private matter. He took the position that a landlord who availed himself of government powers and government financial assistance was under the same constitutional obligation as the government itself not to discriminate against citizens because of their race. This case, as Abrams has pointed out in *Forbidden Neighbors*, an impassioned book he wrote eight years afterward on housing discrimination in America, clearly stated for the first time the constitutional dilemma posed by a partnership between government and private enterprise – a kind of partnership that was being entered into increasingly often for urban development projects of various kinds. The legal issue, he has written, was whether "what the government itself could not do constitutionally it *could* do through an agent using its power and aid," and the moral issue was which ethics would prevail in this partnership – the higher public ethics of the government or the private ethics of the marketplace. Abrams lost his case in the Court of Appeals by a four-to-three decision, but the litigation excited much public concern, and in 1950 the New York State Legislature passed a law applying the principles he had laid down to all projects built with government aid. (A few years later, Abrams found himself administering and enforcing this law as chairman of the New York State Commission Against Discrimination.) Since then, of course, the City Council and the New York State Legislature have gone even further, and it is now against the law here to discriminate against a tenant on racial or religious grounds in any apartment house or development, private or public.

Before Abrams became chairman of the State Commission Against Discrimination in December 1955, he served Governor Averell Harriman's administration for a year as the State Rent Administrator. Here, he headed a chaotic organization whose function was to deal with about a half-million complaints a year. These came from tenants who were angry about their landlords, their rents, their services, or about rat and insect infestations of their buildings, and from landlords claiming financial losses, demanding rent increases, and vituperating against the behavior and base character of tenants. Emotions ran high. Occasionally, Abrams' morning mail would include a whopping cockroach that an irate tenant had captured and sent along to dramatize his complaint. No rats were ever received, mercifully, but one of Abrams' predecessors once got slugged by a tenant just as he was stepping out of his limousine to enter the commission's offices; thereafter, rent commissioners always sneaked in and out the back way. In theory, Abrams has always disapproved of rent control, as a measure that discourages incentive to new construction and private enterprise, but during the acute housing shortage that then prevailed he felt it to be necessary. At one point, when he learned that a deal was being arranged between Democratic and Republican leaders in the legislature quietly to scuttle rent control, Abrams raised such a public furor that the deal had to be called off.

At the State Commission Against Discrimination, when Abrams took over, the tempo was very different from what it was at the Rent Control Commission. Everything went smoothly and quietly. Voices were not raised. The prevailing tone was one of tranquillity, order, conciliation, caution, gentility, respectability. Only a few hundred complaints came in each year, and they were processed with grave decorum. This was the way the agency had operated since its establishment, in 1945, as a result of the passage of the bipartisan Ives–Quinn bill prohibiting discrimination in employment. At the time, this was a legislative experiment without precedent; the New York State Commission Against Discrimination was the first agency of its kind to be established in this country. In administering the law, the emphasis was placed on doing nothing that would alarm the general public or offend powerful interests, and this was probably sound strategy at the outset, for the success of the law depended almost entirely on the degree of public cooperation it could command. Aggressive administration was not needed at the beginning anyway; the mere existence of a law stating, for the first time, that "practices of discrimination against any of its inhabitants because of race, creed, or color or national origin are a matter of state concern" and that "such discrimination not only threatens the rights and proper privileges of its inhabitants but menaces the institutions and foundation of a free democratic state" had a powerful effect. Major corporations, whose respectability was an important part of their stock in trade, had no wish to be lawbreakers, so they immediately began making significant changes in their hiring practices. One such firm was the Metropolitan Life Insurance Company. This company carried life insurance policies on two and a half million Negroes throughout the country – and up until quite recently had been one of the few major firms willing to regard Negroes as insurable human beings. But though it considered them insurable, it had never considered them employable, even in the menial capacity of janitor or charwoman. Not a single Negro employee of any sort was to be found in the home office or in any of its thirteen hundred district offices, including the ones in Harlem and other Negro areas. Nor, if the law had not been passed, would any change have been made, the company's officers have since conceded. But when the law *was* passed, the officers met and decided that it was their duty not only to comply but to do so wholeheartedly. Everybody within the organization was informed unequivocally of this decision. There would be no subterfuges, no secret marks designating race or religion on personnel cards; there would be no special considerations in hiring, assignment, or promotion. Within a decade after this decision, Metropolitan Life was employing in its home office some six hundred Negroes (exact figures were not available, since no records of the employees' race were kept) in a wide variety of positions, including some on the junior supervisory level. From all over the country, executives of other corporations came to Metropolitan Life's home offices to learn how this had been achieved and to see for themselves how it was working out. Abrams later said, "If the law had done nothing more than make it possible for Metropolitan Life to change its hiring practices, it would still have been a most important piece of legislation." The New York experiment was watched closely, and within ten years nine states and some thirty cities passed similar laws.

But by the time of Abrams' appointment to SCAD there were many who felt that New York had lost its leadership in the battle against discrimination. Even among those who had initially favored caution, the quiet, conservative approach was considered to have accomplished its purpose and to be no longer appropriate. Among civil rights organizations, New York's SCAD had fallen into some disrepute. It was said that it worked so quietly that most Negroes did not even know it existed, and so slowly that by the time it issued a ruling the victim had forgotten what it was he had complained about. Negroes were no longer as gratified as they had been a decade before by a company's willingness to hire a token Negro as a stenographer, or even to promote a Negro to a junior supervisory position. Housing segregation, with all its disagreeable consequences, had come to be recognized as a major problem, and, partly as a result, new powers and responsibilities had been entrusted to SCAD by the state legislature. The agency was now responsible for preventing racial discrimination in housing built with public assistance and in all sorts of public accommodations, and also for preventing discrimination in employment on account of age or sex. Governor Harriman's appointment of Abrams was explicitly intended to breathe new life into the agency. Abrams was supposed to shake things up, and he did. In an interview shortly after taking up his new position, he remarked, "At the Rent Control Commission, my job was to make order out of chaos. Here, I would say, my job is to make chaos out of order."

Abrams' appointment created a stir that his subsequent activities did little to abate. A few months after he took office, Oswald Heck, the Republican leader who was Speaker of the Assembly, objected that Abrams was too much of a zealot to head so sensitive an agency. A semantic fracas ensued, with arguments over whether Abrams was or was not a "zealot," and whether that was a good or a bad thing to be. Fourteen civil rights organizations drafted a letter to the press backing Abrams and demanding to know when zeal had come to be a liability for those in public office, and Governor Harriman startled a group of businessmen and industrialists gathered for luncheon at the Bankers' Club in order to discuss discriminatory employment practices by addressing them as "fellow-zealots." As for Abrams, his comment on the accusation was, "Well, now I can truly say I've been called everything from A to Z." Some months later, on Abrams' first anniversary as head of SCAD, he received in the mail letters of commendation from two disparate sources. One was from the militant Negro labor leader A. Philip Randolph, president of the Brotherhood of Sleeping Car Porters. It read, "May I say that your leadership of this Commission represents a fine and constructive force in the worldwide movement for human rights." The other letter was from Thomas Jefferson Miley, executive vice-president of the Commerce and Industry Association of New York, an organization representing possibly the greatest concentration of wealth in the United States. Miley wrote, "If you had asked a group of businessmen ten years ago, the things that you have accomplished in the past year would have been considered impossible. You're a great leader and, to my mind, a man of great integrity. It has been a delight to work with you." Abrams read the two letters, gazed at the ceiling, blew a thoughtful cloud of cigar smoke into the air, and said to his secretary, "Take a poem, Miss Kaslow." The poem went:

> When Randolph and Jefferson Miley
> Both praise a zealot so highly,
> Then this zealot, by Heck,
> Should not his zeal check,
> But foster it ever more spryly.

Under Abrams, who served as chairman of SCAD until Nelson Rockefeller took over from Harriman in 1959, the agency's case load soon tripled. No longer did the Commission bask in quiet obscurity. The civil rights and civic organizations were pleased with the new turn of affairs, and made sure that Abrams knew it. He himself was less satisfied, and said he sometimes thought that citizens' groups ought to be goading him harder. Once, after a session with the Legislature at which he felt his proposals had been less bold than they should have been, he was heard to exclaim, "How I wish I were out of office for a couple of days! Boy, would I blast me!" He sought to improve on the slow, haphazard, case-by-case approach that the Commission had theretofore relied on, and to bring about industrywide agreements affecting tens of thousands of people at a stroke. Instead of waiting to take steps after a complaint had come in, he had his Commission initiate investigations wherever they appeared to be warranted. He set up a research program to analyze in some depth the nature and causes of discrimination in the State. And he applied all his ingenuity to the thinking up of what he calls "gimmicks" – administrative devices or economic instrumentalities to effect social change. One gimmick was an arrangement he made with the New York City Department of Licenses providing for revocation of the licences of private employment agencies – some of which had been less than scrupulous – if they did not abide by the law. Another gimmick was an agreement he worked out with the Federal Housing Administration and with the Veterans Administration to bar federal assistance to any builder found violating the state anti-discrimination law. This represented the first time the federal government had agreed to act in support of a state's civil rights law. Contrasting Abrams with his predecessors, Herbert Hill, the labor relations secretary for the National Association for the Advancement of Colored People, said, "At last the agency has a real expert at its head, not just a well-meaning but cautious gentleman with his heart in the right place. The Commissioners before him would merely say, 'Bring us in your complaints, Mr Hill, and we'll process them.'"

In 1956, an outcry arose when it was discovered that banks and insurance companies consistently refused to take the risk of making housing and improvement loans in Harlem and other ghettos, and Governor Harriman sought Abrams' advice. Abrams thought there was little to be gained either by threatening to punish these financial organizations or by appealing to their selflessness. Instead, he set about devising an instrumentality that would not only minimize the risk for them but hold out the possibility of new profits. He called it the Mortgage Facilities Corporation, and defined it as a kind of banking syndicate, or cooperative, in which all the major banks and insurance companies would participate. The scheme was endorsed by the Governor, the banks and insurance companies agreed to try it, and a revolving fund of twenty million dollars was established by the state legislature. Governor Harriman considered the creation of the Mortgage Facilities Corporation an impressive example of Abrams' practicality on behalf of the ideal.

Harriman, though he had never met Abrams before appointing him to his cabinet, soon became fond of his company, and there was a kind of meeting of spirit between these two men of very different backgrounds. Once, after a late-afternoon session at the Governor's Mansion, Harriman invited Abrams to take a dip in the pool with him, and Abrams remembers that scene as illustrating two contrasting approaches to life. "The Governor didn't have to impress anybody, and he never had had to," Abrams says. "He just lay on his back and floated while I, the ambitious underling, raced furiously up and down the pool with the windmill stroke I had learned at Bershadsky's Baths until I was absolutely exhausted."

Despite all his work at SCAD, Abrams still found energy while there to keep an eye on the housing situation on every level, from the local to the global. Every Friday, he went to Cambridge for the day to conduct classes at MIT, and during his summer vacations he would take on UN missions, leaving New York not for the cool seashore but for the slums of some tropical country so hot, crowded, dirty, and noisy as to make New York City in the summer seem by comparison a paradise. One summer he went to the Philippines, and another summer his mission took him to Pakistan, where he arrived in the middle of a heat wave. For one steaming day after another, the temperature hovered around a hundred and five degrees. Swallowing salt tablets to ward off heat prostration and handfuls of sulfa pills as a protection against dysentery, Abrams bustled about the country, visiting almost every city of any size and inspecting its slums, its new developments, its refugee camps, and its flimsy shacktowns and squatters' communities. He was in Pakistan for four weeks, during which time, teaming up with Dr Koenigsberger, who had accompanied him on five UN missions, he drafted a housing and planning law, drew up a memorandum on financing the program and outlined in detail a constructive approach to coping with the squatter problem. Then, his vacation over, he flew back to New York, looking thoroughly refreshed. Encountering one of his staff members in the corridor as he stepped out of the elevator on the morning he returned to work, Abrams greeted him cheerfully with "Hi, Dick! Now, about those airlines that are resisting hiring Negroes for flight positions," picking up – like the irrepressible Bearded Lady, in Stravinsky's "The Rake's Progress," who resumes in mid-syllable the aria she has interrupted in the previous act – right where he had left off a month before.

Abrams has headed Columbia University's Division of Urban Planning only since the fall of 1965, having at that time given up his connection with MIT. He enjoys teaching, and he is good at it. He is easy and informal with his students, and he keeps himself readily accessible. After class, he may linger for as long as half an hour, surrounded by students who are eager to go on discussing the questions he has raised. The students place particular value on his wide range of practical experience, for very few of their professors have been as active in the non-academic world as Abrams. Columbia's Urban Planning Division has never been a very strong one, and it is Abrams' aim to strengthen it. Enrollment in the Division has already increased fourfold since his appointment. An Institute of Urban Environment has been established, under his aegis, and, with the help of a $400,000 grant from the Ford Foundation, he has introduced several courses on housing in underdeveloped areas – the first such courses to be given in an American university – and hopes to train a crop of young experts who can be of help to the developing nations in the way that he himself has been in his missions for the UN. When a friend asked Abrams if he could be said to be passing on the torch, he replied, with a smile, "No, just spreading the light." He deems it important to have his students come to grips with real affairs rather than devote their time merely to theoretical exercises. He arranged for them to work on a planning job for Nassau in the Bahamas and on planning new communities in Staten Island and Queens. He has not eschewed theoretical exercises completely. Two of his assignments were for the students to draw up plans for Heaven and for Hell. Predictably, Hell inspired the more interesting designs.

At sixty-five, Abrams gives no indication of having contemplated retirement, or even of having contemplated slowing down. He still regards a vacation as a fine time for a strenuous mission for the UN or some other agency. During his spring vacation last year, he went to Chile to make an overall evaluation of that nation's housing programs. Last summer, he traversed the Alaskan tundra to advise the state government what ought to be done about the Eskimos' housing, and a few weeks ago he was in Calcutta for the Ford Foundation to give his opinions on the shelter problems of India. In between, he managed to draw up a seventy-thousand-word report for Philadelphia, in which he offered the novel proposal – immensely simple in its conception though highly sophisticated in its financial and procedural details – that the best and cheapest way for Philadelphia to provide additional housing for the poor would be for the city to buy up habitable existing houses, of which many are available at prices between two and five thousand dollars, and then simply resell them to impoverished families at minimal mortgage rates. Abrams calculates that this would bring home ownership within the reach of families with incomes as low as $3150 a year.

In his rare gloomy moments, Abrams is given to citing what he calls his Reforms Perversion Theory, which is simply that all reforms are sooner or later perverted. "Slum clearance gets perverted into Negro clearance," he says. "Urban renewal becomes a device for profiteering without risk. Zoning becomes racial zoning. What's the use?" As he goes on in this fashion, a discouraged look comes to his face, and his eyes cloud. This transformation lasts for perhaps thirty seconds. Then Abrams remembers an idea for some new reform, and he begins passionately expounding it.

Notes

1 A portion of the original article has been omitted here that dwelt with Abrams' 1965 book, *The City is the Frontier*, and his suggestions for improving New York City.

2 A brief portion of the original article has been omitted here that dealt with housing reform in New York City prior to 1901.

18 From civic worker to city planner: women and planning, 1890–1980

Eugenie Ladner Birch

> We scorn this ill-conceived conference. While the profession claims
> to be trying to humanize its practice, the Conference panel topics
> and the resource people are a denial of this claim. Discussions of the
> inner city, of minorities in the profession of land use policies and of
> neighborhood planning all affect women and community people
> intimately. Women who are a legitimate constituency and an
> invaluable resource have been dealt with by the Conference only as
> "wives" of "delegates", shunted off to . . . department stores and
> museums . . . (only) 15 to 20 per cent of all planners and urban
> specialists are female. Why indeed are not all planning commissions
> 50 per cent female to accurately represent the constituencies of the
> urban community? We deplore the planning that is done by men. It
> takes little account of the needs of women (who) should be the
> guiding force for human communities.[1]

This sharp critique, read at the 1970 annual meeting of the American
Society of Planning Officials (ASPO) by a representative of the newly
formed Women's Caucus, was thoroughly predictable in its timing and
content. Paralleling similar protest from women in other occupations, it
reflected the impact of the mid-century feminist movement on the planning profession. Not since the pre-suffrage days at the turn of the century
had women been so vocal about their needs and concerns.[2] Much of the
action resulted from a quiet revolution in female roles, expressed by the
increasing participation of women in the labor force (by 1970 43 per cent
of all women were working) and by a growing discontent with what some
women considered the forced domesticity of the suburbs (documented so
vividly by Betty Friedan in the *Feminine Mystique*).[3] The National
Organization for Women (NOW), founded in 1966, and aided by the anti-
sex discrimination clause to Title VII of the 1964 Civil Rights Act, began
to press for equality in education and employment. Women defined
themselves as an oppressed minority and shaped their protests on the
civil rights model.[4] Part of their campaign was to publicize evidence of
sexual discrimination. This tactic gained the attention of many professional groups, including the planners, whose examinations of their own
field led to organized outrage. The statement of the Women's Caucus,
then, grew out of this reformist urge.

Aside from professional discrimination, a second and equally significant theme in the Women's Caucus petition was the claim to gender-related expertise. Women, they stated, should be the "guiding force for human communities."[5] In the tradition of the late nineteenth century, the protesters listed activities where domestic knowledge gave women dominance. Access to work for the now heavily female labor force, for example, and questions of residential planning should be included in women's issues along with more conventional concerns: child care, community services, and employment conditions.

While these two themes, professional access and gender-related expertise, reflected the unique mid-century version of American feminism, they had not appeared independently but were the product of the previous eighty years. Furthermore, they echoed another refrain recently proclaimed in the planning profession: the need to recognize the field's pluralistic nature, a view articulated by Paul Davidoff and Thomas A. Reiner, whose essay "A choice theory of planning" was well accepted in the profession by 1970.[6]

The actions of the women planners of the 1970s reflected the larger trends of society and their profession, just as did the work of their predecessors who helped advance the cause of planning in the early twentieth century. An evaluation of female participation in planning must therefore draw both on the history of planning and on general women's history. It also requires an analysis of two phenomena in the history of planning: first, its rise as a profession encompassing an area of expertise, an educational tradition, and a self-regulating component; and second, its acceptance by the public as a legitimate exercise of government power.

In the first area, professional development, women clearly had little direct impact.[7] Through 1940 only one woman held full membership in the American Institute of Planners, the field's credentialling society.[8] (By the same token, few women participated in the growth of any of the traditional professions including law, medicine, architecture and engineering.[9]) However, some individual females did make important indirect contributions in shaping the field. As librarians, executive secretaries, and in other positions, they helped form the intellectual content and participated in the administrative aspects of the field. The careers of Theodora Kimball Hubbard, Charlotte Rumbold, and Elisabeth Herlihy illustrate this type of activity. In the second area, acceptance by the public, women played a far more important role, garnering community support and providing financial backing at critical points. Into this category fall club activity, philanthropy, and public relations, all open to women. The work of the General Federation of Women's Clubs, the Russell Sage and Spelman Foundations, and Harlean James of the American

Civic Association exemplify this aspect. Finally, the fact that there were enough women to form a caucus in 1970 is evidence that women did enter the profession during the postwar period. They entered slowly, however, and despite equal training did not advance as quickly as their male counterparts. They would provide the critical mass of supporters for the call for reform.

Women and planning at the turn of the century

Planning was the product of late nineteenth-century progressive reform efforts. Although it had many roots one of its earliest tangible forms was the 1893 Chicago World's Fair which many regard as a visible precedent for the wave of civic improvement then sweeping the country that culminated in the planning movement in the early twentieth century. Drawing from many strands, from municipal arts to sanitation, cities of all sizes sought to create well-ordered, beautiful urban environments administered in an economic and rational manner. By the late 1920s planning which originated as a private-sector effort had become a legitimate exercise of local government power.[10]

Its primary concern was to direct the physical development of the city. Several organizations promoted its aims – the American Civic Association (ACA) founded in 1904, the National Conference on City Planning (NCCP) created in 1909, the American City Planning Institute (ACPI) formed in 1917, and subsections of the American Society of Civil Engineers (ASCE), and the American Institute of Architects (AIA).[11] The emerging field was explained to supporters and practitioners in periodicals such as the *American City Magazine*, started in 1909, and *The City Plan*, originated in 1915, and its successor, *City Planning Quarterly*; and in several basic books including Benjamin Marsh's *An Introduction to City Planning* (1909), Charles Mulford Robinson's *The Improvement of Towns and Cities* (1907), John Nolen's *Replanning Small Cities* (1912), and *Carrying out the City Plan* (1914) by Flavel Shurtleff and Frederick Law Olmsted, Jr.[12]

At this time, the technical aspects of city planning practice were clearly in the male domain and were taught in schools of architecture or engineering. At first professionals in these areas purveyed their services to private groups, primarily chambers of commerce, the most notable example being Daniel Burnham's contract with the Commercial Club of Chicago to produce a comprehensive plan. Later, with the proliferation of planning commissions, they consulted directly with cities.

City planning spread rapidly because it was sought by urbanites, who by 1920 were the majority of the nation's population. The demand did not rise spontaneously but derived from multiple sources.

Historians have documented the role of businessmen's groups but few have outlined the quite substantial contributions of women. In the thirty-year span between 1890 and 1920, groups of women had become highly active in civic affairs. Predominantly college-educated, a rarity at the beginning of the period, they created clubs to recapture the intellectual life and companionship of their undergraduate years, to justify their education and partly to seek the control over their environments that would ultimately lead to their enfranchisement in 1920.

The club network was vast.[13] By 1909 for example, the General Federation of Women's Clubs claimed 800,000 members in more than 495 affiliates.[14] In addition, women belonged to other groups, such as the American Association of University Women, the Women's Division of the National Civic Federation, local municipal art societies, and general civic improvement organizations.

Despite much public skepticism, the movement of women into public affairs gained momentum. In 1912, the *American City Magazine* dedicated a complete issue to the phenomenon. In a lengthy preface, entitled "The old order changeth," the editor sought to reassure his subscribers (90 per cent men): "How needless was the widespread fear that woman's attempt to spell the task (of civic work) would work havoc to the social structure." In fact, he claimed, the opposite occurred because the distinctive feminine view, "often the reverse of man's" had made "the ideal city a practical reality . . . (for) we are coming to learn that the term city implies of necessity concentration of population but it does not of necessity imply ugliness, squalor or disease."[15]

At this time, a clear division existed by mutual consent between men's and women's civic activities. In the effort to gain acceptance, women had consciously claimed certain urban problems as their own. For example, likening the metropolis to "a home, clean and beautiful," Eva Perry Moore, longtime president of the General Federation of Women's Clubs, maintained that congestion and competition, two earmarks of the early twentieth-century city particularly affected mothers because they hindered homemaking efforts. Therefore, she argued, women should extend their domestic roles to ameliorate the municipal environment. In specific terms, they should view their urban mission as achieving the "City Cleanly, City Sanitary, and City Beautiful." Although the "vast army" of club workers whom Moore addressed were essentially elite, they, like all good progressives, believed their efforts would reach across the social structure to provide "a future gain to every class of society."[16]

One of the first national efforts to be organized by women was at the 1893 Chicago World's Fair. The planning of the Exposition had been delegated by Congress to an all-male commission headed by Daniel H. Burnham. Nevertheless, women gained a foothold by forcing Congress to appoint a 115-member Board of Lady Managers, who were to award the site and an appropriation for a women's headquarters building on the fairgrounds. The Board, headed by Bertha H. Palmer (wife of a wealthy Chicago hotelier) who had been long involved in civic work, soon expanded the women's narrow mission. With Burnham's consent they sponsored a national competition for the design of the Women's Building, as the project was bluntly called, awarding the commission to a 22-year-old MIT graduate, Sophia G. Hayden, who later won the Fair's Artist's Medal for her design. All the work in the building was done by women. For example, the Board commissioned Mary Cassatt, the expatriate American artist, and Mary MacMonnies, the wife of Frederick MacMonnies who sculpted the Fair's fountain, to execute two massive murals for the main gallery.

Not content merely to sponsor a resting place for female visitors, as Congress had envisioned, the Board made their building as important as the other exhibition halls. They filled it with gender-related resources, including a 7000 volume library, a survey of women's social and economic position in forty-seven countries, and a model kitchen filled with appliances designed to lighten domestic chores. In addition, the Board financed the nearby Children's Building, for daycare. Once the Exposition opened, they scheduled lectures, conferences, and demonstrations.[17]

Like their counterparts in the growing, locally based civic movement, the Lady Managers succeeded because of the personal influence of their leaders, their strong organization, and their care to frame their work in terms of women's domestic functions. Using a conservative definition of female roles, they brought their interests into the public view under the cloak of domesticity: in addition to examples of women's crafts they also provided demonstrations about women's suffrage and the entry of women into the professions.

Male observers supported the women's claim that their civic work was merely an extension of their domestic duties. While the *American City* editor writing about the 1912 "women's number" implored his readers to "examine this issue with care," he bid them to "place it within the proper context." Every woman she reminded them, "realizes that she cannot make an ideal *home* without the right kind of house."

This much the American woman has known for generations, [he continued] but a greater vision is now being raised before her . . . she has come to realize that no home liveth unto itself alone. She has come to see that the physical things of the city affect every home in it and that to her, as the homemaker, the improving of these municipal conditions is of vital concern.[18]

Within municipal affairs clubwomen of the time had diverse interests. The General Federation therefore devised separate departments (Civics,

Health, Education). However, early on the whole Federation came to support city planning, believing that their independent efforts in sanitation, hygiene, playground construction, child welfare, and outdoor art could be accomplished only within a broader framework. By 1912, Alice Davis Moulton, chairman of the Federation's Civic Department, had articulated their position:

To designate any one phase as the fundamental requirement in a movement so pregnant with virtual issues as the civic movement is most difficult, but authorities on civics agree that a city plan is a fundamental requirement for comprehensive civic improvement.[19]

Pledging the backing of the national Civic Department, she called for the local branches to contribute the grass-roots support necessary for the expansion of planning into municipalities. She bid her followers to "secure universal interest in city planning (and give) an impetus to civic betterment that ultimately would lay the cornerstone for the future."[20]

As women became increasingly secure of their place in civic affairs, they enlarged the scope of their interests and undertook increasingly sophisticated projects. Correspondingly, as their efforts grew more ambitious, their support for city planning became more significant. In the beginning, they had concentrated on high visibility, short-term, easily defined commitments. Clean-up campaigns were typical; for these efforts they organized parades, rallies, refuse collection days, and planting ceremonies for all citizens, young and old. They soon moved to more substantial endeavors, often raising funds for them. In 1914 Zona Gale reflected on the significance of this trend: "the most potent and least indirect way of cooperation at present in woman's power is actually to inaugurate and pay for the particular advances which they are advocating." Using traditional means, such as holding bazaars, serving home

Although the disenfranchised women had no direct political or economic clout they argued that their impartial views on planning and other reform issues were untainted by selfish motives and therefore more impressive. Typical was the accomplishment of Whytheville, Virginia women who despite having "to contend with man's tendency to subvert everything to a monetary basis," had successfully campaigned for a town park. In the same mode, Mildred Chadsey, chief inspector of the Cleveland Bureau of Sanitation, claimed "women can successfully divorce work from politics," thereby making their projects respectable. Many men concurred with this assessment. George B. Dealey, vice-president and general manager of the *Dallas News*, attributed women's civic achievements to their "sincerity of purpose." Furthermore, he recognized a certain rationale in their choice of projects when he reported that they "have never undertaken an enterprise that was not vital, timely, and practical (which) did not appeal to the public as sane and just."[21]

cooked meals at county fairs, and performing in "ladies minstrel shows" they raised thousands of dollars in countless communities to support their chosen causes.[22]

Park projects were a frequent choice. Observing that "only too often American villages have grown up into towns and become great cities before it was remembered to set apart suitable space for a community rallying center, the real-estate excesses having swallowed up every last vacant lot," they condemned the thoughtless greed of their male counterparts and called for more open space to relieve congestion and minimize the insalubrious effects of competition. These sympathies coincided with park schemes proposed by professional planners. For example, in Dallas, Texas, the women's clubs equipped two playgrounds and paid the salaries of recreation supervisors in two problem neighborhoods. In the process they created a recreation association which soon affiliated with the city's Park Board and Board of Education to promote the park system called for by George E. Kessler in his "City Plan for Dallas." In conjunction with the early twentieth-century parks movement, they supported "social centers" – the use of neighborhood schools for off-hour recreational and assembly purposes – long before this idea become the nucleus of the neighborhood unit concept articulated by Clarence Perry and adopted by technical city planners in the 1930s.[23]

The unity between women and professional city planners is even more closely drawn in the analysis of civic beautification schemes. From Los Angeles to Tampa to Lock Haven (Pa.) city residents moved to improve their town centers. Women's clubs frequently stimulated professional efforts to replan an area, often consulting with leading designers John Nolen and Charles Mulford Robinson.[24]

In later years Ladislas Segoe, longtime Cincinnati planner, related the continuity of the tradition of women's clubs support for planning well into the twentieth century:

The typical start of a planning program in a community had its origin in some members of a garden club, who read something maybe in a foreign publication about something called planning and next, taking the Cincinnati newspaper, they found out that there is a guy called Segoe in Cincinnati who was a planner. Now we had to have some speaker at the garden club . . . so why not call up this Segoe guy and see whether he is willing to come . . . and talk to us about planning? Well, the date had been agreed upon, the speech was dutifully made, and then nothing happened for several months, and then you got a call from the League of Women Voters . . . and after that . . . then came a call from the members of some other . . . club . . . Then . . . somebody . . . suggested if I come down for a day that he could introduce me to somebody in the city hall . . . Now by that time . . . the groundwork had been laid . . . and . . . planning had managed to take root.[25]

With increasing involvement in civic affairs, women gained recognition as legitimate forces in the community and participated in the activities and boards of local and national organizations. As early as 1909, Richard Watrous, secretary of the American Civic Association, ascribed "to the enthusiasm, the untiring efforts and practical suggestions" of women the "splendid headway attained by general improvement propaganda." In his opinion, their most important accomplishment was to promote the vision of a desirable urban environment. "Hundreds of cities, that have distinguished themselves for notable achievements," he claimed, "can point to some society . . . of women that have been the first inspiration to do things."[26]

Additional examples of women's participation in a sphere wider than the clubs come from many cities. For example, at St Louis in 1912 women had prominent positions on the program of a three-day civic conference. In Los Angeles, they occupied two slots on the five-member board of the Municipal Art Commission, the body that ordered the first city plan for the west coast metropolis. And in Boston, they contributed a major demonstration at the famed "Boston 1915" exhibition, sponsored by leading businessmen of the city.[27]

Although the general population unquestioningly accepted women's skill in specific domestic-related areas, popular sentiment strictly circumscribed their performance in the public arena, on the basis that their primary duties were familial and their services supplementary. Consequently, while women would provide the "head and heart" in municipal affairs, men were to be the administrators and implementors of urban policy.[28] The most common view saw women contributing their leisure time to this work. In 1912, the editor of the *American City* magazine clearly expressed this sentiment when he discussed the role of members of women's clubs. Noting that in American cities there were "thousands of women whose housework did not need all their time," he argued that such women had "time and ability for the research and experimental work which should usually precede any radical enlargement of municipal activities." When they had demonstrated "the wisdom of their pioneer work," he concluded, "they may properly turn over to the city the administration of the enterprise . . . and direct their energies to other community needs."[29]

Most women agreed with this limited role. A few, however, did not, and turned their expertise into full time professional positions. Caroline Bartlett Crane of Kalamazoo, Michigan, for example, marketed herself as a "municipal housekeeper" and consulted on street cleaning in over fifty cities.[30] Wisconsin activist Zona Gale defined and promoted the paid position of "civic organizer" and wrote a handbook, *Civic Improvement in the Little Towns*, for those communities unable to afford a professional.[31] Finally, by 1916 the American Civic Association had hired an energetic young woman, Maud Van Buren, as a community organizer. In this job she traveled widely, lecturing and giving advice on organizational strategy, and wrote extensively instructing women to become informed about town ordinances and municipal budgets. She urged them to participate in city planning decisions and to question public officials about the priorities set by their expenditures. Yet even she couched her pleas in familiar terms: "The budget, the city's financial measures for each year, is surely not beyond the comprehension of the woman who conducts her own household expenses on a systemized basis."[32]

A few rare voices called for more women to join the professional ranks. In 1912 Cleveland chief inspector of the Bureau of Sanitation Mildred Chadsey observed that "town planning, transportation, street cleaning and lighting, water supply, sewage systems, and garbage disposal are all questions of 'domestic economy.'" It seemed only logical and fitting, she concluded, "to find women specialists along these lines, as well as men."[33] Yet as the second decade of the twentieth century closed, although women were beginning to make some professional inroads, they did not gain entry to city planning.[34]

By 1917, the city planning movement had divided into two wings: the citizen participants, who remained in the broadbased National Conference on City Planning and its affiliated group, the American Civic Association (ACA); and the professionals – twenty-four men in all – who created the American City Planning Institute (ACPI). The ACPI was consciously created to "study the science and advance the art of city planning" by means of discussions of technical subjects at meetings limited to qualified participants whose credentials had to include specified professional education, several years of paid city planning experience, and a vaguely defined "comprehensive view" of the city. Although torn by internal differences about the precise definition of these criteria, the original members were clear about one item: they were professionals, not reformers or citizen activists.[35]

Women simply did not qualify for membership in the ACPI. They had no professionl education, their practical experience was volunteer, their projects tended to be narrowly focused, not comprehensive in scale, and they were avowed reformers who always left technical decisions to the experts. Thus as the movement split into the two sectors, women continued to participate in the citizen wing. In fact, the ACA would soon hire a young women, Harlean James, to head its daily administration.

As the practitioners adopted their professional stance, they tended to become more efficiency-minded and less humanistic, being concerned mainly with overall land use issues, traffic engineering, and zoning. Perhaps the diminished attention to the social welfare and aesthetic aspects of the field could be related to the lack of female participation in the ACPI. More likely, however, was the overall decline of citizen participation in the public sphere. As the general move for reform in the progressive era petered out, would-be crusaders, male and female, turned to personal self-fulfillment rather than social change. After 1920 women tended to be far less active in the civic affairs of their clubs and their communities.

In the planning field, the emerging professionals focused on differentiating between the lay person and the expert; seeking consulting jobs as well as professional standing, they identified a marketable product – the master plan and its implementing arm, the zoning ordinance – which only they could prepare. In this way they widened the gulf between the professional and the ordinary citizen, removing themselves from the arena of civic action and citizen input, and thrust themselves into the government advisory role which constituted most of their business in the 1920s.

Women and planning in the 1920s

With the decline of interest in civic affairs in the 1920s, middle- and upper-class women devoted themselves to domestic issues, especially marriage and motherhood. A symbolic end to their earlier agitation for social reform was the achievement of female suffrage in 1920. The strategists for the enfranchisement campaign had early opted to keep their work narrowly focused on the vote, eliminating from discussion other issues relating to more basic structural reorganization of female roles, a policy wise in the short term but imprudent in the long term. Consequently, after the passage of the Nineteenth Amendment, the leaders declared victory and submerged their efforts by transforming their activist lobbying group, the National American Women's Suffrage Association (NAWSA), into the non-partisan League of Women Voters.[36]

Concurrently, other female club and organizational networks tended to focus on domestic issues. In 1929, for example, the American Association of University Women disbanded its ten-year-old National Housing Committee, which had supported a federal workers' housing program, and replaced it with another more directly concerned with campus affairs.[37] Despite this trend, the civic clubs did not completely die out. Some of them carried on with a narrowed focus and became more institutionalized by hiring executive secretaries to oversee their daily administration. Representatives from the previous generation of well-educated, single women frequently filled these low-paying although highly responsible positions.

Despite their lack of participation in the professional side of planning, women were not totally without influence in the planning movement. A few, such as librarians and executive secretaries or clericals who advanced in rank, participated through their positions as service professionals.

Plate 18.1 Theodora Kimball Hubbard.

The careers of four are illustrative of this activity: Theodora Kimball (1897–1935), librarian of the Harvard School of Design and later wife of Henry V. Hubbard, head of the first planning degree program; Charlotte Rumbold (1865–1960), lobbyist, administrative assistant, and citizen activist in Cleveland; Harlean James (1877–1969) executive secretary of the American Civic Association (later the American Planning and Civic Association) for almost forty years; and Elisabeth Herlihy (1880–1953), secretary of the Boston Planning Commission from its inception in 1913 until her appointment to the chair of the Massachusetts State Planning Board, a position she held until 1950.

More than a librarian, Theodora Kimball used her position as a vehicle to make major intellectual contributions to the newly emerging planning field. After education at the Girls' Latin School of Boston and graduation from Simmons College, she joined the staff of the Harvard Library in 1908. At age twenty-nine, seeking additional professional training, she returned to Simmons to earn that institution's first master's degree in library science.[38]

Although involved in her field, she was clearly more interested in academic pursuits and turned to writing, until her untimely death in 1935. By 1917 she had co-authored textbooks in city planning and landscape architecture. After that she edited two volumes of the professional papers of Frederick Law Olmsted, Sr; produced the annual survey of city and regional planning, which had first appeared in 1912 in *Landscape Architecture* and later *City Planning* journals founded by Hubbard; assembled city planning bibliographies for the *American City* magazine, the *National Municipal Review*, the US Department of Commerce Advisory Commission on Zoning and the President's Conference on Homebuilding and Homeownership; and produced numerous book reviews for *City Planning* of which she was an editor.[39]

Kimball wrote her most significant book, *Our Cities Today and Tomorrow*, an outgrowth of her annual surveys, in collaboration with Hubbard whom she had married in 1924.[40] Both the book and the reports synthesized city planning progress in the United States and defined the central issues of the field. Kimball wrote not as a reporter but as a critic, assigning priority to topics she considered crucial. The reports usually started with her assessment of current progress, based on the number of zoning and planning commissions founded, outstanding publications, and the status of special concerns: regional planning, transportation, parks and recreation, and civic center development. She favorably reviewed implementation schemes such as zoning and capital budgeting and provided ample illustrations of model projects. She compiled practical instruction material for practitioners and students of the new field.

Kimball established a scholarly tradition emulated by many women. Among them were Katherine McNamara, Kimball's protégé and successor at Harvard, whose career spanned several decades; Lucille Keck, librarian of the Charles E. Merriam Library at the Chicago offices of the American Society of Planning Officials (ASPO) and its sister organizations; and Mary Vance, former head of the Council of Planning Librarians who expanded the field's research potential by editing thousands of planning-related bibliographies.

A second group active in the field were executive secretaries of planning or civic organizations. While it is difficult to judge the influence of these women because of the ephemeral nature of their work, Charlotte Rumbold and Harlean James do stand out. Both had a strong commitment to citizen-based efforts, a personally based network of contacts in planning, a strong organizational legacy, and a series of legislative accomplishments. They were both unmarried college graduates who entered planning through an initial interest in housing reform.

Rumbold, born in St Louis and educated at the University of Missouri, immersed herself in civic activities, including supervision of a pioneering housing study for St Louis. She later became Supervisor of Recreation, a municipal position from which she resigned in 1915 after a battle with the city council who refused to pay her at an equal rate with a male counterpart.[41]

Following the unpleasantness in St Louis, she resettled in Cleveland where she had moved to supervise a slum survey. Through this work she became interested in city planning and took an administrative position at the Chamber of Commerce, combining two functions, assistant secretary and secretary of the City Planning Committee. In 1919, she helped found the Ohio Planning Conference (OPC), a citizen-based group dedicated to the propagation of planning. For more than two decades, Rumbold was the OPC's guiding light. Serving in various capacities (secretary/treasurer, 1919–25, vice-president 1925–8, president, 1928–30, and secretary 1938–43), her most notable efforts were as a registered lobbyist in the 1920s.[42] Supported by contributions from OPC's meager five-hundred-dollar annual budget, she successfully rallied support for the basic state enabling legislation to establish local planning commissions, comprehensive zoning, and subdivision regulations.

Although interested in local planning through the 1930s, as indicated by her tenure on the Cleveland Planning Commission, Rumbold devoted much energy to housing, working for the first laws authorizing public housing, state park development, and state planning.[43] After her retirement in 1943 she continued to support the citizen role in planning until her death in 1960. Early in her career, she had made a clear distinction between citizens and technical planners, in which she emphasized the important role of citizens "who want to learn not to make a city plan . . . but how to put a city plan in force."[44] It was to this constituency that she directed her efforts.

Sharing Rumbold's views was Harlean James, executive secretary of the American Civic Association (ACA). She too believed that public education in city planning was crucial to the advance of the field. Many early city plans "lay unused on the shelves of public libraries or hidden in the back of desk drawers" she observed. Planners tended to "despise the homely, everyday knowledge of the residents in the towns and cities in which they were working," putting forth proposals which could "be easily challenged by ordinary everyday people with no special knowledge and little insight into the future." She therefore urged the ACA to create linkages between citizens and professionals.[45] Like Rumbold, she had developed these ideas from her own experiences as a long time

Plate 18.2 Harlean James.
Source: Department of Manuscripts and University Archives, Olin Library, Cornell University.

worker in civic affairs. Born in 1877, she graduated from Stanford University in 1898 and became the executive secretary of the Women's Civic League of Baltimore. In this position she encountered a wide range of issues from health to housing to public art. She next served as executive secretary of the United States Housing Corporation, the wartime defense housing agency. After the Armistice, she took the same position with the American Civic Association. Her interest in city planning, which had been stimulated in Baltimore and later enriched by her experience with the enlightened designs of the defense housing settlements, inspired her prior to her ACA assignment to write a popular book, *The Building of Cities.*[46]

James was an energetic woman of executive ability who made the ACA an influential force in planning. Working closely with its successive presidents, particularly Frederic A. Delano, the wealthy Chicago businessman who was among the original sponsors of the Chicago Plan of 1909 and uncle of the rising politician Franklin Delano Roosevelt, she focused ACA activities on the major issues of local comprehensive planning and protection of natural resources. In furthering these efforts, James organized nationwide support for the passage of the federal legislation creating the National Capital Park and Planning Commission (later the National Capital Planning Commission) in 1926. She also urged US Secretary of Commerce Herbert Hoover to form the Division of Building and Housing which issued the exemplary state enabling legislation for planning and zoning, and she actively supported the workof the National Park Service, the Department of Interior agency that the ACA had strenuously lobbied for prior to her arrival.[47]

As executive secretary, James edited a steady stream of publications including the monthly *Civic Comment* and the *American Planning and Civic Annual* which featured commissioned essays and an extensive annotated honor roll of civic achievers. She was a prolific author of articles, news notes, book reviews for sympathetic journals, textbooks, and other propagandistic materials. Her *Land Planning in the United States for City, State and Nation*, commissioned by noted land economist Richard T. Ely, was a factual readable book which blended the most current technical information with homely, practical advice.[48]

James' most important work, however, was the least tangible. During her thirty-seven year tenure at the ACA, she built an extensive network of legislators, planning professionals, and civic leaders by whom the force of her opinion would be felt in planning issues, most notably in land use decisions in Washington, D.C. In 1954, her long association with the ACA gained a measure of national recognition when ASPO gave her one of its three awards for that year.[49]

Among the other ASPO award winners in 1954 was Elisabeth Herlihy,

Plate 18.3 Miss Elisabeth Herlihy and Mrs Moore of Boston, 1926 National Conference on City Planning, St Petersburg, Florida.
Source: Olin Library, Cornell University.

also cited for her thirty-seven-year career as a Massachusetts planning official. Herlihy, who had the distinction of being for many years the sole woman member of the American City Planning Institute, had entered planning through an unusual route. The precocious daughter of Irish immigrant parents, she graduated as valedictorian of her high school class at age fifteen. After secretarial training in Boston she remained there to work. In her spare time she wrote short stories and essays, many of which appeared in *The Republic*, a publication owned by John F. Fitzgerald. When Fitzgerald became Mayor of Boston he hired her as his secretary. She quickly rose to chief clerk where she reigned over much of the city's administrative work. In 1913, she briefed Fitzgerald about newly passed city planning enabling legislation and persuaded him to make her secretary of the commission, a position she held until 1935 when she was appointed chair of the Massachusetts Planning Board. (She remained on the Boston City Planning Commission, as a commissioner until her retirement in 1950.) In addition, in 1924 she became clerk of the Board of Zoning Appeals created to administer the city's first comprehensive zoning ordinance.[50]

Through this administrative work, attendance at American planning meetings, and frequent study trips abroad, Herlihy taught herself planning.[51] In 1927 the American City Planning Institute (ACPI) overlooked her lack of official credentials when it admitted her as a member, although many of her ACPI colleagues disagreed with her basic attitudes toward planning as summarized in a newspaper comment: ''There's nothing sacred about planning . . . it's just common sense.''[52]

Over the years, Herlihy gained the respect of her colleagues, who admired her staying power through successive mayors. They also recognized her power as the *confidante* of the leaders who relied on her advice for planning and zoning commission appointments and other sensitive land use decisions. "Mayors came and went," one observer noted, "but Elisabeth Herlihy was as permanent as the planning board."[53]

In addition to her administrative duties, Herlihy worked hard to publicize planning. "There is scarcely an organization in Boston nor a city or town in the metropolitan district she has not spoken to," was one contemporary description, and she was credible to realtor and women's clubber alike.[54] Her faith in citizen support, akin to the approach of Rumbold and James, led her to be a founder and executive committee member of the Massachusetts Federation of Planning Boards, which by 1929 had a membership of 107 towns representing four million people. She also operated on the national level, serving on committees for the ACPI and as a director of the ACA and ASPO. A contributor to *City Planning* and the *American Planning and Civic Annual*, she focused her writing on administration and public relations.[55]

These three women, who based their activities on citizen organization, politics, and administration, had counterparts in many other American cities. Secretaries of city planning commissions were traditionally women. Anne Robertson of New Orleans, Edyth Howard of Des Moines, and Grace Bartlett of Honolulu are examples. Although they did not advance in rank as Elisabeth Herlihy, they played important local roles in the functioning of the planning commissions. Executive secretaries and other civic employees were also frequently women. Edith Sampson's edition of *Municipal Facts* for Denver and the work of A. Edmere Cabana of the Buffalo City Planning Association quietly nurtured public support for planning. Finally, like Rumbold and Herlihy, women did have prominent positions on commissions or associations, as may be seen in the examples of Albion Fellows Bacon, chairman of the Evansville (Ind.) commission, and Gertrude Bosler Biddle, a director of the Tri-State Regional Planning Federation. All in all, women participated in planning in the 1920s not as technical practitioners but publicists, administrators, and lobbyists. Barred from professional participation by social convention, they used rather low level or unpaid jobs to advantage in establishing a presence.[56]

Women and planning in the Depression

The 1930s saw a sharp decline in the advances made by employed women. Men were favored over women, particularly married women, for the few jobs available: the federal government refused to employ more than one wage earner in a family, while twenty-six states passed legislation prohibiting the employment of married women. A 1936 Gallup Poll found that 82 per cent of its respondents disapproved of spouses working when their husbands were employed. By 1940 the labor force was 25 per cent female. Nonetheless, professional schools set quotas for female admissions, medical schools for example, restricting women to 5 per cent of a class and by 1940 women professionals fell to the 1920 level of 12 per cent.[57] The planning profession reflected this trend. Until well into the 1940s, the ACPI had only one female full member (in 1932 Harlean James had joined Elisabeth Herlihy on the roster but only as an associate member).[58]

Nevertheless, some slow changes occurred in the late 1930s, related to the evolution of the planning profession itself which was beginning to have enough adherents to merit the creation of independent degree programs. In 1929, Harvard received funds from the Rockefeller Foundation to found a school of city planning. By 1937, the Massachusetts Institute of Technology, Cornell, and Columbia had followed suit, establishing programs within their schools of architecture. The Institute was the most significant program for women because it had regularly admitted women since its inception. (Harvard, in contrast, refused to admit women to its School of Design until a later date, directing females to the Cambridge School of Architecture which drew heavily on Harvard for its faculty.) Furthermore, in 1937, the exclusively female Lothorp School of Landscape Architecture, under the direction of a recent MIT graduate, John A. Parker, directed some of its students to the Institute when it moved from its Groton campus to quarters at MIT. In 1940 MIT granted master's degrees in city planning to Flora Crockett (c. 1914–1979) and Jane S. Rodman (b. 1914), its first female planning students.[59]

Crockett and Rodman typified women planners of the period. Crockett, who had earned an architecture degree at MIT in 1937, married a Briton, Gordon Stephenson, and returned to England with him. Stephenson held a series of government positions including chief planning officer of the Ministry of City Planning until he became professor of planning at the University of Liverpool in 1948. Subsequently he taught in Canada and Australia. Crockett, accompanying him on these ventures, not only raised a large family but practiced planning in a variety of forms. She supervised the evacuation of British children during the war, collaborated with Stephenson in his written work and co-authored two books and several reports.[60]

A similar pattern was followed by Rodman, who had an undergraduate degree from the Lothorp School/Simmons College joint program and married Richard L. Steiner. Steiner's career took them to Washington, D.C., where he worked at the United States Housing Authority, while

Rodman completed her master's thesis, a study of a multiracial community near Howard University. At the outbreak of the war they moved to Jacksonville, Florida, where Steiner was a housing officer in the United States Navy. In the five years they were there, Rodman held a variety of jobs ranging from designing camouflage for the Corps of Army Engineers to working for a private planning consultant, George Simon. In this period the couple started a family. Following the war, they went to Baltimore where Steiner worked for the city's redevelopment agency and Rodman had her third child. Given the demands of domestic life, Rodman did not work until 1947, when she joined the Baltimore County Planning Department. She remained with the agency for fifteen years, her tenure broken for a five-year period with the birth and early childhood of her fourth child. In 1962 she retired again, deciding to spend a few years at home with her rapidly growing children, and in 1968 she and Steiner divorced. As a result of her disillusionment with planning for its failure to achieve the orderly development of the county, she did not return to work. In 1972, however, she joined the Peace Corps, which exploited her planning experience even though she did not request a professional position. Assigned to Gambia, she directed the national planning office until 1977 when she returned to the United States.[61]

A contemporary of the MIT graduates, Chloethiel Woodward Smith (b. 1910), represents a different career pattern. She trained in architecture at the University of Oregon and in 1933 earned a city planning degree at Washington University. After working in Seattle, Portland, and New York City, she became chief of research and planning for the Federal Housing Administration, a position she held for three years before entering private practice. Like many of her contemporaries, she married, bore children, and shaped her career to her husband's, but she differed in having a well-established reputation before her marriage. Resettling in Washington, D.C., in 1946, she opened her own firm, Chloethiel Woodward Smith Associates, which specialized in architecture, urban design, and planning.[62] Her work has included the award-winning designs for the Washington, D.C. South West Urban Renewal Area, new town plans for Algeria, the American Embassy in Paraguay, and the Crown Tower and Crown Court in St Louis, Missouri.[63]

Unlike the single or childless career women of the previous generation, these women planners sought to blend marriages and children with their work. Although they often collaborated or worked in fields related to their husband's, in the interest of family solidarity they took secondary positions and compromised their employment opportunities. Their professional accomplishments, though notable, were accordingly less dramatic than they might otherwise have been.

Other well-educated but not professionally trained women continued to participate at the periphery of the profession, taking leadership positions in areas defined as female concerns, in particular aesthetics and housing. The case of aesthetics is seen most clearly in the campaign to regulate highway construction and roadside improvements in the 1930s. By the middle of the decade, when car ownership had risen to 25,000,000, middle-class Americans had become increasingly reliant upon automobiles. The rush to build a satisfactory highway network resulted in uncontrolled land development characterized by the ugly, chaotic strips bordering the roads so graphically recorded in the 1939 movie, *The City*.[64] In 1933, Mrs John D. Rockefeller, gave a grant to the American Civic Association to support the general improvement of the highways.[65] Overseen by Harlean James, the project soon caught the interest of professional planners. The ACPI created a Committee on Roadside Improvements whose members included Alfred Bettman and Robert Whitten, noted Ohio zoning experts, and E. P. Goodrich, a principal in the Technical Advisory Corporation, a consulting firm. This group made substantive legal and design suggestions which were taken up by the ACA.[66]

Concurrently, Elizabeth B. Lawton (1973–1952), a Vassar graduate long interested in conservation, created the National Roadside Council and worked with the ACA and ACPI. She directed extensive roadside surveys to gather data for planners and legislators, edited the *Roadside Bulletin*, lectured widely, and aided lobbying efforts to restrict billboards and require landscaping.[67] Harlean James committed the ACA's resources to the cause in order to integrate the work of the professional planners, the Council, and citizens' groups. She purposely defined the issue as one where women, the backbone of the ACA membership, could claim superiority. Although clearly delineating their role, she none the less viewed it in essentially the same manner as had been set forth a generation earlier. "The addition of women voters should bring their influence to bear in projects involving beauty," she thought, for women "seem to observe inharmonies of color more generally than men. . . . There seems to be very good promise that we may advocate projects in city planning because they add to the beauty of a city or because they protect the natural beauty of the landscape."[68] The roadside campaign received generous attention at regular ACA meetings. In addition, Rockefeller funds supported conferences for the three special interest groups – citizen activists, lobbyists, and planners.[69] The tradition of relegating this issue to women would be continued a generation later when President Johnson's wife, Lady Bird, gave strong personal support to highway beautification.

In a second area, housing reform, women had more success relating their work to the planning profession, but the linkage did not occur until the 1930s. Leaders in the field included Edith Elmer Wood (1871–1945),

Mary Kingsbury Simkhovitch (1867–1951), and Catherine Bauer (1905–1964). Although they had always considered housing a major part of comprehensive planning, professional planners regarded the subject as too narrow and refused to rank it with transportation, recreation, or city center development. Thomas Adams, Director of the Regional Plan for New York and its Environs (RPA) and an active policy-making member of the ACPI reflected this view in a letter to Wood during the late 1920s. In response to her criticism of the preliminary RPA reports, which gave little attention to housing, Adams wrote that housing was regarded as inherent in the whole physical structure of the city and not a separate question.[70] Wood considered this stance absurd. "The city planning and housing movements in most European countries are so closely intertwined," she observed, "that this relationship is taken for granted. In the US they have had separate origins and run generally parallel courses without making much contact."[71] This was a perceptive diagnosis. Although both the movements had their roots in the progressive era, the "housers" of the 1930s tended to be social workers associated with settlement houses who promoted general welfare issues, whereas the planners tended to be technicians associated with the design and engineering professions and were interested in urban order and efficiency.

One small segment of the professional planners, the Regional Planning Association of America (RPAA), attempted to connect the issues. Not surprisingly, the RPAA members, who included Clarence Stein, Lewis Mumford, and Robert Kohn, practiced in New York City and were more closely involved with local housing than the planning movements. Propagandists for the British garden city principles, they built two communities, Sunnyside Gardens, New York and Radburn, New Jersey, as model residential prototypes.[72]

The wide gap between the housers and the planners which the RPAA began to narrow, continued to close in the 1930s. The passage in 1932 of the National Industrial Recovery Act (NIRA) with its provisions for housing and slum clearance, aroused the interest of the technical planners. By 1934, they helped create the National Association of Housing Officials (NAHO), a group financed by the Spelman Fund, a Rockefeller subsidiary. At the first annual NAHO meeting old time planners Harland Bartholomew, Jacob Crane, and Walter Blucher, pulling slum clearance and housing into their sphere of interest, sought the counsel of housers.[73] Among the experts consulted was Catherine Bauer, author of the encyclopedic *Modern Housing* and head of the Labor Housing Conference, an American Federation of Labor lobbying group.[74] Bauer was a vocal advocate for the next thirty years, as planners wrestled with the implementation of housing and renewal policy.

Untrained in planning, Bauer had come to her influential position through an unconventional route. After graduating from Vassar College in 1926, she worked at a New York publishing house where she met Lewis Mumford. Under his tutelage she developed interests in urbanism and architecture and joined the RPAA. Later, after engineering the successful legislative campaign for the 1937 Wagner–Steagall Housing Act, she became Director of Research and Information in the newly formed United States Housing Authority (USHA), a position she held for two years. In 1940 she resigned from the USHA and joined the faculty at the University of California at Berkeley, where she met and married architect William Wurster who in 1943 became dean of the MIT School of Architecture. Bauer accompanied him to Cambridge, holding an appointment at the Harvard School of Design. After they returned to California in 1950, she rejoined the faculty at Berkeley. From this position she monitored the American planning and housing movements which for all intents and purposes had merged.[75] A prolific writer and harsh critic, she called for a clearer statement of national housing goals. In her view, the planners had bungled the issue by confusing slum clearance aims, city fiscal exigencies, and housing needs. She indicted the planners for their heavy reliance on design approaches which she believed neglected basic human needs.[76]

Although she had a dramatic impact on the ideology of the profession and prepared the way for the redefinition of the field that occurred in the mid-1960s, she remained only an honorary member of the American Institute of Planners (the ACPI had adopted this name in 1938) probably because she did not meet the organization's strict educational requirements for full membership.[77]

Women and planning through war and peace

The entry of the United States into the Second World War dramatically altered the condition of the working woman. New jobs were generated while the draft created vacancies in the labor force. No longer regarded as intruders in the labor market, women were called upon to join in the war effort, and Rosie the Riveter and the WAC became familiar figures as 8,000,000 women entered the labor force. When peace came the new employees and their employers were in a quandary. On one hand, the returning soldiers would need jobs; on the other many women wished to continue working. Although the matter was resolved with massive layoffs of the female workers, the war effort left an important legacy. Women, by demonstrating that they could be responsible, reliable workers had begun to break down discriminatory employment barriers: by 1952 2,000,000 more women were employed than at the peak of the war. Most were relegated to low-paying, low-level jobs, however, and although in the professional arena female participation increased in some fields, the overall picture was negative. By 1960, women held only 11 per cent of professional positions, and most professional schools retained some form of quota on female admissions.[78]

Opportunities in the planning field paralleled these trends. During the war women had gained some new positions. For example, with a high percentage of the AIP membership in the armed forces, Barbara Terrett, assistant to the director of the American Society of Planning Officials, became executive secretary of the AIP and editor of the *Planners' Journal*, a position she held for two years. Women also found jobs in planning, drafting, and survey work associated with the war-stimulated growth of urban areas, such as Hampton Roads, Virginia.[79]

Finally, with ASPO's 1946 declaration that a "desperate shortage of planners" existed and "that if all the planners still in service were released tomorrow there still wouldn't be enough of them to fill the available jobs," the number of planning schools proliferated. One consequence was that this provided additional opportunities for entry but the increase was small.

For example, from 1941 to 1960 the MIT program graduated fifteen women, 7 per cent of their total, while the University of North Carolina had 12 female graduates between 1946 and 1960, 10 per cent of the total.[80]

During the 1950s, the female graduates of the postwar planning programs began to show up in the AIP membership roles as women jumped from two in 1940 to seventeen in 1951. The male representation rose from 170 in 1940 to over 900 in 1951. The female growth rate was proportionately much higher, but of course their absolute numbers remained low. Furthermore, in comparison to other professionals such as lawyers, doctors, and even engineers, women planners still constituted a much smaller percentage of the total.[81]

Although the number of women was too low to allow statistical analysis of their career patterns, the records of a few demonstrate the nature of their participation in the field. They were often encouraged to specialize in areas such as housing where they were presumed to have credibility. For example, in 1948, a Department of Labor publication, *The Outlook for Women in Architecture and Engineering*, noted that "in the field of home and apartment design . . . and in public housing, women have shown special interest and facility."[82]

The women had a mixed reaction to such career prescriptions. Being a minority, they wanted to prove themselves as professionals equally qualified as their male counterparts. Yet some were not averse to use their specialized gender-related knowledge to appear more expert in certain planning situations. Carol J. Thomas, founder of her own consulting firm, Thomas Planning Services, is representative. She entered planning by an indirect route and was an early example of a type which became increasingly important in later years, the returning housewife. A Vassar College student who majored in political science, Thomas married early, had two children, and accompanied her college professor husband on various assignments, eventually residing permanently outside Boston. In 1950 she was denied admission to graduate training in public administration at Harvard because the school was reluctant to admit an older married woman seeking a part-time program. She then took planning courses at MIT where she met a number of prominent planners and at joint MIT–Harvard gatherings, including Arthur C. Comey who offered her part-time work, a proposal she accepted because she had children at home (and subsequently her husband had contracted a serious illness that required her presence at home). Thomas eventually parlayed her freelance work into a steady business and she established her own firm in 1956. In forming the company, Thomas blended her technical expertise as a planner with her prior domestic experience. Capitalizing on her seventeen years as a suburban housewife – ''Who knows her community better than a woman?'' she claimed – she specialized in land use and environment planning.[83]

Dorothy Muncy, a Washington-based planner, represents a woman who defied the feminine stereotypes. When she graduated from high school in the midst of the Depression, she could not afford to attend college. She worked at the newly formed New Jersey Housing Authority and later the county offices of the Works Progress Administration (WPA) until she saved enough money to attend the University of Chicago where she studied social sciences. After two years she took a job with the national WPA Women's and Professional Division where she was exposed to planning related projects including the Real Property Inventory. During the war she worked for the National Youth Administration, undertaking a study of service needs for women in the event of their official draft into the labor force.

After the war, Muncy married and moved with her husband to Boston, where she completed her education. She was the first woman admitted as a planning student at Harvard's School of Design and subsequently earned three degrees, including a Ph.D in city planning. She specialized in industrial land use issues because she believed that postwar economic growth would be tied to industrial expansion, which in turn would generate the tax revenue to subsidize public housing. Like most married women of this period, she shaped her career to the needs of her family. When her husband was transferred to Philadelphia, she went to work under Edmund Bacon in the Planning Department; when he was moved to Washington, D.C., she followed, wrote her doctoral dissertation, published articles based on her findings, and developed a consulting practice built on her industrial location expertise.[84]

The tradition of non-professional women making a critical intellectual contribution to the field, in the manner of Kimball and Bauer, was continued into the 1960s by Jane Jacobs (b. 1916), the author of *The Death and Life of Great American Cities*.[85] An associate editor of the *Architectural Forum* and married to an architect, Robert H. Jacobs, Jr, she had long been an observer of planning practices and source of community opposition to several ill-conceived Greenwich Village projects. Stimulated by a concern over what she considered the major failures of planning (slum clearance, urban renewal, and public housing) she tried to educate the professionals in urban dynamics. Her highly personal book defined the essence of city life as human interaction in the haphazard, physically disordered but socially workable, small-scale heterogeneous neighborhood. (Much of her evidence came from matters to which she, as a woman, was especially sensitive: childhood development, community ties, neighborliness, aesthetics, and issues of personal physical safety.) Her vision was rapidly adopted by the profession, which integrated her views into its own theory and promoted federal legislation favoring neighborhood preservation.[86]

Planning and women in the 1970s and 1980s

A massive entry of women into the workforce began during the late 1960s. Stimulated by the resurgent feminist movement and the consequent affirmative action legislation, it was bolstered by federal enforcement programs and sympathetic judicial decisions. Concurrently, the national economy had so eroded that by the mid-1970s the "second paycheck" became necessary for maintaining the expectations generated in earlier years. By 1976, 47 per cent of all women and 50 per cent of all mothers with minor children were in the labor force. Nevertheless, women workers did not achieve a commensurate economic advance, and their overall economic position actually declined. In 1973 women's earnings were only 57 per cent of men's. This trend was repeated in the professional arena as well, where the median income for women was $9093, compared to $14,306 for men. Professional women earned only 63.6 per cent as much as men.[87]

The planning profession followed the same pattern. Women entered the field in great numbers and with relative ease. The changes in public opinion which had generated the movement of women into all areas of the labor market held for planning as well. More important, however, was a dramatic transition that had occurred in the profession: by 1976 97 per cent of planners were employed in the public sector; the remainder earned their income as publicly funded consultants. This employment pattern forced the planning profession to be more responsive to governmental affirmative action pressure than others, such as medicine or law. In 1976 women earned 28 per cent of all planning degrees, up from 7.5 per cent in 1968.[88]

Despite their high rate of entry, female planners, like their counterparts in other professions, encountered discrimination. In 1971, ASPO reported: "At no point are female planners' median salaries equal to their male counterparts' despite equal educational background and the same amount of planning experience."[89] Three years later ASPO reported that only eight women planning directors were recorded in their survey of 670 planning agencies.[90] Although the figure reflected to some degree the small pool of female planners who had enough seniority to reach the highest executive positions, when combined with the earnings figures it demonstrated the pattern of discrimination described by the Women's Caucus whose protest was recorded at the beginning of this chapter.

On the basis of this evidence, women convinced ASPO and the AIP to endorse employment and salary guidelines designed to redress the inequalities.[91] In 1974 HUD and ASPO sponsored a publication, *Planning Women and Change*, which outlined the feminist issues that had arisen in the profession: conditions of employment and definition of specific feminine concerns to be incorporated in the planning process.[92]

By 1979 women constituted a large enough block in the AIP to create a technical department, the Planning and Women Division. This had been preceded by the formation of a Women's Rights Committee in 1971 whose members contributed to the later effort. In 1980, the Division received HUD funding to sponsor a competition entitled "Planning for the changing needs of women" and produced a book documenting demonstration projects for child care, housing design and finance, transportation access, and other issues reflecting basic female concerns.[93] This inaugurated an effort to include a new perspective in planning practice, a view that had been lost years before in the separation of the National Conference of City Planning (NCCP) and the American City Planning Institute (ACPI) in 1917.

By 1980, then, women had been brought into the profession through the dissolution of educational barriers. General societal trends, not any indigenous movement from within the profession, had caused the change. When women gained access, some used their position to articulate the gender-related concerns which they had formerly voiced in other vehicles, such as civic organizations and reform associations.

Women and planning: an overview

Clearly, women as a group had few representatives among professional planners until the postwar period. Barriers to their entry were the same as those that prevented all women from having professional careers in the first half of the twentieth century: the socially approved custom of denying or limiting admission to advanced training programs; public opinion which defined the proper female role as domestic-centered and thereby restricted employment possibilities through formal and informal mechanisms; and women's own views of their societal position as wives, mothers, and volunteer workers. The long careers of Elisabeth Herlihy, Flora Crockett, Jane Rodman, and Chloethiel Woodard Smith were unusual.

In the non-professional arena, women had a much longer and more significant record of activity. Their presence as allied professionals or volunteers was in keeping with societal norms, and they used this convention to participate in planning. As librarians, writers, lobbyists, and propagandists they helped to create a receptive public opinion for planning and to define the field for the professionals. The work of Kimball, Rumbold, and James are representative of these efforts. Others built their credibility by claiming areas of presumed female expertise, such as housing reform, neighborhood design, and billboard control, to inject their perspective into segments of the field. Thus the writings of Bauer and Jacobs, based on domestic knowledge, were adopted and translated into professional concerns, particularly in the area of urban renewal.

In the postwar period, women who formerly would have supplied the armies of volunteers or allied professionals gained entry to the field. The feminist movement and federal government affirmative action policies stimulated major changes in all female employment patterns and were clearly reflected in the planning profession. In some instances, the new entrants brought a consciousness of their heritage of gender-related expertise and bid their male colleagues to integrate this perspective into planning practice.

A new era of women's history has begun, as documented in the statistical evidence of educational attainment, employment, wage scales, and professional association membership. An assessment of other impacts on professional practice will have to wait until women have been involved for a longer period.

Notes

1 "Report of the Women's Caucus" (1970) *Planning 1970*, Chicago, ASPO, pp. 297–8.
2 See William H. Chafe (1972) *The American Woman: Her Changing Social Economic and Political Roles, 1920–1970*, New York, Oxford University Press, for a general discussion of women's changing position in American society.
3 Chafe, *The American Woman*, p. 26; B. Friedan (1963) *The Feminine Mystique*, New York, W. W. Norton Company.

4 For a discussion of the anti-sex discrimination provision of the 1964 Civil Rights Act see Sheila M. Rothman (1978) *Woman's Proper Place: A History of Changing Ideals and Practices 1870 to the Present*, New York, Basic Books, pp. 231–42.

5 The full quotation in which this phrase appeared articulated the full definition of how women should contribute to planning. It read: "We deplore the planning that is done – by men. It takes little account of the needs of women; of their access to employment; of their requirements for child care facilities; of the kinds of homes that would be livable for them; of the kinds of communities and usable services that would make the role of wife and mother more humane. The Conference has seriously downgraded the social environment of the city as a theatre for interaction and a central focus for planning. The principal actors in the residential community are women – they should be the yielding force for human communities." (Report of Women's Caucus, p. 298)

6 Paul Davidoff and Thomas A. Reiner (1962) "A choice theory of planning," *Journal of the American Institute of Planners*, 28, 103–15.

7 Although Mary K. Simkhovitch, head of New York City's Greenwich Street Settlement House, was a guiding light in the creation of the New York City exhibition on the problems of congestion whose success would stimulate the first meeting on the National Conference on City Planning and Problems of Congestion in Washington in 1909, her participation is diminished in the succeeding years. No other notable women appear at this time. For details about the early planning movement, see Mel Scott (1969) *American City Planning since 1890*, Berkeley, University of California Press; Jon A. Peterson (1967) "The origins of the comprehensive city planning ideal in the United States, 1840–1911", Ph.D dissertation, Harvard University.

8 Elisabeth Herlihy was elected a full member of the ACPI in 1927. (See 1939 "Roster," *Planners Journal*.)

9 Barbara J. Harris (1978) in *Beyond Her Sphere: Women and the Professions in American History*, Westport, Conn., Greenwood Press, discusses this point in chapters IV and V.

10 See John Nolen, "Twenty years of city planning progress in the United States," in National Conference on Planning, *Planning Problems of Town, City and Region*, Washington, D.C., and Theodora Kimball Hubbard and Henry Vincent Hubbard (1929) *Our Cities, Today and Tomorrow*, Cambridge, Mass., Harvard University Press, for precise data on numbers of cities having comprehensive plans, zoning ordinances, and city planning commissions.

11 See Eugenie Ladner Birch (1980) "Advancing the art of planning, planners and their organizations, 1909–1980," *Journal of the American Planning Association*, vol. 46 for details.

12 See Donald A. Krueckeberg (1980) "The story of the Planner's Journal 1915–1980," *Journal of the American Planning Association*, vol. 46 for an explanation of the rise of planning literature.

13 Chafe, *American Woman*, pp. 16–17; Rothman, *Woman's Proper Place*, pp. 63–74.

14 Mrs Frank A. Pattison (1909) "The relation of the women's club to the American city," *The American city*, 1, 129–30.

15 "The old order changeth" (1912) *The American City*, 6, 803.

16 Eva Perry Moore (1909) "Women's interest in civic welfare," *The American City*, 1, 44; Pattison, "The relation," p. 130; Mrs Edwin F. Moulton (1909) "Municipal housekeepers," *The American City*, 1, 123–4.

17 Susana Torre (ed.) (1977) *Women in American Architecture: A Historic and*

Contemporary Perspective, New York, Whitney Library of Design; Jeanne Madeline Weiman (1981) *The Fair Women: The Story of the Women's Building, World's Columbian Exhibition, Chicago, 1893*, Chicago, Academy Press, 1981.

18 "The old order," pp. 801–2.

19 Alice Davis Moulton (1912) "A city plan a fundamental requirement," *The American City*, 6, 803.

20 ibid.

21 Mary Walton Kent (1912) "From the Southern woman's point of view," *The American City*, 6, 905: Mildred Chadsey (1912) "A woman Chief of Sanitary Police," *The American City*, 6, 873; George B. Dealey (1912) "The kind of civic work that secures newspaper cooperation," *The American City*, 6, 883.

22 Mrs George E. Bird (1916) "The parade that inaugurated a village clean up campaign," *The American City*, 14, 162–6; "Points from the women" (1909) *The American City*, 1, 133; Zona Gale (1914) "How women's clubs can cooperate with the city officials," *The American City*, 8, 537.

23 Mrs Edwin F. Moulton (1911) "Township parks," *The American City*, 4, 217–18; Mrs Caroline Bayard Alexander (1912) "The children at play, effective playground work at small cost," *The American City*, 6, 848; Dealey, "The kind of civic work," *The American City*, 6, 883. Mrs Amalie Hofer Jerome (1911) "The playground as a social center," *The American City*, 5, 33–5; Harriet Lusk Childs (1915) "The Rochester Social Center," *The American City*, 12, 18–22; Anna Pendleton Schnenck (1915) "The need for neighborhood centers in American cities," *The American City*, 12, 337–40; Edward J. Ward (1914) "Where suffragists and anti's unite," *The American City*, 10, 519–24.

24 Mrs Ross W. Barrows (1912) "A women's club which raised money for a city plan," *The American City*, 6, 861–2; Mrs Imogen B. Oakley (1912) "The more civic work, the less need of philanthropy," *The American City*, 6, 805–13; John Williams Mitchell (1916) "Los Angeles: in the making," *The American City*, 2, 149–57; Elisabeth Asker (1913) "The Tampa Civic Association – its aims and work," *The American City*, 7, 619–21; Zona Gale (1913) "The club that studied America," *The American City*, 8, 624–6; Mrs Flora Radcliffe Harmon (1912) "Working for a permanent city plan," *The American City*, 6, 217.

25 Ladislas Segoe to Sydney H. Williams, Cincinnati, May 23, 1978 (Tape 2).

26 Richard B. Watrous (1909) "The American Civic Association," *The American City*, 1, 62.

27 "The Civic Conference in St Louis" (1912) *The American City*, vol. 7; "Los Angeles," p. 149.

28 Helen Marie Dermitt (1912) "The value of co-operation between man and women in public work," *The American City*, 6, 844; Mrs T. J. Bowlker (1912) "Women's home-making function applied to the municipality," *The American City*, 6, 869–70.

29 "The old order," p. 805.

30 Mrs Caroline Bartlett Crane (1912) "Some factors of the street cleaning problem," *The American City*, 6, 895–7.

31 Gale wrote in 1911: "If our actual organization is to keep pace with our dream, then we must realize that no dream can continue indefinitely on volunteer work alone. . . . The work has grown too large for the hands of volunteers . . . if we are to get . . . a fair proportion of efficiency from the splendid, unselfish desire now awake and alive in club women who are civic workers then we must introduce into our work that to which every volunteer work should grow: the co-operation of trained and paid organizers," *The American City*, 11,

92–3; Zona Gale (1913) *Civic Improvement in the Little Towns*, Washington, D.C., American Civic Association.
32 Florence C. Floore.(1916) "A state-wide civic campaign," *The American City*, 14 (3), 280; Maud Van Buren (1915) "Why women should study town ordinances and town budgets," *The American City*, 12, 411–12; Maud Van Buren (1915) "Women and town improvement," *The American City*, 12, 104.
33 Chadsey, "A women chief," p. 872.
34 Harris, *Beyond Her Sphere*, p. 138.
35 For details see Scott, *American City Planning*, and Birch, "Advancing the art and science."
36 Chafe, *American Woman*, p. 29; Rothman, *Woman's Proper Sphere*, chap. 3.
37 Edith Elmer Wood (n.d. "Memorandum for The Committee on Housing," Edith Elmer Wood Collection, Avery Library, Columbia University.
38 "Mrs H. V. Hubbard, landscape expert," *Boston Transcript*, November 8, 1935, "Mrs T. K. Hubbard dead in Milton," *Boston Herald*, November 9, 1935; Henry Lefavour, "Theodora K. Hubbard," *Boston Transcript*, November 14, 1935. "Theodora Kimball Hubbard, a biographical minute" (1936) *Landscape Architecture*, xvi, 53.
39 See, for example: Theodora Kimball (1916) "What to read on city planning," *The American City*, 14, 466–7; Theodora Kimball Hubbard, "Survey of city and regional planning in the United States," *City Planning*, I (1925), 7–26; II (1926), 87–116; III (1927), 111–54; IV (1928), 89–153; V (1929), 80–96; VI (1930), 199–225; VII (1932), 113–20.
40 T. K. Hubbard and H. V. Hubbard, *Our Cities Today and Tomorrow*.
41 Charlotte Rumbold papers, Missouri Historical Society, St Louis, Missouri; "Miss Charlotte Rumbold," *Cleveland Press*, July 6, 1960.
42 Michael Simpson (1969) *People and Planning: A History of the Ohio Planning Conference*, Bay Village, Ohio: Ohio Planning Conf., pp. 9–26, 57.
43 Interview, Evalina Briers, January 17, 1981; Charlotte Rumbold (1932) "Promoting planning in Cleveland," *City Planning*, VIII, 13–15; Charlotte Rumbold (1930) "The Highway Plan for the Cleveland Region," *American Civic Annual*, Washington, D.C., pp. 122–5; Charlotte Rumbold (1931) "Beyond the billboards lies America," *The Clevelander* (June), pp. 15–19.
44 Charlotte Rumbold (1926) "The Ohio State Conference on City Planning," *City Planning*, 2, 51–2.
45 Harlean James (1932) "Public education in city planning," *City Planning*, VIII, 29.
46 United States Housing Corporation Records, 1917–1952, The National Archives, Washington, D.C.; Harlean James (1917) *Building of Cities*, New York: The Macmillan Co.; Harlean James (1915) "The Baltimore Flower Market," *The American City*, 8, 390–2; Harlean James (1912) "Baltimore backyards: a study of gardens and garbage," paper presented to the eighth annual meeting of the American Civic Association.
47 Harlean James (1920) "Federal City Planning Bill passed the House," *City Planning*, II, 141–2; Harlean James (1926) "National Capital Park and Planning Commission," *City Planning*, VI , 200; Harlean James (1926) *Land Planning in the United States for the City, State and Nation*, New York: The Macmillan Co., p. 79.
48 ibid.
49 "ASPO Award Winners Harlean James and Katherine McNamara," (1954) *Planning* (October), p. 57. (Herlihy was awarded the citation posthumously.)
50 Interview, T. E. McCormick, Boston, Massachusetts, July 18, 1980; Interview, John T. Howard, July 10, 1980; Lois Kennedy, "People you ought to know,"

Boston Herald, September 13, 1929; Andrew F. Donnell, "State Planning Board puts your home on the map," *Boston Sunday Post*, October 3, 1937; "Elisabeth M. Herlihy," *New York Times*, October 29, 1953.

51 Interviews, T. E. McCormick; John T. Howard.

52 Louis M. Lyons, "Planning is just common sense says the women who heads our first State Planning Board," *Boston Globe*, May 3, 1937. In 1926 Flavel Shurtleff, executive secretary of the AICP, wrote to John Nolen reflecting upon the Herlihy membership: "I may say that the case of Miss Herlihy is the only one where the applicant has not strictly technical qualifications. However, her long experience as Secretary of the City Planning Board of Boston seems ample."

53 Lyons, "Planning is just common sense."

54 Kennedy, "People you ought to know."

55 See for example, Elisabeth M. Herlihy (1925) "Boston zoning – its first birthday," *City Planning*, I, 81–5; Elisabeth M. Herlihy (1936) "Planning for the Commonwealth in the Massachusetts State Planning Board," *Planning Forum*, 2, 3–7; Elisabeth M. Herlihy (1931) "Boston's Master Highway Plan," *Proceedings*, National Conference on City Planning, pp. 81–4; Elisabeth M. Herlihy (1950) "Everyday planning and zoning problems," *Bulletin of the Massachusetts Federation of Planning Boards*, vol. 10; Elisabeth M. Herlihy (chairman) (1938) "The administration of a planning office," *American Planning and Civic Annual*, Washington, D.C., pp. 251–8; Elisabeth M. Herlihy (1930) "Planning for Boston – 1630–1930," *City Planning*, VI, 1–13.

56 Mrs Grace Bartlett (1925) "City planning in Honolulu," *City Planning*, I, 179–80; Raymond W. Blanchard (1932) "Ten years of city planning in Evansville," *City Planning*, VIII, 77; A. Edmere Cabana (1936) "The Buffalo zoning campaign," *City Planning*, II, 42–7; "Who's who in civic achievement" (1929) *American Civic Annual*, Washington, D.C., pp. 245, 330.

57 Ryan, *The American Woman*.

58 "1937 Institute Roster," *Planners' Journal*, III, 26–8.

59 Interview, John T. Howard.

60 Gordon Stephenson (1979) "Class notes, 1938," *News Department of Urban Studies and Planning*, II, 19.

61 Interview, Jane Rodman, January 25, 1981.

62 Torre, *Women in American Architecture*, p. 117.

63 Chloethiel Woodard Smith and Associated Architects (n.d.) *Architecture, Urban Design, Planning*, Washington, D.C.

64 For further description, see Scott, *American City Planning since 1890*.

65 George B. Ford (1933) "A program for roadside improvement," *American Civic Annual*, Washington, D.C., pp. 184–7.

66 Committee on Roadside Improvements (1933) "Roadside improvement," *City Planning*, IX, 181–6.

67 "Our contributors" (1930) *American Civic Annual*, Washington, D.C., p. 399; Interview, Mrs Frances Utter, Vassar Alumnae Association, January 6, 1981.

68 James, "Public education in city planning," p. 31.

69 Flavel Shurtleff (1941) "Report from the American Planning and Civic Association," *Planning Broadcasts* (January), p. 120.

70 Thomas Adams to Edith Elmer Wood, December 1, 1928, Edith Elmer Wood Collection, Avery Library, Columbia University.

71 Edith Elmer Wood (1929) "Slums and the city plan," *The American City*, XLI, 93.

72 E. L. Birch (1980) "Radburn and the American Planning Movement: the persistence of an idea," *Journal of the American Planning Association*, 46, 424–39.

73 "Delegate List," National Association of Housing Officials, Baltimore, October 1934, Edith Elmer Wood Collection, Avery Library, Columbia University.

74 For an excellent discussion of Bauer's early housing career, see M. S. Coe (1975) "Catherine Bauer and the public housing movement: 1926–1937", Ph.D dissertation, George Washington University.

75 Susan Cole (1980) "Catherine Krause Bauer," in B. Sicherman and C. H. Green *Notable American Women*, Cambridge, Mass.: Harvard, pp. 66–8.

76 Sara White, "Land ownership to Pose Problem," *Boston Traveler*, June 17, 1943, p. 4; Catherine Bauer, "The Dreary Deadlock of Public Housing," *Architectural Forum* 48 (May 1957); Commission on National Goals, *Goals for Americans*, Englewood Cliffs, NJ: Prentice-Hall, 1960. "Redevelopment: a misfit in the fifties," in Coleman Woodbury (ed.) (1953) *The Future of Cities and Urban Redevelopment*, Chicago; (1950) "The increasing social responsibilities of the city planners," *Proceedings American Institute of Planners* and (1950) *Institute of Professional Town Planners Joint Meeting*; (1961) "The belated challenge and changing role of the physical planners" (Keynote address, Annual AIP Conference, 1961), *Proceedings*, Washington, D.C., 1962, pp. 2–13.

77 American Institute of Planners (1961) *Membership Roster*, Washington, D.C.

78 Harris, *Beyond Her Sphere*, pp. 150–6.

79 American Institute of Planners (1943) "Statement of the ownership" *Journal of the American Institute of Planners*, ix, inside cover; American Society of Planning Officials, "Minutes," 1943, Walter Blacher papers, Olin Library, Cornell University.

80 "Education" (1946) *Planning*, xii, 49; John A. Parker, "Memorandum to Eugenie Birch," July 18, 1980; John T. Howard, Interview.

81 American Institute of Planners (1951) *Handbook and Roster*, Washington, D.C., p. 2ff.; Epstein, *Women's Place*, pp. 200–1.

82 US Department of Labor, Women's Bureau (1948) *The Outlook for Women in Architecture and Engineering*, Washington, D.C., US Government Printing Office, pp. 5–1, 5–7. In 1970 the Women's Bureau published an updated brochure, *Why Not Be An Urban Planner?*, picturing female professionals participating in a wide variety of specialties.

83 Carol J. Thomas, Interview, October 17, 1980; Joan Millman, "The lady does planning," *Boston Sunday Herald Traveler*, February 6, 1972.

84 Dorothy Muncy, Interview, January 29, 1981.

85 Jane Jacobs (1961) *The Death and Life of Great American Cities*, New York, Random House.

86 ibid; John E. Zuccotti (1974) "How does Jane Jacobs rate today?," *Planning* (June), pp. 23–7.

87 Harris, *Beyond Her Sphere*, p. 182.

88 Jacqueline Leavitt (1978) "Women in planning: do the numbers really matter?," unpublished paper, Division of Urban Planning, Columbia School of Architecture and Planning (January), p. 8.

89 Karen Hapgood (1971) *Women in Planning: A Report on Their Status in Public Planning Agencies*, Chicago, p. 8.

90 Leavitt, "Women in planning," pp. 8–9.

91 Constance Lieder (1974) "Women in planning: guidelines to be monitored this year," *AIP Newsletter* (January), p. 34.

92 Karen E. Hapgood and Judith Getzels (1974) *Planning, Women and Change*, Chicago: ASPO.

93 Joel Werth and Mary Deal (1980) *Planning and Women: A Competition for Projects*, Chicago.

Index

Entry numbers in bold type refer to plates and figures, those in italics to tables.